STUDIES IN THE
HISTORY OF CULTURE

*The Disciplines
of the
Humanities*

STUDIES IN THE
HISTORY OF CULTURE

The Disciplines

of the

Humanities

Essay Index Reprint Series

BOOKS FOR LIBRARIES PRESS
FREEPORT, NEW YORK

First published 1942

Reprinted 1969 by arrangement with the
American Council of Learned Societies

STANDARD BOOK NUMBER:
8369-1170-9

LIBRARY OF CONGRESS CATALOG CARD NUMBER:
70-86728

PRINTED IN THE UNITED STATES OF AMERICA

FOREWORD

THE twenty-one papers in this volume form the body of a tribute presented to Waldo Gifford Leland, Director of the American Council of Learned Societies, in recognition of his distinguished services to the history of culture and to the cooperation of the humanities. They were chosen for each Society by its Secretary in consultation with its delegates, the design being to present an example of each discipline, often in its relations with another discipline. The arrangement of the very far ranging material is in general chronological, not so much as regards the subject matter treated in each paper, but rather the order in which the various disciplines came to affect the history of culture.

PERCY W. LONG

Chairman of the Conference of
Secretaries, and editor of this book

December, 1941

TABLE OF CONTENTS

TABLE OF CONTENTS

EYES THAT SEE AND EARS THAT HEAR

CAMPBELL BONNER
University of Michigan

I N A testimonial to a scholar who has for many years worked vigorously and unselfishly for the coördination of the various humanistic
disciplines, no theme is more appropriate than community of labor
and mutual helpfulness among the workers in different fields. Such coöperation must necessarily take different forms; and it may be doubted whether
collaboration among students of the humanities can ever be deliberately
planned, from the beginning of an undertaking, with the same confidence
in efficient performance and ultimate success that a group of scientists can
expect. A biologist, a chemist, and a physician can plan and carry out an
investigation into a problem of nutrition, and we are daily more indebted
to such enterprises; but when a Hellenist, a historian, and a philosopher
concern themselves with a problem in the interpretation of ancient life
and culture, their contributions must, as a rule, be made separately, and
the synthesis may require a long period of mutual criticism and gradual
modification of particular points of view. The stature of a humanistic
scholar may perhaps be measured by his ability to combine with the
mastery of his own specialty a breadth of view based upon sympathetic
understanding of the methods of other workers.

In this kind of labor for a common good, classical philology serves
many interests besides those which are its own, namely the criticism,
interpretation, and illustration of Greek and Roman authors. Not only
were the foundations of historical method laid by the Greeks, but even
now historians are incurring a heavy debt to the fundamental work of
classical philologists upon new or neglected texts, especially inscriptions
and papyri. Religion and theology have also profited by the contributions
of classical philologists. Our ideas, not only of Greek and Roman religion,
but also of the later phases of the Egyptian and Syrian religions, have
been revised by classical scholars; and the union of philological competency with theological interest has resulted in a better understanding
of the beginnings and development of Christianity. One may also advert,

though illustration is unnecessary, to the contributions of classical philology to the history of the arts and of science.

So many are the auxiliary parts that philology has played, and played with a good will, that it sometimes becomes necessary to protest against a tendency to confuse coöperation with servitude—a confusion that is at its harmful work in a realm where the voice of scholarship is not heard. Classicists have sometimes been amazed to find that their colleagues in history spoke and wrote as if the reader of texts could scarcely aspire to speak a word of weight in the interpretation of happenings in the ancient world. Fortifying themselves with the magical words "historical method," departments of history have taken the ancient world into their own camp. A philologist may be an authority on Thucydides or on historical inscriptions, but in most American universities he may not lecture on Greek history without attaching himself to a history department. And yet that professional mystery, "historical method," was largely the work of sixteenth and seventeenth century scholars whose natural province was the elucidation of Latin and Greek texts. Fortunately the more enlightened university administrations are showing a wholesome tendency to break down partitions and to encourage plural affiliation of scholars whose interests lead them across departmental frontiers. From another side, the Council of Learned Societies, by fostering a sense of common interests, has done much to obliterate boundary marks that have proved to be obstacles to good understanding and loyal coöperation among all students of the humanities.

The inadequate tribute to a friend and colleague which this paper presents does not merit the title of a study in the history of culture. In fact, it is merely the outcome of a relapse—not without a comfortable feeling of relief—into his own field, on the part of a student whose efforts have been lent for several years to theology and the history of Christianity. If the labor of those years can claim consideration as a service to "divine philosophy," this little paper belongs chiefly to the Hellenist, and in a very small way, to the critic of poetry.

It is likely that many teachers of Greek have felt a certain impatience, in conversation with laymen or even with their own students, when it became apparent that they thought of the Greeks as alive only in certain great moments, or else as living their whole lives at a level far higher than ordinary men can hope to reach. In this reverent, but very hazy vision of antiquity, Athens is a stately city peopled by august, olive-crowned figures, walking among copses of laurel set off here and there by an altar or a statue of marble, and talking philosophy or reciting episodes of Homer or singing lyrics from Pindar or the tragedians. Now this mirage of false classicism is a weariness of soul to the true Hellenist. There are able critics of ancient art who like to turn from the austere simplicity of Phidias to the quaint, amiable charm of archaic sculpture, or to the winning homeliness of Hellenistic genre-work; and there are teachers of Greek who, with somewhat similar feelings, and with an added spice of mischief, like to take students who have been introduced to Greece through Homer, Plato, and Euripides and plunge them into Aristophanes, to learn there the true inwardness of ancient Athens, with its confused medley of sights, noises, and smells. It can do the over-serious student no harm to walk for a while in the thick of the shouting, sweating, gesticulating, grimacing crowd that he will meet in the comedies of Aristophanes. He may, now and then, be uneasily aware that he is in low company, and he may dislike the habits and disapprove the morals of some people that he will encounter in the plays. But in time he will calmly accept the simple truth that it was men like that, of the earth and very earthy, who admired the rugged greatness of Aeschylus and the dynamic oratory of Pericles, and loved the beautiful serenity of Sophocles' vision of life.

Nobody can live long at the height of his greatest efforts; and appreciation of Greek life and literature is prone to flag when it is directed exclusively to the high moments of history or the greatest works of poetry. It may be a salutary experience to consider how the Greeks behaved in moments of relaxation, and to see how they looked at little things. Much can be said about the lesser amenities of Greek culture; about amenities of speech, the language of courtesy, the good-natured give and take of conversation; about amenities of conduct or behavior, about the little kindnesses, the acts of generosity, of compassion, of self-sacrifice among friends and compatriots; about the instances of love and tenderness that mark the family, despite a social tradition of female inferiority and despite the influence of slavery. This paper, however, deals with amenities of a simpler and more palpable sort, and calls attention to the keenness of the Greek eye for certain little matters of every-day experience; how children, animals, plants, and various inanimate things looked to them, and how they recorded in words what they saw.

Keen perception, taking in at a glance the essence of what is seen or heard, and coupled with the power to suggest in words essential forms, colors, movements, and sounds, is a part of all poetic talent of the first order. There is no need to enlarge upon its importance; and to illustrate the generalization from the more familiar works of the great poets would entail much threshing of old straw. Homer's brilliant similes are obvious examples, and I touch upon three, chosen at random, only to show the kind of thing that I mean. Achilles compares the dejected Patroclus to a baby girl that runs beside her mother and begs to be taken up, plucking at her mother's dress and looking up at her with tearful eyes. Ajax, as he slowly retreats before the Trojans, turning back now and then to put the pursuers to rout, is like a stubborn ass, over whose back many a cudgel has been broken, that breaks away from the small boys that are driving him and gets into a cornfield, where he eats his fill and then, and then only, allows himself to be beaten back into the road by their puny blows. Odysseus' boat is driven hither and thither by veering winds, as the autumn north wind drives over the plain thorn-plants caught together in clumps or balls (like the tumble-weeds of our western plains). In each instance the vision of child, animal, plant behavior is clear and unerring.[1]

With just such faultless sight and limpid words Sappho describes the fair grove of apple trees where an altar smokes with fragrant incense, there is a cool plashing of water, heard among the apple-boughs, a shade of rose-bushes, the sound of rustling leaves, the sight of a flowery meadow, and the odor of parsley. Even Pindar can stoop from his soaring song of gods and heroes to see how the tender skin of an infant laid among flowers is tinged by the yellow and purple light reflected from pansies.[2]

This kind of perception is naturally less to be observed in the great tragedians, because they are concerned chiefly with the clash of wills and

---

[1] *Il.* 16. 7–10; 11. 558–562; *Odyss.* 5. 328–330.

[2] The passage of Sappho, in which frs. 5 and 6 (Diehl) are now united, has been reconstructed on the basis of an ostrakon on which Medea Norsa discovered the text. Her treatment of it in her *La scrittura letteraria greca* (Pubblicazione della R. Scuola Normale Superiore di Pisa) lists the discussions of the text that had appeared up to 1939.—Pindar, *Olymp.* 6. 55.

purposes, and with the fateful consequences of error and guilt. To find fit images for conflict and ruin a dramatic poet is likely to turn to the harsher aspects of nature, as when Sophocles, thinking of the swelling tide of crime in the house of the Labdacids, compares it to a storm sweeping over the darkness of the sea, rolling up the dark shingle from the depths, and roaring against the wind-beaten headlands. Even when a figure is suggested by some simple and beautiful object in nature, it is sometimes used to heighten by contrast the effect of a scene of horror, as when Clytemestra says that a jet of her husband's blood, bespattering her as she dealt him the third murderous blow, gladdened her even as the sown land rejoices in the heaven-sent moisture at the birth of the bud; or as when in Euripides' *Medea*, the aged Kreon, bending over the body of his daughter, seared by the hidden fire of Medea's poisoned robe, is caught by the bewitched garment and held gripped to the dying girl "as ivy is held by the shoots of the bay-bush."[3]

Still, there is plentiful evidence that the great dramatists sometimes glanced aside from their subjects not only to observe, but also to enjoy little things; and when they did so they described them with the same vivid and scrupulous accuracy that they applied to the motives of tragic actions. Some suggestion that I can no longer trace led me recently to look over the fragments of the lost plays of Aeschylus and Sophocles, and most of the examples that I use are drawn from them.[4]

The fragments of Aeschylus, which are much less numerous than those of Sophocles and Euripides, give us little, but enough to serve as useful samples. What could be more vivid than the line in which he draws a picture of decrepit age—"a weak old man, loin-racked and wrenched with pain"? In another place he describes, quite accurately, a berry-bush which at one time has upon it fruit in all three stages—white, red, and black. Again he seems to be fascinated by the sounds of certain musical

---

[3] Soph. *Ant.* 582–592; Aesch. *Agam.* 1389–1392; Eur. *Med.* 1211–1214.

[4] By reason of the circumstances in which the fragments of Aeschylus and Sophocles are found, that is, as brief quotations in other writers, the sense connection in many of them is obscure, and the difficulties of interpretation are often complicated by corruptions of the texts. Since they are cited only for the interest of their literary contents, textual problems are ignored, and in one or two instances abbreviated and simplified versions have been given in order to avoid discussion that would be out of place here. The fragments of Aeschylus are cited by the numbers in Sidgwick's Oxford text, those of Sophocles by Pearson's edition, which I have followed in questions of doubtful interpretation.

instruments and by the way they are made and played: "One held in hand a lathe-worked flute and swelled the melody tossed from his fingers' ends." In its way, this merits comparison with Milton's famous verses about an organ player:

> His volant touch
> Instinct through all proportions, low and high,
> Fled and pursued transverse the resonant fugue.

Milton's description is more learned and technical, not more clear.

For a bit of homely domestic truth to life, note these words about the preparation for a feast:

> This pig, a fine fat-suckled one
> I'll lay upon the sputtering roasting-pan;
> What better morsel could a man desire?

The words would have made Charles Lamb lick his lips.[5]

Sophocles in the *Aleadai* wrote:

> Down the steep rocky crags a wandering deer,
> Lifting its nostrils and its spiky horns,
> Came on unfearing.

Elsewhere in one line he shows us a kite, screaming as it swoops down upon an altar and carries off a morsel of meat without breaking its flight:

> ἰκτῖνος ὡς ἔκλαγξε παρασύρας κρέας.

In the *Aegeus* he notes how, though all other foliage is still, "the wing of a breeze" stirs and tosses the head of a tall poplar. Like Aeschylus he was interested by the three colors of blackberries; but the point of his allusion to them lies in the succession of these colors in the single berry, not in the presence of berries of different color on a bush at the same time. Like Homer, and like many minds that keep something of the freshness of their childhood, he was fascinated by the drifting of thistle-down:

> Like to the down from aged thistle blown.

Even for creeping things he had a patient and observant eye. He describes ants as "four-winged, black-hided, pinch-girt at waist." In another

---

[5] In the order in which they are mentioned, the fragments of Aeschylus are nos. 361, 116, 57, 309; for the lines of Milton, see *Paradise Lost* 11, 561 ff.

passage he compares something to "a woodlouse rolled up to the size of a pea." Adults who have forgotten what a woodlouse is were probably well acquainted with them when they were between five and ten years old. The woodlouse is the small grayish crustacean (not a true insect) that one is likely to find under stones or planks that have lain for some time on damp ground; children like to prod the creatures and see them roll up into little balls. They are familiarly called wet-sows, pill-bugs, and other quaint names.

There is a curious proof of Sophocles' interest in technical processes in an isolated line where a warrior who has been in a hot affray says "my shield is as full of eyes as a *ligdos*." Now a ligdos is the clay casing of the wax models which were used in casting bronze statues by the *cire perdue* process; and since the melted wax had to be poured off, the upper surface of the ligdos was perforated. It is plain that Sophocles had looked on at this process—perhaps when Phidias made one of his masterpieces. Not only does the choice of the word show his interest, but it testifies to his preference for exact comparisons; for the coarser punctures of the ligdos would be much more like the spear-holes in a shield than would the fine meshes of a sieve, which less careful writers would seize upon as an obvious comparison.

When we come to examples of Sophocles' observation of human behavior we find him no less acute and vivid. He sees the goat-herd abroad at dawn plucking twigs for his goats to browse on, the fisherman at work trapping purple-mollusks with his weels of woven rushes; he hears the morning hum of shuttles, which wakes the household from sleep. There is a curious passage in which he compares the mingled pleasures and pains of love to the scene "when frost comes in bright weather and children seize a solid lump of ice; at first they feel a new pleasure, but at last the melting mass can scarce be dropped, nor will it remain firm in their hands." To anybody who has seen a group of Athenians of today frolicking in one of their infrequent snows, the figure is immediately convincing. Note next this sketch of babyhood from the satyr-play "Little Dionysus," spoken, it would seem, by the comical old Silenus:

When I bring him food he forthwith strokes my nose, and lifts his hand up to my bald-spot, sweetly smiling.

This is the same Sophocles who gave us the grand tragic figures of Electra, Oedipus, and Antigone.

The list of examples from Sophocles may be fittingly closed with a passage from the *Tympanistai* in Headlam's version:

> Ah, what joy
> Can out-joy this—to reach the land, and then
> Safe-lodged, with happy drowsing sense to hear
> The rain-drops pattering on the roof outside!

The feeling of cosy comfort after hardships has not often been so happily described.[6]

When a casual search of these scanty fragments yields so many illustrations, it is certain that many more could be added from familiar texts. One remembers Archilochus' little four-line sketch contrasting the tall, strutting general, shaven and curled, with the little sturdy, stout-hearted, bow-legged commander whom the poet favors; Euripides, pausing in the midst of a story of intrigue to note the red feet of a poisoned pigeon; or returning to a wondering mood of childhood when he speaks of the "endless" reflections in a mirror; or fixing almost photographically the posture of the Corinthian princess in *Medea* as she looks over her shoulder and down at her ankle to see the fall of her skirt; or, again in the *Medea*, telling of the sweet breath and soft skin of the children, which all but blunt the murderous mother's purpose. Aristophanes has the eye not only of a humorist but of a consummate artist; witness his delicate picture of the spring-time sports of the happy youths, "when plane-tree whispers to elm," and the words of his homesick rustic, who longs for the old-time ways on the farm, for the figs, the myrtle-berries, the sweet new wine, but does not forget "the pansy-bed beside the well."[7]

This quality of clear sight and swift, convincing delineation of what is seen is not confined to the poets. One remembers Xenophon's genial description of the tribal dances in the sixth book of the Anabasis; and for

---

[6] The fragments of Sophocles are nos. 89, 767, 23, 395, 868, 29, 363, 35, 502, 504, 890, 149, 171, 636. The first of those, no. 89, is a striking illustration of the difference between poetic truth as shown in the picture of the deer's behavior, and scientific accuracy; for the grammatical gender shows that Sophocles, like some other Greek poets, thought that a doe might have antlers. This blunder, which was observed by Aristotle and by the ancient commentators, is discussed by various modern editors. Pearson's notes on fr. 89 give the references.

[7] Archilochus fr. 60 Diehl; Eur. *Ion* 1207, *Hec.* 926, *Medea* 1166, 1075; Ar. *Clouds* 1008, *Peace* 577 f.

clear imaginative vision of what he could not actually have seen, Thucydides' account of the sortie from Plataea on a night of storm and bitter cold is beyond compare.[8] To discuss many vivid passages in Lysias and Plato would carry this paper beyond reasonable limits of space, and it must now be closed with two general comments.

It may have occurred to some readers that these examples of accurate and minute vision are not unlike a well known tendency of Hellenistic literature and art—the tendency to use for artistic purposes simple things that come within our every-day experience, the tendency that has caused the phrase genre-work to become a cliché in discussions of the art and the poetry of the Alexandrian age. There were undoubtedly forerunners of Alexandrianism; Euripides is often considered one of them, and the words that Aristophanes puts into his mouth,

οἰκεῖα πράγμαθ' εἰσάγων, οἷς χρώμεθ', οἷς ξύνεσμεν

might almost serve as a motto for Hellenistic art.[9] But some of the examples that were cited from Aeschylus and Sophocles also show an interest in familiar things. Perhaps it may be significant that many, though not all, of the examples from the two elder tragedians are fragments of lost satyr-plays. That would suggest that they manifested this faculty of observation of familiar things less in their tragedies than in the humorous tail-piece to the group of tragedies; it would then seem to be a product of a somewhat relaxed exercise of poetic power—the dramatist in milder mood. Thus the reflection naturally presents itself that this important characteristic of later Greek literature is no novelty, for it has been present from the beginnings; but that what we think of as one phase of Alexandrianism is really a matter of emphasis upon familiar things, and conscious exploitation of them for their own sake; whereas in the older writers such genre-work as we find is subordinate to a broader and bolder grasp of poetry—a neat handmaid serving a goddess of superhuman majesty and beauty. It is another proof that in the study of literary history it is wrong to set up too substantial partitions between chronological periods. What comes plainly into view on the farther side of the partition has been on the hither side all along, but beneath the surface, or at least less conspicuous to the view.

---

[8] Xen. *Anab.* 6. 1. 4–10; Thuc. 3. 20–24.

[9] "Bringing in familiar things, things that we use and live with"; Ar. *Frogs* 959.

The second of these closing remarks has to do with the aesthetic value of such naturalistic vision as we have been considering. Certainly it would be an error to take it as a principal criterion of great poetry, which must deal with the deeper passions and aspirations of the soul. But to make such poetry at home in the world, the poet must show that he does not lose sight of the simple, homely things that enter so largely into our lives, and are often deeply entangled in our affections. Without this kindly perception of little things, poetry is likely to become merely philosophy in verse; without the higher vision it may become a chronicle of trivialities. The greatest poets will be found to do the one thing and not leave the other undone. The permanent vitality of Greek poetry is due largely to that accurate observation of simple things which is merely a part of the Greek zest for life. That boundless zest is of the essence of great poetry; and it is a quality in which no later people has equalled the Greeks. So long as that is recognized, the works of Hellenic poets will never cease to be the nursery of their spiritual descendants.

THE RÔLE OF THE CANAANITES IN THE HISTORY OF CIVILIZATION

W. F. ALBRIGHT

The Johns Hopkins University

AS our title stands, it may seem rather restricted in scope, since the Canaanites are known to most people only as the unhappy precursors of Israel in Palestine. However, if we remember that the word "Canaanite" is historically, geographically, and culturally synonymous with "Phoenician"[1] the title immediately becomes more impressive, since it also deals with the rôle of the Phoenicians in the history of civilization. For convenience we shall employ "Canaanite" below to designate the Northwest-Semitic people and culture of Western Syria and Palestine before the twelfth century B.C. and the term "Phoenician" to indicate the same people and culture after this date.

First and last the Canaanites played a very important part in the history of civilization. In the third and second millennia they bridged the gap between Egypt and Mesopotamia and to them we undoubtedly owe much of the slow, but constant, transfusion of culture which we find in the ancient Near East. Across the Canaanite bridge went innumerable techniques and motifs, to say nothing of countless ideas and ways of expressing them. Through the conquest of Palestine by Israel and of Syria by the Aramaeans these two peoples became in large measure the heirs of Canaanite culture. The subsequent history of Israel, with all its significance for the world, would have been very different without this initial Canaanite influence. Forced out of Palestine and most of Syria in the thirteenth and twelfth centuries, the Phoenicians turned their energies seaward and became the greatest mariners and traders of all time, if we

---

[1] The evidence is very complete, consisting of explicit statements in classical writers from Philo Byblius to Stephanus of Byzantium and of coins from Laodicea south of Tyre bearing the inscription *l-l'dk' 'š b-kn'n*, "Belonging to Laodicea which is in Canaan"; see especially Eduard Meyer in the *Encyclopaedia Biblica*, III, p. 638, with corrections by Meyer in *Geschichte des Altertums*, II, 2², p. 63, n. 2, and additions by F. M. Th. Böhl, *Kanaanäer und Hebräer* (1911), p. 5.

may relate their accomplishments to the extent of the known world. It is true that there has been a strong tendency in the last half-century to be-little the classical traditions of early Phoenician expansion and influence on the Greeks. Just why the Hellenes should have been so eager to at-tribute their achievements in the arts of peace to the Phoenicians unless the tradition was very strong, remains unclear. Recent discoveries, a number of which will be presented for the first time in this paper, prove that the reaction against classical tradition is not warranted by the facts, though the reaction against modern exaggerated deductions from classical tradition is indeed justified.

I. The Rediscovery of the Canaanites

In the late sixteenth and seventeenth centuries Phoenician coins and inscriptions began to be collected and published, but no progress worth mentioning was made in their interpretation. After the discovery of several Graeco-Phoenician bilinguals in Malta and Cyprus more success-ful efforts at decipherment were made almost simultaneously by Swinton and Barthélemy (1750–1758); the work of the French scholar was much more methodical and successful than that of his English colleague. On the whole little progress was made by their successors, except in increasing the number of available inscriptions and in publishing more accurate copies, until the brilliant work of Gesenius, *Scripturae linguaeque Phoeniciae monumenta quotquot supersunt* (Leipzig, 1837), appeared.[2] In this epochal book he collected all accessible documents in accurate copies and inter-preted them on the basis of sound epigraphical method, profound gram-matical knowledge, and balanced judgment.

Gesenius's decipherment and publication of all known texts was fol-lowed closely by Movers's four-volume work, *Das phönizische Alterthum* (1841–1856), which collected everything then known about the Phoe-nicians and their colonies, utilizing the results of his great predecessor's research. Movers has been unduly criticized in some quarters for his hazardous conjectures and especially for his wild etymologies. However, he was in these respects only a child of a generation which was so dazzled by the rapidity of philological and archaeological discovery that it fol-

---

[2] For an account of the previous literature and of the progress of research before his time see Gesenius, *op. cit.*, pp. 1–9.

lowed mirages with as much confidence as it did solid horizons. We still draw freely from the vast reservoir of information which Movers brought together and sifted, mainly from classical sources. During the fifteen years which elapsed between the first and the fourth volume of his work such remarkable epigraphic progress was made that much of his work was speedily antiquated. Among the many new inscriptions which came to light were the Sacrificial Tariff of Marseilles (1845), the funerary text of Eshmunazar (1855), and several new inscriptions from Phoenicia which had been recovered by the expedition of Renan in 1860–1861. The wealth of new documentation naturally antiquated Gesenius's grammatical sketch and made possible a sound new study by Schröder (*Die phönizische Sprache*, 1869), which remained standard up to the appearance of Z. S. Harris's *Grammar of the Phoenician Language* in 1936. In 1881 the first part of the great *Corpus Inscriptionum Semiticarum* was issued, entirely as a result of the enthusiasm and organizing capacity of Renan; this work is still in progress, though greatly slowed down since the First World War and now far behind the progress of epigraphic discovery. Seventeen years later appeared Lidzbarski's solid *Handbuch der nordsemitischen Epigraphik* (1898), which was speedily followed by Cooke's *Text-book of North-Semitic Inscriptions* (1903); Phoenician epigraphy was now established on a firm basis, which has had to be extended but seldom rebuilt in the past forty years.

Meanwhile excavators were engaged in the archaeological recovery of the Phoenician past. Renan's pioneering expedition of 1860–1861 was followed rapidly by its publication in *Mission en Phénicie* (1864). Numerous minor excavations were undertaken between 1887 and 1914 by Turkish, French, and American archaeologists. The end of the World War found the French ready to undertake systematic excavations in Syria. Of the many archaeological enterprises which they carried out between 1921 and 1939 we may mention in particular the work at Byblus under Montet and Dunand (1921—), at Ugarit under Schaeffer (1929–1939), at Khadattu (Arslan Tash) under Thureau-Dangin (1928), at Hamath on the Orontes under Ingholt (1931–1938), at three mounds in the Plain of Antioch under McEwan (1932–1937), at Mari under Parrot (1933–1939), and at Alalakh under Woolley (1936–1939). Other major and minor excavations have contributed their quota to the recovery of ancient Syria; we have mentioned only those which have been of most value for our knowledge of Canaanite history and civilization. Curiously enough, excavations in Syria have thrown most light on the Bronze Age and the Hellenistic-Roman period; the earlier Iron Age, from the twelfth to the fourth centuries B.C., has been something of a step-child in Syrian archaeology. In Phoenicia itself scarcely any intact remains of the pre-Hellenistic Iron Age have been discovered, and even Byblus has yielded almost no fresh information of importance bearing on the Iron Age except for the tomb of Ahiram. The Phoenician strata of Tyre, Sidon, and other great cities lie so deeply buried under later accumulations that it will probably be long before they are explored. Our knowledge of Phoenician culture must, therefore, still come mainly from discoveries made outside Phoenician soil.

The task of synthesizing the monumental data and writing a history of Phoenician art and architecture, etc., was first seriously undertaken by Perrot and Chipiez as a part of their monumental history of ancient art. Vol. III, dealing with Phoenicia and Cyprus, came out in 1885 in both a French and an English edition, and still remains the most complete and best illustrated treatment of the subject. While the massive volume by the two French historians of art cannot be considered as a critical history of Phoenician art in the modern sense, it must always hold a high place in the history of the subject, in spite of its mistakes and its *naïvetés*. In 1912 it was to a considerable extent antiquated by Poulsen's important book, *Der Orient und die frühgriechische Kunst*, which still remains standard, in spite of the tremendous influx of new material from Arslan Tash, Samaria, Megiddo, and elsewhere. We shall discuss the curious oscillations of scholarly opinion on Phoenician art and its originality relative to Aegean art below, in part V of our study.

While archaeological research in Syria was dormant and while Phoenician epigraphy was developing slowly toward scientific status, archaeologists began excavations in Palestine which were to prove of very great importance for our knowledge of the Canaanite prehistory of the Phoenicians. In 1890 Flinders Petrie began the epochal excavation at Tell el-Hesi; his initial six-week campaign at that site was followed by stratigraphic excavations at many Bronze-Age sites, such as Gezer, Taanach, Megiddo and Jericho. After the First World War excavations were resumed with increasing momentum and a vast body of archaeological data was gathered and analyzed, until the chronology of ordinary Bronze-Age

artifacts is better established in Palestine than in any other country of
the Near East except Egypt, in spite of the paucity of datable inscriptions. Sites like Megiddo, Beth-shan, and Jericho, like Lachish and Tell
el-'Ajjul, like Tell Beit Mirsim and Beth-shemesh, like Bethel and Ai,
have yielded many of their secrets and have enabled us to write a history
of the evolution of Canaanite material culture. We shall not enter into a
detailed discussion of this topic, since it has often been undertaken elsewhere[3] and is only incidental to the theme of the present paper.

II. The Canaanites Before the Seventeenth Century b.c.

There is no object in dealing in this paper with the origin of the Phoenicians. The time is past when we need discuss the Erythraean theory of
Herodotus, or the derived speculations of Lieblein and other Egyptolo-
gists of the nineteenth century who connected "Phoenician, Punic" with
Egyptian Punt (probably Eritrea and Somaliland),[4] or the more recent
hypotheses of Virolleaud, Dussaud and others, who bring both Canaanites
and Israelites from the dry Negeb, south of Palestine.[5] Nor need we stop
to consider the prehistoric state of Phoenicia and Palestine[6] or the question of the home of the Semites. The Canaanites may well have been
settled in Palestine and Southern Syria as early as the fourth millennium,
and we now know that their predecessors in the land were not appreciably
dissimilar in race, judging from skeletal remains.[7] The oldest towns in
this region, whose foundation is dated by clear archaeological evidence
before 3000 b.c. at the latest, already bear such excellent Canaanite

---

[3] E.g., Albright, *The Archaeology of Palestine and the Bible*, New York, 1932–1935; "The
Present State of Syro-Palestinian Archaeology" in the *Haverford Symposium on Archaeology and the Bible*, New Haven, 1938, pp. 1–46.

[4] See the detailed discussion and refutation by R. Pietschmann, *Geschichte der Phönizier*
(1889), pp. 121 ff.

[5] See Albright, *Bull. Am. Sch. Or. Res.*, No. 71 (1938), pp. 35–40; R. de Langhe, *Eph.
Theol. Lovan.*, 16 (1939), pp. 245–327; J. Pedersen, *Berytus*, 6 (1941), pp. 63–104. For
Dussaud's views on the Negebite origin of the Phoenicians see especially his paper "Les
Phéniciens au Négeb et en Arabie d'après un texte de Ras Shamra" (*Rev. Hist. Rel.*, 108,
1933, pp. 5–49) and his later discussion, *Les découvertes de Ras Shamra et l'Ancien Testa-
ment* (1937), especially pp. 55–63.

[6] On this subject see Albright, *Jour. Pal. Or. Soc.*, 15 (1935), pp. 199 ff., and *Haverford
Symposium*, pp. 6 ff.

[7] Cf. *Bull. Am. Sch. Or. Res.*, No. 60 (1935), p. 3 and *Haverford Symposium*, p. 7.

names as "Jericho," "Beth-shean," "Beth-yerah," "Megiddo." The
Phoenician cities, such as Accho, Tyre, Sidon, Sarepta, Byblus, Arce,[8]
Simyra, virtually all have good Semitic names, often names which may
be called specifically Canaanite. Even in the extreme north of Canaan,
Ugarit, Gabala,[9] and many smaller towns bear names which are cer-
tainly or probably Canaanite. On the other hand non-Semitic names like
"Arvad" (Arwada), Wallazi (Ullazi),[10] appear in Northern Phoenicia in
the fifteenth and fourteenth centuries B.C., and may be much older.

While we still lack any direct monumental evidence from Mesopotamia
bearing on Syria south of Mount Amanus until the Ur documents of the
twenty-first century B.C.,[11] our Egyptian material is now far richer than
it was twenty years ago. The excavations at Byblus have yielded dated
Egyptian inscriptions extending as far back as Nebka (Khasekhemwi),
the last king of the Second Dynasty, and a number of characteristically
Thinite objects have been found in the débris of an early temple. Early
Egyptian remains at Byblus belong mostly to the Fifth and Sixth Dynasties, when the cedar trade was most active and Byblus had practically
become a colony of Egypt. At least as early as the Sixth Dynasty we find
ships used for Mediterranean traffic called "Byblus (ships)," *kbnyt.* In
Palestine excavations are also yielding an increasing number of objects
imported in early times from Egypt; the royal Canaanite acropolis at Ai,
for instance, has furnished a considerable number of Egyptian stone

---

[8] The name *'Irqatum,* *'Irqata* already appears in the execration texts from the beginning
of the second millennium; see Albright, *Jour. Pal. Or. Soc.,* 8 (1928), p. 245, and *Bull.
Am. Sch. Or. Res.,* No. 81, 18.

[9] Gabala (modern Jebeleh) is probably the *Gb'l,* i.e., *Gab'al* (cf. Heb. *gib'ôl*), of the
Ugaritic inscriptions. The name *Ugarit* itself is clearly connected with that of the com-
posite mythological figure *Gapnu-wa-Ugâru,* "Vineyard-and-Field," in which the second
element cannot be separated from Accadian *ugâru,* "field," which seems ultimately to be a
Sumerian loanword, like a number of other common words in Ugaritic Canaanite. The
name is to be pronounced *Ugârîtu* (nominative) for older **Ugârîyâtu,* with a phonetic development which is regular in Ugaritic. The corresponding South-Canaanite form would
normally be *Agôrît,* transcribed in Egyptian syllabic orthography as *A-ku-ri-ta* (with the
accusative ending, as usual in Egyptian transcriptions).

[10] See Albright, *Voc. Eg. Syl. Orth.* (1934), p. 47, X.A.1.

[11] For the new low chronology of Mesopotamian history which is employed in this paper
see especially the writer, *Bull. Am. Sch. Or. Res.,* No. 77, pp. 25–30 and Sidney Smith,
Alalakh and Chronology (London, 1940). Unpublished material makes this chronology certain within very narrow limits (see also Neugebauer, *Jour. Am. Or. Soc.,* 61 [1941], 58 ff.).

bowls of the Third Dynasty, found in a sanctuary belonging to about the middle of the third millennium.[12] Canaanite pottery and other objects occur in the royal tombs of the First Dynasty and more such material will unquestionably be discovered as excavations proceed.[13] At least two Canaanite loan-words are known in early Egyptian: one, ka(r)mu, "vineyard," appears in hieroglyphic texts of the Second Dynasty while the other, qamḥu, is found in the Fifth Dynasty.[14]

There can no longer be any doubt that the Egyptians actually claimed political suzerainty over most of Canaanite Palestine and Syria in the Old Kingdom. As we have seen above, Byblus was virtually an Egyptian colony from the reëstablishment of the Thinite empire by the Memphite king Nebka, Zoser's predecessor, to the collapse of the Memphite empire under the long-lived but weak Phiops II. According to the minimum Egyptian chronology which we follow here,[15] this period lasted over four centuries, from cir. 2600 to cir. 2200 B.C. Several Egyptian invasions of Canaan are attested during the Fifth and the Sixth Dynasties. Under Phiops I of the Sixth Dynasty no less than five rebellions against Egyptian rule are said to have taken place and a force of several myriads was required to crush one of the rebellions in question.

Between 2200 and 2000 B.C. we find a rapid decline in the density of sedentary occupation in Palestine, both east and west of the Jordan.[16] This decline, which reached its lowest point about the end of the third millennium, cannot be separated from the contemporary Babylonian reports of aggression on the part of the nomadic Western Semites, whom they called "Amorites" (i.e., Westerners).[17] Before the end of the Third Dynasty of Ur the movement of Semitic nomads into Babylonia had become sufficiently significant to be mentioned in year-names and documents, and the Larsa Dynasty, which arose in southern Babylonia im-

---

[12] Cf. *Jour. Pal. Or. Soc.*, 15, p. 210.

[13] For a partial list of the now available material, including especially inscribed objects, see Rowe, *A Catalogue of Egyptian Scarabs*, etc. (Cairo, 1936), pp. xiii ff.

[14] *Jour. Pal. Or. Soc.*, 15, pp. 212 f.

[15] See the references given by the writer, *From the Stone Age to Christianity* (1940), pp. 319 f., n. 23.

[16] See *Jour. Pal. Or. Soc.*, 15, 217 ff., abundantly confirmed by subsequent discoveries.

[17] Accadian *Amurrī(y)um* is adjectival from *amurrum*, "west," a Sumerian loanword (as shown by the form, though the Sumerian pronunciation of the ideographic *MAR-TU* is still unknown).

mediately after the fall of Ur III (cir. 2020 B.C.) was founded by Amorites. In the twentieth century or at the beginning of the nineteenth we find Amorite dynasties replacing native Accadian rulers at Babylon, at Eshnunna in northeastern Babylonia, and at Mari on the Middle Euphrates. The Mari documents, from the early eighteenth century, illustrate the Amorite occupation of most of Mesopotamia with a wealth of detail.[18] In them we find that practically all the region between the Taurus and the Zagros, between the coastland of Syria and the highlands of Elam, is dominated by princes with Amorite names. The region of Mari, which was still Accadian in the twenty-first century, to judge from proper names, had become overwhelmingly Amorite. Amorite dynasties were likewise installed in such Syrian cities as Aleppo and Qatna (el-Mishrifeh northeast of Emesa).

The evidence of the Egyptian execration texts from the Twelfth Dynasty (cir. 2000–1800 B.C.), which have been greatly increased in number and importance by Posener's recent publication, shows that Palestine was still dominantly in the hands of nomads with characteristic Amorite names about 2000 B.C., and that it became rapidly urbanized during the following two centuries, strictly in accord with the results of excavation.[19] The execration texts, combined with the data from Mari and from Byblus itself, make it possible for us to draw some extremely interesting conclusions about the political history of Byblus at this time. In sharp contrast to virtually all of the Palestinian and Phoenician towns mentioned in these documents, no princes or chieftains of Byblus are named, only its Asiatics and its clans. Since the execration texts come down at least into the early nineteenth century, it would seem that Byblus was then ruled by a council of elders, not by princes, as we know to have been the case after about the middle of the nineteenth century or a little later.[19a] It is very interesting to note that some, at least, of the cities of the

[18] For full bibliographic references to M. Parrot's sensational finds, as well as to the publication of texts by Dossin and others, see the writer's sketches, *Bull. Am. Sch. Or. Res.*, No. 67, pp. 26–30; No. 77, pp. 20 ff.; No. 78, pp. 23–31. For the emerging historical picture see the writer's account, *From the Stone Age to Christianity*, pp. 109, 111 f., 120 ff.

[19] See *Bull. Am. Sch. Or. Res.*, No. 81, pp. 16–21; 83, pp. 30–36.

[19a] In the second half of the nineteenth century we have Abi-shemu (or Abi) and his son Yapi-shemu-abi. Contemporary with Seḥetepibreʿ, the fourth king of the thirteenth Dynasty, we probably have Yakin-ilum (*Jour. Pal. Or. Soc.*, 2, 120, where I erroneously identified him with Amenemmes I), followed by Yantin-ʿammu (Antin) and perhaps by Ilum-yapi (*Jour. Pal. Or. Soc.*, 15, 226).

Egyptian Delta were at a slightly earlier time also governed by their own magistrates and enjoyed fiscal autonomy.[20] It is hard to avoid seeing some connection between the gerontocratic organization of the cities of the Delta in the early twenty-first century B.C. and the similar political structure of Byblus in the twentieth century, especially since the same word *whyt*, "clan," is employed with reference to both. The "republican" constitution of the cities of the Delta may safely be regarded as a result of the civil wars and Asiatic raids which reduced Egypt to a state of anarchy in the 22nd century, when the cities had to protect themselves as best they could. Since Byblus had previously formed part of the Egyptian Empire, it was natural enough that it should follow the example set by the ports of the Delta, with which it was so closely bound by ties of commerce.

Before the end of the third millennium, perhaps even before the close of the Sixth Dynasty in Egypt, the Canaanites had invented a syllabary of their own, clearly modelled to some extent after the Egyptian hieroglyphic system and containing at least eighty characters.[21] A considerable number of inscriptions in this script, all on stone or copper, has been discovered by Dunand at Byblus; the finding of one inscription on copper in the ruins of the Egyptianizing temple of the Old Empire is decisive for the general date of the script. The writer is inclined to consider the weathered inscription on a reused stela from northern Moab as an example of the same script; reasons for dating the original stela in the late third millennium have been given elsewhere[22] and there is no denying the fact that the traces do remind one strongly of the Byblian syllabary of the same age. It is quite possible that this script would have become standard in Canaanite and Amorite territory if it had not been for the conquering march of Accadian cuneiform in the first centuries of the second millennium.

There can be no doubt that the Canaanites were physically enriched

---

[20] See J. Pirenne, *Journal des Savants*, 1937, pp. 14–17. Some details of Pirenne's treatment must be modified (e.g., his reference to Athribis and some lexical points), but there can be little doubt that he is correct in the main.

[21] Cf. provisionally *Bull. Am. Sch. Or. Res.*, No. 60, pp. 3–6, together with Dunand's subsequent observations, *Mélanges Maspero*, I, pp. 567–571, and *Fouilles de Byblos*, I, pp. 30 (on No. 1140) and 158 (on No. 2334).

[22] See *Jour. Am. Or. Soc.*, 56 (1936), p. 129, n. 8. Several of the semi-legible signs on the Balû'ah stela have close analogies in the Byblos syllabary.

by the afflux of fresh blood from the east and we may perhaps suppose that they would have built up a civilization of their own in the next two or three centuries if it had not been for the pressure of Egypt from the south and of Mesopotamia from the east. The execration texts have demonstrated conclusively that the Egyptian pharaohs of the Twelfth Dynasty claimed suzerainty over Palestine and Phoenicia. That they not only claimed it but also exercised it has been shown by the discoveries at such sites as Byblus, Ugarit and Qatna in Syria, to say nothing of previous discoveries in Palestine, recently increased in number by finds at Megiddo.[23] We now know that political pressure from Babylonia did not begin until the early eighteenth century, in the time of the weak pharaohs of the Thirteenth Dynasty. However, owing in large part evidently to the occupation of nearly all Mesopotamia by the Amorites between 2000 and 1800 B.C., cultural contacts between Syria and Mesopotamia were so close as to produce a virtually identical culture from the Orontes Valley to the Zagros Mountains. This has been proved beyond cavil by recent excavations at Mari and Alalakh.

The collapse of Egyptian power in the early eighteenth century gave the Canaanites freedom to develop the cultural influences which had been streaming from Egypt and Mesopotamia during the preceding two or three centuries. The new culture of the Middle Bronze II was surprisingly rich in many respects, but it remained too syncretistic to possess a really independent artistic life, in this respect foreshadowing the cultural history of Iron-Age Phoenicia. The royal tombs of the late nineteenth century at Byblus still exhibit slavish cultural dependence on Egypt; it was not until about the middle of the eighteenth century that the Canaanites finally broke away, as shown especially by the ceramic and glyptic arts, which reached an extraordinary level of excellence at this time.[24] Our data

---

[23] Cf. *Jour. Pal. Or. Soc.*, 1935, pp. 220 f., and Wilson, *Amer. Jour. Sem. Lang.*, 1941, pp. 225–236.

[24] *Ibid.*, pp. 217, n. 73, 222; Frankfort, *Cylinder Seals* (1939), pp. 259 ff.; Watzinger, *Denkmäler Palästinas*, I, pp. 45 f. In this connection it may be emphasized that Strata E-D at Tell Beit Mirsim and Strata XII–IX at Megiddo have yielded proportionately many more beautiful objects than have any other strata in these sites (we except, of course, occasional hoards like the ivories of the twelfth century, on which see below). According to ceramic experts who have examined Palestinian wares of all ages, the Middle-Bronze II pottery is unequalled before the Greek period, both in beauty of form and in technical excellence. This is also true of the goldsmith's art and of jewelry, to say nothing of faience,

nearly all come from Palestine; Syrian sites hitherto excavated show a very remarkable lacuna, for reasons on which we shall presently touch. Sporadic finds in Phoenicia (especially at Ugarit) show that the focus of the new Canaanite civilization was really there and that Palestine was in general only an outlying district of it. It would seem that the ruling princes of Byblus in the eighteenth century were of Amorite, not Canaanite stock, but this point is of comparatively little significance, since the racial and linguistic difference between the two peoples can scarcely have been appreciable.[25] Their difference in culture was mainly due to the simple geographical fact that the Amorites were strongly influenced by Mesopotamian civilization, while the Canaanites were almost equally affected by Mediterranean and by Egyptian material culture.[26]

III. THE CANAANITES FROM THE SEVENTEENTH TO THE TWELFTH CENTURY B.C.

The elusive problem of the racial origin of the Hyksos conquerors of Egypt has now been substantially solved by the new data from Mari and Ugarit. Contrary to general opinion it turns out that all of the Hyksos names now known are certainly or probably Canaanite or Amorite.[27] Ma-

---

work in metal, etc. We need only refer to the objects found in patrician houses and tombs at Gezer, Jericho, Beth-shemesh, Tell Beit Mirsim, Tell el-'Ajjûl, Megiddo, Ugarit, to demonstrate our point.

[25] The linguistic difference between Amorite as reconstructed from personal names and words preserved in Old-Babylonian tablets, especially at Mari, and Canaanite is so slight that far-reaching conclusions are futile. Albrecht Goetze has very recently tried to show that the North Canaanite of Ugarit was really an Amorite dialect (*Language*, 1941, pp. 127–138), but this is again going too far; moreover, the cultural connections of Ugarit are mainly with Phoenicia, not with the Euphrates Valley. That the dialect of Ugarit was in some respects more closely related to the Amorite of the Euphrates Valley than it was to the South Canaanite of Phoenicia proper and Palestine we may well grant. It is also probable that the semi-nomadic East Canaanites (Amorites) swept through the coastal regions of Syria and Palestine, leaving a solid deposit of personal names. Thus, for example, a name like *Yantin-'ammu*, name of a prince of Byblus about 1760 B.C., both of whose elements are characteristically Amorite, the first phonetically, the second semantically (since the use of *'ammu*, "clan, kindred," in personal names was characteristic of Semitic nomadic groups), certainly suggests Amorite intrusion of some kind into Byblus.

[26] For excellent illustrations see Schaeffer, *Ugaritica*, pp. 19 ff., 53 ff.

[27] See below for several illustrations of this fact. Many names, such as *'Anat-har*, *Ya'qob-har*, *'Abd*, *Naḥmân*, etc., were already known to be Canaanite-Amorite, but the

netho was, accordingly, right in designating the Hyksos as "Phoenicians,"[28] and the Egyptians of the New Empire were essentially correct in calling them *'Aʒmu*, a name otherwise applied only to nomadic or semi-nomadic Semites. The hypotheses of recent writers, including the author of this paper, who would make them dominantly Hittite or Hurrian or Indo-European, thus prove to be unfounded, though it would be rash indeed to insist that there were no non-Semitic groups among the foreign conquerors of Egypt.[29]

Three dynastic groups of Syrian rulers of Egypt in the Second Intermediate Age are known. The first group consists of an obscure succession of "rulers of foreign lands" named *'Anat-har* (probably the *'Anata* of the Turin Papyrus), *Ya'qob-har*,[30] *Samuqena*,[31] *Bablimma*,[32] etc. That this group preceded the Fifteenth Dynasty is certain from the evidence of stratigraphy,[33] glyptic style,[34] and the Turin Papyrus.[35] The six kings of the Fifteenth Dynasty form the second group, but only the names of the last three are preserved in hieroglyphic form.[36] Under them was established an

---

rest defied explanation and Hurrian or Indo-European theories were current. Now we can add *Samuqena, Khayana, Bablimma (Nablimma)*, etc., to the list of Hyksos names of Semitic character. The mysterious Ugaritic names ending in *n*, to which the first two of these names belong, turn out, not to be Hurrian as thought by Thureau-Dangin, nor South-Anatolian (Luwian) as conjectured by the writer, but simply Canaanite. It may now be demonstrated that nearly all of them have hypocoristic endings, properly *ânu, âna*, which become *yânu, yâna* after an initial element ending in *i* (e.g., *Iliyâna, Shamshiyâna, 'Ammiyâna, Akhiyâna, Nuriyânu, Zukriyâna*), except where there is an initial *ya* in the name, in which case the ending becomes *inu (enu)* by dissimilation. Where the initial element ends in a consonant the ending remains *ânu*. This observation, illustrated by scores of examples, eliminates nearly all of the puzzling names in *n* from the supposed non-Semitic category.

[28] Eduard Meyer's skepticism about the Manethonian origin of this datum may now be corrected, since the datum in question is correct.

[29] See especially *Jour. Pal. Or. Soc.*, xv (1935), pp. 227 ff.

[30] Cf. *Jour. Bib. Lit.*, 1935, p. 191, n. 51 for the second element. The first element (biblical "Jacob") is found in personal and place-names attested in the eighteenth and the fifteenth centuries.

[31] *Jour. Pal. Or. Soc.*, xv, p. 229.

[32] *Ibid.*, p. 227, n. 107.

[33] *Ibid.*, p. 227.

[34] *Ibid.*, p. 227, n. 107.

[35] Farina, *Il papiro dei re* (Rome, 1938), pp. 49–56.

[36] The monuments of Apophis I and of Khayana are now quite numerous. The name

ephemeral Hyksos empire, ruled by such kings as Apophis I and Khayana, monuments of whom are found scattered over the Near East from Crete to Babylonia; this dynasty may now be dated cir. 1720–1610 B.C.[37] The third group, which may be perhaps termed the Sixteenth Dynasty, consisted at least of two Apophids and a king named *Shurk*,[38] or the like; it lasted not over fifty years, until the expulsion of the Hyksos in the latter part of the reign of Amosis I. It is scarcely accidental that our knowledge of the relative chronology and the material culture of the Hyksos age comes mainly from Palestine, since the focus of their power must have remained in their native land.

There is both archaeological and documentary evidence pointing to a great migratory movement or movements from the northeast into Syria between 1750 and 1600 B.C.[39] As a result of this movement Hurrian and Indo-Iranian tribes flooded the country. By the fifteenth century we find most of eastern and northern Syria occupied predominantly by Hurrians and Indo-Iranians. Even as far as southern Palestine non-Semitic groups are in the ascendancy. Megiddo, Jerusalem and Ascalon are all ruled by princes with Anatolian or Indo-Iranian names. The cranial type at Megiddo, which was previously Mediterranean in character, now becomes brachycephalic Alpine.[40] In the seventeenth century great rectangular

---

Apapa may be an Egyptianized Canaanite hypocoristic name like *Ababenu* (*Syria*, xviii, 249 ff.), presumably from an original name beginning with *abu*, "father"; Canaanite *b* often appears as *p* in Egyptian. The name *Khayana* seems to occur at Ugarit; see *Syria*, xix, 138, line 11, where we find the name *Ḥyn-m*. The name of the last king of the dynasty is at least partly preserved on the Turin Papyrus as reconstructed by Farina, who reads *Ḥ3-mw-dy*, transcribed by him *Ḥemeṭe*. The writer tentatively proposes a different reading for the second and third hieratic signs: [*ʾA?*]-*ḫu-du-ri*, corresponding to a Canaanite or Amorite *Aḫu-ṣûrî*, "The Brother is my Rock."

[37] According to the Turin Papyrus it lasted 108 years and presumably began with the occupation of Tanis, which formed an era in Egypt, commencing about 1720 B.C. If this view is correct it came to an end some twenty years before the capture of Babylon by the Hittites and may have just preceded the invasion of Northern Syria by Khattusilis I of the Hittite Empire (on this see Hardy, *Am. Jour. Sem. Lang.*, 1941, pp. 193, 213 f.).

[38] *Jour. Pal. Or. Soc.*, 15, p. 227, with references to Borchardt's publication, according to which *Sh3-r-k* and an Apophis were respectively contemporary with the grandfather and the father of a Memphite priest who flourished under Amosis I.

[39] Cf. *Jour. Soc. Or. Res.*, 1926, pp. 243 ff., 267 f.; *Jour. Pal. Or. Soc.*, 1935, pp. 223 ff.; *Bull. Am. Sch. Or. Res.*, No. 78, pp. 30 ff.

[40] See A. Hrdlička in Guy and Engberg, *Megiddo Tombs*, pp. 192 ff.

earthworks, after the model of older earthworks from Europe and Central Asia, were built in different parts of Syria, Palestine, and Lower Egypt; their chronological association with the Hyksos is certain and their connection with horse-drawn chariotry is obvious.[41] Horses and chariots were introduced into Western-Asiatic warfare by the Hittites between the twentieth and the eighteenth centuries, but the strong and speedy chariots which became so universal in the Late Bronze Age seem to have been introduced by the Indo-Iranians slightly later.[42] The first emergence of the latter in our available sources must be dated in the late seventeenth century, when several "Hurrian" kings bear clear Indo-Iranian names.[43]

It would, therefore, appear that the Canaanites of the Late Bronze Age were a much more mixed people than their ancestors of the Middle Bronze Age had been and that they were influenced by even more complex cultural trends. The extraordinary development of Aegean civilization inevitably led to the corresponding expansion of sea-trade, which already plays a respectable rôle in the Mari archives,[44] whereas there is no clear trace of it in the business documents of the Assyrian merchant colonies in Asia Minor in the twentieth century B.C. Objects of import are found increasingly in Egypt, Syria and the Aegean after the nineteenth century. During the following centuries trade expanded more or less steadily, reaching a climax in the fourteenth century B.C., and falling off notably in the thirteenth and especially in the twelfth, as we shall see. Thanks to the new wealth brought by trade, the Canaanites were able to develop a very high degree of material civilization, best known to us from Ugarit. Canaanite

---

[41] For recent literature on this subject see especially *Ann. Am. Sch. Or. Res.*, XVII (1938), pp. 28 f., n. 2, where necessary references are given.

[42] Dossin, *Revue Hittite et Asianique*, fasc. 35, pp. 70 ff.; Albright, *Bull. Am. Sch. Or. Res.*, No. 77, p. 31. On the subject of the early history of the horse and chariot in general see especially J. Wiesner, "Fahren und Reiten in Alteuropa und im alten Orient" (*Der Alte Orient*, 38: 2-4, especially pp. 22-44). However, though this monograph appeared in 1939, the Mari Tablets and other recent discoveries have already rendered both Wiesner's data and his chronology antiquated in vital respects. For example, there is still no clear evidence of horse-drawn chariots in Western Asia before the beginning of the second millennium.

[43] *Bull. Am. Sch. Or. Res.*, No. 78, p. 30, where P. E. Dumont has made some important observations, since confirmed by the study of new material from the Nuzi documents, to be published by P. M. Purves.

[44] Dossin, *Syria*, xx, pp. 111 f.; Albright, *Bull. Am. Sch. Or. Res.*, No. 77, pp. 30 f.

sculpture was at its height in the sixteenth century and the art of the gold-smith attained its peak in the following two centuries. The excavations in Cyprus, especially at Enkomi, have vividly illustrated the distribution of Canaanite works of art there. In northern Mesopotamia, too, Canaanite art was in demand, as we know from the excavations at Assur and Kar-Tu-kulti-Ninurta,[45] etc.

During these centuries Phoenicia became the center of the manufacture of purple dye and of embroidered textiles. The murex shell-fish was doubt-less native to the Syrian coast as well as to the coasts of Asia Minor and the Aegean, but the earliest evidence for the existence of the purple indus-try comes from the fifteenth century and is found in the Nuzi documents from eastern Mesopotamia.[46] At Ugarit it became highly developed in the next two centuries, as we know from Schaeffer's excavations at Minet el-Beida,[47] as well as from two tablets, one in Accadian and the other in Ca-naanite cuneiform.[48] Speiser has recently shown that the Greek name "Phoenicia" must refer to the purple industry ($\phi o \iota v \acute{o} s$ = "purple"),[49] and the writer believes that the name "Canaan" itself is a Hurrian expression meaning "Belonging to (the land of) Purple."[50] The purple industry must

---

[45] See Andrae, *Die jüngeren Ischtar-Tempel in Assur* (1935), pp. 78 ff., 106 ff., etc., where thirteenth-century objects imported from Canaan or imitated from Canaanite models are illustrated and described.

[46] See Speiser, *Language*, 1936, p. 124.

[47] Cf. Schaeffer, *The Cuneiform Texts of Ras Shamra-Ugarit* (1939), pp. 22 f., 38. There has been no detailed report so far.

[48] Thureau-Dangin, *Syria*, xv, pp. 137 ff. and Virolleaud, *Syria*, xix, pp. 131 ff. The Canaanite tablet has not been entirely understood by Virolleaud. It deals with eight and two-fifths talents of wool delivered by (not "to"; cf. the Accadian *ina qâti . . . așû* which corresponds exactly to Canaanite *bd . . . ys'a*) Shumeminu to the weavers for the purple industry ('*argamannu*, just as in Hebrew).

[49] Speiser, *ibid.*, pp. 121–126. Contrast Bonfante's labored criticism in *Classical Philology*, 1941, pp. 1–20, which substitutes wholly impossible speculations.

[50] Since this explanation is new a brief explanation is in order. Besides the word *arga mannu* (which seems to be derived from Anatolian *argam- [Hittite *arkammas*, "tribute"]), "red purple," we find Accad. *uknû*, "lapis lazuli" (somehow related, it would seem, to Greek κύανos) used at Ugarit for "blue purple" (later Assyrian *takiltu*, which also appears in Hebrew). The Canaanite equivalent of *uknû* is '*iqna'u*, also meaning primarily "lapis lazuli." Borrowed by the Hurrians (in the accusative form or without ending) it would appear as *ikna, and with the Hurrian ending -*ǧǧi* (cuneiform -*ḫḫi*), used to form adjectives of material and provenience (e.g., *šinniperuḫḫi*, "ivory," in cuneiform transcription, de-

then have been dominant in Phoenicia when the Hurrians came into close contact with the coast before the sixteenth century; we may perhaps date its rise to a place of economic importance in the eighteenth century, after the Mari documents. The only other valuable natural resources possessed by the Canaanites were the coniferous woods of Lebanon and Casius, exported to Egypt (the Mesopotamians can scarcely have come into direct contact with the Canaanites on the eastern slopes of Amanus, from which the former drew most of their coniferous timber), so their foreign trade may well have been dominated at that time by the purple garment industry.

It is still quite impossible to outline the reciprocal relationship between Minoan, Mycenaean, and Phoenician sea-power and commerce. In spite of the artistic and intellectual superiority of Minoan culture, the Cretans seem to have been lacking in enterprise, if we may judge from the fact that Asiatic and Egyptian imports into Crete seem to be more numerous from cir. 1600 to cir. 1400 B.C. than Minoan imports into Egypt and Canaan. Whether the piratic activities of the Lycians (who were doubtless not alone), known to us from the Amarna Tablets, had anything to do with the comparative slackness of trade, we cannot say. In any event, it is certain that an unparalleled period of Mycenaean trade expansion eastward began with the fall of Cnossus and continued until the irruption of the Sea-peoples toward the end of the thirteenth century. For a century and a half, from cir. 1375 B.C. to cir. 1225 B.C.[51] enormous quantities of Mycenaean

---

rived from Accad. *šinnipiru*, "ivory") it would become *$iknaǵǵi$ or *$knaǵǵi$ (cun. *Kinaḫḫi*, Phoen. *Kna'*, "Land of Purple"). The Nuzi Accadian *kinaḫḫu*, "purple," is simply Hurrian *$knaǵǵi$ with Accadian nominative ending. With the determinative ending -*ni* the word becomes *$knáǵǵini$, whence Accadian *Kinaḫni*, Heb. *Kná'an*. It is possible that the ending is not the Hurrian adjectival suffix, which appears as *ḫ* in Ugaritic transcription ('*en trḫn = enna duruḫḫina*) and should be voiceless if the rules worked out by Sturtevant and Speiser operate here, but the gentilic, which appears as *ǵ* in Ugaritic transcription (e.g., *Ttb Ḫlbǵ = Tešub Ḫalpaḫi*) and should be voiced according to Speiser and Sturtevant. In this case *$knaǵǵi$ (for *$kna'ǵi$?) would mean originally "Belonging to (the land of) Purple." The etymology is not, however, affected by this possible substitution of suffixes. J. Lewy has proposed a similar etymology, "Land of Reeds," in *Rev. Et. Sém.*, 1938, pp. 49–54. Ours is quite independent.

[51] For the date at which Mycenaean ware began to be imported in appreciable quantities into Palestine and Syria see the writer's remarks, *Ann. Am. Sch. Or. Res.*, XII, §60, corrected by the revised treatment *ibid.*, XVII, §87. The recent publication of the pottery

vases were imported into all parts of Canaan, from Ugarit and Qatna in the north to the Negeb of Palestine in the south.[52] In these vases were brought mainly perfumes and cosmetic products.[53] Since few Syrian vases of this age have been found in the Aegean area, we must resort to guessing the nature of the Syrian merchandise received in exchange. A fair guess would be that manufactured goods such as purple garments and furniture (see above) and natural products such as grain and spices (e.g., myrrh and balsam, both mentioned in the Amarna Tablets) formed a large part of the bartered Syrian merchandise. What other manufactured goods and natural products were imported into Canaan from the Aegean at that time is not yet clear.[54]

All branches of Canaanite art and craftsmanship which we can follow from century to century through Palestinian excavations, show pronounced —often catastrophic—decline between their height about the sixteenth

---

from the Fosse Temple at Lachish is in agreement with this general date, as is also Sjöqvist, *Problems of the Late Cypriote Bronze Age* (1940), pp. 194 f. The end of the period is marked by less clear-cut evidence from stratigraphy; decisive is typology, since Mycenaean granary and close styles are entirely missing. For details see especially Mackeprang, *Am. Jour. Arch.*, 1938, pp. 537–559, and Daniel, *ibid.*, 1940, pp. 553 ff.

[52] On this pottery, which he calls "Levanto-Helladic," see now Sjöqvist, *op. cit.*, pp. 65 ff., 92 ff., 212. His contention that the Mycenaean ware in Syria and Palestine was made by local colonies of Mycenaean potters is very unconvincing, especially in view of the identity of wares and techniques between "Levanto-Helladic" and native Aegean pottery (see pp. 65 f.). It is quite possible that there were such colonies in Cyprus (with reference to which Sjöqvist is less than clear) and even in Ugarit (with Schaeffer), but Syrian potteries would have been compelled to use Syrian clays. Ancient potters were not so skilled that they could duplicate exotic wares; numerous examples show that they preferred exterior camouflage to laborious efforts to duplicate materials. The view that Mycenaean vases found in the eastern Mediterranean were actually imported from the Aegean seems still most probable, though it may well require modification with regard to Cyprus (see now especially Sjöqvist, *op. cit.*, p. 212!).

[53] Here we must enter a vigorous protest against the theory that Mycenaean pottery was exported *en masse* empty from the Aegean. We must surely assume an active basic trade in perfume; cf. Sjöqvist, *op. cit.*, p. 29, on the similar use of base-ring ware. Of course, open bowls and cups could not be so used but they need much less space. Moreover, it is likely enough that perfume manufacturers in the Eastern Mediterranean sometimes ordered empty vases in which to pack their own substitutes for the Syrian market.

[54] On Mycenaean influence and imports at Ugarit see especially Schaeffer, *Ugaritica* (1939), pp. 72–106.

century and their lowest point about the end of the thirteenth.[55] This fact becomes particularly clear when we examine successive groups of pottery made in Canaan and not imported from outside, when we compare the sculpture and glyptic art of the period 1600–1400 with that from the thirteenth century, when we compare tomb-groups and patrician houses or fortifications from earlier and later phases. Ugarit shows the same general picture in this respect as Beth-shan and Tell Beit Mirsim, in spite of the fact that Ugaritic wealth seems to have been greater, rather than less, in the thirteenth century than in the sixteenth. Explanations for this general situation are not hard to find, though each must remain strictly limited in its validity and there may be additional causes which we cannot control. The oppressive weight of heavy Egyptian taxation and corrupt administration during the long period of the New Empire, from cir. 1550 to cir. 1220, must be placed first in any catalogue, since it is only too well attested by Egyptian sources, vividly illustrated by the Amarna Tablets.[56] Hittite rule in the north from cir. 1370 to cir. 1220 was much less centralized, local administration being largely in the hands of several hereditary kings belonging to the Hittite imperial family. Nor is there any evidence that Hittite officialdom was organized on anything like the bureaucratic plan which the Egyptians had inherited from the Pyramid Age. Canaanite social organization did not lend itself to the development of crafts and guilds, since it combined an aristocracy of "chariot-warriors," partly non-Semitic in origin,[57] with a lower class composed partly of half-free serfs or coloni (*khupshu*)[58] and partly of slaves. A true middle class seems to have been wanting. In other words there was apparently no class or stratum of the population which was in a position to undertake enterprises on its own initiative or which could be fired with ambition to change its ways and develop along new lines. A third reason, which must not be discounted because of its relative intangibility, was probably the extremely low level of Canaanite religion, which inherited a relatively very primitive mythology and had adopted some of the most demoralizing cultic practices then existing in the Near East. Among these practices were human sacrifice, long

---

[55] Cf. *Ann. Am. Sch. Or. Res.*, XVII (1938), §77.

[56] Cf. Albright, *The Archaeology of Palestine and the Bible*, pp. 99 f.; *From the Stone Age to Christianity*, pp. 155 f.

[57] *Archiv für Orientforschung*, VI, pp. 217 ff.

[58] See I. Mendelsohn, *Bull. Am. Sch. Or. Res.*, No. 83 (October, 1941).

given up by the Egyptians and Babylonians, sacred prostitution of both sexes, apparently not known in native Egyptian religion though widely disseminated through Mesopotamia and Asia Minor, the vogue of eunuch priests (*kumru, komer*),[59] who were much less popular in Mesopotamia and were not found in Egypt, serpent worship to an extent unknown in other lands of antiquity. The brutality of Canaanite mythology, both in the tablets of Ugarit and in the later epitome of Philo Byblius, passes belief; to find even partial parallels in Egypt and Mesopotamia one must go back to the third millennium B.C. The reasons adduced to explain Canaanite decline in the Late Bronze Age may at least be called impressive, and their cumulative force cannot be disregarded.

Canaanite literature has been partly recovered by the excavations of Schaeffer at Ugarit and the publication of many tablets by Virolleaud. Three mythological epics, Baal and Anath, Danel and Aqhat, and Keret, contained a number of tablets each, over half of the extant remains of which have been published. All other literary remains are religious, including abstracts of myths, rituals, and hymns. Verbally and stylistically these specimens of Canaanite literature show striking similarity to Hebrew poetry, especially to such early poems as the Song of Deborah[60] and the Lament of David over Jonathan,[61] and to poetic literature from the Exilic and Postexilic ages (on which see below). There can be no doubt whatever that Hebrew poetic literature was under immeasurable obligation to Canaanite poets of the Bronze Age, who fashioned the vehicle and cultivated the style which have given biblical verse most of its formal appeal. There are striking parallels between the prosody and the style of Canaanite and of early Accadian poetry, especially Accadian poetry of the so-called hymnal-epic category, which clearly goes back to pre-Sumerian times for its roots. The bulk of Accadian verse arose, however, as translation or adaptation of Sumerian originals and, even when the language shows strong stylistic influence from hymnal-epic sources, the result bears little similarity to Canaanite or to Biblical Hebrew poetry. On the other hand, Ca-

---

[59] Albright, *From the Stone Age to Christianity*, p. 325, n. 46.

[60] See already *Bull. Am. Sch. Or. Res.*, No. 62 (1936), pp. 26–31. Subsequent discoveries in the Ugaritic field have materially increased the number of parallels: e.g., there are many instances of the climactic parallelism first isolated by Burney and now found to be characteristic of Canaanite verse (cf. Gordon, *Ugaritic Grammar*, 1940, p. 80, §12. 5–6).

[61] See Ginsberg, *Jour. Bib. Lit.*, 1938, pp. 209–213.

naanite poetry was strongly influenced by Hurrian models[62] and by Hurrian poetic devices,[63] as might have been expected, in view of the symbiotic relation in which many Canaanite and Hurrian groups lived in the late Middle and the Late Bronze Ages. There is increasing evidence for influence of some kind from Canaanite literature on early Greek, presumably exerted through South-Anatolian intermediation, but our data are still isolated and subject to eventual reinterpretation.

In the Late Bronze Age there were at least two consonantal alphabetic scripts which had been devised by Canaanites for their own use. The cuneiform alphabet is still known only from Ugarit and Beth-shemesh, but there can be little doubt that it was more widely used at one time—perhaps in the sixteenth and fifteenth centuries. There is no adequate reason to suppose that it was anything but an original Canaanite invention, the work of a man who was acquainted with the idea of writing on clay in wedges, as well as with the hieroglyphiform alphabet of Canaan in the late Middle Bronze, which employed only consonants.[64] We may perhaps suppose that he knew little or nothing about the details of either script, since he would otherwise presumably have modelled his new script more directly after cuneiform or have devised only one *aleph* sign instead of three, each with a different vowel.[65] The other alphabetic script was the direct progenitor of later Phoenician, but there is little reason to believe that it was directly influenced by the earlier syllabic script of Byblus.[66] We now

---

[62] See Ginsberg, *Orientalia*, VIII, pp. 317 ff.; see also a forthcoming paper by Goetze in *Jour. Bib. Lit.*, 1941.

[63] E.g., the frequent stylistic device of the use of graduated numbers in Canaanite poetry, often as "seven . . . eight," appears also in Hurro-Hittite verse, as pointed out by Friedrich.

[64] Cf. the writer's remarks in *The Haverford Symposium on Archaeology and the Bible* (1938), pp. 18 f. On the one hand Olmstead goes too far in trying to derive the cuneiform alphabet from the early Phoenician in Sprengling. *The Alphabet*, Chicago, 1931, pp. 57–62; and Ebeling goes too far on the other in deriving it from Old Babylonian cuneiform (*Forschungen und Fortschritte*, 1934, pp. 193–194). B. Rosenzweig's recent effort to improve on Olmstead (whom he does not mention), *Zeits. Deutsch. Morg. Ges.*, 92 (1938), pp. 178 ff., cannot be regarded as successful.

[65] On the problem of the three alephs see especially Friedrich, *ibid.*, 91, pp. 322, and Eissfeldt, *Ras Schamra und Sanchunjaton* (1939), pp. 58 ff.

[66] Cf. Dunand, *Mélanges Maspero*, I (1934), 569 ff. (subsequent discoveries have added two more characters to the list of correspondences); contrast the writer, *Bull. Am. Sch. Or. Res.*, No. 60, p. 5.

possess a number of short inscriptions in this script from the Late Bronze Age, all datable to the period 1400–1200 B.C. and all partly, if not wholly, decipherable.[67] We also possess at least three inscriptions in the same script from Middle-Bronze Palestine, between 1700 and 1500 B.C., as well as a considerable number of more cursive graffiti and inscriptions from Sinai, to be dated in the same general age.[68] It is a remarkable commentary on the versatility of the Canaanites of the Middle Bronze Age that they should have invented at least two original alphabets in which to record their transactions, in spite of the fact that they were already familiar with at least three more complex scripts, Accadian cuneiform, Egyptian hieroglyphics, and Byblian syllabic characters. It is an equally striking commentary on their imitative propensities that in the Late Bronze Age they failed to employ either alphabet generally, but preferred the complicated Accadian cuneiform system, even for ordinary business transactions.

IV. The Canaanites in the Transition from Bronze to Iron

In the thirteenth century the decadent Canaanites were rudely disturbed by the movements which brought the Israelites into Palestine and the Aramaean tribesmen into Syria. The Israelite invasion seems to have begun about the middle of the century and to have reached its climax about 1230 B.C.[69] By the end of the twelfth century, at the latest, the Israelites had established themselves firmly in the hill-country of Palestine, from Laish and Abel, due east of Tyre, to the extreme south. Closely fol-

---

[67] Cf. the writer's sketch, *Bull. Am. Sch. Or. Res.*, No. 63, pp. 8–11. In the past five years a new inscription in this category has been found at Megiddo and other efforts at interpreting the inscriptions have been made, particularly by Obermann. The writer hopes shortly to publish some suggestions for improved readings.

[68] For the most recent and complete bibliographic sketch of the Palestinian inscriptions see Yeivin, *The History of the Jewish Script* (Hebrew), I (1939), pp. 89 ff. For the latest account of the Proto-Sinaitic documents see Butin, *Excavations and Protosinaitic Inscriptions at Serabit el Khadem* (Kirsopp Lake, *Studies and Documents*, VI, 1936), pp. 31–42. The writer still adheres in principle to his own tentative proposals for decipherment (*Jour. Pal. Or. Soc.*, 1935, pp. 334 ff.), but considers the material as insufficient to permit a decision at present.

[69] For the most recent account of the movement see the writer, *Bull. Am. Sch. Or. Res.*, No. 74, pp. 11–23. For an admirable popular account of the state of our knowledge at present see G. E. Wright, *The Biblical Archaeologist*, Vol. III, No. 3 (1940).

lowing the Israelites came the irruption of the Sea Peoples, who swept over the Eastern Mediterranean basin like a flood in the half-century which began cir. 1225 B.C. After devastating the Hittite Empire, as well as the coast of Syria and Palestine, they were defeated by Rameses III in a great land and naval battle on the Egyptian coast (1188–1187 B.C.). However, the Egyptians were quite unable to dislodge the invaders from the occupied territory, and the Philistines took permanent possession of the Canaanite territory in the south, from Gaza to south of Joppa, while the Tsikal[70] settled further north at Dor. Ugarit was certainly destroyed at this time and Tyre was probably destroyed soon afterwards, since it was just as much exposed to a sufficiently powerful attack by sea as it was protected by its insular situation from land invasion. Shortly after these two formidable invasions the Aramaean[71] tribesmen from the Syrian Desert occupied much of the Canaanite hinterland of Phoenicia, from Hauran to the Eleutherus Valley, but details escape us entirely; we know only that the Aramaean movement reached its climax in the eleventh century.

These invasions reduced the extent of Canaan along the coast by about three-fifths, from over 500 km. in a straight line to less than 200. In the south the Canaanite border was pushed north from Raphia to the Ladder of Tyre; in the north it was pushed south from the northern boundary of Ugarit (Mons Casius) to just north of Arvad. In later times the Phoenicians regained the coast of Palestine as far south as Joppa, but they never recovered any appreciable part of the hinterland, which was lost for good. At a conservative estimate they lost *nine-tenths* of the region over which Canaanite culture had once prevailed. What a terrific shock this must have been cannot easily be appreciated today. On the other hand, they were forced by circumstances and enabled by the march of civilization to exploit their mountainous hinterland of Lebanon to an extent not previ-

---

[70] According to the writer's system of transcription (*The Vocalization of the Egyptian Syllabic Orthography*, p. 65, xx. A. 14), the name appears in Egyptian as *Tsi-ka-ra* and *Tsi-ka-ar*, but there is no distinction made in these texts between *l* and *r*. This people may be identical in name with the classical *Sikel*, who later gave their name to Sicily.

[71] In the writer's opinion the Aramaeans of the Assyrian inscriptions from 1100–800 B.C. were North-Arab tribesmen who were occupied in settling down in Syria and Northern Mesopotamia and who adopted the local Northwest-Semitic dialect of the Upper Euphrates region. In other words the people were in part originally Aramaeans but the language was a later acquisition.

ously possible. Thanks to the then recent discovery of the uses to which plaster made with slaked lime could be put, they were able to dig cisterns everywhere and to line them with true lime plaster, impervious to water.[72] As in Israelite Palestine this made it possible, not only to develop intensive cultivation of the rich coastal lands of the Libanese Riviera, but also to build villages in the mountains, as well as to provide for a much larger population on such islands as Tyre and Arvad. In coming centuries it would similarly make it possible for the Phoenicians to colonize waterless islands all over the Mediterranean, thus giving them well protected stations for their expanding commerce. The vast forests of Mount Lebanon made it possible to build great navies and the discovery of iron there[73] enabled the Phoenicians to build their ships and arm their sailors without interference from outside.

Another factor of importance for the new colonizing activity of the Phoenicians was the invigoration of the decadent Canaanite stock by fresh blood, especially from the hardy mountaineers of Syria and the equally hardy peasants of northern Israel, who were drawn into Phoenician service by its tempting emoluments. We need not go as far as Slousch[74] and Rosen[75] to recognize the great significance of these sources of man-power.

The destruction of Ugarit in the north and apparently of Tyre in the south made Sidon and Byblus the leading—perhaps the only autonomous —states of Phoenicia. In the Bible the Phoenicians were thenceforth called "Sidonians," and "Sidonian" appears in the Homeric poems as a synonym of "Phoenician." Both in the Bible and in Phoenician and Assyrian inscriptions kings of Tyre (e.g., Ittoba'al I, Hiram II, and Elulaeus) are designated as "kings of the Sidonians." Eduard Meyer has explained this as

---

[72] For many years the writer has endeavored to find proof of the existence of Bronze-Age cisterns in Palestine, hitherto without success. It is also quite certain that true lime plaster has not yet been identified by experts before the Iron Age, all older samples being of gypsum or hydraulic plaster.

[73] Cf. Albright, *Archaeology of Palestine and the Bible*, p. 215, n. 75.

[74] N. Slousch(z), *Les Hébraeo-Phéniciens*, Paris, 1909. According to him the Phoenicians who colonized the Western Mediterranean were mainly of Hebrew origin. This goes much too far, but the Song of Deborah, v. 17, proves that the Danites took service as sailors in the early eleventh century (*Bull. Am. Sch. Or. Res.*, No. 78, pp. 7 ff.).

[75] See Rosen and Bertram, *Juden und Phönizier* (1929), who lay their emphasis mainly on an alleged amalgamation of the Phoenician colonists in the Mediterranean with the Jews in the Hellenistic-Roman period.

due to a great expansion of Tyre at the expense of its sister-city, Sidon, after the reign of Hiram I (cir. 969–936 B.C.),[76] but this is quite an unnecessary supposition. Justin, probably quoting Timaeus, tells us that the Sidonians founded Tyre after a defeat at the hands of the king of Ascalon.[77] Moreover, Sidonian coins of the Seleucid age call Sidon "mother of Kambe (Carthage), Hippo, Citium (in Cyprus), and Tyre." Since Carthage and Citium (also called "Carthage," i.e., New Town, *Qart-ḥadasht*) were both Tyrian colonies, their mention proves clearly enough that the Tyre of this list is none other than the Phoenician city itself. It follows that some time after the reoccupation of Tyre as a Sidonian settlement in the early twelfth century (the traditional era of Tyre was 1198–1197 B.C.) it became the official seat of Sidonian government, the capital of the Sidonians. During these centuries, then, the terms Tyrian and Sidonian are merely synonyms. Between 950 and 850 B.C. the territory controlled by the Sidonian state was extended southward as far as Carmel and northward as far as Tripolis; this period saw the climax of Sidonian power, as far as Phoenicia proper was concerned.

Owing mainly to the lack of deep excavations at Sidon, as well as to the virtual impossibility of carrying out effective work at Tyre, we know nothing about early Sidonian history from inscriptions. On the other hand, a whole series of inscriptions, recently discovered at Byblus by Montet and Dunand (including two previously discovered but misinterpreted for lack of parallel material), enable us to reconstruct a partial list of Byblian kings in the eleventh and tenth centuries. The two latest rulers in this list, Abi-ba'al and Eliba'al, are dated by the reigns of their Egyptian suzerains Shishak I and Osorkon I to the second half of the tenth century. The inscriptions of Ittoba'al (on behalf of his father Ahiram) and Yehimilk have been erroneously dated back to the thirteenth or the twelfth centuries B.C., whereas they cannot be earlier than the eleventh and may even belong to the beginning of the tenth.[78] These inscriptions show a most striking prog-

---

[76] *Geschichte des Altertums*, II, 2 (2nd ed.), p. 126.

[77] It may be, as often thought, that the king of the Ascalonians was a Philistine. Another suggestion, that someone confused the Tsikal (Phoen. *Skl-*) with the Ascalonians (Phoen. 'ṣqln-), is very unlikely.

[78] The writer has hitherto dated the Ahiram Sarcophagus too high, owing mainly to his efforts to keep from breaking too violently with the date of Montet, accepted by Vincent and by most other scholars who have written on the subject (Spiegelberg and Lidzbarski

ress toward flowing cursive on the part of the Canaanite alphabet; such examples as the *mem* of Yehimilk and the *aleph* of Ittoba'al show that the scribes not only imitated cursive script successfully on stone but also some times employed extreme cursive forms which failed to obtain general

excepted). For his successive discussions, during which he lowered the date from the thirteenth century to about 1100 B.C., see especially *Jour. Pal. Or. Soc.*, 1927, pp. 126 f.; *Archiv. für Orientforschung*, v (1929), p. 150; *Bull. Am. Sch. Or. Res.*, No. 63, pp. 8 f. There are two main lines of intrinsic evidence: (1) the resemblance in content, throne, costume, etc., to an ivory plaque from Megiddo (Loud, *Megiddo*, Pl. IV), which cannot be later than cir. 1150 (see n. 108), is too great to allow a very great interval between them; (2) the argument from script prevents our assuming too great an interval between the Ahiram Sarcophagus and the second half of the tenth century. A date around 1050 would best suit the intrinsic indications. The extrinsic argument is based mainly on the latest pottery found in the filling of the chamber and the shaft, which is emphatically stated by Montet and Vincent to be contemporary with the burial (or at most not long subsequent). The sherds published by Montet and Dussaud contain some Late-Bronze examples, but there are also a considerable number of geometric sherds. In the total absence of stratigraphic data for the chronology of this ware from Phoenicia itself, we must resort to comparison with parallels in Cyprus and Palestine. The sherds in question are mainly black-on-red, and appear to be most closely related to pottery from the White-painted II phase of Gjerstad, which the latter assigns to the tenth–ninth century. His date for the beginning of White-painted I (cir. 1050) is either too low (Sjöqvist raises it to cir. 1075) or indicates that there was a considerable lag between putative Phoenician prototypes and Cypriote imitations (assuming that the latter are secondary to the former, which remains to be proved). It seems likely that Cypriote White-painted I really began about 1100 B.C. and that similar ware (ultimately adapted from Mycenaean prototypes) was in use even earlier in Phoenicia. At Megiddo Shipton has recorded a vase (*Notes on the Megiddo Pottery of Strata VI–XX*, §15, p. 6) which cannot be later than the first half of the eleventh century (probably not later than cir. 1075) and which bears strikingly close resemblance to vases of Cypriote White-painted I. At Gibeah the writer discovered a sherd said by Gjerstad to belong to White-painted I in the ruins of the citadel of Saul (*Ann. Am. Sch. Or. Res.*, IV, p. 87, No. 7), in no case later than cir. 1020 B.C. Cypriote Black-on-red I, to which the Byblus sherds seem to belong, may then have come into use by the middle of the eleventh century even though coeval (roughly speaking) with White-painted II. It must be emphasized that the ointment juglets of the type figured by Gjerstad (*Cyprus Expedition*, I, Pl. cxxxvi: 6) and assigned by him to Black-on-red I, are found in Palestinian deposits of the eleventh century (Albright, *Ann. Am. Sch. Or. Res.*, XII, §95, p. 72).—If then we may date the Ahiram Sarcophagus about the middle of the eleventh century we are far enough removed from the Palestinian inscriptions of the thirteenth century (see above, n. 67) to allow time for drastic changes in forms of letters, and yet not so far from the Abiba'al-Eliba'al dedications that we cannot explain the close resemblance to them in its script.

vogue and rapidly went out of use. It is evident that writing was intensively cultivated by the Phoenicians of that day, as vividly illustrated by Zekarbaʿal's receipt of 500 papyrus rolls from Egypt as part payment for cedar wood (cir. 1080 B.C.).

We can state with considerable confidence that Phoenician commercial expansion in the Mediterranean did not seriously begin until after the time of Zekarbaʿal, as we may infer from the data found in the Report of Wenamun, special envoy from Egypt to Byblus, about 1080 B.C. In the first place, piratic activity on the part of the Sea Peoples was still acute. In the second place, Cyprus appears as a land quite outside the political spheres of both the Egyptians and the Phoenicians. Thirdly, we find an explicit statement about the mercantile organization prevailing in Wenamun's time. In the harbor of Byblus were twenty ships (not all there at once) which were in *khubûr* relationship with Smendes, prince of Tanis. At Sidon there were fifty ships in a similar relation to a man with the non-Semitic name *Wrktr* or *Wlktr*.[79] From the context and from the meaning of the word *khubûru* in Accadian and Ugaritic (and of the derived *shbêr* in Coptic) we must suppose that it has some such meaning as "trading company."[80] Thanks to the *khubûr* it was possible to find the necessary capital

---

[79] There is no warrant whatever for the usual transcription with initial *b* and the reading *Birket-el.* For some fanciful—and extremely ingenious—speculations see Eisler, *Zeits. Deutsch. Morg. Ges.*, 1924, pp. 61 ff.

[80] The meaning was correctly given by the writer in *Vocalization*, p. 18, n. 77, but the etymology there proposed is false. The correct etymology was given *Bull. Am. Sch. Or. Res.*, No. 63 (1936), p. 28, n. 27, where an article on the subject was promised. The article in question has not been written but the conclusions have now been in large part anticipated by Rosenthal, *Orientalia*, 1939, p. 231 f. and by Brandenstein, *Zeits. f. Assyr.*, 46 (1940), 87, n. 1. Schroeder (*Zeits. f. Assyr.*, 35, p. 49) was clearly right in explaining Assyrian *bît ḫubûri, bît ḫuburni, bît ḫiburni* (the latter two being Hurrianized forms with the Hurrian demonstrative particle *-ni*) as *Proviantmagazin*, "storehouse for grain." With this rendering would agree the Assyrian documentary evidence, the building inscriptions (according to which this building had thick double walls, necessary for insulation against moisture), the Keret Epic of Ugarit (in which Keret gets wheat for the *bt ḫbr*), and the references in Proverbs. In Accadian *ḫubûru* means "company, community, assembly," and Hebrew *ḫbr* (for *ḫbr) has the same meaning in the Maccabaean coins, as pointed out by Rosenthal. There were demonstrably two Semitic stems with similar meanings, *ḫbr* and *ḫbr*. Coptic *šbêr*, "companion, partner," bears the same relation to older Egyptian *ḫubûra*, "company, partnership," that Phoenician *mmlkt*, "king," bears to older Canaanite *mmlkt*, "kingdom." Semantic parallels are legion.

with which to build and outfit trading fleets, as well as to protect them after they were built. These merchant fleets were still employed mainly in trade between Egypt and Phoenicia; there is no hint of a developed commerce with more distant lands, such as the Aegean. In fact, we may very probably assume that trade between Syria and the Aegean was still mainly in the hands of the Sea Peoples and their congeners.

V. THE PHOENICIAN PROBLEM

Attentive study of Greek and Latin historical sources, in the absence of archaeological or epigraphic check, could only result in the attribution to the Phoenicians of a dominant rôle in the early history of the Mediterranean, before the beginning of Greek colonization, and even to some extent after it. Such solidly established historical facts as the Phoenician origin of the Carthaginians, who controlled the Western Mediterranean for more than three hundred years, and as the Phoenician origin of the letters of the Greek alphabet seemed to authenticate the sweeping statements of ancient writers. After the decipherment of Phoenician there was a strong tendency to go even farther than classical sources in making claims for the Phoenician origin of Mediterranean civilizations. Men like Movers, followed by third-rate etymologizers, filled the Mediterranean with Phoenician colonies and geographical names. All Greek art and culture were derived from Phoenician sources.

The discovery of the Mycenaean civilization which began with Schliemann's excavations at Mycenae in 1874 was not long in effecting a complete *volte-face*. After a brief period during which the astonishing new finds were naïvely attributed to the Phoenicians, such savants as Milchhöfer and Salomon Reinach came out strongly (both in 1883) in favor of their autochthonous character. In 1893 Reinach published his famous brochure, *Le mirage oriental*, and though he was opposed by Helbig (1896) and others, the sensational finds at Cnossus after 1900 carried the day completely and no competent archaeologist has since dared to take up the cudgels again on behalf of the Phoenicians in the second millennium B.C.[81] Meanwhile Beloch went so far (1894) as to deny that the Phoenicians exerted any in-

---

[81] There are of course some exceptions, even among archaeologists of standing, like Dörpfeld (see below), but one would hesitate to apply the term "competent" to a man who had fallen so far behind the main body of scholarship.

fluence at all on Greece and Greek commerce in the early first millennium B.C.; according to him Herodotus and Thucydides were either romancing or were misinformed. Beloch's point of view was most recently and most forcibly presented in the second edition of his *Griechische Geschichte* (1913). He maintained (Vol. I, Chap. VII) that there was no evidence whatever, either archaeological or literary (since he considered all contrary statements in Greek writers as based on "haltlosen Kombinationen"), for admitting the existence of any Phoenician colonies or trading stations in the Aegean region at any period. At most he would only admit that the Orientalizing style of the eighth century and later, as well as the adoption of the Phoenician alphabet (which he attributed to the ninth century), pointed to commercial relations of some kind in the age of the first Greek colonies and of the Greek epics (according to his chronology). In discussing the Phoenicians in the Western Mediterranean (Chap. XXII) he went still further: Phoenician colonization in pre-Punic times was very much less important than generally supposed and there is no valid archaeological or literary evidence to carry it back before the seventh century. In other words, the earliest Greek settlements in the Western Mediterranean were earlier than (or as early as) the oldest Phoenician factories. Beloch expressed himself skeptically about the official Punic date of the foundation of Carthage (814 B.C.), which he was unwilling to place before the seventh century, or the eighth at the earliest. Biblical references to Tarshish proved nothing, he claimed, for the period before the Deuteronomic redaction of Kings in the sixth century B.C. Other scholars went still farther, and even the Phoenician origin of the Greek alphabet was regarded with increasing skepticism. Dussaud expressed the attitude of a whole school of thought when he denied that the Greeks borrowed their alphabet from the Phoenicians and maintained that both obtained it from a common source, which was probably the Minoan script.[82] Subsequent discoveries have brought about a change of view on Dussaud's part, as we shall see.

Unfortunately for the legitimate claims of the Phoenicians their defense has been too often in the hands of scholarly phantasts. V. Bérard's *Les Phéniciens et l'Odyssée* (1902–1903, 1927–1928) gathered an enormous mass of material in support of his thesis that "the Phoenicians, coming from the Red Sea to the shores of our sea [the Mediterranean] about the

---

[82] Dussaud, *Les civilisations préhelléniques* (1910), pp. 296–300.

30th to the 25th century B.C. were from the sixteenth to the eleventh century the principal agents of the spread of Pharaonic influence in the waters of the Levant."[83] It may safely be said that Bérard's influence would have been negligible if it had not been for his great prestige in French intellectual circles and for the fresh enthusiasm of his presentation. The distinguished historical architect and archaeologist, L. Dörpfeld, went to the most absurd lengths in attributing Greek geometric art to Phoenicians who lived in Greece side by side with the Hellenes during the second millennium B.C.,[84] but since Dörpfeld not only lacked historical judgment but also denied the validity of modern ceramic chronology (!) his views exerted no influence among specialists, though they created much confusion outside the latter's ranks.

Among serious scholars a reaction was inevitable. In 1912 the eminent Danish classical archaeologist, F. Poulsen, published *Der Orient und die frühgriechische Kunst.* In it he collected all accessible archaeological evidence for Phoenician metallurgic and glyptic art, especially ivory carvings. Ivories and metal vases came mainly from the excavations at Calah (Nimrud) in Assyria, from Cyprus, Crete, Olympia in Greece, and from Etruria. From their chronological and geographical distribution, from their common repertoire and technique, as well as from the extraordinary amount of borrowing, mainly from Egypt, but also from Assyria and Syria-Anatolia, he deduced that all these objects were either Phoenician in origin or were made under direct Phoenician influence, in imitation of Phoenician originals. The outbreak of the First World War before the book (printed at the end of 1912) had become generally known, delayed critical examination of the work and allowed it to be ignored in some quarters. However, subsequent discoveries of rich collections of ivories of the same type at Arslan Tash, published in 1931, and at Samaria (published in 1938), as well as the further study of the Nimrud collection, have brought such cumulative evidence for the correctness of Poulsen's position that only strong partisans can oppose it any longer.[85] We will discuss the chronological development of this category of art below.

---

[83] *Op. cit.,* Vol. 1 (1927), p. 7.

[84] See Dorpfeld, *Alt-Olympia* (1935), *passim.*

[85] Among classical scholars who support Poulsen's position may be mentioned particularly V. Müller and C. Watzinger; see especially the latter's sketch in Walter Otto's *Handbuch der Archäologie* (1938), pp. 805–812.

In 1929 Eduard Meyer published a brief, but important paper on some problems of Phoenician history,[86] followed in 1931 by an extremely valuable detailed treatment in the new edition of his *Geschichte des Altertums*. Meyer examined all available documentary material with his usual acumen, and in general reached very sound conclusions. However, he seems to have overshot the mark in accepting Timaeus's date for the foundation of Utica near Carthage in 1100 B.C. One serious weakness in his otherwise admirable historical sketch was his neglect of the accumulating archaeological data and his disregard of what archaeologists had contributed to the solution of the question. To be sure, since the conclusions of archaeologists were based on negative evidence they were not entirely reliable, as we shall see, so Meyer's results could scarcely have been improved by drawing on them.

Recent archaeological research tends to reject the standpoint of Eduard Meyer with respect to the time of Phoenician commercial activity in the Mediterranean and to adhere to the attitude of Beloch, almost wholly on negative evidence. Thus the eminent Catalan authority, P. Bosch-Gimpera,[87] followed closely by Rhys Carpenter[88] and Pierson Dixon,[89] thinks that Phoenician trade with Spain began in the eighth century and was at its height in the seventh, when the Phoenician colonies in Spain were established. Shortly after the middle of the sixth century the Phoenicians lost their commanding position in the Western Mediterranean and were replaced by the Carthaginians. The foundation of Carthage is placed by these authorities at least a century later than the traditional date, i.e., not before the end of the eighth century. Phoenician penetration of the Aegean is restricted to the eighth century and Carpenter brings the date of the adoption of the Phoenician alphabet by the Greeks down to the end of the eighth century, about a century and a half later than Beloch's date.[90] In his *History of Cyprus* (1940) Sir George Hill declares that "we have no direct or indirect evidence of the presence of Phoenicians in Cyprus before

---

[86] "Einzelne Fragen der phönizischen Geschichte" (*Sitz. Preuss. Akad.*, 1929, pp. 204–206.

[87] "Fragen der Chronologie der phönizischen Kolonisation in Spanien" (*Klio*, 1928, pp. 345–368).

[88] Cf. *loc. cit.*, p. 368.

[89] *The Iberians of Spain* (Oxford, 1940), pp. 23–27.

[90] *Am. Jour. Archaeol.*, 1933, pp. 8–29.

the eighth century."[91] Olmstead reflects the same point of view when he dates the beginning of Phoenician expansion in the Western Mediterranean in the ninth century and its climax in the eighth and seventh.[92]

Epigraphic discoveries published within the past two years have, however, changed the situation materially. At the end of 1939 A. M. Honeyman published an archaic Phoenician inscription in the Cyprus Museum, in the study of which the writer had collaborated with him.[93] The writer then studied it anew, with a facsimile copy, and showed that it cannot be later than the ninth century and belongs probably to the first half of that century.[94] The stone is local red sandstone. This discovery pushes the date of the effective Phoenician colonization of Cyprus back more than a century, since the Baal-Lebanon dedication can scarcely be dated before cir. 750 B.C. and the five-letter graffito on a vase of red bucchero ware[95] belongs epigraphically to about the same time, or somewhat later.

Much more unexpected than this discovery were the results of a careful reëxamination of the earliest Sardinian inscriptions, undertaken by the writer after he had repeatedly despaired of any success whatever in this direction. It turns out that the interpretation of the Nora stone has been hopelessly handicapped in the past by three things: (1) scholars relied on recent copies of the weathered surface, presupposing erroneous underlying characters; (2) correct interpretation would have been almost impossible before the Cyprus inscription and other archaic texts had yielded previously unknown or little known forms of characters and meanings of previously misunderstood words and phrases; (3) previous students had all wrongly assumed that the inscription was virtually complete, which is not the case at all. On careful examination of photographic reproductions, assisted materially by the oldest facsimile copies by Arri and Euting, the characters prove to be almost identical with those of the Cyprus inscription. The script of the Sardinian inscriptions is rather more archaic and cannot be dated later, unless we assume a most improbable lag. The lan-

---

[91] *Op. cit.*, pp. 96–104.

[92] *History of Palestine and Syria* (1931), pp. 404–406. For still lower dates (agreeing substantially with Beloch) see Myres in the *Cambridge Ancient History*, III, pp. 642 f. (nothing in Spain before the late seventh century, Sardinia occupied about the same time).

[93] *Iraq*, VI, 106–108.

[94] *Bull. Am. Sch. Or. Res.*, No. 83 (October, 1941), pp. 14–22.

[95] For references see Hill, *op. cit.*, pp. 102 f.

guage of the Nora stone is pure Phoenician, representing exactly the combination of earlier and later elements which we should expect in a document from the ninth century. The stone is local, so there can be no doubt about its local origin. The characters are monumental in size and the original inscription was considerably over a metre in height and about a metre and a quarter (over four feet) in width. The contents strongly suggest a public decree. It is evident that Nora must have been a town of considerable importance in the century before the foundation of Carthage! The two other archaic Sardinian inscriptions are both fragmentary but enough is preserved to show that their script is even more archaic than that of Nora and may well go back to the beginning of the ninth century. Moreover, the Bosa fragment, though found at a site a hundred kilometres away in a straight line, exhibits the same monumental script (with characters 12–15 cm. high) as the Nora stone and accordingly should also belong to a public decree. If the writer's interpretation is correct, Nora then bore the Phoenician name "Tarshish," meaning "Smelting Plant, Refinery."[96] What Phoenician refineries of the period were like has just been shown for the first time by Glueck's excavation of a great copper refinery of the tenth and ninth centuries, operated by slave labor, at Tell el-Kheleifeh, biblical Ezion-geber on the Gulf of 'Aqabah.[97] There were doubtless at least as many Phoenician settlements which bore the name *Tarshîsh* as there were "New Towns" (*Qart-ḥadasht* = Carthage).

There can be little doubt that further study of the material in local museums in the Western Mediterranean region, systematic excavations in North Africa, Sardinia, and Spain,[98] and actual excavation in sites of the Early Iron Age in Phoenicia itself, will increase the amount of recognizable early Phoenician material in the West. Even now, it is clear that the

---

[96] The formation *tafʿil* is common in Accadian and was frequent in Northwest Semitic as well; *taršîš* seems to be derived from Accadian **taršîšu*, from the stem *rašâšu*, "to melt, be smelted," cognate with Arabic *ršš*, "to trickle, etc., of a liquid." This etymology will be discussed in detail elsewhere.

[97] Glueck, *The Other Side of the Jordan* (New Haven, 1940), pp. 50–113; *Bull. Am. Sch. Or. Res.*, No. 79 (1940), pp. 2 ff.

[98] It must be remembered that there have been virtually no systematic, scientific, excavations in Spain, aside from the German work at Numantia, that there has been only a little scientific excavation at Carthage and none in other Phoenician sites of North Africa, and that the Sardinian towns which were occupied by the Phoenicians remain archaeologically virgin.

Spanish ivories of Carmona, which are identical in technique and repertoire with the Phoenician ivories of comparable age, belong to the eighth
or even the ninth century rather than to the seventh, where they are
usually dated.[99] Of course, they may have been exported somewhat later
to Spain. On the other hand, the famous Praenestine bowl, often dated in
the eighth century, belongs in the seventh, as proved both by its artistic
relations and by the characters of the Phoenician epigraph.

The following historical sketch of Sidonian expansion will illustrate the
conclusions which we have reached with regard to the solution of the
Phoenician problem. As we have pointed out above, there is no reason to
suppose that Sidon and Tyre formed distinct states during the period of
colonization; it is rather almost certain that Tyre was refounded by the
Sidonians in the early twelfth century and remained a Sidonian city until
the late eighth century B.C., when a separate dynasty was set up at Sidon
under Assyrian tutelage.[100] It is clear that Sidon had not attained her later
significance in the time of Wen-Amun and Tyre is not mentioned at all
(see above). We may safely suppose that the colonial expansion of the
Sidonians began in the second half of the eleventh century, while the
Philistines and Tsikal were occupied with their struggle against Israel
and were unable to offer serious competition in the Mediterranean. It began undoubtedly with Cyprus, where the colony of "New Town," almost
certainly Citium, was founded. If the writer's interpretation of Josephus's
quotation from Menander of Tyre is correct, the people of Citium rebelled
against Hiram I (cir. 969–936 B.C.).[101] The Honeyman inscription (see

---

[99] On these ivories (now published in full as *Early Engraved Ivories*, New York, Hispanic
Society, 1928) see especially Poulsen, *op. cit.*, pp. 52–54. He justly compares the warrior's
helmet in Figure 47 with the helmet on a well-known silver bowl from Amathus in Cyprus,
probably to be attributed to the eighth century. The elaborate decoration in Fig. 49 is
very closely related to some of the Samaria ivories (cf., e.g., Crowfoot, *Samaria*, Pl. xxi)
from the ninth century. For the figures above the geometrical panel see especially *Samaria*,
Pl. xi: 1.

[100] Sennacherib, Taylor Prism, col. ii: 34 ff. For the subsequent reduction of both Sidon
and Tyre to the status of Assyrian provinces see Forrer, *Die Provinzeinteilung des as-
syrischen Reiches* (1921), pp. 65 ff. The province of Sidon was established about 676 B.C.,
the province of Tyre in 668.

[101] Josephus quotes Menander on Hiram twice: in one case the text reads τοῖς τε Ιυκεοις
(ηυκαιοις, ηυκεοις, etc.); in the other it reads ὁπότε τιτυοις (τιτυαιοις, Ιυκεοις, titiceos, etc.).
Gutschmid cleverly emended the text to read τοῖς τε 'Ιτυκαίοις, referring to the men of

above) at all events proves effective Phoenician penetration in the early ninth century.

It is not necessary to suppose that the Phoenicians established any colonies in the Aegean. The dangers of piratic raids in this region must have discouraged them from serious attempts at economic control; we may rather suppose that they contented themselves with temporary trading "factories" under local Greek protection. On the other hand, we may safely trace their earliest colonizing activities in the Western Mediterranean back to the end of the eleventh century or the very beginning of the tenth. The more important routes were undoubtedly well known to the more adventurous seamen of the Eastern Mediterranean, since they had been traversed intensively by the Sardinians, Tyrrhenians,[102] and other Sea Peoples in the late thirteenth and the twelfth centuries. As we have seen above, Sardinia was already colonized by the Phoenicians early in the ninth century, and there seems no reason to doubt that the smelting plants of Nora dated back to the age of Hiram I, if not earlier. One would expect a period of several generations before the colonies of Nora and Bosa could develop to the point where monumental edicts in stone would be set up. In Sardinia we may safely suppose that the Phoenicians followed in the traces of the Sea Peoples, whose exploitation of their island metals they continued. North Africa and Spain were, however, more remote and in all probability less known. We may, therefore, set up the provisional order of colonization: Cyprus—Sicily (first on such islands as Malta and Motya, in agreement with Thucydides)—Sardinia (Nora and Bosa)—Africa (Utica)—Spain (Gades and Tartessus). By the middle of Hiram I's

---

'Ἰτύκη, Latin *Utica*, but this is at best only plausible (against it see Beloch, *op. cit.*, p. 251). The writer proposes what seems to him a much more rational emendation: τοῖς τε Κιτίοις, from which the manuscript readings may be derived by assuming only the simplest types of scribal error.

[102] It is now hypercritical to reject the identity of the Sardinians and the Etruscans with the corresponding Sea Peoples. With the Graeco-Roman *Sardin-*, *Sardan-*, Phoenician (ninth century) *šrdn* cf. Egyptian *Ša-ar-di-na*, *Ša-ar-da-na* (the writer's transcription) and with Graeco-Roman *Turs-* (Τυρρ-, *Turs-*) cf. Egyptian *Tu-ur-ša*, *Tu-ru-ša* (cf. Latin *Etrusc-*). It is not necessary to go into the strong archaeological arguments here, since they are well known. Where the ancestors of the later Tyrrhenians or Etruscans were between the twelfth and the eighth centuries is another question, but they may well have settled in Italy as early as the tenth century, in spite of the negative evidence of archaeology, since relevant material still comes almost exclusively from tombs.

reign, about 950 B.C., we may suppose that Gades and Tartessus had been founded.[103] It is significant for the probable lack of any local civilization that both these towns received Phoenician names.

Just as the date of the beginning of Phoenician colonization in the West must be pushed back two or three centuries earlier than the dominant view now allows (though a century later than Meyer's date), so the date of its close must be raised from the middle of the sixth century to the end of the eighth century B.C. The foundation of Carthage in the late ninth century was the beginning of the end, since the Carthaginians must soon have begun to compete with the mother country—and they were not the only colony strong enough to become a serious competitor. The conquest of Phoenicia by the Assyrian kings of the late eighth and the early seventh century proved fatal to Sidonian independence, and the contemporary wave of Greek colonization[104] weakened Phoenician maritime power still farther. Finally, the Chaldaeans dealt Phoenician maritime ambitions the *coup de grâce* when they captured Tyre in 572 B.C., after a

---

[103] It is true that the accounts of Solomon's mercantile activities do not refer to Tarshish, but only to a "Tarshish fleet" which was sent to Ophir in the extreme south to bring back gold, silver, ivory, and two kinds of monkeys, both with Egyptian names. Moreover this expression probably means only "refinery-fleet" (see above and note 96) i.e., a fleet which traversed the Mediterranean at regular intervals, bringing smelted ores home from the Western mines. The word "Tarshish" appears in extant literary sources only from the seventh century on, but in our earliest references, especially in an inscription of Esarhaddon (*Tar-si-si* [pronounced by the Assyrians *Taršiš*] is the actual reading of the original, not an emendation, as still thought by Hill, *History of Cyprus*, p. 106), it already appears explicitly as the farthest limit of the Mediterranean or of the Phoenician colonial empire. But since the neighboring Gades was believed by the Greeks to vie with Utica in age and since the mines of southern Spain were much more important than those of Sardinia, where a "Tarshish" was established not later than the early ninth century, it is hypercritical to reject a date in Hiram's reign or even earlier for the Phoenician settlement of Tartessus. In this connection it may be observed that the phonetic relation between *Taršiš* and *Tartes-* is almost exactly like that between Phoenician *Qarthad-* and Greek *Karkhad-* (later Ionic-Attic Καρχηδών), "Carthage"; the dissimilation in question has been explained by J. Friedrich. The Greek ending is obviously formed on the analogy of a very widely diffused group of pre-Hellenic place-names. Biblical Tarshish was located in Sardinia by W. W. Covey-Crump in *Jour. Theol. Stud.*, 1916, pp. 280 ff., but on inadequate toponymic evidence (Tarshish = Tharros at the mouth of the Thyrsus).

[104] The age of Greek colonization must apparently be lowered somewhat, as a result of the general lowering of the date of late geometric pottery; this fact has been repeatedly stressed by Rhys Carpenter.

siege of thirteen years.[105] The Greek colonies in the West now entered into the Phoenician heritage. Carthage was not ready, it would appear, to carry the burden of empire for several generations yet. In Tartessus there was a brief, but apparently a brilliant, period of native autonomy under the semi-legendary Arganthonius.[106] In Cyprus local Phoenician dynasties were set up at Citium and Salamis on the eastern coast. But the day of the Phoenicians was over. With the subsequent Canaanite renaissance under Carthage we are not concerned here.

V. The Diffusion of Phoenician Culture

After this reconstruction of the history of Phoenician expansion we may profitably turn to survey the development of Phoenician art and the chronology of Phoenician cultural influence on other Mediterranean peoples. Owing to the synthetic character of Phoenician art, which borrowed from elsewhere and continued to borrow new repertoires and new motifs down to the very end of its autonomous existence in the sixth century B.C., it is not only difficult but dangerous to attempt a coherent history of its development. We must content ourselves for the present with classifying the available material according to the evidence furnished by datable groups of homogeneous objects.

The oldest large group of ivories belonging to the Canaanite Iron Age was discovered in 1937 at Megiddo by Gordon Loud, on behalf of the Oriental Institute.[107] These ivories belong to the latest of a series of Canaanite palaces, the last of which was destroyed not long after cir. 1150 B.C. (in or immediately after the reign of Ramesses VI).[108] Unfortunately they do not form a homogeneous group from a single article of furniture or a suite, but represent a miscellaneous collection. Some of the strips of inlay in Plates 58–61 may go back to the fifteenth century or even earlier. However, it is clear that the overwhelming majority of the pieces

[105] This date has been fixed by Eissfeldt, *Ras Schamra und Sanchunjaton* (1939), pp. 4–8.

[106] Cf. Schulten, *Tartessos* (1922), *passim*, and *Klio*, XXII (1928), pp. 284–291. Schulten's historical methods are generally questionable.

[107] *The Megiddo Ivories*, Chicago, 1939.

[108] On the date see *Bull. Am. Sch. Or. Res.*, No. 78, p. 8; *Am. Jour. Archaeol.*, 1940, p. 548a. Watzinger (in Otto, *Handbuch der Archäologie*, p. 807) seems to have misunderstood the provisional reports of the excavators; at all events he has dated the destruction of the ivory palace a century too late (cir. 1050 B.C.) because of an erroneous identification of the fire which destroyed Stratum VI with the fire which ended VII.

in the collection belong to the first half of the twelfth century, like the model pen-case in Pl. 62, which is dated by an inscription to the reign of Ramesses III (1195–1164 B.C.). The remarkable plaque on Pl. 4, bearing a scene which exhibits striking points of contact with the Ahiram Sarcophagus (see above, note 78) is among the latest characteristic pieces and may provisionally be dated cir. 1150 B.C., though it may be a little earlier, of course. While Egyptian influence on the Megiddo ivories is strong, it is not nearly as pervasive as it later became and these pieces, like the roughly contemporary ivories from Enkomi, are excellent examples of the artistic syncretism of Syria in the Late Bronze Age. Such stray objects as have come down to us from the eleventh century, like the Ahiram Sarcophagus, still reflect the same artistic tradition.

After a gap of over two centuries we find Syro-Phoenician art well illustrated by the ivories from the Southeast Palace at Nimrud (Calah) in Assyria, which belong to the outgoing tenth century and perhaps to the beginning of the ninth, as has been shown by Barnett.[109] Resemblances in detail to the finds at Enkomi, Byblus, and Tell Halaf have been pointed out by Watzinger[110] and others; we may add that there are some resemblances to the Megiddo ivories, though not very striking. Closely following this group in point of time are the Samaria ivories and the ivories from Arslan Tash, which are epigraphically and stratigraphically dated to the ninth century, probably to the second half.[111]

Soon after these ivories, probably, come the major part, if not all, of the remarkable collection made by Bonsor from tombs in the valley of the Guadalquivir, near Carmona. As we have seen, these pieces are most closely related to the ivories from Samaria and to an eighth-century bowl from Cyprus. The combs in this collection are particularly striking, since they carry on the Megiddo tradition even in detail (e.g., the zigzag line decorating the frame of the central panel), though at least three centuries later.[112]

---

[109] *Iraq*, II (1935), pp. 179 ff.

[110] *Op. cit.*, pp. 807 f.

[111] For Samaria see the discussion by Crowfoot and Sukenik, *Early Ivories from Samaria* (1938), pp. 1 ff., 6 ff. For the Egyptian background, which is "all-pervasive" (Crowfoot's term), in the art of the Bubastite period (late tenth and ninth centuries) see Crowfoot's remarks, pp. 49–53.

[112] See also Poulsen, *op. cit.*, pp. 54 ff.

In the eighth century the syncretistic tendencies of Iron-Age art reach an all-time high, with the fusion of Egyptian and Mesopotamian elements which characterizes the art of the earlier group of silver bowls from Cyprus and Greece and of the bronze shields from Crete. To this period belong the earliest known Greek imitations of Phoenician work, abundant in Crete, Rhodes, Ionia, and illustrated by inferior work on the Greek peninsula itself.[113]

The Saite renaissance in Egypt was accompanied, it would seem, by a new wave of Phoenician adaptation and imitation, best known from the Barberini and Bernardini tombs at Praeneste in Etruria.[114] One of these bowls bears the name of its maker, Eshmunya'id son of 'Ashta, in characters belonging to the seventh century, probably to its latter half. The Egyptian borrowings of this phase do not limit themselves to specific religious groups and decorative motifs as in the Bubastite period (ninth century), but extend to copying whole scenes of action from the walls of tombs and temples, together with quantities of meaningless hieroglyphs. The Barberini group and contemporary finds elsewhere represent the last and least original phase of Phoenician art. Thereafter it lost all claim to autonomous existence and by the early fifth century, if not earlier, it was completely absorbed by triumphant Greek art.

It cannot be accidental that the period when Phoenician art[115] most powerfully affected the Greeks was also the time at which the alphabet was borrowed. Thanks to our steadily increasing knowledge of the development of the Phoenician alphabet, both lapidary and cursive, and to

---

[113] On this material see especially Poulsen, *op. cit.*, and Kunze, *Kretische Bronzereliefs* (1931).

[114] C. Densmore Curtis, "The Bernardini Tomb," in the *Memoirs of the American Academy in Rome*, III (1919).

[115] Phoenician influence on Greek art extended also to architecture, where it was undoubtedly strong but perhaps in part indirect. There are still serious gaps in our documentation, especially in Phoenicia. The best single illustration of this influence is the Aeolic-Ionic capital, which may be traced back to the eleventh century at Megiddo and to the ninth at several Palestinian sites. The early Hellenic parallels with the Phoenician Temple of Solomon have often been noted and pan-Hellenic archaeologists have tried to explain them away by denying the age and authenticity of the account of the Temple in Kings. However, it becomes clearer all the time that it must have been typically Phoenician: see especially Watzinger, *Denkmäler Palästinas*, I (1933), pp. 88–95, and Wright, *The Biblical Archaeologist*, IV (1941), pp. 16–31.

recent discoveries of early seventh (or late eighth) century graffiti at Hymettus,[116] we can speak with a confidence not hitherto possible. The early chronology of Ullman (eleventh or even twelfth century)[117] and others is absolutely out of the question. These scholars reach their conclusions by comparing individual characters, regardless of their period, and striking the highest chronological average, whereas we must, as recently emphasized by Rhys Carpenter,[118] compare whole alphabets taken from actual inscriptions and not eclectically reconstructed. Carpenter, working with insufficient data and basing his conclusions solely on lapidary inscriptions, thinks that the alphabet was borrowed from the Phoenicians toward the end of the eighth century; the writer, with more material and a cursive prototype, would date this event in the early eighth century or possibly the late ninth.[119]

The blows of fate *per Assyrios*, which put an end to the territorial ambitions and the merchant empire of the Phoenicians in the late eighth and the early seventh centuries B.C., brought with them a renewed interest in the literature of the Canaanite past.[120] There was a literary renaissance which may have attained its climax in the sixth century. To this renaissance belongs the enigmatic figure of Sanchuniathon, who collected the religious records and the mythological poems of his people, as we know from a Greek sketch, written in the first century A.D. by Philo of Byblus. To the same period we may perhaps attribute the Tyrian history from which Menander of Ephesus drew material for a Greek adaptation in the third (?) century B.C.

Our ideas about Phoenician religious literature would be exceedingly hazy if it were not for the documents of Ugarit, from about 1400 B.C. The mythological epics of Baal and Anath, of Danel and Aqhat, of Keret, etc., unquestionably reflect a common Canaanite literary heritage, as we can tell both from the many reminiscences of them which we find in Philo Byblius and from their strong literary influence on the Israelites

---

[116] See Blegen, *Am. Jour. Archaeol.*, 1934, pp. 10–28.

[117] *Ibid.*, 1934, pp. 359–381.

[118] *Ibid.*, 1933, pp. 8–29.

[119] A student of the writer's, Mr. John V. Walsh, is preparing a dissertation on this subject, to which we may refer for a full discussion.

[120] See Albright, *From the Stone Age to Christianity* (1940), pp. 242 ff., *Jour. Bib. Lit.*, 1941, pp. 209 f.

(see above). This influence is most abundant and most direct in the Exilic and Postexilic ages, as can easily be seen by analyzing the biblical poetic literature in which it appears. If we pass over a few of the earliest documents, which illustrate Canaanite influence at the beginning of Israel's history, we find it in the later prophets (but not in Hosea, Amos, the original parts of Isaiah, etc.), especially in Ezekiel, Habakkuk and the Exilic parts of Isaiah and Deutero-Isaiah, the Psalms, Proverbs, Job, Song of Songs, etc.—everywhere in works or passages dating in their present form from the period 650–350 B.C. It can now be proved that substantial parts of Proverbs are direct borrowings from Phoenician sources.[121] The case of the Psalms is more difficult, since some of them may go back to early Israelite times and direct Phoenician influence on Israelite music in the age of David and Solomon is increasingly likely.[122] However, most of the close literary parallels (aside from Psalms 29, 68, etc.) are found in the latter books of the Psalter, which in general belong to a comparatively late period. There can no longer be any doubt that the Bible has preserved much of the best in Phoenician literature, especially lyric and gnomic. Without the powerful influence of Canaanite literary tradition, we should lack much of the perennial appeal exerted by Hebrew poetic style and prosody, poetic imagery and vivid description of natural phenomena. Through the Bible the entire civilized world has fallen heir to Phoenician literary art.

---

[121] See provisionally Albright, *Jour. Pal. Or. Soc.*, 1934, p. 134, n. 175; Ginsberg on the origin and development of the graded numerical aphorism in *Minḥal David* (1935), pp. 76–82.

[122] The writer dealt with this subject in a still unpublished paper presented before the Society of Biblical Literature in December, 1940.

SOME SOURCES OF INTELLECTUAL AND SOCIAL PROGRESS IN THE ANCIENT NEAR EAST[1]

E. A. SPEISER
University of Pennsylvania

LATEST advances in the study of the past have lent fresh emphasis to the traditional view that the oldest known historic civilizations evolved in Egypt and Mesopotamia. It is equally clear that intellectual and social progress in these two centers kept pace with material developments. The question of relative priority is injected all too often into discussions on this subject. For the time being, at least, such a question is not capable of a satisfactory solution. It is doubtful indeed whether an answer can be expected at all, in view of the dynamic character of both civilizations and the consequent diffusion of vital innovations and inventions from the one center to the other. There are, however, certain characteristic aspects of progress in the two respective areas which stand out by contrast, and it is to one particular set of such contrasted characteristics that I wish to address myself at present. I refer to the background of progress in science.

The following remarks will embody four main propositions: (1) Available evidence points to Mesopotamia as the oldest center of scientific observation permanently recorded. (2) Whatever its immediate objectives, this activity comes to include such widely separated fields as education and language study, jurisprudence, and the mathematical and natural sciences. (3) The divers elements in this broad advance are basically interrelated. The common underlying factor is a concept of society whereby the powers of the state are restricted and the rights of the individual receive a corresponding degree of emphasis. (4) It is significant that under

---

[1] The substance of this paper was presented before the University of Pennsylvania Bicentennial Conference and published in a volume on *Studies in the History of Science* (University of Pennsylvania Press, Philadelphia, 1941) under the title of "Ancient Mesopotamia and the Beginnings of Science." The present is a revised and somewhat expanded version of that paper.

the opposed order of authoritarian Egypt early scientific development differed in scope as well as in degree; although notable in selected fields, such as medicine and engineering, it lacked the breadth and balance manifested in contemporary Mesopotamia.

It should be made plain at the outset that the scientific detail cited in this statement is negligible in amount and derivative in character. My principal objective will be rather to demonstrate that there were forces in the social structure of early Mesopotamia which tended to promote intellectual progress. The results happen to constitute the first recorded evidence of scientific performance known to us today. To this extent we are justified in touching here upon the beginnings of science, including the natural sciences. But this account is concerned not so much with the results as with the background: a combination of forces conducive to concerted intellectual activity rather than the disciplines affected by that activity. The background provides us in this instance with the all-important starting point. It is thus more significant than the eventual achievement.

Our interest, then, will center on a given cultural stage at which there were at work forces that led to extensive scientific developments and provided the predisposition to these developments. Accordingly, we shall ignore the sporadic achievements of a still more remote age, for instance, the invention of the wheel, the introduction of the brick-mold, and perhaps the use of instruments in effecting accurate geometric designs on very early forms of painted pottery. We may have here Mesopotamian inventions which were to play substantial parts in the subsequent progress of engineering, architecture, and possibly geometry. But these inventions represent isolated contributions of discontinuous civilizations which scarcely had any immediate bearing on intellectual progress. This statement will confine itself, therefore, to subjects which had a common origin in a well-defined period and area; which involve from the start habits of observation, classification, and analysis; and which enter then and there upon a continuous course of development.

The locale of our inquiry is Lower Mesopotamia, the land of Ancient Sumer. More specifically, it is the area which extends southeast from the environs of Babylon, past Uruk—the biblical Erech—and on along the Euphrates to the metropolis of Ur. The time is the middle of the fourth millennium B.C. The period can be established with relative accuracy be-

cause it coincides with a clearly stratified cultural stage that is marked
off sharply by distinctive material remains. Soon thereafter we begin to
get inscribed records which tie up before long with regnal years and thus
afford data for an absolute chronology.

Our first inscribed documents come from a building level dated to about
3500 B.C. and constituting one of a long series of strata which represent
the remains of ancient Uruk. It is among these documents, written on
clay, that we find a small collection of scientific records, the earliest known
to man to date. That similar records of still greater antiquity will ever
turn up outside Mesopotamia is improbable. All available evidence favors
the conclusion that the scientific notations with which we are concerned
were compiled as a direct consequence of the introduction of writing
itself. To be sure, this evidence applies only to the script of Mesopotamia.
But writing from all the other ancient centers of civilization is demonstrably later. In Egypt it follows by some centuries the appearance of
script in Mesopotamia, and the earliest evidence of writing in India is
well within the third millennium B.C. As for China, there is nothing to
indicate that its script antedates the second millennium. It follows, therefore, that the scientific notations on our earliest Mesopotamian tablets
constitute not only the first evidence of intellectual activity in Sumer but
at the same time also the oldest recorded effort of this kind from anywhere in the world. With this significant fact in mind let us turn now
briefly to the records themselves.

What is it that would justify the use of the term "scientific" as applied
to a few of the primitive inscribed documents from Mesopotamia? The
answer is bound up with the nature and purpose of these special texts.
Each contains lists of related entries. But these lists have nothing in common with the customary inventories of a strictly economic type. They
serve an intellectual rather than material purpose. They are to enjoy,
however, the sort of continuity and diffusion that will set them off sharply
from the usual run of business documents which can claim only ephemeral
and local importance. The lists in question are destined to be copied and
recopied for many centuries and in more than one city or country. Actual
samples of such copies, often modified and expanded but still in a clear
line of descent from the very first prototypes, have been dug up in Mesopotamian sites of much later age, and in the foreign Elamite center of
Susa. We have here the beginning of a family of scholarly documents

notable at once for their continuity, distribution, and purposeful adherence to an established tradition.[2]

In this recording of accumulating experience and the manifest applicability of such records to centers separated by time and space we have the essential ingredients of scientific performance. What branches of science did that activity include? We shall see presently that the primary purpose of the lists under discussion was to aid in the preservation of the knowledge of writing. Before long, philological studies become an added objective, owing largely to the complex ethnic and linguistic background of early historic Mesopotamia. But natural sciences, too, soon come in for their share of attention.

For regardless of their original purpose, our lists happen to include, quite early in their history, groupings of birds, fish, domestic animals, plants and the like. It is worth stressing that these compilations presuppose careful observation and imply organization and analysis of the accumulated data.[3] As part of the cumulative tradition of the land these compilations are subject to expansion and revision. Moreover, such texts lead in course of time to the independent study of the subject matter involved. The fields thus affected are zoology and botany, and later geology and chemistry. The first recognition of all these subjects as so many separate disciplines may be traced back, therefore, to the oldest inscribed documents of Mesopotamia. That recognition was due ultimately to the fact that man had just discovered in writing a way to arrest time and was bending all his effort and ingenuity to the task of keeping this method alive.

The subsequent progress of the individual sciences just mentioned has to be traced by specialists. We are concerned at present with the initial impetus alone and the time and circumstances in which that impetus arose. A few details, however, may be brought out in passing for purposes of illustration. In the light of the foregoing remarks botanists should not be surprised to learn that many of the terms which they use today go back to Mesopotamian sources. These terms include "cassia" (cuneiform

---

[2] These facts are brought out in full by A. Falkenstein whose *Archaische Texte aus Uruk* (Berlin, 1936) is the basic work on the earliest documents from Mesopotamia, cf. especially pp. 43 ff.

[3] Careful observation is evidenced also by the accurate drawings of the early pictographs, particularly where exotic animals or specific plants are concerned.

kasû), "chicory" (*kukru*), "cumin" (*kamûnu*), "crocus" (*kurkânu*), "hyssop" (*zûpu*), "myrrh" (*murru*), "nard" (*lardu*), and probably many others. The zoological compilations which are available in cuneiform contain hundreds of names systematically arranged and presented in two columns, the first giving the Sumerian term and the other its Akkadian counterpart.[4] The scholastic tradition in chemistry[5] results in such texts as the one which has come down to us from the early part of the second millennium B.C., wherein a formula for glazing pottery is preserved in the guise of a cryptogram so as to remain hidden from the uninitiated.[6] The importance of the natural sciences for the study of medicine is self-evident; it was not lost on Babylonian and Assyrian medicine.

So much for the indirect benefits derived from the lists under review. But the primary objective of these compendia was not neglected in the meantime. On the contrary, the direct results are reflected in an immensely fruitful advance in another field of intellectual progress.

It was indicated above that our lists were conceived as a means of maintaining the knowledge of script. By the very nature of its origin in concrete pictographs, early writing was an elaborate medium which comprised thousands of items. To each new prospective user it represented a code which could not be deciphered without the right key. The lists were calculated to furnish that key. They were analytical catalogues of signs arranged according to outward form. Since each sign was at first a reflection of something specific in the material world, these catalogues came to constitute systematic arrangements of related objects; hence their incidental value for the natural sciences, as we have just seen. The immediate purpose, however, of the sign-lists was pedagogical; they are our oldest manuals of a basic branch of education.

With the study of the script there was linked perforce the study of language. It is evident from the material at hand that the pictographs were not meant merely to be seen but to be sounded. They were associated with concrete words or groups of words on an auditory rather than visual basis. This is made clear by the ability of the early writers to use given

---

[4] See B. Landsberger (with I. Krumbiegel), *Die Fauna des alten Mesopotamien* (Leipzig, 1934).

[5] On this subject cf. R. Campbell Thompson, *A Dictionary of Assyrian Chemistry and Geology* (Oxford, 1936).

[6] R. C. Thompson and C. J. Gadd, in *Iraq* III (1936), pp. 87 ff.

graphs for purely phonetic values. For instance, the first lists contain a graph which appears to represent a carpenter's drill and thus comes to be sounded as *ti*. Now Sumerian had a word for "life" which also was pronounced *ti* in certain positions. But the concept "life" is not as readily depicted by a pictograph as a concrete artisan's tool. The protohistoric Sumerian did not hesitate to use the tool-sign when he wanted to express the word "life."[7] It is this freedom in the use of specific pictorial symbols for abstract phonetic values that accounts for the rapid progress of Sumerian writing as a medium for recording any required type of utterance. After the Semitic-speaking Akkadians had joined the Sumerians in building up the civilization of Mesopotamia the resulting bilingual background caused linguistic studies to rise to exceptional heights.

The deep-rooted respect for scholarly tradition, implicit in a conscious dependence on the contributions of the past, had much to do with the unprecedented achievements of ancient Mesopotamia in the field of linguistics. For it meant that Akkadians, Babylonians, and Assyrians alike must fall back upon records in the wholly unrelated tongue of Sumer. The knowledge of that language had to be preserved for cultural reasons long after its speakers had lost all political power and eventually disappeared from the scene altogether. For the first time in history translators are busily at work to commit their renderings to writing. This activity called for the creations of various auxiliary manuals: syllabaries giving the phonetic value, form, and name of each given sign; vocabularies containing the Sumerian pronunciation, word-sign, and Akkadian equivalent of each word or group of words; lists of synonyms, commentaries on selected word-signs, interlinear translations, and the like. Nor was this all. The scientific analysis of Sumerian took the form of grammatical works arranged in paradigms according to parts of speech and explicit down to such minutiae as the place of the accent. Differences in the dialects of Sumerian were carefully recorded. And most of this formidable apparatus was available and in use more than four thousand years ago! It is to this apparatus that we of today owe our knowledge not only of the various dialects of Sumerian and Akkadian but also of such languages as Hittite, Hurrian, Urartian, and Elamite. As linguistic material these languages may be of interest only to a small group of specialists. But as the media

---

[7] Cf. note 2, p. 38.

for expressing the thought of a large portion of the ancient world over a period of three millennia—a period one and a half times as long as the whole of the present era—they have a deep significance for the whole of the civilized world.

The foregoing outline has had as its main theme the demonstration that many forms of scientific progress in Mesopotamia were influenced and linked together by a scholarly tradition which was in turn a byproduct of the invention of writing. Our survey has not included thus far mathematics and astronomy, two fields for which Mesopotamia has long been celebrated and is today honored more than ever before owing to the discoveries of modern investigators.[8] It goes without saying that these two subjects were affected no less than the other disciplines by the same forces which made for a broad cultural advance in general. But the primary cause of the extraordinary development of mathematical and related studies in Mesopotamia is to be sought, I believe, in conditions which antedate the introduction of writing. In fact, I would add, the origin of writing as well as the interest in mathematics are to be traced back in this instance to a common source. This source will be found inherent in the society and economy of the proto-historic Sumerians.

We know today that the Sumerians came upon the idea of writing through their use of the cylinder seal. Such seals were engraved with a variety of designs and were employed as individual personal symbols for religious and economic purposes, say, with temple offerings. In this representational function the decorative motifs on the seals come to be applied also to cities, temples, gods, all for purposes of identification; the designs are thus converted into graphs. Their employment is gradually extended to represent animals, plants, and objects in general. The graphs are soon associated with specific words and the gap between picture and word is bridged. The next step is to divorce the given sign from the specific underlying picture and to use signs not only for complete words but also for component syllables, the advance leading thus from the concrete to the abstract, as was illustrated above. Complete flexibility of the new medium is attained very early in the third millennium when administrative and historical documents are produced with equal ease. It is scarcely a coin-

---

[8] Especially Otto E. Neugebauer, whose paper on "Some Fundamental Concepts in Ancient Astronomy" is included in the *Studies in the History of Science* (cf. note 1).

cidence that this advanced stage of writing should mark for us the beginning of the historical age.

When we look back now on the successive stages in this complex process, a process which could be sketched here only in its barest outlines, an interesting fact comes to the fore. The early Sumerians had not set out at all to invent anything like writing. They were driven to this result by a combination of peculiar circumstances. The outcome had hardly been planned or foreseen. The achievement of the discoverers lay chiefly in their ability to recognize and seize their opportunity. This they did with no little ingenuity and perseverance. But they had this opportunity to begin with because of the way in which their society functioned. The underlying system can now be reconstructed from a wealth of diversified evidence. Only a rough summary can be attempted at present.

We have seen that the immediate ancestor of Mesopotamian writing was the cylinder seal which was first and foremost the Sumerian's mark of ownership. Impressed on clay or cloth it served to safeguard in the eyes of gods and men one's title to possessions or merchandise. We have here a clear indication of a strongly developed sense of private property and thereby of individual rights and individual initiative.[9] The curious shape of the cylinder seal, original with the Sumerians, is explained by its employment as a mark of individual ownership. For such objects are well suited to cover uneven surfaces with their distinctive designs.[10]

Wholly consistent with this economic origin of writing is the fact that the earliest written documents are given over to temple economy. Later texts branch out into the field of private business. Both these uses testify independently to the importance of property rights. Records of a non-economic character are the last to appear in the developmental stages of script, except for the lists discussed above which served as direct aids to writing. The first inscribed documents were used, accordingly, for economic ends, precisely as the cylinder seals themselves. It is easy to understand why the oldest pictographs were so often identical with the designs on the seals.

It follows that Mesopotamian writing, the oldest script known to man, was the unlooked for outgrowth of a social order founded on the

---

[9] Cf. E. A. Speiser, "The Beginnings of Civilization in Mesopotamia," Supplement 4, *Journal of the American Oriental Society*, Vol. 59 (1939) pp. 17 ff. (esp. 25–28).

[10] See H. Frankfort, *Cylinder Seals* (London, 1939) p. 2.

recognition of personal rights. This basic feature of Sumerian society is attested overwhelmingly in cuneiform law, perhaps the most characteristic and abundant expression of ancient Mesopotamian civilization. In the last analysis this law rests on individual rights. Under this system proof of ownership becomes a vital necessity. Incidentally, the rigid requirement of such proof is the principal reason for the hundreds of thousands of legal documents recovered from the buried sites of Mesopotamia; the forces responsible for the introduction of writing emerge as the main factor in the subsequent popularity of this means of communication and attestation.

The law applies to ruler and subjects alike. The king is at first no more than a "great man," as is shown by the Sumerian etymology of the term and the form of the corresponding pictograph. He may become the administrator of a vast empire, but even then he is still the servant, not the source of the law and is responsible to the gods for its enactment. There is here no encouragement of absolute power. The law is the constitution which guides the ruler and safeguards the subjects. The king cannot increase his holdings by the simple process of requisition or expropriation. Even members of the powerful Sargonid Dynasty, which flourished about the middle of the third millennium and strove to raise kingship to a superhuman status, had to pay for the lands which they would have. An impressive business record of Manishtusu, a member of that dynasty, testifies to the absence of special privileges in transactions of this kind.

This brings up the question of the divine rights of kings which some works of a general character still read into Mesopotamian history. Careful study of the entire material[11] shows conclusively that this view cannot be upheld. It is true that under the Sargonids attempts were made to arrogate for the king the prerogatives of the gods. The success of the founder of the dynasty, Sargon of Akkad, in establishing a mighty empire may have served as an incentive to such aspirations. At any rate, the deification of the king was never a complete success. The effort is repeated towards the end of the third millennium, and sporadic attempts in the same direction are made a few centuries later. None of these ventures left a permanent impression on Mesopotamian civilization. Each in turn was to fail to strike root; it was a thing alien and unassimilable. One need point only

---

[11] Cf. R. Labat, *Le Caractère Religieux de la Royauté Assyro-Babylonienne* (Paris, 1939).

to the fact that the Assyrian kings, whose conquests bespeak unprecedented military power, are foremost in their subservience to the gods whose aid they ceaselessly invoke.

Mesopotamian literature provides ample independent evidence of the limited powers of the ruler. This is true not only of the human kings but also of the leaders in the divine hierarchy, which is no more than an idealization of conditions on earth. In heaven and in the netherworld alike the ranking gods draw their authority from the "assembly" in which ultimate power is vested. Just so, the great hero Gilgamesh, legendary king of Uruk, has to consult the elders of his city. And Uta-Napishtim, the hero of the Mesopotamian account of the Flood, tells us plainly that he must have the consent of the city which he rules before embarking on a journey: "What am I to say to the city, the people and the elders?"[12] The rule of the city is vested in "the people and the elders," the identical source of power which we are to recognize, thousands of years later, in "the senate and the people." The system of government, then, is a rule by the assembly or delegates of the citizens. We may call it politocracy.[13]

We have seen that this system was capable of promoting intellectual progress on an extensive scale. Its inherent vitality is attested by the ease with which this order maintains itself for tens of centuries in spite of a succession of political changes under the Sumerians, Akkadians, Gutians, Babylonians, Kassites, and Assyrians. Nor is its further expansion hindered by ethnic or linguistic barriers. Distant and unrelated peoples are attracted time and again to the orbit of the civilization of Mesopotamia. Among the newcomers we find the Elamites, the Hurrians, and the Hittites, the last-named a people of European ancestry and Indo-European speech. Incidentally, it is to the influence of Mesopotamia upon the Hittites that we owe today our oldest records of any Indo-European language. The newcomers proceed to copy the laws, use the script, and enjoy the other benefits of the adopted civilization.

To sum up, there existed an intimate relation between intellectual progress in Mesopotamia and the mainspring of historic Mesopotamian

---

[12] Gilgamesh Epic, Tablet xi, line 119.

[13] Similar conclusions, based on cuneiform literary sources, but proceeding from different illustrations, were presented by Dr. Thorkild Jacobsen at the meeting of the American Oriental Society held in Chicago in April, 1941. The independent nature of our respective results tends to enhance their validity.

civilization. Underlying all was a social order resting on the rights of the individual, embodied in a competitive economy, and protected by the supreme authority of the law. This system brought about the evolution of writing, henceforward a decisive factor in the progress of civilization and its diffusion across the changing ethnic and political boundaries. We have here the essentials of a truly cosmopolitan culture notable for its assimilatory power and distinguished by a dynamic science broad in scope and balanced through the inner unity of its component elements.

Would this story of intellectual and social development have differed appreciably under another type of civilization? The answer is hinted in one of history's greatest experiments. The one center possessing a culture of comparable antiquity but dissimilar social and economic background was Egypt. Here the king was a god and as such the absolute ruler and titular owner of all that his realm contained. Under this concept of government there was no room for unqualified recognition of private property or the all-embracing power of the law. The pharaoh was dictator of a state genuinely and thoroughly totalitarian. The pyramids bear lasting and eloquent testimony to his enormous authority.

We are not concerned here with the respective merits of two contrasted forms of government. Our interest is confined to the effect of coexistent civilizations upon scientific progress in the two centers under comparison. The perspective of more than five thousand years cannot but help deepen our appreciation of the debt which modern life owes to both Egypt and Mesopotamia. By the same token, however, we are now able to view objectively some of the differences between their respective achievements.

The established superiority of Mesopotamian mathematics may be attributed, in part at least, to the stimulus of the local economy, so different from the Egyptian. Opposed concepts of property ownership and the basic rights of the individual were responsible for the intensive pursuit of legal studies in the one instance and their subsidiary rôle in the other. The astounding accomplishment of Mesopotamia in the field of linguistics had no adequate counterpart in Egypt. We have seen that in Mesopotamia progress in linguistic studies, not to cite now other branches of science, was linked perforce with the development of writing. But was not Egyptian writing a correspondingly potent factor?

If this question cannot be answered with complete confidence it is largely because the origin of the Egyptian form of script is still open to conjecture. Some details, however, are clear and beyond dispute. The earliest inscribed records of Egypt are some centuries later than the first written documents of Mesopotamia. In Sumer we can follow the successive paleographic stages step by step, whereas in Egypt the formative period of writing must have been short indeed, to judge from the available material. Moreover, writing left in Sumer a clearly marked trail which leads back to a specific social and economic set-up; in Egypt there is no such demonstrable relationship. Because of all these facts, and in view also of the commercial and cultural links known to have existed between Egypt and Mesopotamia at the very period under discussion, it is logical to assume that Egypt acquired the idea of writing from Mesopotamia. Differences in the form and use of the signs would correspond, then, to the manifest differences in the art and languages of the two cultural centers. On present evidence, any other assumption would leave too much to coincidence.[14] In the final analysis it is not so much a question of the mere use of script as of the conditions responsible for the original appearance of writing.

At all events, Egyptian writing, regardless of its origin, inevitably played its part in the notable progress of Egyptian science. What we miss here, however, is the scope and inner unity of scientific advance which we have found to be characteristic of Mesopotamia. That unity was the product of a tradition which is traceable ultimately to a particular concept of life. In totalitarian Egypt a different set of values attached to life and government and tradition. Is this the reason for an effort that seems more sporadic, greater perhaps in its power of concentration on specific objectives, but also more conspicuous for its omissions? Over a period of millennia this appears to be a justifiable comparative appraisal of the results achieved in intellectual and social matters by the two oldest historic civilizations.

---

[14] For an Egyptologist's statement on this point see Siegfried Schott, in Kurt Sethe's *Vom Bilde zum Buchstaben* (1939) pp. 81 ff.

ESKUALHERRIA[1]

GEORGE SARTON
Harvard University

A FRENCH nobleman was speaking somewhat indiscreetly of the antiquity of his family to a Basque peasant. "We date back," said he, "to more than five centuries ago." The old peasant answered quietly: "We no longer date back." This answer was typical of his people, for it is quite true that, though they have remained very faithful to their family and community traditions, their origins are lost in the mists of time and so distant that counting centuries has no meaning; and it is equally true that they are proud. Theirs is the natural pride of mountaineers who have succeeded in keeping their freedom and their traditions unviolated from time immemorial. Until the French Revolution on the French side, and for almost a century longer on the Spanish side, they have enjoyed their own "fueros" and remained practically their own masters. There is a saying that every Basque freeholder is a nobleman. This is not a phrase; it is (or was until recent times) a fact. Their ancestral house, however humble, is their castle. Many of these houses bear magnificent coats of arms. One may see these not simply in the Calle Mayor of Fuenterrabía or other show places, but as well in some of the smallest villages lost high up in the mountains. The traditions pertaining to the hereditary manor of each peasant are just as strict as those which rule the aristocracy of England. There is at any time but one lord of the house, the "etšeko jaun," and one appointed heir, the "etšeko seme." But among the Basques, the heir is not necessarily the eldest son; it may be a younger son or even a daughter, as the "etšeko jaun" decides for the good of the house. This heir is often chosen in childhood, and from that time on he shares to some extent the distinction which belongs to the master. Indeed it is he who will be the lord when the father dies, and to him will be handed down the responsibility of protecting the ancestral home. Of course, since

---

[1] Meaning "pais vasco," the Basque country. Basque words in this article are spelled as in the Diccionario vasco-español-francés por el presbítero Resurrección María de Azkue (2 vols. quarto, Bilbao 1905–1906).

the French Revolution and the promulgation of the Code Napoléon, a good deal of this has become theoretical: the legal obligation to divide the estate almost equally between all the children has made it very difficult and sometimes impossible to carry on the tradition; many old homes have been ruthlessly broken and transformed into kinds of hostelries where the generations pass without ever staying long enough to root themselves. Yet most peasants, being helped in this by the clergy, find roundabout ways of doing what they consider to be their ancestral duty without violating the letter of the law. And, in spite of all, they preserve, deep within them, that instinct of race, that pride of family, which stiffens men and helps them to walk straight and go through life without hesitancy. Such traditions, mind you, represent a considerable economy of moral energy.

The Basque country—Eskualherria, as they call it in their own language—is situated at the western end of the Pyrénées around the corner of the Bay of Biscay. The coastline extending from the mouth of the Adour to that of the Nervión, or from Bayonne to Bilbao, is about sixty miles long. The ideal line which separates the real Basque country from Gascony, Béarn, and Spain follows for a while the River Adour, then in a southeasterly direction the River Bidouze, passes between Mauléon and Oloron (Oloron is not Basque but Béarnais), then touches Féas and Aramits and passes a little east of St. Engrace and of the magnificent gorge of Cacouëta. That line crosses the main watershed and the political boundary near the Pic d'Anie (8215 feet). It then proceeds almost due south towards the Ebro, which it joins a little south of Tudela and follows as far as Logroño; hence it rejoins the Nervión after encircling Vitoria and Orduña. The main Pyrenean watershed divides the Basque country into two unequal parts, of which the larger by far is in Spain. Though mountaineers can cross the range at a great number of points along the innumerable little paths which are so easy for goats and smugglers but so hard for ordinary pedestrians, there are only three roads allowing wheeled vehicles to pass from France into Spain: the magnificent road along the Atlantic which joins Biarritz and San Sebastián, and two real mountain roads, the one crossing the pass of Velate and the other the famous col of Roncesvalles, where the Basque peasants defeated the rearguard of Charlemagne's army. The profile of the Pyrénées is very different on the northern and on the southern sides. On the northern, that is, on the French side, the slope is rather precipitous and the plain is very near to the main watershed; on the Spanish side, on the contrary, the mountains extend to a far greater distance. In other words, the Pyrénées cover a far greater area in Spain than in France, and it is for that very reason that the Basques, who are essentially a mountain people, are three or four times more numerous on the Spanish side. Of course, the Pyrénées must not be conceived as one single ridge; there are many secondary ridges, parallel and lateral, especially in the Spanish territory, and the Basque country is thus naturally divided into various sections or provinces. Students of the Basque dialects and of Basque architecture and folklore can easily distinguish seven provinces, to wit: three in France, Labourd, main city Bayonne, Lower Navarre, main city Saint-Jean-Pied-de-Port, Soule, main city Mauléon; and four in Spain (which I cite again as much as possible from west to east), Bizcaya, main city Bilbao, Guipúzcoa, main city San Sebastián, south of these two Aláva, main city Vitoria, and finally Upper Navarre, main city Pamplona. However different many details of their houses or clothing or speech may be when one passes from one province to another, even to the nearest one, the essential is the same throughout. As they put it, "Zazpiak bat,"[2] the seven are one. In spite of the mountains which keep all but the most vigorous, as it were, prisoners in their own district, in spite of administrative boundaries, the Basque country is one unit, the Basque men and women are substantially the same everywhere, speaking the same language, playing the same games, dancing the same extraordinary dances, having the same dreams, the same longings, the same attachments.

Who are these people who have succeeded in preserving their traditions and their language and in keeping their individuality amidst powerful neighbours? To be sure, many external aspects of their lives have been slowly adapted to the standards of the nations to which they politically belong. For example, on the French side post offices are like all such offices in the French country, and on the Spanish side like the Spanish ones. But underneath that administrative varnish, the Basque people remain the selfsame people here and there. Who are they? Whence do they come? From what source have they drawn the strength to resist alien

---

[2] Bat means one and zazpi means seven. Zazpiak means the seven, *a* being the definite article singular, *ak* the definite article plural. Ezkualdun = Basque; Ezkualduna = the Basque, el Vascongado; Ezkualdunak = the Basques.

traditions? The last question is the easiest to answer. The spring of their force is obviously the purity of their race and their legitimate pride in it. But this does not carry us very far. Whence came that strange race, so deeply different from its nearest neighbours? How often have I asked myself that question while wandering along the byways of Eskualherria, from Tardets to Mauléon and Saint-Jean-Pied-de-Port, to Cambo, to Saint Jean-de-Luz, to Azpeitia, to Pamplona—? When I saw the handsome women carrying, with such stately gait, pitchers of water on their heads or exchanging gossip at the fountain, or the grandmothers spinning wool with no instrument but a distaff, or the young peasants walking a few steps ahead of their pair of oxen or cows, holding their long goad across their shoulders with both arms extended as if crucified, when I heard the characteristic creak of the solid wooden wheels of their wagons—even now when memory brings back to my mind those pleasant pictures or those familiar noises—above all, when I see again with the mind's eye the humblest but not the least lovable creatures of that country, the sweet-eyed donkeys, so unassuming and so patient, I ask myself, where did those people come from and how did they manage to stay, almost unviolated, in this tiny corner of western Europe?

The mystery of their origin is deep. Leaving out of account some of their own apocalyptic explanations, various theories have been developed by learned scholars of many countries, but none of these theories has proved sufficiently convincing to obtain the assent of more than a small clique. Are the modern Basques descendants of the original Iberians[3] or Ligurians, or not? It should be noted that ancient writers speak of a strange people living on both sides of the Western Pyrénées, but none of them gives us certain means of identifying that people with Eskualdunak. And those Iberians or Ligurians themselves, where did they come from? Who knows? Some would have it that they came from North Africa and were somewhat related to the fairer Berber tribes. They migrated to southern Spain and later to France, being finally pushed back south of the Garonne by the Visigoths. According to others, they hailed from the Caucasus, or even from Armenia, in the vicinity of Lake Van, where they

---

[3] The connection between the Basques and the Iberians was determined a long time ago by Wilhelm von Humboldt: Prüfung der Untersuchungen über die Urbewohner Hispaniens vermittelst der vaskischen Sprache (200 p., Berlin 1821). It has been confirmed by later investigations, but the proof is not complete.

might have been at some remote time neighbours of the Etruscans. . . .
They migrated northwards across the Aras River and the Caucasus, then
westwards to their present home. This theory would account for the
presence across Europe of many place names which are said to be of
Basque derivation. According to still others, the Eskualdunak came from
Northeastern Asia, whence they migrated to the Pyrénées by way of
Georgia, while some others of their original neighbours were passing into
North Africa. . . . None of these theories is proved; none, I am afraid,
is provable, and the origin of the Basques will ever remain a secret.

Such filiations indeed can be established only in three ways: the purely
anthropological, that is, the comparison of body measurements; the
archaeological, the comparison of buildings and tools, if such exist, also
the comparison of rites and lore and customs; and finally, the linguistic,
the comparison of languages. In the present case, but little information
can be obtained by means of the first two methods, but one might naturally expect the third method to give us abundant results towards the
solution of the riddle. For the Basque people have a language of their
very own. Unfortunately, that language (Euskera) is so much their own
that it is absolutely unique in its kind. Neither its vocabulary nor its
structure reveals sufficient congruous similarities to suggest close and
sure relationship with any other language, living or dead. We cannot even
say, as was done before, that Euskera belongs to the Ural-Altaic languages of the Finno-Ugric type (like Magyar and Finnish), and if we
could say that, it would not help us very much, for who can tell where the
Finns and the Magyars came from? One thing is very certain: Euskera
is a primitive language, and this would tend to prove its antiquity, its
remoteness with regard to time or to space, or to both. The Basques are
most probably pre-Aryan: either they are descendants of the European
aborigines, or they came to Europe before the Aryan invaders. It has
been observed that the names of cutting instruments are all derived from
the word *sitz*, meaning hard stone or silex, and this would suggest a
neolithic origin. Again, their language reveals that their original week
was one of only three days. Some of the most fervent Eskualdunak maintain that Euskera is one of the languages which derived directly from
the confusion of Babel; some others claim that it is the very language used
in heaven. Let us hope that this last claim is unfounded, for it would be
a terrible handicap for all people who did not have the good luck to be

born in the Basque country. That language is indeed extremely difficult.[4]
There goes a story that the Devil tried to learn it and spent many years
in the Basque mountains for that very purpose, but he never succeeded in
knowing anything beyond a few swear words.

If we must give up the hope of knowing the origin of that people, do
not the recorded annals of the past tell us much of its history? In this
respect, too, our knowledge is unfortunately very meagre. Though there
are now many scholars in various countries who take a deep interest in
Basque problems, no scientific history has yet been written. Their first
appearance upon the European stage is evoked by the fateful name of
Roncesvalles. Who does not remember these two beautiful lines in one
of Alfred de Vigny's greatest poems?

> Roncevaux! Roncevaux! Dans ta sombre vallée
> L'ombre du grand Roland n'est donc pas consolée!

Is it through that "port"—one of the very few openings in the gigantic
Pyrenean wall that the Northern Tribes invaded Spain in the fifth century, that the Saracens passed from Spain into France three centuries
later, that Charlemagne marched his armies to the conquest of Saragossa.
The mountain dwellers had apparently no partiality either for Muslim or
Christian; all alike were equally hated when they intruded upon the sanctity of their mountain homes. Thus, on the fifteenth of August, 778, they
defeated and massacred at Roncesvalles the rearguard of the Frankish
army; it is there and then that the hero Roland, a margrave of Brittany,
found his glorious death. This made such a strong and lasting impression
upon the French that as late as the end of the eleventh century, that is,
three centuries later, it became the subject of that great poem, the *Chanson
de Roland*—perhaps the noblest epic of mediaeval Europe. To cross the
Pass of Roncesvalles (3960 ft.), to stop at the old Augustine monastery,
where every traveller is entitled to a simple but brotherly hospitality, is to
any historically-minded person one of the most delightful experiences of

---

[4] "What we express in English by the three forms *have, has, had* requires one hundred
and fifty different forms of the verb in Basque; the forms vary not only as in English with
present and past time, and not only as in Latin with the different subjects, but also according to various direct and indirect objects." Holger Pedersen: Linguistic science in the
nineteenth century (p. 124, Harvard Press, 1931). Willem J. Van Eys: Grammaire com-
parée des dialectes basques (546 p., Paris 1879). Christian Cornelius Uhlenbeck: Beiträge
zu einer vergleichenden Lautlehre der baskischen Dialekte (Amsterdam 1903).

life. This monumental abbey dates back at least to the thirteenth century; it was—and still is considered by the Spaniards—one of the most famous sanctuaries of Christendom. It was one of the many places of rest and safety which the pilgrims bound for Santiago de Compostela (in far-away Galicia) needed so much, and without which such distant pilgrimages would have soon become impossible. Travellers in southern France meet from time to time fortified churches built by the Hospitallers or by local initiative, where the weary pilgrim could find an asylum, forget for a moment the dangers and hardships of the journey, breathe a while in peace, and gather new strength for the coming days. Nowhere was such an asylum more needed than here, in the very heart of the mountains, amidst a hostile nature and men even more hostile, bent upon considering every stranger invading their fastnesses as a legitimate prey.

Speaking of this reminds me that the earliest document containing explicit[5] references to the Basque people and their language is a manuscript of the first quarter of the twelfth century, the so-called Codex Calixtinus.[6] This is a sort of guide-book composed by a pilgrim to Santiago de Compostela for the benefit of other pilgrims. It quotes for the sake of illustration a few Basque words which any Eskualdun can easily identify. It is only from that time on (the twelfth century) that the history of the Basque people can be reconstructed with any accuracy, but such history is of necessity very complex. However much the Basques had in common—and they had in common the very essentials: language and religion, traditions relative to the main events of life—they were disaggregated by their rugged mountains, they had no political unity, no unity at all except that implicit and secret unity resulting from the similarity of their circumstances and of their aspirations and from their equal distrust and contempt of all dwellers of the surrounding plains.

When a mountain range separates two countries, the main profession of its inhabitants is preordained: they are bound to be smugglers. But smuggling across treacherous mountains is not simply a profession; it is a fine art, a royal sport. It is easy to understand how it must fascinate those who practise it, even if it fails to give them more than a bare sustenance. The exhilaration of such a life, of all the thrills and dangers of

---

[5] In his life of Charlemagne, Einhard (d. 840) speaking of the ambush of Roncesvalles calls the aggressors Wascones; he has but little to say of them.

[6] G. Sarton: Introduction to the History of Science (vol. 2, 254, 1931).

crawling along precipitous paths in the depth of moonless nights, has been beautifully told by Pierre Loti in *Ramuntcho* (1897), a very good novel which everyone interested in the Basque country should read. In a sense one might say that all the Basque mountaineers are smugglers, for, if they do not all of them take part in the smuggling—this very hard work is necessarily left to the strongest men—they all abet it. Even the church is, if not openly, at least secretly, on the side of the smugglers. If not, none of the younger men could ever obtain the absolution of their sins, and they would drift away from the church, which does not seem to be the case. Reckless smugglers are generally good churchgoers; whenever nights are sufficiently dark, they run such extraordinary risks that they feel more deeply the need of some miraculous protection. They say that, years ago, whenever carabineers were detected about a frontier village, the sexton would set the church bells going to give warning to all the smugglers of the neighbourhood. And even now the people shout otsoa! otsoa! (wolf! wolf!) almost under the very nose of the poor officers of the law.[7]

The Basques are Roman Catholics and intensely devoted to their church. Their religion is the main inspiration, the light, of their life. The church is also the most powerful guardian of their traditions, and one might say that if they lost their faith, they would abandon those traditions at one and the same time. Go and attend mass in one of their churches, and you will notice that theirs is not largely a religion of women, as in many parts of France, but a religion of men. The womenfolk and the children occupy the floor, but the men—clean-shaved men with strong, austere faces—sit in the galleries, and one can see behind them hanging in a row upon the wall their bérets (or birettas), their round black caps. In the bigger churches there are many tiers of galleries, as many as four or even five (opposite the altar) in Saint-Jean-de-Luz. The church then suggests a theatre, a sort of Elizabethan stage. This effect is reinforced (in Saint-Jean-de-Luz, for instance) because the main altar is on a very high platform, so high indeed that the vestry can be placed under-

---

[7] An interesting illustration of the popular connivance at smuggling is given in the book Atheka-gaitzeko by J. B. Dasconaguerre (Bayonne 1870), telling the story of the famous Labourdin smuggler Ioannes Anchordoquy, generally called Ganich (diminutive of Ioannes). The book obtained considerable popularity. See Julien Vinson: Essai d'une bibliographie de la langue basque (2 vols. Paris 1891–1898; vol. 1, 335–341).

neath, though it is itself almost on the same level as the nave. Basque altars are generally of the Spanish type, decorated with a number of spiral columns of marble or gilded wood and statues of saints, some of them dressed up like dolls, all glittering with gold and silver and jewels.

Even as in Brittany, the intense loyalty of the people to their church does not entirely hide their pagan origin. Some of the older cemeteries contain tombstones in the shape of discs, bearing symbols referring to the profession of the departed—crude images of his tools—and other strange marks, but in some cases (it must be admitted, very rarely) no cross, no Christian symbol of any kind. These tombs suggest clearly pre-Christian origins. The Basque country has always been a hotbed of superstition. During the black days of the witchcraft delusion it flourished there in a most terrible fashion, and caused thousands of people to lose their mental balance or their life, or both. Even to this day the superstitious nature of the Eskualdunak reveals itself continuously. They will make a sign of the cross each time that some new action of importance, real or symbolic, is undertaken, as, for instance, before giving the first stroke of their scythe at the moment of reaping, or before cutting a new loaf of bread. In fact, they cross themselves as often and as casually as Muslims utter the basmala. Some of the superstitions which still obtain, at least in remote villages, are very touching. For example, when a man is about to die, one of the tiles of his roof is taken away by his neighbour in order that the liberated soul may depart and fly to heaven more easily. And as soon as the soul is departed, the widow and the young heir go to the beehives and say formally to the bees: "O bees! we inform you that the master of the house has just died." To neglect such a rite might bring bad luck to the home.

I said above that their religion is the main source of inspiration of Eskualdunak. That is absolutely true, but I ought to add that their instinct and pride of race are so great as to form an integral part of their religion. The ancestral hearth is still a reality in most Basque villages, at least in those which are not on the main roads of traffic, in spite of the fact that their isolation becomes smaller year by year and that foreign customs are continually forced upon them. To the uncontaminated Basque mind the salvation of his soul and the preservation of his home are duties of equal importance. I have already mentioned the custom, which the Code Napoléon has not yet succeeded in uprooting, of handing down the paternal estate to one of the children, fair compensation being conceded to the others. If one of the children becomes a priest or a monk, he readily abandons his claim to the estate, if not at once at least by a written will, in order to facilitate the transmission of the estate unbroken. This tradition might be regarded as the fundamental tradition of their life, because it involves directly or indirectly all the others. For example, the authority granted to the master of the house and vicariously to his appointed heir, and the respect so spontaneously shown to them, implies an unusual amount of family discipline and indirectly of social discipline. It implies at the same time a good deal of self-respect. They know their duties but they know also their rights, and they are ready to react vigorously if some authority not implicitly recognized by them tries to pile more obligations upon their shoulders. Another interesting result of their views on inheritance is that many of the younger sons emigrate to the Americas, especially to Mexico and the Argentine, where their habits of hard work, frugality, and thrift bring them not unusually an amount of prosperity which would have been undreamed of had they remained at home. Many of these "Americans" return to their homeland to spend the balance of their life and enjoy their wealth among their old neighbours. The preservation of paternal estates has often been due to the generosity of the enriched exiles. The importance of the ancestral home is well indicated by the fact that each home has a name and that the inhabitants are known by that name, even when the family name is different, as happens when the heir was a woman who acquired a new legal name by marriage. Another aspect of the home sanctity is revealed to us by their great reverence for the hearth itself and for the fire that dwells in it. It is the duty of the mistress (or shall we call it her privilege?) to light or to revive the fire in the morning, no hand but her own must attend to that. And when they fear bad luck they throw a handful of salt into the hearth. You see, the hearth is not a common thing but a sort of domestic altar, and the fire that burns in it, a living member of the family, a symbol of its unity and holiness.

One of the readiest ways of understanding the soul of a people is to investigate its literature. This is unfortunately very difficult in the present case, because the Basque language is so difficult and practically unknown abroad, but even more because their literature is very largely a spoken,

not a written, one.[8] They are still in the Homeric stage and will probably
ever remain there, that is, as long as their traditions can withstand the
growing pressure from the outside world. It is much too late indeed to
pass from the spoken and relatively unconscious stage where they are
now to the more purely literary one: the country is too small, the literary-
minded people too few, to create the written language and help it push
its way into the world without being smothered by its powerful neighbours,
the French and Spanish languages. It makes one sad to think that the
Basque literature has no chance of development, and even that any attempt to develop it along more conventional lines would hasten its death
—but such is its fate. In the meanwhile it is, in its humble fashion and
within the limits of its own mountains, a very living language. There is
something very austere in the Basque character, and their literature is
very different from those of the Latin peoples which surround them, in
that it is far less rhetorical and hyperbolic, far more direct and simple.
This does not mean that it is jejune. Those who understand it (I do not!)
say that it is a great joy to hear the Basque improvvisatori (plain peasants,
mind you, not different in other respects from their neighbours) taking up
almost any subject and discussing it at great length *in verse*. This is
usually done at the end of one of those generous Basque dinners, duly
sprinkled with cider and wine, which leave the audience in a receptive
and indulgent mood, ready to applaud enthusiastically every happy con-
ceit of their favourite poets. Another highly characteristic feature of
Basque literature is the acting on holidays in almost every village of "pas-
torals," little plays which seem to be the direct descendants of the mediaeval mysteries. It is clear that the mysteries have survived in those mountains because of their oral, or at any rate unprinted, tradition, which
alone can preserve popular literature in a plastic and living shape, without drying it up and killing it.

An account of Eskualherria, however brief, would be essentially incomplete if it did not refer to their main recreations: their dancing and jump-
ing, so original and so primitive, but above all their great national game,
which is played with equal fervour wherever Eskualdunak are assembled
(even in South America), the game of pelota. This is played with a ball,
which is thrown against a wall either with the naked palm, or by means

---

[8] This statement is qualified in the appendix, Notes on Basque literature.

of a wooden racket or a wickerwork glove which looks like a fantastic claw. It is a splendid game, which calls for a great deal of strength, agility, and skill and admirably brings out these qualities. There is a wall especially built for that purpose in every village, and the best players are the heroes of each community (they are very often also the best smugglers). The games, generally played on Sundays, attract young and old alike, men and women, and are by far the main interest of the parish while they last, and the main subject of conversation for a long time afterwards. The piety of the people is well illustrated by the fact that, however intense their interest in the game, if the Angelus happens to ring, they will stop playing at once, remove their bérets, and remain perfectly still until the bells have ceased to call. This sudden stop of a most vigorous game, perhaps at a very exciting moment, is exceedingly impressive.

But the pelotari—as they are called—are not the only heroes of Eskualherria. That small nation, lost in the fastnesses of the Western Pyrénées, has contributed more than its share to the essential task of mankind: the creation of spiritual values. As we might expect, their main contributions have been made in the religious field. And but few words are needed to indicate them. It will suffice to say that San Ignacio de Loyola, that undaunted soldier of Christ, who founded the Society of Jesus in 1534, and San Francisco Javier, the Apostle of the Indies, were both of them genuine Basques. I visited, in September 1925, the birthplace of St. Ignatius near Azpeitia, and this enabled me to cross one of the wildest and most beautiful parts of the Spanish Basque country. It is strange to think that Jansenism, a religious doctrine which made considerable stir during the second half of the seventeenth century and was largely directed against the Jesuits, was also to some extent a Basque production. Jansenius himself, bishop of Ypres, was a Dutchman, but his greatest friend and champion, Jean Du Vergier de Hauranne, later abbot of Saint Cyran, was a Basque, and the pair spent many years in Bayonne, reading St. Augustine and concocting their new theology.

The Basque country is mainly a mountainous country, but it touches the ocean; sixty miles along the Gulf of Gascony are theirs to look at and listen to the sea, and dream of it. That is more than enough to draw them out! The same physical and mental qualities which made of them such successful smugglers caused those of them who lived nearer to the seashore to become audacious sailors. Basque seamen were among the first to explore the forbidden Atlantic; they were also among the first cod- and whale-fishermen. Crossing the little village of Guetaria (in Guipúzcoa) on my way to Loyola, I was shown the monument dedicated to the memory of the greatest Basque sailor, Juan Sebastián de Elcano, who was in command of the only ship of Magellan's fleet that came back in 1522 after a three-year absence. Elcano was thus the first man to navigate around the world. And a little further, along the same wonderful coast, another surprise awaits the traveller, the beautiful villa (Santiago-echea, meaning the house of St. James) built by the master painter Zuloaga upon the shore of Zumaya. That house contains not simply his studio, but a little museum, wherein Zuloaga has collected many of the Spanish paintings and articles of virtu which he knows so well and loves so deeply. He has built also a strange little chapel, more Spanish in taste, however, than Basque. (It is true the Basque taste in religious matters is very much Hispanized.) But Zuloaga himself is a real Eskualdun, and very conscious of it; he has promised full assistance to the Basque museum, which has been established at Bayonne and is already, in spite of its youth, very remarkable. His own art combines in a masterly way the passion, the warmth, and the spice of Spain with the greater austerity and reticence of his native soil. Any country, especially such a small one, which has given to the world an Ignacio de Loyola and an Ignacio Zuloaga, a Francisco Javier and an Elcano, each of these representing many others less brilliant but equally devoted to the highest ideals of their race—any such country may be justly proud of itself. It has not joined the comity of nations empty-handed; poor as it was, as far as material goods were concerned, it has given far more than it has received.

Notes on Basque Literature

My reflections concerning the poverty of the Basque literature may raise objections on the part of readers who understand "literature" in a strictly philological sense, i.e., as a collection of texts. There is an abundance of Basque texts, but the literature—the bonae litterae—is very restricted indeed. Apart from poetry, songs, and proverbs, the vast majority of Basque writings are devoted to Catholic apologetics or edification. Much of that "literature" is artificial, in the sense that it was written for the people rather than by the people. As was noted by Julian Vinson (1843–1926), a life long student of everything pertaining to Eskualherria, "Les livres de piété traduits en basque sont tous remarquables par la bizarrerie du style. . . . "[9] The bulk of Basque books is religious propaganda, often mixed with political propaganda, anti-Revolutionary during the Revolution, imperialistic under Napoleon, then royalist, anti-Carlist, etc., always anti-Protestant. Many books speak of the greatness of the Basque country, chiefly Guipúzcoa, but that is always combined with religious edification. There are also many almanacs the purpose of which is as much to reiterate the catechism as to indicate the cycles of Moon and church.

In justice to the Basque people one should remember that their language has always been handicapped by the constant rivalry of three other languages of international prestige, to wit, Latin, French and Spanish. Every educated Basque is well acquainted with at least one of these languages, and more probably with two. Moreover, there was never a political union of their provinces, nor any chance for any dialect to dominate and eclipse the others and thus obtain the dignity of a standardized language.

The number of Basque-speaking people was never very large. Prince Louis Lucien Bonaparte estimated it in 1873 at 800,000 (660,000 in Spain, 140,000 in France). It cannot be much larger now; it may be smaller. On account of the segregation of groups of people in many valleys the dialectal diversity is exceptionally high. Prince Bonaparte divided Basque in three main dialectal groups, fifty dialects (plus four written ones), twenty-five subdialects broken into fifty "varieties" and half a score of "subvarieties." The language is very ancient, but its tangible monuments are relatively recent. Some place-names can be dated back to the eighth century,[10] but that is not very early; we have the Codex Calixtinus (XII–1) mentioned above and a few Basque sentences jokingly quoted by Rabelais (Pantagruel, ch. IX, pr. 1532; Gargantua, book 1, ch. v, pr. 1534). The first Basque book was printed only in 1545,[11] and the total

---

[9] Vinson (vol. 2, p. viii, 1898).

[10] The information given in this paragraph down to here is derived from Georges Lacombe: La langue basque, in Antoine Meillet et Marcel Cohen: Les langues du monde (319–326, Paris 1924)

[11] Modern reprint with French translation (86 p., Bordeaux 1847); more accurate re-

number of books printed in the sixteenth century amounts only to seven. The first book (fig. 1) is a collection of poems called Linguae Vasconum primitiae edited by Bernard Dechepare, priest of Saint-Michel-le Vieux (Bordeaux 1545). The most remarkable monument of the Basque language

FIG. 1. Title-page of first book printed in Basque. Bernard Dechepare: Anthology of poetry in Low Navarrese dialect [28 leaves, Bordeaux 1545]. Vinson (1891, p. 1–5).

is the translation of the New Testament written for Jeanne d'Albret, queen of Navarre, by Jean de Liçarrague (or Ioannes Leiçarraga) and printed in La Rochelle 1571 (figs. 2, 3). This was the third Basque work to be printed and the first having a Basque title page. Its appearance was

print, Poésies basques de Bernard Dechepare d'Eyheralarre, edited by Abel Hovelacque and Julien Vinson (72 p., Bayonne 1874).

paradoxical, for while the Basques are deeply Catholic, this, their first great work, and in many respects the greatest ever to appear in their language, was of Protestant inspiration. Many Basques established in La Rochelle had been converted to the Reformation; Leiçarraga was a "minister of the reformed church of Béarn"; he prefixed to his Calvinistic translation a long dedicace in French to queen Jeanne dated August 22, 1571. Many Protestant books printed in Antwerp and other places were smuggled into France and Spain during the sixteenth century, and this Basque New Testament was one of them. Leiçarraga's version was in the Labourdin dialect, as was later the whole Bible printed by the English Bible Society, under the patronage of Prince Louis Lucien Bonaparte (London, 1859–1865). This prince, a nephew of Napoleon, was deeply interested in the Basque language and caused various parts of the Gospels and the Song of Songs to be translated into many dialects, Biscayan, Central, Guipúzcoan,[12] Marquina, Eastern Low Navarrese, South High Navarrese, Spanish Navarrese and Souletin. These partial versions were issued during the years 1856–68.

A complete New Testament was published in Guipúzcoan (Bilbao 1931); otherwise all translations of some extent (including at least the four Gospels) were in Labourdin. The first of all was the Calvinistic New Testament of 1571, then a Catholic version of the Four Gospels was made in 1740 by Ioannes Haraneder, priest in Saint-Jean-de-Luz, and after being revised by two Labourdin priests it was finally published in Bayonne in 1855. A New Testament translated from Greek into Labourdin was issued in 1828. Thus from the point of view of Biblical translations, Labourdin was by far the outstanding dialect; yet the vernacular Bible was generally associated with Protestantism and the abundant Catholic literature was more partial perhaps to Guipúzcoan and other dialects of the Spanish side than to Labourdin.

In the year 1571 which witnessed the publication of the first Basque New Testament, the same author, Ioannes Leiçarraga, published two other books under a single cover, the first of which is a calendar, the other a book of Christian (Calvinistic) instruction for children. The title of the Calendar is characteristic (see fig. 4).[13]

---

[12] A version of St. Luke in Guipúzcoan had been made before by Oteiza and edited by George Borrow (Madrid 1838).

[13] A critical edition of the three Basque books of 1571 by I. Leiçarraga, the N.T.,

IESVS CHRIST

GVRE IAVNAREN
TESTAMENTV
BERRIA.

MATTH. XVII.

Haur da ene Seme maitea, ceinetan neure atseguin ona
hartzen baitut, huni beha çaquizquiote.

ROCHELLAN.
Pierre Hautin. Imprimiçale.
1571.

FIG. 2. Title-page of the third Basque book, the first with a Basque title. The title reads: The New Testament of Our Lord Jesus Christ. Matthew XVII "This is my beloved Son in whom I am well pleased; hear ye him." La Rochelle, Peter Hautin printer, 1571. (568 leaves). Printing was completed on Sept. 24. Labourdin dialect, with some Low Navarrese expressions. As stated in his preface, the translator, John of Leiçarraga, avoided forms of speech which were too local, for he tried to be understood by as many people as possible. Long description in Vinson (pp. 5–38, 1891).

FIG. 3. First page of the Gospel according to St. Matthew in the Basque Bible of 1571.

Aside from this calendar the first scientific book in Basque, and for aught I know the only one, was a translation in the Labourdin dialect of Saint-Jean-de-Luz of a French treatise on navigation, "Les voyages aventureux du capitaine Martin de Hoyarsabal, habitant de Çubiburu,

KALENDRERA,
BAZCO NOIZ DATEN,
ILHARGVI BERRIAREN
eta letra Dominicalaren eça-
gutzeco manera-
requin.

+ *
*

*Beſta deitzen direnetaric-ere batzu eçarri içan
dira, ez Igandeaz berce egun ſanctificatzeco-
ric delacotz, baina ferietaco, hatu-emanetaco,
eta aſco berce gauçataco egun iaquinac eta be-
reciac dituztenéc cerbitzu dutençat.*

ROCHELLAN.
Pierre Hautin, Imprimiçale.
1 5 7 1.

FIG. 4. Title-page of fourth Basque book, divided into two parts, a calendar and a Christian ABC. The second part is dated La Rochelle, October 1, 1571. The title of the first part here reproduced means "Calendar, with the manner of knowing the date of Easter and the New Moon and the domini-cal letter. One has added some of the so-called holydays, not because it is necessary to sanctify another day than the Sunday, but in order that the people who must choose and know the days for the fairs, the deliveries to be made or received and many other things, may make use of it. La Rochelle, Pierre Hautin, printer, 1571." It contains Easter tables, golden numbers and dominical letters from 1572 to 1623, various eras, the year and its parts, calendar (total 16 p.). Vinson (1891, pp. 42–46).

contenant les reigles et enseignemens nécessaires à la bonne et seure navigation" (Bordeaux 1579; revised edition, Bordeaux 1633). The trans-lator was Piarres (Peter) Detcheverry or Dorre; his work was printed in Bayonne 1677 (fig. 5). It is fitting that the only scientific treatise in

---

calendar and ABC was published by Th. Linschmann and Hugo Schuchardt (Strassburg 1900).

LIBVRVHAUDA JXASOCO

NABIGACIONECOA.

MARTIN DE HOYARZABALEC
egiña Francezes.

Eta PIARRES DETCHEVERRY,
edo DORREC efcararac emana,
Eta cerbait guebiago abançatuba.

BATONAN.

FAUVET, Imprimerian Carmeſſeteco aldean.
1. DC I X.X VII

FIG. 5. Title-page of first and last scientific book printed in Basque (Labourdin dialect of Saint Jean-de-Luz). The title reads "This book is the one on sea navigation, done in French by Martin de Hoyarsabal and put into Basque by Peter Detcheverry or Dorre, with something added to it. Bayonne, Printed by Antoine Fauvet near the Carmelite monastery, 1677" (172 p.). Vinson (1891, pp. 129–132).

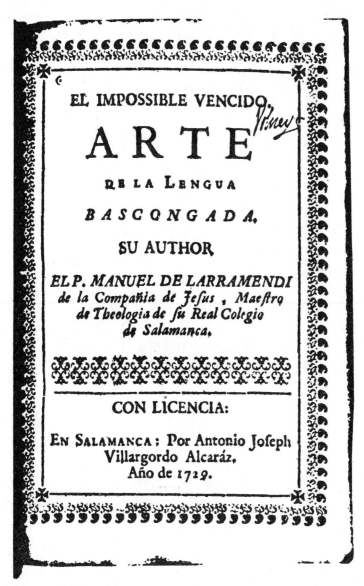

FIG. 6. Title-page of the first elaborate grammar of the Basque language (small octavo, xxxvi+404 p., Salamanca 1729). It is dedicated to the very noble and loyal province of Guipúzcoa. Title-page reproduced from the copy in the Harvard College Library, which I was privileged to use.

Basque should be a treatise on navigation, for the Basque nation was a cradle of navigators; as sea captains can hardly be expected to be scholars, it is natural that they would desire a vade-mecum printed in their own tongue. The book of 1677 filled that need.

The first good instruments for the study of Basque were forged by the Jesuit father, Manuel de Larramendi (1690–1766), born in Guipúzcoa, who was professor of philosophy in Palencia, Valladolid, Salamanca, confessor to the dowager queen Mary-Ann of Neuburg, and spent the end of his life in Loyola. His elaborate grammar (450 p.) was published in Salamanca 1729 (fig. 6) and his tri-lingual dictionary (Spanish, Basque, Latin) in San Sebastián 1745 (2 vols., c. 1050 p.).[14] Father Larramendi was the first scientific regulator and organizer of the Basque language and this gave considerable prestige to Guipúzcoa.

Among other eighteenth-century publications, I shall only mention two items. A comic opera, "El borracho burlado," was played in Vergara 1764 under the patronage of the court of Peñaflorida. The dialogue was in Spanish but the songs in Basque; that is, Spanish was considered to be the language of gentle conversation, Basque, that of poetry.

The other item is a complex one. It is a whole group of revolutionary official publications in French or Basque, or in both languages. The first is the Cahier des vœux et des instructions des Basques-François du Labourt pour leurs députés aux Etats généraux de la Nation (Bayonne 1789). There are many others ranging from 1789 to 1795; most of them have been reprinted in Bayonne 1874–1887.[15]

Many Basque publications are translations, e.g., there are many versions of the Imitation of Christ and of the Spiritual exercises of San Ignacio; a Latin anthology (Quintus Curtius, Sallustius, Tacitus, Cicero, Livius) was translated in Tolosa 1802, some fifty fables of Aesopos in San Sebastián 1804, a part of Plautus' Poenulus in 1828, selected fables of La Fontaine in La Réole 1848.

Considering the fact that the Basque printing presses have been kept busy since 1571 for propaganda purposes, I wonder what they have been concocting during recent years? It is true that our age of intense propaganda is not satisfied any more with printing but needs the help of the

---

[14] All the books reproduced in this article, except Larramendi's grammar, are exceedingly rare, that is, only very few copies are known to exist. The grammar is not uncommon.

[15] Vinson (p. 248–252, 1891).

radio. However, 'verba volant, scripta manent'; the first part of that old proverb applies beautifully to the winged words of the radio. It will be interesting later on to find out how much and what kind of propaganda was printed in Basque, and which dialects were favored.

It is curious that no scientific book was published in Basque except the Hoyarsabal translation of 1677, no book on mathematics or medicine. This confirms the dependence of Basque on other languages, Latin, French and Spanish. The small languages can exist only for the heart's needs, for common life and poetry. That may seem little, but it is very much.

THE MONETARY REFORM
OF ANASTASIUS I AND ITS
ECONOMIC IMPLICATIONS

ROBERT P. BLAKE

Harvard University

FROM the numismatic standpoint it is obvious that the coinage of the emperor Anastasius I forms a turning point in the history of the currency of the later Roman Empire.[1] A fairly extensive literature, though much scattered *more numismatico*,[2] exists on this particular aspect, but the economic implications of the reform have not been studied with the same attention. In fact the bearing of the reform upon contemporary conditions and its reception by the population of the empire have been, it would appear, largely neglected, perhaps under the illusion that merely different flans and modules were used and nothing else.[3] We propose in the present paper to investigate its other aspects and to ascertain how it was integrated with the rest of the emperor's administrative program.

It is a matter of common knowledge that the gold and silver currency of the Roman empire, which had been placed on a sound basis by Augustus, began to deteriorate after Marcus Aurelius. Deterioration proceeded apace in the third century, and in the reign of Gallienus, for all practical purposes, a complete collapse ensued, and the Empire de facto went into bankruptcy. Aurelian, Diocletian and Constantine, by a series of meas-

---

[1] Wroth makes this reform the beginning of Byzantine currency proper (Warwick Wroth, *Catalogue of the Imperial Byzantine Coins in the British Museum*, I, London, 1908. Introduction p. xii). J. Sabatier, *Description générale des monnaies byzantines frappées sous les empereurs d'Orient depuis Arcadius jusqu'à la prise de Constantinople par Mahomet II* (St. Pétersbourg 1862), Count I. I. Tolstoi, *Monnaies byzantines*, St. Pétersbourg, 1912–1914, and Hugh Goodacre, *Coinage of the Byzantine Empire*, London, 1928-33, prefer the reign of Arcadius as a starting point, but this date was chosen so as to fit on to H. Cohen's *Description historique des monnaies frappées sous l'empire romain*, as Wroth, l.c., p. xi points out. A strong body of experts had held Wroth's view (l.c., xii and note 1).

[2] To be cited below in the notes.

[3] This is certainly the implication in Wroth, l.c., p. xiii.

ures, which are by no means clear in detail individually, nor in their causal connection with one other, finally established a sound gold currency, whose unit, the solidus or *nomisma*, remained dominant and undepreciated until the 11th century.[4] We are still far from possessing a complete understanding of how this was effected, and the investigations recently made by numerous scholars have brought to light sundry problems, particularly connected with the issue and circulation of copper-bronze currency in the empire during the 4th and 5th centuries, which still await satisfactory answers. The general question is additionally complicated by the fact that no large scale work has been done by modern numismatists upon this later bronze currency. The British Museum Catalogues do not yet cover this period. The older general works are out of date and admittedly incomplete. The statistics on size and weight of various issues are very fragmentary, and the literary evidence scattered and indefinite. Sufficient work, however, has been done to adumbrate the main lines of development, and to introduce some logical order into what has hitherto appeared to be a hopeless mass of amorphous confusion. We shall preface our remarks by briefly sketching what appears to have been established with reasonable probability.

If we commence our survey of Roman currency with the period of the Severi, we are confronted with the following situation. The imperial coinage of gold and silver, both being debased to varying amounts as compared with the previous standard of fineness, were supplemented at an earlier period on the silver, and more widely later on the bronze level by a series of provincial and especially of municipal issues, which ran current along with and, it would seem, on a parity with, the imperial copper currency. Egypt had a special currency of its own. The Severi in particular seem almost to have made it a point to increase the amount of local copper-bronze or brass currency in circulation by freely granting the right of coinage to the many new municipalities which they founded or to which they gave municipal rights. The administrative reasons for this are

---

[4] A general sketch in H. Mattingly, *Roman Coins from the Earliest Times to the Fall of the West Roman Empire*, London, Methuen, 1927. The British Museum Catalogue does not yet cover the later empire, nor does the repertorium of Mattingly and Sydenham, *Roman Imperial Coinage*, London, 1923 f., treat the later period. With the exception of J. Maurice's *La Numismatique constantinienne* (Paris 1908–1912) we are badly off for detailed studies of the fourth and fifth century currency.

far from clear, but the facts are indisputable. The debasement of the currency, according to Gresham's law, led to the disappearance of the old, full-value coins, which were either hoarded or exported. This is tantamount to saying that the fluid reserves of precious metals in the empire were seriously depleted, and with the growing demoralization in the state, the normal accretion from mining operations tended equally to diminish.[5]

There has been a great deal of discussion of the gold exports from the Roman Empire to India,[6] which were unquestionably a drain on the resources of the state, but much less has been said about the equally important outflow of silver. Kubitschek[7] has pointed out the importance of this factor, and the rarity of the silver coinage of the later period brings additional indirect testimony on this point. We should not overestimate it, however. We have not to do here with any silver famine, such as affected the majority of the Islamic world from 1000–1250 A.D.

Students of the later Roman Empire have come to realize, thanks to the penetrating and acute investigations of the late Gunnar Mickwitz[8] and of other scholars,[8a] that the fourth century likewise was marked by a series of inflationary crises, less widespread, perhaps, than those of the preceding epoch, but locally at least just as violent. The causes underlying these phenomena differ somewhat from those of the third century, and some understanding of them is a necessary preliminary step in comprehending the problem which we intend to discuss in detail. Constantine, we know, succeeded in establishing the gold currency on a sound basis, and in theory, if not wholly in practice, the silver as well.[9] At the

[5] Cf. Pauly-Wissowa *RE* s. v. Bergbau, Supplementband IV, cols. 108–155.

[6] Literature in E. H. Warmington, *The Commerce between the Roman Empire and India* (Cambridge, 1928), pp. 272–318.

[7] Der Übergang von der vordiocletianischen Währung im 4 Jhd., *Byz. Zeitschrift* 35 (1935), 340–374, esp. pp. 350–351.

[8] Geld und Wirtschaft im spätromischen Reiche, Societas Scientiarum Fennica, Commentationes Humanarum Litterarum, IV. N° 2, Helsinki, 1932. Also his study, Die Systeme des römischen Silbergeldes im IV Jhdt. n. Chr. (Same series, VI. 2 (1933)), is very interesting, though certain points made in this have by no means found general acceptance. See F. M. Heichelheim, *Wirtschaftsgesch. des Altertums*, notes p. 1127–1128.

[8a] The later work has been in large measure a development from, or a criticism of, the ideas advanced by Mickwitz. Especially to be noted is Kubitschek's article (cited above note 7).

[9] Maurice, *Numismatique constantinienne I*, Introduction, passim; Mattingly, *Roman Coins*, 223 f.

basis of his reforms he put the sexagesimal system, finally enabling this to triumph over the decimal, which underlay Aurelian's reforms.[10] He struck the solidus as 1/72 of a Roman pound, using, it would appear, the 12 ounce unit, and not the aberrant weights which bob up here and there, both before and after this time. It is clear that the amount of gold available for coinage was sufficient to meet the needs of the large-scale transactions of the period,[11] which were predominantly carried out by the government.[12] The amount of silver in circulation appears to have been small,[13] to judge by the rarity of the coins, and to a considerable extent it may have become merely a *monnaie de compte;* but tied as it was to the more precious metal, it had little effect upon the general situation.

The copper-bronze currency, however, was quite a different matter. During the earlier empire it had been heavily overvalued,[14] as compared to the gold and silver coinage. I suspect, though I cannot prove it, that the emperors intentionally increased the amount of copper in circulation[15]

---

[10] Good remarks on this point by B. Hilliger, Argyrismus und Denarismus im römischen Münzwesen von Caracalla bis Diokletian, *Numismatik* 2–3 (1933–1934), 141–145 (article never completed).

[11] This may have been brought in by the confiscation of the temple treasures, as Mattingly thinks (*Roman Coins*, p. 259) and by acquisitions in war, but it seems somewhat dubious. The temples had been largely plundered before. The Eastern trade at this period, with its export of finished textiles, esp. silk, was much less of a drain on the resources of the state than it had been under the earlier empire, when the purchase of raw materials took place in India for cash. While the mines were less intensively worked, some precious metal was produced in the empire, and the supply from Africa, paid for as previously and also later in trade goods was still available. Some continuing source of supply must be assumed since the gold reserves were not seriously depleted. The fact that silver was current in the Iranian area had its effect, no doubt, in fostering the export of Roman silver coins eastward rather than the gold currency.

[12] The later Roman state manufactures have not been satisfactorily studied. The literature is gathered by Heichelheim, l.c., pp. 1185 f.

[13] See above note 7.

[14] See. J. W. Kubitschek, *Byz. Zs.* 35 (1935), 355 and also his article Gold und Silber im 4 Jhd. n. Chr., *Num. Zs.* 46 (1914), 604.

[15] The bronze and copper currency had always been considered a local affair, as the countless local issues show. We have no evidence that the government, imperial or provincial, ever controlled at all the amount of the currency so issued. The explanation is probably that the difficulties of transporting quantities of money were so considerable and so risky that it was necessary to have a large number of mints supplying local needs, whose circumferential circulation was largely limited to the district.

in order to extricate themselves from their financial difficulties, and that certain measures, such as the issue of the so-called Antoninianus, had as one of its basic aims the devaluation of the copper currency, as Hilliger asserts.[16] Under stable conditions it might have been possible to attain this end by legislative means, but political chaos, military disasters, economic disorder and social unrest intervened or supervened, and depreciation went on in a series of minor crises throughout the fourth century. It did not result from the stabilization of the gold currency, as the first of these crises took place during the years 307–311 A.D., before the coinage of the solidus, as we can see from the Egyptian documents.[17]

It also behooves us in this connection to remember the mixed ancestry of the copper coinages which circulated in the empire. They were the mongrel progeny of highly divergent ancestors: the degenerated currencies of the Hellenistic monarchies, as in Egypt; the issues of the Roman provincial governors and the coinage of the cities to whom the emperors had granted this privilege. While the silver coinage of the empire remained of full weight and good alloy, the bronze currency played the modest part which was assigned it of enabling payment of minute sums and execution of petty transactions. Sufficient amounts were coined for local needs, and as long as an ample supply of gold and silver was available and exchange readily accomplished, the total amount in circulation might vary very considerably without affecting the economic equilibrium.

This brings up a matter of considerable importance for our general problem. In what economic category or categories are we to place this copper or bronze currency? Is it fractional currency or is it token money? Was it definitely related arithmetically to the higher values and other metals and guaranteed by the government as receivable in unlimited quantities for the discharge of debts and the payment of taxes—legal tender unlimited in its nature—or was it token money with a limited sphere of validity? We possess no specific data on this point, but converging lines of evidence seem to show that *de facto*, if not *de jure*, its status seems to have oscillated considerably during the period which we have been surveying. Bearing in mind, then, this dual possibility, we shall endeavor to trace the development during the fourth century.

---

[16] See Benno Hilliger, Argyrismus und Denarismus, l.c. (cf. note 10).

[17] See Mickwitz, l.c., p. 99 ff. and A. Segrè, *Circolazione monetaria e prezzi nel mondo antico*, Roma, 1922 (Rassegna numismatica italiana no. 13), p. 47 f.

It is clear first of all that a catastrophic fall in the value of the copper currency took place during this period. We find our evidence for this almost wholly in the papyri: literary data are very nearly non-existent. These periods of inflation coincide only in part with periods of political confusion and disorder, so that *a priori* we cannot aver that these latter were the dominant reason for the fall in value of copper-bronze. The coins do not bear any mark of value, and the equation of the various terms mentioned in our sources and in our documents with the known types is extremely difficult; opinions diverge radically. There is some attempt, it would appear, to distinguish between the values of the coins by the size of the flans, but whether this was a 5:2:1 ratio, or whether the basic unit represented 10:5 or some other figure, we have no means of knowing.

A further point which often has not been emphasized sufficiently in the discussion is that the Egyptian materials may give us a somewhat exaggerated picture of the results of the inflation, because during its course the old Egyptian billion coins were replaced by the imperial bronze currency, and this can well have accentuated the results of the depression. It is striking that our literary sources do not indicate any extreme discomforts arising from these causes.

The process of adjustment seems to have reached a certain measure of stability in the days of Julian the Apostate (ca. 360).[18] The value of the solidus expressed in copper oscillated somewhat, but the unit (now called νούμμιον) appears to have been fixed. At the end of the century (395 A.D.)[18a] the government gave up the attempt to differentiate between denominations, and until Anastasius' day the small bronze coin was usually the only one minted, and the amount issued seems to have been small.

It is not improbable that certain issues were demonetized during this period, though the evidence for this, apart from the *damnatio memoriae* of unsuccessful or defeated usurpers, is rather scanty, but it is usually clear from the finds that certain series remained in circulation for a long time.

A fundamental reform in those chaotic conditions was carried out by the emperor Anastasius I in the year 498, four years after his accession

---

[18] Cf. Mickwitz, l.c., p. 112–3.
[18a] Cod. Theod. IX. 23.2 (395 A.D.).

to the throne. Anastasius abandoned the small copper coin which had been minted by his predecessors, and replaced it by a new series of an entirely different type. So far as is known, he coined no small pieces of the earlier model. The differences consisted in the following points:

1) A different alloy was used, giving a ruddy surface which is largely proof against chemical disintegration.[19]

2) The flans were much larger and thicker than the coins of preceding emperors, with approximate correspondence in their relative weights to the denominations which were marked upon them.

3) The coins were issued in four different denominations, which were quintuple multiples of a basic unit, M = 40, K = 20, I = 10, E = 5 and a unit piece.[20]

4) Two series of coins were issued, one larger and one smaller. Whether these were simultaneous or whether one preceded the other is uncertain.[21]

5) The coins are marked with the device of the mint which issued them.

We can easily understand how Anastasius, a representative of the civil bureaucracy, and himself a capable financier, felt himself impelled to put an end to the chaotic currency conditions which had existed under his predecessors, and did so early in his reign. The reform proved to be a successful one, as his successors followed it with only minor deviations well down into the seventh century. The nature of the coins themselves indicates up to a point, we feel, what the emperor's intentions were, but the statements of his motives preserved in the literary sources are hedged about with difficulties of interpretation which are puzzling in the extreme.[21a]

---

[19] This ruddy color is commented upon by Cassiodorus Varia i. 18.

[20] The unit piece is quite rare. See Wroth, l.c., plate II. 2 and Tolstoy, l.c., under Anastasius, no. 69.

[21] The proportional relation in weight among the different denominations is approximately the same in both series, but the smaller is half the size of the larger.

[21a] The supply of copper coinage during the latter half of the fifth century was clearly insufficient, both in the east and in the west, but was more acute, it would appear, in the West. In this connection the remarks of Lorenzina Cesano on the bronze coins circulating in Italy at the fall of the Western Empire and under the Ostrogoths are much to the point (Rivista Italiana Numismatica 20 (1913), 542–543): "Quanto alla rozzezza dei tipi i pezzi cosidetti vandalici nulla hanno ad invidiare ai bronzetti coniati contemporaneamente nel resto del mondo romano; per la quantità si è già detto che era minima, in-

What do the coins themselves tell us? It is reasonably clear that we have an attempt on the part of the government to reach the following ends:

1) The copper coinage represented a small subdivision of the dominant unit—the solidus.

2) For convenience in payments, these were issued in larger units (40/20/10/5).

3) From their size, shape, color of the metal and general appearance they were intended to, and did replace, an older currency of one *Nominale* only.

4) The presence of the mint mark shows that the state exercised some control over their issue.

To draw further deductions from the actual coins would seem to be hazardous: let us now turn to a consideration of the literary evidence so as to evaluate, if possible, the aims of Anastasius in carrying out the reform, and the effects of the reform upon popular opinion.

The late J. B. Bury[22] drew attention to the neglected passage in the chronicle of John Malalas of Antioch,[23] where this currency reform is mentioned, which had been largely overlooked in recent discussions. We learn from it that the person in charge of the operations was John the Paphlagonian, surnamed Caïaphas, the *comes sacrarum largitionum*. The text reads: Ὁ δὲ αὐτὸς Βασιλεὺς προεχειρίσατο κόμητα λαργιτιώνων ἐν Κωνσταντινουπόλει τὸν ἀπὸ ὑπάτων Ἰωάννην τὸν Παφλαγόνα τὸν λεγόμενον Καϊάφαν, ὅστις ἅπαν τὸ προχωρὸν κέρμα τὸ λεπτὸν ἐποίησε φολλερὰ προχωρεῖν εἰς πᾶσαν τὴν Ῥωμαϊκὴν κατάστασιν ἔκτοτε. Bury suggests reading προχωροῦν (which was apparently the original reading of the Oxford ms. See Bury in Byz. Zs. 6(1897), p. 229) or πρόχειρον. The first suggestion is preferable, I think, but the second is possible; from the economic standpoint the result is the same. What Bury did not entirely see was the purport of his own emendation:

---

sufficiente, onde si suppliva coi frammenti di monete dei periodi precedenti, coi tondini non coniati, ed infine colle cosidette *contraffazioni*. . . . La riforma di Anastasio perfezionata da Giustiniano, nel campo economico è massimamente importante avendo apportato se non un termine, un rimedio a tale stato esiziale di cose per esso essendo di nuovo messa in circolazione in quantità straordinaria la moneta di bronzo di più moduli con segno di valore, la data e il luogo di emissione."

[22] J. B. Bury, *A History of the Later Roman Empire*[2] I, 448, and note.

[23] Johannes Malalas, l. xvi, ed. Bonn 400. 16–21 = Migne, P. G. 97, Col. 593A.

He says: "He converted all the small copper currency into *follera* which circulated henceforward in the Empire."

I should render it: "He made all the current small change of low denomination into *follera* for circulation henceforward in the Roman state."

Bury did not take into account the implications of the word προχωροῦν[24] which shows that we have to do with a calling-in or demonetization of the existent currency. Λεπτὸν may also mean "of light weight," but I prefer the rendering given above; compare the widow's mite in the Gospels.[25] Κατάστασιν might be translated literally as "set-up."

We must now examine the much discussed passage of Marcellinus Comes in his chronicle under the year 498. We quote the text as it stands in Mommsen's edition: Monumenta Germaniae Historica, Auct. Antiq. xi (Berol. 1894) Chronica Minora ii, p. 95. 10–11.

Nummis quos Romani Terentianos vocant Graeci follares, Anastasius princeps suo nomine figuratis placibilem plebi commutationem distraxit.

Mss.

placibilem N; placabilem cett. *placente Scaligero et all.* Phollares *Babelon;* phollerales *Scaliger* Terentianos] teruncios *vel* teruncianos *multi* computationem direxit *Nipperdey:* commutationem instruxit *Mommsen;* implacibilem plebi commutationem instruxit *Mommsen*

Bearing in mind the wise adage ascribed to Moritz Haupt: "*Jede Verbesserung, die nur möglich und nicht überhaupt notwendig ist, ist ganz zu verwerfen,*" let us see what sense can be made out of the passage as it stands. The meaning appears to be as follows: "Through the coins, marked with his (*or* their) (own) name, which the Romans call *Terentiani*, the Greeks *follares*, the emperor Anastasius interfered with a (form of) exchange which was agreeable to the populace."

---

[24] In the later κοινὴ προχωρεῖν was sometimes used in the technical sense of "to pass current," "to be accepted at the rate of." Stephanus quotes in addition to another Malalas passage Sextus Empiricus 254, ὥσπερ ἐν πόλει νομίσματός τινος προχωροῦντος and the Periplus Maris Erythraei (ed. Fabricius p. 88. 11–12), ἀπὸ οὗ μέχρι τοῦ νῦν ἐν Βαρυγάζοις παλαιαὶ προχωροῦσι δραχμαί. Additional testimony is afforded by the papyri: Preisigke (Wörterbuch s. v.) quotes Pap. Amh. 133.18, οὐ προχωρεῖ ὁ πυρός, εἰ μὴ ἐκ δραχμῶν ἑπτὰ Pap. Lips. 64. 12, τὰ δηληγατευθέντα ἐπὶ τῆς ια' καὶ ἐπὶ τῆς ιβ' ἰνδικτίωνος προσήκει προχωρῆσαι.

[25] Mk. 12, 42-44; Luke 21, 1–4.

The majority of scholars prefer to read *teruncianos* for *Terentianos*.[26] *A priori* it seems far more likely that the appellation should have been derived from the weight of the coin rather than the name of the engraver who cut the die. We accept, then, this emendation. Apart from it there are three main points where opinions differ as to the choice of readings and the interpretation of this passage: these are:

1) suo nomine
2) commutationem . . . placibilem
3) distraxit

We shall now take these up in order:

1) Does *suo* refer to the coins (Mommsen) or to Anastasius (Pinder and Friedländer)?[27] Grammatically speaking either interpretation would be possible, though the second would be the more usual one. It seems somewhat hard to see why or how the issuance of a coin inscribed with the emperor's name could have caused much inconvenience to the populace, for the emperors in the fifth century customarily put their names on the coins. We have pointed out above that the small bronze and brass in the earlier period did not have the denomination engraved upon them. In this connection Anastasius' new issue marked a revolutionary break with earlier custom. All the above considerations incline me towards Mommsen's opinion.

Readings 2) and 3) belong together, and the interpretation depends upon what view scholars hold of Anastasius' aim in promoting the measure. *Commutatio* is translated in the Thesaurus Linguae Latinae as *pretium* in

---

[26] Some scholars have endeavored to see in *Terentianos* a denominative from a putative die-cutter Terentius. Some parallels can perhaps be found for such an appellation in numismatic history, but it seems incredible that the Roman West should have called a coin minted in the east by the name of the man who cut the die there. A safer assumption would be that it had something to do with ⅓ of an ounce. The reading *follares* in the Mss. needs no emendation: the Latin suffix *-arius* was widely current in Greek and the *-is -in* forms could easily be taken back as third declension.

[27] Mommsen's original emendation is in *Beiträge zur älteren Münzkunde herausgegeben von M. Pinder und J. Friedländer*, Bd. 1, Heft 1–11, Berlin, 1851, in the article "Die Follarmünzen" (pp. 123–131); ibid., p. 124, n. 2, Nipperdey computationem direxit: Mommsen, ibid. instruxit, "Distraxit verstehe ich nicht." p. 135 in note of editors: "Schlägt der Verfasser nachträglich die Verbesserung vor implacabilem etc." Here also (pp. 135–6) they raise objections to *suo nomine* (Momms. p. 124 referring to Anastasius).

this particular passage. Other parallels are quoted there, but all are taken from the OT or the NT and represent the Septuagintal συνάλλαγμα or ἄλλαγμα: these words do *not* mean "price" in the ordinary sense, but "return," "profit," what one gets back on a transaction. The usual meaning of *commutatio* in Latin appears to be that of a change, alteration or movement to another state or position, e.g., *commutatio rerum*. The natural interpretation here seems therefore to be that of exchange, and I have so translated it. *Distrahere* fundamentally means "to pull apart, divide," and in the transferred sense, "to divide, prevent, hinder"; in any case the concept of completing an action does not enter into the picture.

If, however, we assume that Anastasius did something which pleased the populace, we must then adopt one of the various emendations which favor this view; computationem direxit Nipperdey; commutationem instruxit Mommsen or <im >placibilem[27a] Mommsen. Of these from the palaeographical standpoint, the last is unquestionably the easiest to explain.

Before we endeavor to choose between these two alternatives, let us first see if the attitude of Marcellinus toward Anastasius in general yields any implication of the attitude he took on this particular matter. Marcellinus, it would appear, wrote his chronicle in Constantinople.[28] It contains rather more than the usual amount of *omina et portenta* which one expects in literature of this type, but over and above this, if one examines the laconic notices covering the 27 years of Anastasius' reign, it is clear that the author felt a strong animus against the emperor. This appears to have a threefold origin: 1) Marcellinus was closely associated with Justinian; 2) Marcellinus' religious feelings were lacerated by Anastasius' leanings towards the Monophysites; 3) in secular matters he reflects a sentiment of hostility which appears to mirror that of the population of the capital. *A priori*, therefore, we have no reason for believing that in this instance Anastasius put through a measure of which the city population approved, but rather that the reverse is true.

[27a] Placibilem is the reading of the oldest Ms. (the Tilianus) and is a good Vulgar Latin form, underlying as it does Ital. piacevole (See W. Meyer-Lübke, *Romanisches Etymologisches Wörterbuch*, Heidelberg, 1935, no. 6558).

[28] On Marcellinus in addition to the introduction in Mommsen's edition in the *MGH* see Schanz-Hosius-Krüger, *Geschichte der römischen Litteratur* 4.2, 110–112, and O. Holder-Egger, Die Chronik des M. C. und die oström. Fasten, *Neues Archiv der Ges. für ält. deutschen Geschichtskunde* 2 (1877), pp. 49–109.

In the second place it is clear from the text and is confirmed by the numismatic evidence that the emperor replaced the existent currency by another one. If we read προχωροῦν in the Malalas passage and take it, as we must, as meaning "current,"[29] the inevitable implication is that the copper in circulation was either demonetized or (more probably) called in at a lower rate of exchange as against the currency to be issued, which involves the necessary corollary that the amount of small change in circulation was decreased, perhaps by a very appreciable amount. It is extremely hard to see why the emperor should have wished to increase the amount.[30] Such an action would be tantamount to a partial devaluation of the previous copper currency.

At the same time it does not follow that the effects of this devaluation were either immediate or omnipresent. The new coins were evidently used in governmental transactions and in the payment of taxes, but the others might remain in circulation for some time, especially in the outlying areas.

We are now in a position to evaluate the economic implications of Anastasius' reform. It was an attempt on the emperor's part to bring about a stabilization at a figure not too far removed from current market rates of the ratio between gold and copper by introducing a series of multiple coin units, and by calling in or demonetizing issues of earlier emperors and also by establishing an exchange ratio between them and the dominant coin, the solidus.[31] That the treasury did not lose thereby can easily be imagined, but what discount was made on the older issues is beyond our ken. This was sound policy, both fiscal and monetary, and could, apart from any putative, supervening catastrophe, have been successfully carried out, provided three basic conditions were observed. These were:

1) The solidus must remain of the same weight and fineness;

2) The copper currency must not be over-issued, but issued in sufficient quantity;

---

[29] See above, note 24.

[30] We shall discuss some of the economic implications below.

[31] The best formulation of this point which I have come across is in B. Hilliger, Die Kupferrechnung der spätrömischen Kaiserzeit, Numismatik 1933, pp. 55–60; ibid. p. 60: "Später freilich ist wie die Silber so auch die Kupfermünze mehr und mehr zur Kreditmünze geworden. Das zeigt vor allem auch die Follisprägung des Anastasius und seine Nachfolger, die bis auf Justinian unverkennbar in zwei verschiedenen Gewichtsreihen neben einander zur Ausgabe gelangte. . . . Ja unter Justinian . . . lässt sich mit der Zeit ein deutliches Absinken der Gewichte verfolgen. Allerdings versucht man auch hier

3) It must be freely exchangeable within reasonable limits.

How successful Anastasius was escapes our knowledge, but we find later on in the sixth century ample evidence to show that the ratio was not being held stable. A word about these facts is indicated here.

It had long been known from literary sources and has now been confirmed by the papyri that at various times during the sixth century A.D. in Egypt and elsewhere in the empire, the gold solidus was taken in monetary transactions at a discount; in most instances this is quite small—$2\frac{1}{2}$–4 per cent—but there are cases where it is distinctly larger (up to 25 per cent = a. 602). We find it both in governmental transactions and in private dealings. The most important treatments of this problem are those by J. W. Kubitschek[32] and Ch. Diehl.[33]

It is clear from both the literary sources and the papyri that the gold coin circulating in Egypt was under weight, and that it was currently accepted at a discount. Justinian endeavored to counteract this, as it meant a net loss to the fiscus when the money was transferred to Constantinople. It is to be noted, however, that the phenomena were not confined to Egypt, for Procopius (Anecdota 25)[34] points out that the money changers gave only 180 folles in lieu of the previous 210. This gives a discount of 14.2 per cent. It is impossible to go into the question here in detail, but it seems desirable to point out that we are dealing here with two related but distinct phenomena. First it is clear that light weight solidi were in circulation in Egypt and probably in the rest of the empire as well;[35] secondly we

---

zuweilen der Münze wenigstens äusserlich durch Weisssieden das Aussehen eines höheres Innenwertes zu geben. Dies alles zusammengenommen berechtigt zu dem Schluss, dass schon die blosse Rückkehr zu der Massregel, wieder Wertzahlen auf die Kupfermünze zu setzen, das Eingeständnis enthielt, dass aus dem blossen Gewicht dieser Stücke nichts mehr für ihren eigentlichen Wert zu entnehmen war."

[32] J. W. Kubitschek, Beiträge zur frühbyzantinischen Münzkunde, *Numismatische Zeitschrift* 29 (1897), 163–196.

[33] Ch. Diehl, Une crise monétaire au vi⁰ siècle, *Revue des Études grecques* 32 (1919), 158–166.

[34] Procopius, Anecdota 25 ed. Haury, p. 155. l. 2–8, Ἄδε εἰς τὰ κέρματα τοῖς βασιλεῦσιν εἴργασται, οὔ μοι παριτέον οἴομαι εἶναι. Τῶν γὰρ ἀργυραμοιβῶν πρότερον δέκα καὶ διακοσίους ὀβολούς, οὓς φόλλεις καλοῦσιν, ὑπὲρ ἑνὸς στατῆρος χρυσοῦ προτεῖσθαι τοῖς ξυμβάλλουσιν εἰωθότων, αὐτοὶ ἐπιτεχνώμενοι κέρδη οἰκεῖα ὀγδοήκοντα καὶ ἑκατὸν μόνους ὑπὲρ τοῦ στατῆρος δίδοσθαι τοὺς ὀβολοὺς διεπράξαντο.

[35] These light weight solidi (mentioned by Procopius, l.c.) are particularly common in

have to do here with a further fall in the value of the gold currency which raised the price of the copper coins in terms of the more precious metal. The relation between them had relaxed and the nomisma was being treated as a trade coin rather than a monetary unit. The reform instituted by Anastasius had been only partially successful.

The material on prices and wages in Byzantium which Andréadès,[36] Segrè,[37] and Ostrogorsky[38] have gathered does not throw much light on the effectiveness of Anastasius' reform. Price indications for the fifth century are largely lacking in the papyri, and our data from the sixth century are mostly subsequent to Anastasius. The inflational prices of the early fourth century have vanished and a reasonably stable level appears to have been attained; how much Anastasius' reform actually helped in this matter must remain uncertain in the absence of further data.

We are finally in a position to evaluate how Anastasius' reforms were received by the population of the empire. It is clear that the lower classes whose scanty savings were for the most part in the previous bronze-copper currency, must have been seriously irked by the move. The wealthier citizens and the government undoubtedly found it a convenience, while from the technical angle of the mint masters it marked a great advance.

---

hoards outside the territory of the Empire, and F. Stefan (*Num. Zs.* 70 (1937), 56) has plausibly suggested that they were coined to pay the barbarian tribute. N. Bauer (*Frankf. Münzzeitung* 2 (1931), 227–229) thinks they were barbarian counterfeits. It is noteworthy that tribute is stated in the treaties as far as we know by coins and not by weight of metal. See *Harv. St. in Class. Phil.* 51, p. 22.

[36] A. Andréadès, De la monnaie et de la puissance d'achat des métaux précieux dans l'empire byzantin, *Byzantion* 1 (1924), 75 ff.

[37] See above, note 17.

[38] G. Ostrogorsky, Löhne und Preise im Byzanz, *Byz. Zs.* 1932 (32), 293–333.

TUTUSH, EPHEMERAL SULTAN

GEORGE C. MILES

Princeton University

TUTUSH, son of Alp Arslān, son of Dāwūd, son of Mikā'īl, son of Seljūq, son of Duqāq, son of Chaghri Beg, the Seljūq, is an obscure figure, whose life scarcely spanned thirty years and whose sovereignty, in the East of many rulers and much sovereignty, lasted less than one year. Yet he was close kin to the greatest Turkish kings of the Moslem East—of Persia, Mesopotamia, Syria and Anatolia—grandnephew of the great Seljūq Ṭoghril Beg, son of the warrior Alp Arslān, and brother of the brilliant statesman and patron of arts and letters, Malikshāh. At the age of fourteen he was plunged into high politics, for several years he struggled with a legion of rivals, for nine brief months he claimed the rule over all the lands which his great forebears had ruled, and finally he died in battle far from the land of his childhood, but close to the heart of the Empire.

These ephemeral things happened nearly nine hundred years ago, but even Tutush has left his monuments in the well-documented Islamic world: at Damascus, on a pillar supporting the cupola of the Mosque of the Ummayads,[1] an inscription dated 475 A.H. (1082–1083 A.D.); another dated 487 (1094 A.D.) on the wall of Diyarbekir;[2] and a third inscription, high on the fifth story of the great minaret at Aleppo.[3] This last is undated, but for various reasons it can be assigned to the autumn of the year 487 of the Hijrah. And this leads me to a fourth monument Tutush has bequeathed us, for it also is dated in the late autumn of that year. I call it a monument. Actually it is only a small gold coin, but it recounts a dramatic episode of obscure history and is ample justification of that motto which the American Numismatic Society has adopted—*parva ne pereant.*

---

[1] Max van Berchem, *Inscr. Arabes de Syrie, Mém. Inst. Égypt*, 1897, pp. 12 ff.

[2] Combe, Sauvaget, Wiet, *Répertoire chronologique d'Épigraphie arabe*, Vol. VIII (Cairo, 1937), no. 2804.

[3] Ernst Herzfeld, *Alep* (unpublished), Inscription no. 77; cf. his *AMI*, Vol. VIII, p. 89. For information about this inscription and for much else, I am indebted to Professor Herzfeld.

Dinar of Tutush
Al-Rayy, 487 A.H.

In the rich collections of the American Numismatic Society in New York there is preserved a unique *dinar* struck by Tutush. Not only is it unique in date and mint, but it is, to my knowledge at least, the only coin issued by Tutush existing in any collection, public or private, in the world. Numerous specimens are known of the coinage of his father, Alp Arslān, of his brother Malikshāh, of Ṭoghril and Muḥammad and Barkiyāruq and Sinjar, and of many others of his cousins in the family of Seljūq, but no other coin bearing his name has ever been published. This is enough in itself to warrant its publication, but the circumstances surrounding the striking of the coin are more remarkable still. These circumstances I shall briefly relate. But first the coin itself.[4]

Dinar. Al-Rayy, 487 A.H. *Diameter*: 28 mm. *Weight*: 2.70 gms. (From the Starrosselsky Collection)

Obverse:

عدل

لا اله الا

* الله وحده *

لا شريك له

المستظهر بالله

Inner margin: بسم الله ضرب هذا الدينار بالرى سنة سبع وثمنين واربع مائة

Outer margin: Qur'ān, XXX, 3–4.

Reverse:

لله

محمد رسول الله

° السلطان المعظم

عز الدنيا عضد

الدين ابو سعيد

تتش بن محمد

Margin: Qur'ān, IX, 33.

Thus we learn the following facts: the coin was struck in 487 A.H. (1094 A.D.) at Rayy. The Caliph was al-Mustaẓir, who ruled from early 487 till 512 A.H. (1118 A.D.), and to him, of course, the Seljūq owed nominal allegiance. Tutush called himself "The Great Sultan"—the imperial title—

---

[4] Brief mention of the coin was made in my *Numismatic History of Rayy* (*Numismatic Studies No. 2*, New York, 1938), in a footnote on p. 210. It was discovered among the "unidentifiables" of the Society's collections just as that book went to press.

and used the honorifics " 'Izz al-dunya, 'Aḍud al-dīn" (the Glory of the World, and the Support of Religion). That his filionymic was Abu Sa'īd we know from the biographer Ibn Khallikān and from other chroniclers,[5] but the titles are new ones. In the histories he was known as Tāj al-Dawlah (Crown of the State), and in the inscriptions the honorifics Sirāj al-Ummah and Sharaf al-Millah (Lantern of the People, and Glory of the Nation) are appended. This is not unusual, that the epigraphical protocols should supplement those recorded in the chronicles, and that the numismatic titles should differ somewhat from those in books and inscriptions. But why did Tutush bear the imperial title "al-Sulṭān al-Mu'aẓẓam," and how did it come about that he, whose province was Syria, ruled over Rayy in north-central Persia?

Tutush was born in the month of Ramaḍān, 458 (July, 1066 A.D.), probably in Persia. At the age of twelve, that is in 470, he came to Syria and although only a child his parentage immediately placed him in the full stream of public affairs. His brother Malikshāh, overlord of the Seljūq Empire, gave him Syria to rule and at the age of fourteen he took possession of Damascus. The succeeding years were years of struggle against rival claimants for the sovereignty over various parts of Syria, with especial emphasis on Aleppo, then as now the political key to the northern part of the country. Affairs culminated in 485 (1092 A.D.) upon the death of Malikshāh. Tutush claimed the succession, and the emirs of Syria, with whom he had been obliged until that time to form a coalition, paid him homage. The way was opened to him for wider conquests, and he immediately set out on a campaign which brought under his rule the towns of Nisibin, Diyarbekir, Mayyāfarīqīn and Mosul. Here he was checked.

In the East arose the inevitable rival. It was Barkiyāruq, eldest son of Malikshāh, who, upon his father's death, had been proclaimed sultan at Rayy in Iran. While Tutush had been progressing eastward Barkiyāruq had faced westward. The former's emirs deserted him and he was obliged

---

[5] *Ibn Khallikan's Biographical Dictionary*, translated from the Arabic by MacGuckin de Slane, Vol. I (Paris, 1842), pp. 273–274. For other details of the following sketch I have drawn upon Ibn al-Athīr's *Al-Kāmil fi al-Ta'rikh* (ed. C. J. Tornberg, Leyden, 1864), Vol. x, pp. 136–138, 149–151, 157–159, 166–168, and *passim*; on the *Encyclopaedia of Islām, s.v.* Barkiyārūḳ, Seldjuken, and Tutush (in the German edition); and on G. Weil, *Geschichte der Chalifen* (Mannheim, 1851), Vol. III, pp. 140–142; and use has been made of that convenient handbook of chronology, E. de Zambaur's *Manuel de Généalogie et de Chronologie pour l'Histoire de l'Islam* (Hannover, 1927).

to return to Syria, but in a battle which took place at Tel al-Sulṭān, six leagues south of Aleppo, Barkiyāruq's army was defeated and Tutush remained master of the field. The date was Jumāda I, 487 (May, 1094 A.D.). The two principal emirs who had deserted him, Aqsonqor and Buzān, were executed, and Tutush set forth toward the East once more.

Barkiyāruq was in full flight—he fled from Nisibin in Shawwāl, 487 (October, 1094)—and we can trace Tutush's progress in pursuit through Ḥarrān, Jazīrah, Diyarbekir and Khalāṭ to Azerbayjan, and finally to Hamadan, where he ordered that he be proclaimed sultan in Baghdad, the ultimate in recognition of supreme authority. Barkiyāruq's route had taken him by way of Mosul, Irbil and Kanguvār (the village known to every modern traveller who has made the journey from Baghdad to Teheran), to Isfahan, where the poor boy—he was only thirteen at the time—fell gravely ill of smallpox.

For the history of our coin the dates that have been mentioned are important. The battle at Tel al-Sulṭān took place in May, 1094. Barkiyāruq's flight commenced in October, and Tutush could hardly have arrived in Hamadan before November at the very earliest. It is not clear whether Tutush went immediately on to Rayy, but his recognition in that city was not contingent upon his actual presence there, for as ruler of Hamadan he may have been acclaimed lord of Rayy as well, especially as his nephew's cause appeared to be lost in Isfahan. Thus the *dinar* which has been the cause of resurrecting all these obscure minutiae must have been struck in November or December of the year 1094 (the Christian and the Moslem calendars very nearly correspond in this year).

The end of Tutush's career was near at hand. Not long after his arrival in Hamadan he travelled on to Jurbādhaqān (the present Gulpaygan) and thence to Rayy—or to the vicinity of Rayy. Barkiyāruq, recovered from his illness, had struck northward from Isfahan, and at Gulpaygan in Tutush's rear he had assembled an army of 30,000 men. On the 17th of Safar, 488 (26th of February, 1095), at Dāshilwa[6] in Rayy province, the two rivals met, the followers of Tutush were put to flight, and he himself fell victim to the sword of one of Aqsonqor's men who had sworn that he would avenge his former leader's death.

---

[6] Exact location undetermined. Cf. C. Barbier de Meynard, *Dictionnaire géographique . . . de la Perse* (Paris, 1861), p. 223 (Yāqūt's original is not at hand), and P. Schwarz, *Iran im Mittelalter nach den Arabischen Geographen* (Leipzig, 1926), Vol. VI, p. 802.

So for a few months Tutush had pretended to the titles and prerogatives of emperor. His inscriptions, which have been mentioned above, show how in 475 at Damascus he called himself by the relatively modest title of al-Malik al-Ajall, "the most excellent king," and how after the battle of Tel al-Sulṭān he assumed at Diyarbekir and Aleppo the honorific of full sovereignty in the Seljūq house, al-Sulṭān al-Muʿaẓẓam. Unfortunately there are no other coins to help us trace his temporal growth, but the state of affairs in the East with respect to Tutush's brief appearance in the limelight is revealed in the coinage of certain of the cities of Iraq and Iran. Barkiyāruq struck coins at Baghdad,[7] Isfahan (with his younger brother Maḥmūd),[8] Qumm,[9] Amol,[10] and Nishapur[11] in 486. Sometime in 487— probably early in Muḥarram—well before the issue of Tutush's *dinar* at Rayy, another *dinar* was struck in Barkiyāruq's name at that city,[12] as well as one in Baghdad.[13] The following year, 488, after the temporary eclipse reflected in the coin under discussion, he was once more firmly established at Rayy[14] and Isfahan,[15] and in the ʿAbbāsid capital.[16] Tutush had come and gone.

---

[7] Markoff, *Inventory* (St. Petersburg, 1896), no. 47, p. 370.

[8] Markoff, *op. cit.*, no. 46a, p. 855.

[9] American Numismatic Society (unpublished).

[10] American Numismatic Society (unpublished).

[11] Philip Thorburn Collection.

[12] G. C. Miles, *op. cit.*, no. 246, p. 209 (Bibliothèque Nationale).

[13] *British Museum, Catalogue of Oriental Coins* (London, 1875–90), Vol. III, no. 65; and Aḥmed Tevḥīd, *Meskūkāt-i Qadīmeh-i Islāmiyyeh Qatalōghi* (Constantinople, 1321), Vol. IV, no. 88.

[14] G. C. Miles, *op. cit.*, no. 247, p. 210 (Bibliothèque Nationale).

[15] American Numismatic Society (unpublished); and J. M. C. Johnston Sale (Sotheby, Wilkinson & Hodge, July 16, 1906).

[16] *British Museum, op. cit.*, Vol. IX, no. 65c; Aḥmed Tevḥīd, *op. cit.*, no. 89; J. Gerson da Cunha Catalogue (Bombay, 1888–1889), no. 1315, and Johnston Sale, no. 319.

THE METAMORPHOSIS OF OVID
IN "LE ROMAN DE LA ROSE"

E. K. RAND

Harvard University

I. The Classics in the Thirteenth Century

NOBODY would deny that in the thirteenth century the chief intellectual interest centered in philosophy. The disclosure of a new Aristotle, with new glimpses of Plato, gave a tremendous impulse to new speculation on the problems that had occupied the minds of thinkers from Alcuin to Abaelard. Their successors of the end of the twelfth and of all the thirteenth century must have had a philosphic thrill not less than the humanistic thrill of the scholars of the Renaissance at the discovery of lost treasures of antiquity. No wonder that the minds of philosophers were keen to explore this new world of ancient thought and thus to give old problems a new solution.

The Church of the thirteenth century, with its natural conservatism, at first looked askance at the novel fermentations of ancient thought. But, as has often been remarked, what was at first forbidden was later tolerated and later still prescribed. For the new material, once assimilated, gave richness and depth to Catholic doctrine. Plato and Aristotle, as in the famous fresco at Santa Maria Novella, were taught to sit at the feet of St. Thomas Aquinas.

It has appeared not unnaturally, to some scholars, after an examination of various University programmes of the thirteenth century, that the study of mere literature had suffered an eclipse. The humanistic school of Chartres and Orléans and Tours seemed, in the battle of the arts, to have surrendered to the dialectic laboratories of Paris. It is the old battle of philosophy and poetry, of which Plato had written, or the battle of the present day between science and literature. And science, apparently, then as now, had the upper hand.

I am more and more convinced that this is only half of the story.[1] It is

---

[1] See "The Classics in the Thirteenth Century," *Speculum* IV (1929), 249–269; "A Friend of the Classics in the Times of St. Thomas Aquinas," *Mélanges Mandonnet* (Paris, Vrin, 1930), 261–281.

hard to believe that the seven liberal arts which from the days of Boethius on were regarded not merely as paving the way to the Queen of them all, Philosophy, but as offering the very pabulum on which Philosophy must feed,[2] should have been dumped upon the dust-heap, as certain theorists in education would like to dump the Greek and Roman classics today. There were differences in emphasis, of course. Paris was modern and progressive with the new philosophy, Orléans was ancient and conservative with the old humanism, but to think that the Latin Classics were barred from Education and thus ceased to be read is demonstrably untrue. The manuscripts of Ovid, for one instance, written in the thirteenth century tell a different tale.[3] The reading of the great writers in the vernacular shows a most intimate acquaintance with the old masterpieces. They must have studied them somewhere; perhaps we may think of the establishments that cultivated the new philosophy as akin to our Graduate Schools, in that they did not supersede the standard training but supplemented it.

There was also a new effort to make those masterpieces accessible in translation to an increasingly wide lay public who had not the benefit of Latin. Jean de Meun, for instance, made a version of Vegetius, *De Re Militari*, which would interest knights, and one of the *Consolation of Philosophy of Boethius*, which would appeal to any intelligent reader with a love of poetry, philosophy and spiritual drama. There exist today two late fifteenth century manuscripts of the *Consolation*, one in the British Museum[4] and one in the Bibliothèque Nationale,[5] both deriving from a most sumptuous edition of the version of Jean de Meun. Each is in five little volumes, which contain the Latin text, Jean's translation and his (or somebody else's) commentary. The script is beautifully attractive and the ornamentation is superb. Each contains as a frontispiece an exquisite picture, illustrating some significant moment in the narrative of the book. One can see from the first of these, made familiar in our times by Mr. J. W. Clark's

---

[2] See "How Much of the *Annotationes in Marcianum* is the Work of John the Scot," *Trans. of the American Philological Association*, LXXII (1941), 501–523.

[3] See Dr. Hilda Buttenwieser, "Manuscripts of Ovid's *Fasti*: the Ovidian Tradition in the Middle Ages," *ibid.*, 45–51.

[4] Harl. 4335–4339.

[5] My notes on both these manuscripts are with my friend Emile Van Moé, Librarian in the Salle des Manuscrits of the Bibliothèque Nationale, who, I hope, will devote an extended study to them both.

excellent volume on *The Care of Books*,[6] that the artist who adorned the
British Museum copy partly misunderstood the intention of the original
design, which is patent in the copy at the Bibliothèque Nationale. That
the pictures and the ornamentation in this fifteenth century edition descend from the copy that Jean de Meun presented to Philip the Fair (1285–
1314) would be rash to assert,[7] although that volume, as a gift to Royalty,
was presumably as elaborate in its way. In any case, what may seem to
some the essentially modern idea, illustrated in the *Loeb Classical Library*
and the *Collection des Universités de France*, of confronting an ancient text
with a rendering into the vernacular, is at least as old as the Renaissance.[8]
We also may note that Jean's "Boethius" remained a standard work down
to that time.

Another ancient author, alien in temperament to Boethius yet quite as
dear to the heart and the mind of Jean de Meun, was Ovid. Though Jean
knew no Greek, he was well versed in many of the Latin authors. Since the
little town that gave him birth was not far from Orléans, he may have had
his schooling in that place. Our information about his career is sparse and
uncertain. According to the foremost authority on the subject, Ernest
Langlois,[9] he is not identical with a Jean de Meun (Johannes de Magduno)
who was Archdeacon of Beauce, a member of an aristocratic family, with
residences at Meun and Orléans. Our Jean, also of the clergy, though apparently of humble origin, spent most of his time at Paris. At any rate,
whether there or at Orléans, he had learned to know the Latin classics intimately, his favorites being, if I mistake not, Ovid and Boethius.

---

[6] Cambridge University Press, 1902, p. 159, Fig. 64. See also H. R. Patch, *The Tradition
of Boethius*, New York, Oxford University Press, 1935, pp. 80, 96, Plates IV and V, with the
frontispiece (The Pierpont Morgan Library, MS 222 fol. 1), which shows Jean de Meun
presenting his work to Philip the Fair. The Morgan MS, a fifteenth-century book, shows
a different set of pictures from those in London and Paris just described. Its text should
be studied in the light of the article by Langlois mentioned in the following note.

[7] E. Langlois examines, in the wake of Léopold Delisle and other scholars, "La Traduc-
tion de Boèce par Jean de Meun" in *Romania* XLII (1913), 331–369. What the relation of
the text in the two manuscripts that I have mentioned is to that of the prose version
which Langlois, in agreement with Delisle, decides is that of Jean de Meun, I have no
means of ascertaining. My friend Van Moé could tell us.

[8] That Jean de Meun copied a Latin text of the *Consolation* to accompany his translation does not seem likely, but the matter at least deserves examination.

[9] *Le Roman de la Rose, per Guillaume de Lorris et Jean de Meun*, Tome I, *Introduction*,
Paris, Firmin Didot, 1914, pp. 8–25.

I had at first intended in this paper to lay the chief stress on a certain battle fought out in the mind of Jean de Meun, in which the protagonists are Ovid and Boethius; it suggests that which went on in the youthful mind of Milton between Ovid and Virgil.[10] I have adumbrated that topic in a little book on Ovid published some years ago,[11] and it richly deserves elaboration. But the space at my disposal obliges me to confine my attention to the use, or rather the absorption, of Ovid by Guillaume de Lorris. Thus was involved a magical metamorphosis of the master of metamorphosis himself. This, too, is a rich theme, and a necessary preliminary to a full appreciation of the mind of Jean de Meun.

II. The "Roman de la Rose"

The *Roman de la Rose* is a great and extraordinarily typical work. The terms "mirror" or "embodiment," of the Middle Ages, frequently applied to Dante,[12] are no less apposite for the joint-production of Guillaume de Lorris and Jean de Meun. If we construct a triptych mirror, with the works of Chaucer for the third leaf, we shall find therein a tolerably complete reflection of the whole wealth of mediaeval life and thought, although of course certain most important aspects are more powerfully set forth in other master-pieces, such as the *Chanson de Roland* and the works of St. Thomas Aquinas.

To speak of the *Roman de la Rose* as a joint-production is, of course, not meant to suggest collaboration. Guillaume de Lorris, born also in a little town not far from Orléans, wrote his romance of the rose, little guessing that he should not live to finish it or that another so startlingly unlike in temperament should take up the tale when he dropped it. There is only one other "collaboration" in the history of literature of such startling dissonance; it is that in which Shelley supplied the lost "Prometheus Unbound" of Aeschylus. Guillaume would also have been dumbfounded to see the *dénouement* of his story postponed to a point so many leagues away. When the modern reader learns that the portion composed by Guillaume includes 4058 verses, at the end of which the lover *seems* just

---

[10] See "Milton in Rustication," *Studies in Philology*, XIX (1922), 109–135.

[11] *Ovid and his Influence* in *Our Debt to Greece and Rome* (edited by G. D. Hadzsits and D. M. Robinson, Boston, Marshall Jones Co., 1924), pp. 126–128.

[12] Admirably illustrated in C. H. Grandgent's *Dante* in *Master Spirits of Literature*, (ed. G. R. Noyes and W. M. Hart) New York, Duffield, 1916. See the last chapter, pp. 350–375.

about to pluck his Rose, and that Jean postpones the blessed event till 17,623 more verses have flowed on,[13] he is disposed by the law of antecedent probability to infer that the supplement is inordinately padded. This is a great mistake. All time abandon, ye who enter here. View the course of events *sub specie aeternitatis.* Prepare yourselves by a perusal of *Tristram Shandy,* whose author, trained, if ever a Britisher can be, in French *malice,* may have had as part of his intention, a sly parody of the mediaeval romance. The mastery of leisure may seem impossible in the year of grace 1941, but the mind of the reader must have it if he would comprehend the graces and the subtleties of both parts of the *Roman de la Rose.*

III. Scholarly Works on the "Roman de la Rose"

Before coming to close quarters with our topic I will say a word about our present helps to the study of this work. It is remarkable that it has attracted so few scholarly studies in recent times. Compared with the literature on Dante that is produced every year, the titles of works on the *Roman de la Rose* are insignificant or even infinitesimal. If the proportions were represented by a graph, the two authors of the romance would be shown by a little stump, hugging the earth, while Dante's column would scrape the skies. One reason for this neglect may be that just one scholar has come near to pre-empting the field. Ernest Langlois, of course, had important precursors, notably Hauréau and Gaston Paris, but such was the wealth of his *Origines et Sources du Roman de la Rose,* published in 1891[14] as a harbinger of his edition, the first critical edition, of the text, and such was the elaborateness of the edition when it appeared,[15] with its exhaustive study of the manuscripts, its elaborate introduction, its metri-

---

[13] I am reckoning with the number of verses in the critical edition of Langlois, who has excised 828 verses from the text as given by preceding editors. In the passages quoted in this paper, I will cite line-references from the edition of Marceau, with the corresponding lines in Langlois in parenthesis followed by the letter L. It would have been more convenient for the reader if Langlois had retained between square brackets the lines that he omits, thus preserving the traditional numbering, while indicating the spuriousness of these lines.

[14] Paris, E. Thorin. I will refer to this work as *Origines.*

[15] In five volumes, 1914–1924. See note 9, p. 105. I will refer to the works as *Edition.* Langlois's detailed study of the manuscripts and their classes had appeared in *Les Manuscrits du Roman de la Rose (Travaux et Mémoires de l'Université de Lille,* 1, 7), Lille (Tallandier) and Paris (Champion), 1910. I will cite this work as *Manuscrits.*

cal, phonetic and grammatical disquisitions, with a complete list of the rhymes and studies of sources and influence, that gleanings after Langlois seem peculiarly unpromising. Of course important studies of special topics have appeared,[16] but I can think of no other case in the history of literary studies—certainly none in those on ancient Classical literature—where one man holds such a title to his field. This work of vast learning is also, in a twofold sense, a labor of love; it is dedicated to his faithful *collaboratrice*, Madame Langlois.

Before Langlois the chief editions available to scholars and general readers of the *Romance* were three. M. Méon (Paris, Didot, 1814) was the first in modern times to examine afresh some of the manuscripts. F. Michel (Paris, Didot, 1864) reproduced, with occasional alterations, the text of Méon. He had examined no manuscripts, but he added one feature for which the reader unversed in old French is grateful. *Crede experto*: I mean the renderings of words and phrases into modern French set at the right down the columns of the text. With these stepping-stones, helped by some Latin and less French, I think I have been able to get the meaning and the flavor, though not of all the niceties, of the *Roman de la Rose*. Experts in mediaeval French will, I hope, be merciful to me—and severe. After Michel, M. P. Marteau (pseudonym for I. Croissandeau, Orléans, 1878–1880) repeated more exactly the text of Méon, compounded it with a version in modern French and added an old French grammar and glossary. More recently the translation into English by F. S. Ellis[17] deserves high praise. In the passages I have tested, it both follows the text closely and renders the spirit of the original with great skill. I know of few translations of great poetry in recent years that have come nearer to the mark.

One detail concerning the text invites a brief discussion. In all the editions before Langlois both parts of the poem are divided into chapters of no great length, and each of these is prefaced by a brief summary in verse. These summaries are agreeable stopping-places for the reader in his lengthy journey, but they are dropped by Langlois since the testimony of the manuscript is against them. They descend from the *Editio princeps*, which took them along with its text from some manuscript of the fifteenth century.[18] The use of such summaries was by that time a matter of long

---

[16] Such as the article of Hawkins discussed below, note 25.

[17] London, Dent, 1928.

[18] *Edition*, I, 42 f.

standing. The story begins at least as early as that worthy pedant Gaius Sulpicius Apollinaris of Carthage, a teacher of Aulus Gellius in the second century A.D., who wrote little summaries of the books of the *Aeneid* in dactylic hexameters. These may possibly, though not surely, have accompanied an edition of Virgil's text.[19] A later grammarian, perhaps of the fourth century, palmed off a similar set on Ovid.[20] These became a regular accompaniment of the text of Virgil. They are found as early as the famous *Codex Romanus* (*Vat. lat.* 3867 *saec.* V) and appear in a number of well-known manuscripts of Virgil from the ninth to the eleventh centuries and doubtless in later codices.[21]

The apparent sanction of Virgil and Ovid may well have induced mediaeval Latin poets to equip their own works with such summaries. I will not stop to give instances from the early Middle Ages—someone should gather them all—but mention only the *Alexandreis* of Gautier de Châtillon, published in 1184, all of the ten books of which have summaries of ten or eleven lines in dactylic hexameters.[22] This use of summaries, therefore, had become a tradition considerably before the time of the *Roman de la Rose*, and was continued in the Renaissance, as we see from Ariosto, Tasso and Spenser.

It would not be surprising, therefore, if both Guillaume de Lorris and Jean de Meun had followed the familiar practice. Indeed Langlois did find such summaries in certain manuscripts, particularly in B. N. fr. 1569, an early manuscript (thirteenth-fourteenth century) of the best class.[23] Despite the large number of manuscripts, he has grouped them into three main classes, the third of which is nothing but a conflation of the first two. I am treading on dangerous ground, which angels would hesitate to enter, but it might be suggested that in the archetypes of both these classes the summaries were intended to be written in a distinctive form of script which was left for a specialist in that mode—who neglected to perform his task.[24] Or they might have been put in the margin in both archetypes—and

---

[19] M. Schanz, *Geschichte der römischen litteratur*, III² (Munich, 1905), 170 f., §597.

[20] *Ibid.*, II, 1 (1911), 119, §247.

[21] A. Riese, *Anthologia Latina*, I (Leipzig, Teubner), 7.

[22] Edited by F. A. W. Mueldener, Leipzig, Teubner, 1863.

[23] See *Edition*, I, p. 43; *Manuscrits*, pp. 25–26.

[24] So in B. N. fr. 12786 (thirteenth-fourteenth centuries) the spaces left for miniatures (*Manuscrits*, p. 50) and headings ("rubriques," H. Omont, *Cat. gén. des mss. français*, I [1895], 43) were not filled in.

thus could have been easily omitted in the archetypes of the different families of the two classes, though a few of the early manuscripts might have recovered them from the original. The present set may, of course, have been a somewhat later affair. Even so they should not perish from the earth; they are an interesting specimen of an early editing of this work. Our editor might have left them enclosed in the condemnatory square brackets, or at least put them in his critical apparatus or his notes.

An important contribution to our knowledge of the text has been made by R. L. Hawkins, who gives a careful description of two manuscripts of the *Roman* at Harvard and one at Yale.[25] All-important is "Harvard A,"[26] which not only had a most interesting history (its first owner was the great de Thou) and is most beautifully written, but also belongs to the best class (I), being closely related to Langlois's Ca.[27] I agree thoroughly, after an examination of this manuscript, with Hawkins's date, the early part of the fourteenth century.[28]

One certain feature of the original edition was the division of the text into small sections, or paragraphs. These are devoted in the manuscript Harvard A by the use of capital letters, alternately red and blue—as is frequent in manuscripts of the thirteenth and fourteenth centuries. The same divisions are noted in the other Harvard manuscript, "Harvard B,"[29] an inferior book of the fifteenth century; in this the capitals are always in red. There are minor differences, of course; either manuscript may fail to distinguish the initial now and then. But the use of the same system is plain. And it is that given in the text of Langlois; in that printed by previous editors a few more sections are found.

The number of manuscripts of the *Roman* is large. Langlois catalogued

---

[25] "The Manuscripts of the *Roman de la Rose* in the Libraries of Harvard and Yale Universities," *The Romanic Review*, XIX (1928), 1–24. Langlois (*Edition* I, 49, note I) had included a very brief notice of the Harvard manuscripts on the basis of information communicated to him by Professor E. S. Sheldon.

[26] Ms. fr. 14.5 (cited as Ci by Langlois, *Edition*, II, p. 330).

[27] *Manuscrits*, pp. 246 f.

[28] One palaeographical curiosity is the frequent use of the numerical figure ·I· for the indefinite article *un*. Perhaps to students of French palaeography it may be more common than I suppose. If not, it might possibly serve as an ear-mark for the classification of the manuscripts.

[29] Ms. fr. 14 F.

at least 215 and classified 116 of them.[30] He felt that some might have escaped him, and dwells on the fact that many more must have been lost.[31] The popular work was copied and recopied and adapted to the dialects of different parts of France. A maker of genealogical stemmata is confronted not by clear lines of descent, but by something more akin to a spider's web.[32] Nevertheless, Langlois makes out his three classes,[33] even though many of their representatives may have mixed texts. While carefully avoiding this spider's parlor, we may note the existence, once upon a time, of the following manuscripts.

A. The original text of Guillaume de Lorris, left unfinished.[34]

B. This text supplemented with a brief ending (78 verses) added, according to Langlois[35] before Jean de Meun composed his own.

C. Jean de Meun's original work, composed of Guillaume's part plus his own. This was divided into sections denoted by distinctive initials of some sort. What kind of a manuscript of Guillaume's work did Jean possess?

D. An edition of C in which the redactor added between the two parts the poetical heading that names Jean de Meun and states the fact that between his work and that of Guillaume de Lorris forty years had elapsed.[36] This same editor might have added the versified chapter head-

---

[30] *Edition*, I, p. 49.

[31] *Manuscrits*, p. 2.

[32] *Ibid.*, p. 236.

[33] See above, p. 109.

[34] Langlois, *Edition*, I, p. 4 cites Bibl. nat. fr. 1573 for the text of Guillaume alone. Another hand adds the sequel of Jean de Meun. The date of this manuscript (Ha) is the end of the thirteenth century (*Manuscrits*, p. 29). It belongs to Class I and its dialect is that of Orléans.

[35] *Edition*, I, p. 3. He prints the text in Vol. II, pp. 330–334. He cites one manuscript (Bibl. nat. fr. 12786) in which this conclusion is attached to the work of Guillaume, without the sequel by Jean de Meun. The date of this manuscript (Da) is the end of the thirteenth or the beginning of the fourteenth century (*Manuscrits*, pp. 49–52). It is of Class I. Hawkins (*op. cit.*, pp. 8–9) prints this supplement in the form found in Harvard A, which lacks the initial six verses and differs in other details from the versions published by Langlois and Marteau. It occurs between the parts of Guillaume and Jean and is in the same hand as that of the adjoining texts.

[36]   Cy endroit trespassa Guillaume
      De Loris, et n'en fist pas pseaulme;
      Mais, après plus de quarante ans,

ings, each containing one or more of the paragraphs above described. I could wish once more that Langlois had retained these headings, putting them in square brackets. Marteau retains them, though he, too, recognized in them the work of a later editor. See his edition, II, pp. I, 987. At least, I infer, he was a late mediaeval editor, whose treatment of the text is worth exhibiting for its own sake.

It will doubtless be impossible, after Langlois's testimony, to attempt to restore these various editions, or the archetypes of the redactions in the different dialectal regions of France. But the problem is so new and fascinating to a Classical scholar that I cannot refrain from this attempt to formulate it. A study of its dialectal aspects might even throw some light on the language of the Homeric poems.

IV. GUILLAUME DE LORRIS

Like Jean de Meun, Guillaume was born in a village not far from Orléans. Like him, he had a good schooling in the Latin Classics, and like him, he left little for his biographers to record—except an immortal poem. Langlois has shown in minute detail the literary background of Guillaume, the literary types that entered into the composition of his part of the *Roman de la Rose*, and the authors who had especially influenced him. Langlois[37] observes that Macrobius and Ovid are the only ancient writers who have left any traces in Guillaume's part of *Le Roman de la Rose*. But of course the regular training in the "authors" must have preceded, or accompanied, the special study of any one of them. For his poem he immersed himself in the spirit of Ovid and of various mediaeval poets of love, not because he had read nothing else, but because composing in his romance he kept true

---

Maistre Jean de Meung ce Rommans
Parfist, ainsi comme je treuve;
Et ici commence son oeuvre. (Marteau, II, p. 2.)

The reference to forty years is backed up by Jean himself (Langlois, *Edition*, I, p. 2, note 3). Langlois (*loc. cit.*) enquires whether he began or finished his poem forty years after the death of Guillaume. The phrase "Jehans le continuera / Emprès sa mort" would seem to me to refer to the beginning. The words of the later redactor "Après (emprès?) plus de quarante ans . . . parfist" apparently denotes its completion. How long it took him the redactor does not say (or know?).

[37] *Origines*, p. 74.

to his design, for which the master of dreams and the master of love were his prime concern. His work was written between 1225 and 1240.

The poem is, in its outlines, a romance of an amatory or chivalric type. The tale is of a lover, who after surmounting the obstacles with which the course of true love is beset, wins his beloved. But the characters in the story are not ordinary human beings with human names, but ideas, abstractions, that are invested with human traits. Fair-Welcome, Pity, Generosity speed the lover on his quest, Reason exhorts him to go slowly, Danger, Fear, Evil-Tongue (a foe of fair women) and Jealousy keep him from his post. Jealousy, at the bidding of Shame, builds a high tower of defence, in which Fair-Welcome is imprisoned, and Fair-Welcome is in prison when the story breaks off.

In a narrative of this kind we have that simple variety of allegory of which the essence is personification, only that the personifications, like Pygmalion's statue, become actors in a story. The "allegory" consists in making abstract qualities something that they are not, i.e. persons. They have been transformed, or rather in-formed, embodied. Considering the goal of the process rather than the start, we may call this variety "personal allegory." It descended to the Middle Ages from the *Psychomachia* of Prudentius and many another ancient work. It throve in the Renaissance no less than the Middle Ages. It flavors the *Faery Queene* delightfully, and supplies strength to *Pilgrim's Progress*. It makes a direct bid for universality, and succeeds if its abstract ideals behave like human beings—just as a modern novel fails, if its human characters behave like abstractions.

There is one exception in the application of this personal allegory to the narrative. The fair maiden herself is not identified with some abstract quality, like Beauty. "Beauty" alone could not sum up her qualities. She is, indeed, love ideal and incarnate, but she cannot be too remote; for she inspires and purges the passion of the lover. A happy compromise is found in giving her the semblance of the Rose, who gathers up all that is true and good and beautiful in her fragrance.[38]

But now for the story. The lover strolls forth on a morning in May amidst the fragrance of flowers and the songs of birds. He comes to a

---

[38] Many before Guillaume had compared a maiden to a rose and some had used the flower as a symbol of love, but none, so far as I can gather, had developed the idea with the delicate subtlety displayed in this poem. See Chaps. IV and VI in Langlois, *Origines*, on allegory in general and in particular the allegory of the Rose.

garden-wall, painted with images of Hate, Felony, Avarice, Envy, Hypocrisy and other dreadful vices. They are without; nothing but Joy reigns within. A pleasant party engages in dance and song. Mirth and Gladness and Courtesy are among the company. The God of Love is there, with his five good arrows—Beauty, Simplicity, Candor, Friendship, Fair-Semblance—and his five evil ones—Pride, Villainy, Shame, Despair and Fickleness. The lover, after looking into the Fountain of Love, the very one at which Narcissus once had gazed, is attacked by the Love-God, and is smitten with each of the Good Arrows in turn. He is met by Fair-Welcome, and proceeds upon the quest of the Rose.

As each of the Good Arrows strikes him, the nature of true love is explained. The work at this point becomes an Art of love, drawn straight from Master Ovid, but Ovid amplified and etherealized.

Finally, the story is set in a dream,[39] as happens so frequently in mediaeval narrative. The Middle Ages may have been an "époque de foi naïve,"[40] but so, in the matter of dreams, was classical antiquity. Although mediaeval writers had stories of dreams from a multitude of sources, their sovereign literary model was from the start Cicero's *Somnium Scipionis*, accompanied by the commentary of Macrobius. Guillaume appeals to its authority at the beginning of his work. We start in the atmosphere of a dream, and should probably have wakened abruptly at the end, as Scipio and the lover in Jean de Meun do.[41]

---

[39] See Langlois, *Origines*, Chap. v.

[40] *Ibid.*, p. 55.

[41] One ancient vision that perhaps played a larger part in the vision-literature of the Middle Ages than has been recognized is Ovid's *Amores*, III, 5. The lover dreams that he strays into the country and sees a bull lie down in a cozy nook by the side of his cow—*"feliciter ille maritus."* When he is fast asleep, a crow flies up and pecks at the cow, who has a black and blue spot on her breast. She rises, leaves her husband and makes for a group of admiring bulls. An interpreter of dreams explains the meaning of the vision. The cow is his beloved, the crow an aged *lena*, the bulls are her paramours, he is left cold in his solitary bed, the black and blue spot is her infidelity. The lover wakes in pallid fright and sees naught but the black night before his eyes. Here we have both a vision and an allegorical interpretation, with Ovid's playful mockery. This poem appealed to the mediaeval love of visions and allegory, and I hope, to the mediaeval sense of humor. It not only was read in copies of the *Amores* but had a separate tradition in anthologies. The earliest of these that I know is found in a Leipzig MS (Rep. 1 74), written in the neighborhood of Orléans somewhat before the middle of the ninth century—a most interesting book that

Thus an air of dreamy mysticism pervades the poem—*la douce savor de la rose*. Its leisurely procedure seems natural enough to a reader who has submitted to its spell. The use of abstractions instead of human names contributes skilfully to this effect. For human persons are definite and call for action; abstract qualities are rich in potencies and bid us pause and contemplate. They elude our grasp and we are not sorry that they do. I am by no means certain that Guillaume would have wound up the story quickly, certainly not as quickly as was done by the author of the supplement in seventy-eight verses.[42]

To develop this point for a moment, I venture to suppose that the tower would have offered considerable resistance to the invaders. As far back as v. 1733 (1673 L) the lover was on the point of plucking the Rose—but he was destined to a long postponement. We may also note that Reason does not enter the story till v. 2934 (2840 L) and does not have her say till 3104 (2997 L). Nor does she have much to say. Her speech makes a good enough introduction, but compared with her rôle in Jean de Meun's part of the romance—where Boethius and his pupil Alanus ab Insulis are her champions—she is of very minor importance in Guillaume's plot thus far. It would certainly be natural if she put up some further defence before the castle was taken.

How did the idea for his work come to Guillaume de Lorris? We have seen that this romance of love draws not only on romance, but on three other literary forms or themes in vogue in Guillaume's time—allegory, the art of love and the dream. The fusion is complete. Whatever the author's indebtedness to his predecessors, he has woven what he has taken into his own design, and thus transformed these borrowings. Langlois's studies of the mediaeval precursors of Guillaume in the Latin and the French literature of the Middle Ages leave little to be done, I imagine, in the amassing of imitations or parallel passages. He, of course, pays tribute to Guillaume's genius, but he has not quite brought out the point that I have in mind. One reason may be that in his earlier work[43] Langlois believes that Guillaume had taken the framework of his poem from a work in the

---

not yet has been adequately studied. Whether Guillaume knew this poem would be difficult to prove—but it is altogether in the vein of Jean de Meun.

[42] See above, p. 111. I like the remarks made on this matter by Marteau, *Edition*, 1, lxxxvii–xci.

[43] *Origines*, pp. 32–35, 36, 55, 58.

vernacular, *Le Fablel dou Dieu d'Amours*. But in his subsequent discussion of this matter,[44] Langlois decides that *Le Dieu d'Amours* is the later work. Thereby Guillaume's originality acquires a new lustre.

Whatever his treatment of his mediaeval sources, Guillaume shows himself a master of literary metamorphosis in his adaptations from Ovid. Bits of Ovid's descriptions or characterizations are taken over, but not in such a way as to proclaim their origin and the author's learning; on the contrary Guillaume sometimes eludes the student of his sources for the reason that he turns borrowings into creations. Langlois observes[45] that to Oiseuse is appropriately assigned "le rôle d'introduction à la vie amoureuse" on account of Ovid's precept:[46]

> Otia si tollas, periere Cupidinis arcus.

That is an acute observation. It shows in a flash the intimacy with which Guillaume knew his Ovid. This is indeed the reason why Oiseuse is chosen for a rôle in this romance of love. But we may add that for his portraiture of this pleasantly indolent maiden, Guillaume had a model awaiting his command in Ovid's Salmacis, who, avoiding anything strenuous, like the chase, bathed in her fountain, asked the approval of its mirroring waters for her coiffure, or wrapped in a glistening robe, lay down in the soft grass; her most energetic act was to pick flowers.[47] With this description Guillaume starts, enlarges it with a sumptuous account of the maiden's beauty and her passion for dress, and sums her up with a witticism worthy of Ovid's best:

> E bien paree et atornee
> Ele avoit faite sa jornee.[48]

When she had finished her toilette, she "called it a day."

Similarly, Ovid's story of Narcissus[49] is retold in a manner suited to the poet's purpose.[50] Langlois (*Origines*, p. 71) makes it clear that though Guillaume was presumably familiar with some vernacular form of the story of

---

[44] *Edition*, I, pp. 4–5.

[45] *Edition*, II, p. 301, on line 582 (599 Marteau).

[46] *Remedia Amoris*, 139.

[47] *Met.* IV, 306–315.

[48] 603–604 (569–570 L).

[49] *Met.* III, 339–510.

[50] 1495–1570 (1439–1510 L).

Narcissus, which had a great vogue, he must have turned to Ovid directly. There is in Guillaume nothing of the subtle satire at the expense of Narcissus, who is involved in the rarest kind of love that Ovid ever had to describe; for the poor youth, in love with his image, finds the distinction between *meum* and *tuum* most amusingly difficult to draw. There is the same grace and liquidity in Guillaume's version and there is further the sense of magic; for the pool becomes *La Fontaine d'Amors*, in which Cupid had dropped seeds of love, fatal to youths or maidens who looked within.[51]

Another of Guillaume's borrowings from Ovid appears in the picture of Envy that the lover sees on the outside of the garden wall.[52] This Langlois calls a free copy of Ovid's description[53] and finds it inferior, on the ground that Guillaume spins out into fifty-five verses what Ovid can say in five or six hexameters.[54] We must not forget that a Latin hexameter can comprise the meaning of two verses of mediaeval, or modern, French. As a matter of fact, Ovid's description includes thirteen hexameters (768[b]–782[a]), nor should we neglect the setting in which Envy is placed, her House, or Cave (760–768[a]).[55] Guillaume had no room to paint the House of Envy on his wall, and his description lacks something of Ovid's color for this reason. But it is well-adjusted to the pictures of the other vices, and one of his expansions adds a specific touch to Ovid's phrase. Ovid says simply that Envy cannot look you straight in the face—*nusquam recta acies* (v. 776). Guillaume is livelier than this:[56]

> Lors vi qu' Envie en la pointure
> Avoit trop laide esgardeüre:
> Elle ne regardast neient
> Fors de travers en borgneiant;
> Si avoit un mauvais usage,
> Car el ne peüst au visage

---

[51] *Vv.* 1648–1654 (1588–1594 L). Here Ovid's account of the uncanny fountain of Salmacis (*Met.* IV, 380–388) may have been an incidental spur to the imagination of Guillaume. All this is but one moment in the history of the Fountain of Love in poetry.

[52] *Vv.* 245–300 (205–290 L).

[53] "*Met.* II, 770 ff."

[54] *Origines*, pp. 69–70.

[55] This is one of several Houses or Caves constructed by Ovid, which started in literature a goodly lineage of such abodes, including Chaucer's House of Fame and, one that Ovid would have specially enjoyed, the Cave of Dulness in Pope's *Dunciad*.

[56] 289–295 (279–286 L).

Regarder rien de plain en plain,
Ainz clooit un ueil par desdein.

This is expansion to some purpose. The spiteful closing of one eye is an excellent touch.

Finally, a familiar poem of Ovid's, not mentioned, so far as I can find, by Langlois, may have stimulated the imagination of Guillaume in his story of the Love-God's attack on the lover. I mean Ovid's Triumph of Love.[57] Here we find the lover tossing on his couch through the long night, when he is suddenly smitten by the arrow of Love. These are simple shafts, all of the same variety. But elsewhere Ovid's Cupid has two kinds of arrows, one of gleaming gold, sharp-pointed, which induces love, the other blunt with lead beneath the reed, which deadens love.[58] With this to start from, Guillaume fills the quiver with the ten arrows, Five Evil and Five Good, the effect of which we have already seen.[59] Will Ovid's lover yield? He thinks of young bullocks struggling against the plow, of colts tugging at the bit, and concludes it is better to give in:

Acrius invitos multoque ferocius urget
Quam qui servitium ferre fatentur amor.[60]

He surrenders, then, unconditionally:

En ego confiteor: tua sum nova praeda Cupido.
Porrigimus victas ad tua iura manus.
Nil opus est bello: pacem veniamque rogamus.

Then follows the Triumph of Cupid, in which the lover follows with other recent captives after the chariot:

---

[57] *Amores* I, 2.

[58] *Met.* I, 467–471.

[59] Above, p. 114. Langlois (*Edition*, II, p. 304) quotes *Carmina Burana* (F. A. Schmeller, Breslau, 1894), no. 116b:

Mittit (Amor) pentagonas nervo stridente sagittas,
Quod sunt quinque modi quibus associamur amori:
Visus, colloquium, tactus, compar labiorum.

The date of the poem is uncertain, but this doctrine of the five steps in the approach to love had a vogue in the Middle Ages. I feel certain that I have seen it in some mediaeval commentary on Ovid, but the reference escapes me. It may have been a half-way house between Ovid and Guillaume, the latter refining what he found, in his fashion.

[60] *Vv.* 17–18.

> Ipse ego, praeda recens, factum modo vulnus habebo;
> Et nova captiva vincula mente feram.[61]

Very similar are the musings of Amant, in answer to the cry of Amors:

> Vassaus, pris es.[62]

It is a willing submission:

> Sire, volentiers me rendrai,
> Ja vers vos ne me defendrai.[63]
> Car, se je faz vostre voloir,
> Je ne m'en puis de rien doloir.[64]

Naturally we do not expect the chariot of Cupid to enter the mystic garden, with a formal Roman procession in its train, but a phrase in the God's acceptance of his new recruit,

> Qu' Amors porte le gonfanon
> De Cortoisie e la baniere,[65]

shows that the scene of a Triumph is still in the poet's mind. Let us note also that Ovid includes among the captives *Mens Bona, Pudor*

> et castris quidquid Amoris obest.[66]

Cupid's attendants, on the other hand, are *Blanditiae . . . Errorque Furorque*.[67] These abstractions are as animated as those in the Romance. We note that there Raison (*Mens Bona*) and Honte (*Pudor*) are associated. Honte in fact is the daughter of that noble lady Raison:

> E sachiez que, qui a droit conte
> Son parenté e son lignage,
> El fu fille Raison la sage.[68]

Possibly also the suggestion of an attack on the camp of Love (*castra Amoris*) may be a foreshadowing of the assault in the tower at the end of this part of the *Romance*.

---

[61] *Vv.* 28–29.

[62] *V.* 1958 (1884 L).

[63] *Vv.* 1973–1974 (1899–1910 L).

[64] *Vv.* 1995–1996 (1921–1922 L).

[65] *Vv.* 2020–2021 (1946–1947 L).

[66] *Vv.* 31–32.

[67] *V.* 35.

[68] *Vv.* 2932–2934 (2838–2841 L).

If, therefore, my analysis is sound, the nature of Guillaume's imitation is clear. It is more subtle and creative than that of Petrarch in his *Trionfo d'Amore* or that of Boccaccio in his *Visione d'Amore*. Their method is to take over a whole scene or episode and trim it up anew. Guillaume de Lorris, like Chaucer, selects what suits his design, but the design is already there. To speak in the language made classic by Lowes,[69] various pictures, phrases, ideas, attract the "Falcon Eye," as Guillaume de Lorris absorbs his Ovid. Images taken from various mediaeval works, both vernacular and Latin also sink into the "Deep Well," and various fusions are made there, ready to rise at the creator's call.[70]

The most miraculous of these metamorphoses is the transformation of Ovid's very naughty *Art of Love* into the code that the lover learns in the garden. We sometimes hear that Ovid was tolerated in the Middle Ages because his works were treated to an allegorical interpretation whereby the pleasant myths of old and merry scandal told by a wag like Ovid became as safe as the *Song of Songs* (similarly treated) for theology and Catholic discipline. This kind of interpretation, of course, flourished. It flourished in Petrarch's day in the work of his friend Pièrre Berçuire. It had flourished at Orléans in the century before Guillaume. Master Arnolfus had so expounded Ovid.[71] It is strange that such teaching, which I supposed must have continued at Orléans, ran off the mind of Guillaume like water from the duck's back. There is not one touch of it in his part of *Le Roman de la Rose*, not one touch of anything specifically theological. Tak-

---

[69] In 1905, I had an interesting talk with a graduate student about to take his examination for the doctorate, one John Livingston Lowes. He spoke of the habit of Chaucer and Froissart of taking a suggestion from Ovid, weaving it into material drawn from mediaeval tale or legend, and adding their own inventions. The ideas that he set forth, then, may have been the tiny mustard seed whence waxed a mighty tree in *The Road to Xanadu.*

[70] I have only broached this subject. It should be examined afresh by someone versed in both the vernacular and the Latin literature of the Middle Ages and, of course, in Ovid. Langlois notes various other coincidences with Ovid, and surely more remain.

[71] The work of this teacher of the humanities, who in this respect was hardly more than a name to us before, has been recently put into clear light by Fausto Ghisalberti, in his *Arnolfo d'Orléans, un cultore del Ovidio nel secolo XII* in *Memorie del R. Istituto Lombardo di Scienze e Lettere XXIV* (xv ser. III) iv, Milan, Hoepli, 1932, 157–234. For his allegorical interpretation of Ovid see pp. 201–229, and for selections from his commentary, pp. 201–229. He interprets *historice, moraliter* and *allegorice*—now in this mode and now in that.

ing what he needs from the *Ars Amatoria*[72] and from various mediaeval works on the same theme, such as the scandalous Ovidian comedy *Pamphilus*,[73] Guillaume has devised his own Art of Love. He was helped, of course, by the tradition that had been forming ever since Crestien de Troyes, in the twelfth century, published his translation of the *Ars Amatoria;* this version, unhappily, is now lost. Guillaume's *Roman de la Rose* is the full flower of that tradition.[74] Christian feeling underlies it, for these writers were Christians, and is responsible for the gradual sublimation of Ovid's precepts. No touch of the gross or the sensual remains. The sentiment of love is as pure, and as passionate, as in some of the mediaeval hymns to the Blessed Virgin, the Rose of Heaven, and as in the mystic vision of the Rose at the end of Dante's *Paradiso.*

So Guillaume is writing no *Ovide moralisé;* he presents an *Ovide décidément métamorphosé—sartor resartus.* Perhaps the gay Roman would view the process with some amusement and a mild protest, sympathizing with the Goliard who denounced the union of wine and water:

> Numquam Bacchus adaquari
> . Se voluit,
> Nec se Liber baptizari
> Sustinuit.

But possibly, for Ovid had his serious moments, he would not object that his merry *Art of Love* had led up, through the *Roman de la Rose,* to Dante.

---

[72] Langlois, *Origines*, pp. 71–74 gives the most obvious passages.

[73] Langlois, *Origines*, pp. 27–32.

[74] Gaston de Paris, *La Littérature française au Moyen Age*, Paris, Hachette, 1889, §104 (6th ed., p. 168): "*Le Roman de la Rose*, dans sa première parte, est l'épanouissement de toute cette floraison."

THE ROAD IN OLD JAPAN*

ROBERT BURNETT HALL
University of Michigan

THE road, and by this term it is meant to include those forms and features which are inseparably tied to the road, is a prominent element of the Japanese landscape. Geographically and otherwise the road has been a major integrating force in developing and maintaining the Japanese State. The road has been the primary unifying bond, not only within the different regions of Japan, but likewise has been the most important adhesive which tied one region to another and allowed the development and maintenance of a nation. The condition of the road at any one time has accurately reflected the degree of national cohesion. It has been a measure of the vitality of the central government. Japanese history is the story of the almost cyclic rise and decline of central government—of centrifugal forces predominating for a while only to give way to centripetal ones. Each period is expressed in the condition of the road. A great central highway system disintegrates into an amorphous pattern of local roads and trails which unite again into a consistent whole.

The territorial extension of the road system is also one of several guides to the expansion of empire and political control. The extension of Yamato control outward from the plains of Kinai has been accompanied by an extension of roads to the frontiers of political control.

Japan is an exceedingly mountainous country. The great highways, in a most definite manner, have had their direction pre-fashioned by nature. The trajectories which have predominated throughout historical time were also doubtlessly utilized in prehistoric and probably even pre-human time. Isolation growing out of this same mountainous character has laid a

* The writer is indebted to the Social Science Research Council and the Faculty Research Fund of the University of Michigan for financial assistance given on several field seasons spent in Japan and China during which the data included in this and other articles were gathered. To Mr. Joseph K. Yamagiwa and Mrs. Hanako H. Yamagiwa of the staff of the Department of Oriental Languages and Literatures and to Mr. Ch'i-Yang Ke of the Department of Geography of the University of Michigan he is most thankful for their painstaking care in translating and in the checking of annotations.

particularly heavy responsibility upon the few natural roadways. The main roads of Japan, throughout long centuries, have changed their trajectories only in minor detail and in the means by which they have been operated.

The term Old Japan carries both historical and geographical connotation. It is pre-Restoration Japan—the Japan of the Orient—and so excludes such areas as Hokkaidō and Karafuto which have had their characters largely determined by occidental influence. It is the Japanese islands bordering the Inland Sea—the cradle of civilization which was Japan's.

It is probably safe to assume that in Japan, as in other habitable portions of the earth, earliest man found it necessary to travel from one place to another. Migration, gathering and hunting, war and barter were all motivating forces. Communication by land, then as now, must have tended to concentrate upon the natural passageways between one area and another. Gradually trails and primitive roadways were worn into the rock along the lines of least resistance. As permanent settlements developed, pathways between villages and from one habitable region to another were accentuated. Because of the proximity of most fertile areas to the sea and because of the mountainous character of Japan, coastal water routes competed with and retarded the development of land routes in many places. In other places land and water routes seemed to have supplemented each other. Coastal water routes formed continuations of land routes where the terrain was unusually rugged or where shore lines compelled a too circuitous course by land.

Until the infiltration of Chinese ideas of communication and the beginnings of a centralized government, roads developed and were facilitated as local needs required. Gradually local roads came to be connected and through travel over considerable distances became possible, but certainly nothing like a standardized road system prevailed. There seems not to have been any romantic economic background in Japan leading to the development of early long-distance trade routes, such as developed the Amber Road in Central Europe, the Jade Road from China into Tarim, or the distant quests for lapis lazuli.

There are no extended written records before the early Eighth Century after Christ. The *Kojiki* (Record of Ancient Things) compiled in 712 and the *Nihon-Shoki* (Chronicles of Japan) in 720 A.D., although containing interesting and valuable material and numerous references to roads and travel, must be regarded as mixtures of inseparable myth, legend, and historical fact. They cannot be entirely relied upon nor can they be entirely cast aside. In addition to these early compilations, there is also recourse for the early period to the distribution of prehistoric shrines and the sites of ancient palisades and settlements. Local tradition, too, often helps in re-establishing the patterns of the past. Contemporary studies of particular periods and regions have also proved most valuable.[1]

We can surmise with relative safety that roads led northward into distant Ōu in the prehistoric period. Here are found ancient shrines. Here are the sites of prehistoric fortresses. The campaigns of the Shidō-shōgun, although not mentioned in the *Kojiki*, are vividly described in the *Nihon-Shoki*, Vol. v, and might be taken to indicate the extension of control over four roads and the regions they served. The campaigns of Ōbiko-no-Mikoto via the Hokurokudō and of his son via the Tōkaidō and their meeting at Aizu in Iwashiro, suggests, in spite of many inconsistencies, that early roads led from Yamato to Ōu. The travels of Prince Yamato-dake, as given in both the *Kojiki* and *Nihon-Shoki*, indicate that the Tōkaidō, Tōsandō, and Kiso-kaidō were at least passable. His conquests in Kyūshū, likewise, suggest that communication from the Tōsandō was possible well into Kyūshū. That roads were not continuously good is indicated by the numerous short coastal voyages made and also by the still existent, though ancient, place names—where rugged headlands meet the sea or where deep embayments interrupt land routes—bearing the suffix "zu" or "tsu" (ferry).

In the broader aspects of the ancient road pattern it would seem reasonable to assume that with the migration of the Yamato clan to the plains of Kinai, and with growing political ascendency there, both the land and water routes of ancient Japan gradually gravitated around that center. According to the Kōdaiki, the Sanyōdō was opened in the reign of the Emperor Suizei (c. 10 b.c.–a.d. 20) and the Tōkaidō and Nankaidō were opened during the reign of the Emperor Kōgen (c. a.d. 170–200). There follows in tradition, the extension of central control over Hokuro-kudō, Tōkaidō, Saikaidō and Sanindō under the "Generalissimo of the

---

[1] The writer has used freely of materials contained in the following excellent studies by Japanese scholars: Ōnishi, Seijirō: *Nihon Kōtsūshi Ronsō*; Tokyo, 1939, pp. 3–53; Sakamoto, Tarō: *Jōdai Ekisei no Kenkyū*; Tokyo, 1928. Frequent reference has also been made to the writer's: "Tōkaidō: Road and Region," *Geog. Rev.*, vol. xxvii, no. 3, pp. 353–377.

Four Circuits" in the time of the Emperor Sujin (c. A.D. 240).[2] It would appear then that a gradual development of roadways came at an early date to gravitate outward in every direction from the plains of Kinai. It is only natural, too, that the Sanyōdō, connecting, finally, northern Kyūshū with Yamato, should be the first great road. Thus it remained for centuries or until migration and conquest northward established a new political and demographic equilibrium. Within the Kinai region the details of the developing road pattern changed to conform to each new location of the capital city. Naniwa, Asuka, Ōtsu, and later Nara and Kyōto each became in their time the hub of the pattern of circulation.

Just what the condition of the roads of Japan was at the time of the Taihō-ryō (Civil Code of Taihō, A.D. 702, revised 718) is not clear. That there had been roads of a sort for long centuries is certain. But whether, in the years immediately preceding the code, something like a systematic post road structure had developed, stimulated both by continental ideas and by a gradual centralization of government, is difficult to say with certainty. There is some evidence that the code gave authority to a system which already had come into at least partial existence, rather than itself creating an entirely new structure.

It seems certain that Sir George Sansom was correct in concluding that " . . . there were no good public roads, no canals and hardly any bridges," and that "travel between the capital and distant provinces was difficult and dangerous. . . . the remoter districts were infested with bandits and pirates. . . . "[3] Yet it is reasonable to believe that a good deal had been done by way of improving facilities for transport and communications and that some of the features of the post system, later to be modeled so clearly on the T'ang system, had already been established at least on some roads.

The post system was already an ancient development in China. It was maintained for "the transmission of Imperial orders by stages and couriers." By this system military orders were dispatched, official documents of all kinds were carried from one place to another, and government officers travelled up and down in pursuit of their duties.

It would seem that the first written mention of the post system appears

---

[2] The story of the Shidō-shōgun may well have been simply copied from some Chinese tale. The tradition, however, is believed to form the basis for the later divison of the country into *dō*. The story also proves the recognition of these regions at an early date.

[3] Sansom, G. B., *Japan: A Short Cultural History*, London, 1932, p. 94.

in the book of *Mencius* in which it is stated, "Confucius said, 'The flowing progress of virtue is more rapid than the transmission of imperial orders by stages and couriers.'"[4] The origin of the post system has been placed in the Western Chou[5] but it is difficult to accept the *Chou Li*[6] as authentic either as to date or fact. It seems reasonable to believe, however, that by the fifth century B.C. some sort of an extensive post road system was in operation.[7] Ch'in Shih Huang was credited with building broad roadways reaching to Yen and Ch'i in the east and to Wu and Ch'u in the south. On either side were low "golden" walls planted with green pine trees.[8] In the period of the Han Dynasty posts were divided into two classes—express and ordinary—and a system of post supervisors or *Tu Yu* was established,[9] which prevailed up to T'ang times.

Under the Sui Dynasty, China was reunified and a strong central government developed. The T'ang inherited this favorable situation and further unified and developed the institutions of the state. It was the post road system of this period which furnished the immediate pattern for the road system which was extended and standardized under the Taihō Code in Japan. What were the characteristics of the T'ang system?

The system of *Tu Yu* was abolished and the post roads were put under the *Ping Pu* (Army Department). There were at least two reasons for this: 1, the post system in China was maintained primarily for the army

---

[4] *Mencius*, Book 2, Kung-sun Ch'ou, p. 2. If this statement is accepted in entirety it would indicate an established post system in the time of Confucius (B.C. 551–479). Again, if only the time of writing is accepted the date is moved forward to the latter part of Mencius' life (c. 370–334 B.C.).

[5] Ch'en Yüan-yüan, "T'ang Tai I Chih K'ao," *Shih Hsueh Nien Pao*, Vol. 1, No. 5, p. 61. Frequent reference has been made to this excellent study.

[6] *Chou Li*, Chia Ch'ing Shih I Nien (1806), Shun Te Chang Shih Ch'ing Fen Ke (2nd Ed.). The Western Chou (B.C. 1122–?770).

[7] *Ch'un Ch'iu Tso Chuan*, Chung Hua Shu Chü, Vol. 9, p. 12 (" . . . Viscount Chu rode the posts and assembled the troops in Lin P'in.") and Vol. 21, p. 13 (" . . . Viscount Ch'u, by the posts reached Lo Jui.") Chen Yüan-yüan, *op. cit.*, quotes Ku Yen-wu, a well-known Ch'ing scholar of the seventeenth century, in *Jih Chih Lu*, Vol. 10, *I Ch'uan*, p. 7 as "I assume that the device (of posts) had already been adopted during the period of Ch'un Ch'iu" (B.C. 722–481).

[8] *Shih Chi*, Kuang Hsu Kuei Mao (1903), Wu Chou T'ung Wen Chu (lith. ed.), Vol. 6, p. 14. These roads were said to be 50 *pu* wide (113 feet).

[9] *Wen Hsien T'ung K'ao*, Shanghai, T'u Shu Chi Ch'eng Chu. (lith. ed.), Vol. 63, p. 22.

and for army affairs, and 2, the army had the control and management of horses throughout the Empire.[10] Under the army an array of officials functioned—magistrates, watchmen, etc. At each post there was an *I Chang* or post master.[11] Supervisors made periodic inspections of the posts and their properties.[12] The post masters were held responsible for the animals entrusted to them and were required to report annually the condition of the horses and donkeys of their posts, and all expenditures and surpluses of their post. They were also required to welcome and provide for all persons with authority to demand shelter, food and transportation from their posts.

In general, post stations were to be established every 30 *li* along the post highways.[13] Resting lodges were to be maintained at reasonable intervals between the post stations. In all, 1,639 post stations seemed to have developed, of which 1,297 were land stations, 260 were water stations and 86 performed both land and water post functions. The post stations were established to provide food and shelter for officials, messengers and porters and to provide a succession of transportation by horses, donkeys, porters, messengers, etc. The ordinary post probably provided only indifferent accommodations, but those posts located at convenient points for the travel of many high officials seem to have developed luxurious accommodations. Magnificent buildings and superlative cuisines are frequently mentioned. A distinguishing feature of some water stations was a high watch tower[14] which served both as a look-out and as a landmark.

The number of porters available at any one post depended upon the demand for porter service. In general, it seems one porter was available for every three horses and three porters were supplied with every boat.[15] Porters were drawn from the common people of the locale. The law provided that every adult male was obligated to serve the post for twenty days a year and if special conditions prevailed he could be requisitioned for

---

[10] *T'ang Liu Tien*, Sao Yeh Shan Fang, Vol. 5, p. 15.

[11] *Hsin T'ang Shu, Pai Kuan Chih*, Chekiang Shu Chü, Vol. 46, p. 13.

[12] *Ibid.*, Vol. 46, p. 13 and Vol. 182, p. 7.

[13] *Ibid.*, Vol. 46, p. 13. The *li* was roughly one-third of a mile (1 *li* equals 1,800 *ch'ih* and 3.125 *ch'ih* equals 1 metre) so that posts were planned to be about 10 miles apart.

[14] *Ch'üan T'ang Shih*, Han 6, book 9, *Yüan Chen Shih*, Vol. 17, p. 5.

[15] *T'ang Liu Tien, op. cit.*, Vol. 5, p. 16.

another fifteen days. No man, however, could be compelled to serve more than fifty days in any one year. Men from well-to-do and larger families were requisitioned first. Such men served especially during the periods when agricultural demands were greatest. Those from families with only one man served only in the periods of leisure.

The number of horses also varied according to the demand upon the post. At the *Tu T'ing I* (the post stations of the two capitals) there were 75 horses. Other posts were classified into six grades. A first grade post had 60 horses and a sixth grade post had but eight. In general, post horses were provided by and were the property of the government but under some conditions the populace was obligated by law to provide and feed additional post horses. There were two classes of horses—large and *shu*. The latter were small ponies raised in Ssu-ch'uan and used for rough trails.[16] Post horses were also classed as *I* and *Ch'uan*. The former were for more urgent or express post while the latter were employed for ordinary business.[17] Messengers ordinarily covered four posts in a day on *Ch'uan* horses and six when riding *I* horses. Donkeys were widely employed in T'ang time and were supposed to allow a speed of 40 *li* a day as against 70 *li* by horse.

Communication by water was well developed. There were 260 water post stations and 86 which served both land and water.[18] Three grades of water posts are recorded according to the demand on them, i.e., two, three and four boat posts. Of twenty-one land and water posts recorded, nine had but one boat, five each had two and three boats and two had four boats.[19]

Land was allocated to each post for the support of its horses. The exact amount may well have differed both as to time and place. "Four *ch'ing* were provided for each station"[20] and "the size of the area given each post was according to the number of horses it had, . . . each horse was allowed 40 *mou* and 5 *mou* were deducted if the pasture was nearby, and for horses used in ordinary post only 20 *mou* was allowed."

---

[16] *Ibid.*, Vol. 5, p. 15.

[17] *Ibid.*, Vol. 8, p. 7.

[18] *Ibid.*, Vol. 5, p. 15.

[19] *Ibid.*, Vol. 7, p. 13.

[20] Quoted from Ch'en Yüan-yüan, *op. cit.*, pp. 71–72. One *ch'ing* equals 100 *mou* and 6.07 *mou* equals one acre.

The facilities of the post system were available to all who could identify themselves as legally qualified. Persons on important military business; bearers of urgent reports from and to the provinces; various government officials on government business (and their families under certain conditions); scholars, astronomers, monks and nuns, and Taoists in government service; and official messengers were chief among those entitled to transport, lodging and food at the post stations. Through the post messenger service were conveyed edicts and dispatches concerning the levying of taxes and the calling up of people to public service. Memorials of gratitude to the Emperor and written congratulations on the enthronement of a new Emperor or the selection of a new Empress or Prince were also entrusted to the post service.

Messengers identified themselves by the carrying of credentials, i.e., a silver tablet on which the characters *Ch'ih, Tsou, Ma, Yin* and *P'ai* were carved or a small bronze dragon or an official paper ticket. The number of horses they could command depended upon their rank. Horses had to be exchanged at each post along the route. Rooms at the post stations were allocated in the order of arrival. It seems relatively certain then that some knowledge of the Chinese post system had reached Japan by the Fifth or Sixth Centuries A.D., if not earlier.

To partially substantiate this view there are numerous references to post stations, post horses and post messengers in the older Japanese writings. According to the *Nihon-Shoki*, station roads for the movement of tribute from Kudara (Paikché) were established in the time of Jingō-Kōgō (c. A.D. 363–380). An earlier but less understandable reference in the *Kojiki* states that the Emperor Sujin "sent post messengers [couriers?] in every direction," while a passage in the *Nihon-Shoki* speaks of "riding on a post horse and hurrying to pay homage." These statements are regarded by some as the first indications of post messengers and of the post system, respectively. The *Kojiki* refers to the post messengers during the reigns of at least three emperors. Also in the records relating to the Emperors Kimmei, Sushun, Suiko, and Kōgyoku in the *Nihon-Shoki* are found frequent references to post horses and post messengers. In the Harima-no-kuni Fudoki (section on Kako-no-kōri) there is related the crossing of the ford of Takase in Settsu by a ferry which was operated by an employee of the imperial government. These references obviously are not conclusive and frequently not entirely understandable, yet they do suggest that a beginning had been made in establishing a post road system before the time of the *Taika* Reform.

In Japan, as elsewhere, the development and maintenance of an integrated and standardized road system had to wait upon the establishment of a centralized government. As in Persia, Rome, China and the Inca Empire a strong imperial government found it necessary to establish and control a wide system of post roads in order to facilitate political control, to collect taxes and enforce law. Control of outlying provinces could only be maintained and taxes collected and brought to the support of the central government by tying the peripheral areas to the center through a standardized road system. The problem of taxes was, of course, accentuated as they were paid in kind. Under existing forms of transportation and communication post stations, located at about a day's travel apart, were essential to insure shelter and provide fresh carriers. The differences of time and space have brought different forms, but the essential pattern has been everywhere the same. Because of the exceedingly mountainous character of Japan, which tended to isolate each productive and populous area from all others, and which hindered communication between one region of the country and another, it was particularly essential that communication and transportation be facilitated. Unfortunately Japan, unlike China, has no great navigable rivers. Nor does it have wide lowlands over which canals could be constructed. The advantage which its small size should have given was more than offset by the rugged and complex character of land surface. Difficulty of communication, not distance, long retarded the development of a central government and later militated again and again against its continuity.

Article II of the Taihō-ryō provided for a regulated road system, for barriers, for ferries, and for post horses—both ordinary and special. Mountain passes were to be regulated and travel was to be made safe by guards and watchmen. Bell tokens were to be provided. The Taihō-ryō was the first civil code to be declared throughout the empire. The Taika era had seen the establishment of a highly centralized bureaucracy modeled upon that of the T'ang. Japan's "Golden Age" had dawned. From the continent came Korean immigrants of various kinds and Chinese Buddhist priests, some of whom were highly versed in the engineering practices of their time.

The road system, as it developed, reflected different influences. First and foremost, its prototype was the contemporary T'ang. How nearly a facsimile of Chinese institutions the Japanese of this time could produce has been noted in other studies. In the adaptation of Chinese institutions to Japanese conditions there seems always to have entered a touch of native genius. The introduction of bell tokens, for example, appears to be strictly a Japanese invention. Also, the years of experience preceding the Taihō Code, and especially those following the Taika Reform, produced other modifications and adaptations to Japanese and regional differences, as did the years and centuries following. The remarkable thing is that so complicated a structure as the post road system could have persisted for so long with so few changes. To the end, when it was abolished after the Restoration, it still retained all of the fundamental parts and many of the details of the early Chinese model upon which it had been based.

In attempting to recreate the post road system of Old Japan, almost insurmountable difficulties present themselves. Beyond the inadequacies of the literature, the very nature of the problem itself makes anything like a complete understanding exceedingly difficult. The road is among the most fundamental institutions of a people. As such, it is a vital, complex, and everchanging thing. With every alteration in the environment in which it functions, both temporally and spatially, the institution must adapt itself or fail to survive. In a most persistent way, too, it reflects the individuals who control it. Perhaps the greatest difficulty of all lies in the fact that whereas the literature is explicit and relatively complete in stating the laws by which the system was created and altered, there grew up about the road a mass of convention and tradition and a pattern of behavior, much of which was never legalized, but which nevertheless was as significant in the operation and development of the system as was the law itself.

The post road system in Japan followed upon long centuries in which roads of a sort had gradually developed haphazardly and without central control. With the introduction of the post system from China and the extension of central control over the empire, these old trajectories were utilized, improved and standardized. The post road system was developed by the central government and for its purposes. Its primary function was to facilitate and insure governmental communication and transportation. It was not designed as a public highway system and only more or less fortuitously functioned as one. The purposes of the post system were (1) to provide a succession of men and horses (or boats where necessary) to insure continued and rapid government transport and communication and (2) to provide shelter and food for persons and horses in the government service.

The constituent parts of the post road system of this period included the road itself and land and water post stations. The post station was composed of the post houses and the post rice fields. Within the stations were maintained post horses, in the case of land posts, and post boats in the water posts. Post men, post messengers, and a post master were integral parts. Barriers, although not a part of the post system, were an integral part of the road system.

Three classes of roads were recognized.[21] There was one first class road which connected the imperial capital with Dazaifu in Kyūshū—the Dazaifudō. The Tōkaidō and Nakasendō (Tōsandō), connecting the capital with Kantō and the north country, were roads of the second class. All other roads were small or third class roads. As to the exact condition of the roadbeds, little is known. Largely because of the extremely mountainous character of the country no attempt was made to facilitate transport by wheeled vehicles except in the cities and, at best, locally on the plains of Kinai.[22] The roads were meant only to serve pedestrians and horsemen. They could then be narrow and without hard surface and from those portions of the roads of this period which can be positively identified today, little attention seems to have been paid to steepness of slope. The most direct line, if slopes were possible for men and horses, seems to have been the rule. That the roads, at least in the provinces, were poorly marked and policed is suggested in the *Ise Monogatari*[23] which tells of friends travelling together for safety and of parties losing their ways, even on the Tōkaidō. That many improvements were made cannot be doubted. Fruit trees were ordered to be planted on both sides of the post roads in Kinai, in the seven districts and in the provinces.[24] Any wide-

[21] *Ryō-no-gige, Kyūboku-ryō* in *Shintei-zōho Kokushi taikei*, xxii (1939), p. 275.

[22] *Genji Monogatari* (Arthur Waley's translation). Numerous references occur as to ox-drawn wagons and carriages, but their use seems to have been confined to Kyōto and vicinity.

[23] *Ise Monogatari*, Sec. 9.

[24] *Ruijū Sandaikyaku*, Bokusaiji (A.D. 732), in *Shintei zōho Kokushi taikei*, xxv (1936), p. 298.

spread application of this order is to be doubted, however, as later records fail to recognize the existence of such trees. Ferries and floating bridges were ordered to be improved and extended again and again.

There are numerous references to the activities of priests in road improvement. The priest Gyōgi, for example, travelled through the various provinces and "laid out straight roads and built bridges." The nun Hōkō, of Echigo, devoted much of her energies to the establishment of ferries and otherwise alleviating the suffering of travellers. In fact the priesthood alone seemed to show any interest in facilitating the road for public travel. Local populations seemed to have despised the traveller and to have hindered rather than helped the common traveller.

There seems to have been a steady extension and improvement of the national roads until about the end of the first quarter of the tenth century, when a general national disintegration set in. New roads were added, others were straightened or changed in detail to facilitate their use. In 737, for example, officials were sent to open up a road between Okachi-no-gō and the Idewa palisade. The Emperor Kammu caused the opening of the Hakone-Kaidō, a road to Ashigara was added, and partially new trajectories were ordered on the Tōkaidō. In 797, improvements were ordered on the Nankaidō.[25] Quite a complete record of the national road system is recorded in the *Engishiki* (A.D. 967). The *Engishiki* is a record of the past rather than a pattern for the future. It probably pictures the national road system at shortly after the peak of its development and before serious decline had set in.

A. First-Class or Big Roads

I. The *Dazaifudō* began officially at Yamazaki and ran westward along the northern shore of the Inland Sea to the straits of Shimonoseki and thence across the provinces of Buzen and Chikuzen to Dazaifu. Two branch roads stemmed from it: (1) one began in Harima province and ran northward to Mimasaka, while (2) the other went from the Straits of Shimonoseki eastward through Nagato province to Iwami province where it joined the Sanindō. [The Dazaifudō was the highway of chief importance for the government as it joined the imperial capital with the government center at Dazaifu. This highway had the competition of boat

---

[25] *Nihon ki ryaku* (Enryaku 15).

travel on the Inland Sea. When speed was important the land route was of course preferred.]

B. SECOND-CLASS OR MIDDLE ROADS

I. The *Tōkaidō* began officially at Seta and ran across southeastern Ōmi province through the Suzuka-no-seki, across northern Ise province, and thence east and north, following for the most part close to the Pacific coast, beyond the great *Kantō* plain into Hitachi province. Three branch roads were associated with it: (1) the Iseji which joined the Tōkaidō at Suzuka and ran southward to Ise-dai-jingū (Ise Shrine) and eastward into Shima province; (2) the Kaiji which extended from the Kai provincial seat of government to join the Tōkaidō in Suruga province, and (3) the Kamifusaji which joined the Tōkaidō in Shimōsa province after extending the length of the Bōsō Peninsula from Awa province. Still another road joined the Tōkaidō to the Tōsandō via the Hitachi provincial seat of government and Higashi-Shirakawa in Iwaki province. [The Tōkaidō was unquestionably the second road of importance in this period. It did not become the primary road of the country until the founding of the Kamakura government.]

II. The *Tōsandō* (Nakasendō or Sendō) also began at Seta and ran northward across Ōmi province, by way of Fuwa-no-seki and through Mino province and the mountainous heart of Honshū, north and east through the provinces of Shinano, Kōzuke, Shimotsuke and Mutsu (Iwashiro) to Shiwa castle. There were two branch roads: (1) one connected Akita castle with the Tōsandō at Shibata-no-eki in Mutsu and (2) the other connected the Hida and Mino provincial seats of government with the Tōsandō in Mino province. [The Tōsandō was the sole national highway serving the vast mountainous interior of Honshū beyond Lake Biwa. It parallels the Tōkaidō and historically has supplemented it.]

C. THIRD-CLASS OR SMALL ROADS

I. The *Hokurokudō* skirted the northern shore of Lake Biwa and through the Arachi Barrier entering Echizen-no-kuni, thence followed the coast of the Sea of Japan northward into Echigo province where a ferry continued the route to Sado Island. There were two branch roads: (1) the Wakasaji left the main road in northwest Ōmi province and traversing

Wakasa province rejoined the Hokurokudō at Tsuruga in Echizen province, and (2) the Notoji left the main road in northern Kaga province and ran northward into the Noto Peninsula to the provincial government of Noto. Still another road connected the provincial government of Echigo with that of Shinano and so connected the Hokurokudō with the Tō-sandō.

II. The *Sanindō* cut across Tamba province into Tajima province and thence followed the Sea of Japan coast to Izumo and beyond to reach the Iwami provincial seat of government. Two branch roads stemmed from the Sanindō: (1) the Tangoji left the main road in Tamba province and after reaching the provincial seat of government in Tango rejoined the Sanindō in Tajima province; and (2) the Okiji was a ferry route connecting Oki Island with the mainland and the Sanindō in central Izumo province.

III. The *Nankaidō* began at Yamazaki, as did the Dazaifudō, but ran southward through Kawachi province and thence into the Izumi provincial government and southward to reach that of Kii. By short ferry route between Akashi-no-ura (Harima province) and Iwaya on Awaji Island the route continued across Awaji where another short ferry ride allowed the route to continue to Awa-no-kuni on Shikoku Island and from there it continued across Sanuki province to the seat of government of Iyo province. A branch road ran from Iyo to connect the seat of government in Tosa province.

IV. The *Saikaidō* had a western and an eastern branch. The former ran from Dazaifu, where it joined the Dazaifudō, southward along the west side of Shikoku to reach the seats of government of Chikugo, Higo, and Satsuma provinces. Then it ran eastward into Ōsumi province. The latter left the Buzen seat of government and traversing that province ran southward along the west side of Kyūshū through Bungo and Hyūga provinces to join the western branch in Ōsumi. Several short roads connected the two main branches. One ran from Dazaifu to the Buzen provincial government. Another connected the Chikugo and Bungo governments. Still another ran from Higo province to Bungo province and another connected the main two roads running from Higo across northern Ōsumi into Hyūga. There were two other important branch routes in Kyūshū: (1) the Ikiji stemmed from the main route a little north of Dazaifu and ran westward to the coast of Matsura-no-kōri in Hizen province where a ferry connected it with Iki Island, and (2) the Higoji left the main road in eastern Hizen and ran west and south to the Hizen government where it branched into two routes: (a) one ran straight north and joined the Ikiji in Matsura-no-kōri and (b) the other ran southward through the Shimabara Peninsula and then by ferry was connected with the islands and mainland coast of Higo-no-kuni.

There were unquestionably other roads in Japan in this and earlier periods. The roads enumerated, however, seem to have been the only national post roads at the time of compilation of the *Engishiki*.[26]

The general jurisdiction of the post system in Japan, as in China, was placed under the military department. The specific office was that of Hyōmashi (Office of Military Horses). Wide authority, however, seems to have been given to provincial officers. The *kuni* governor, for example, had the authority to inspect and replace the horses at each post in his province, where messengers came rarely.[27] In fact the power of the *kuni* governors was so great that they often exploited the posts within their jurisdiction at the expense of the general efficiency of the post system and to the suffering of the local population. By Engi time, the *kōri* officials seem to have acquired large powers over local posts. As time went on, there seems to have been more and more civil use and control of the post system in Japan. Whether, as the system developed, the Japanese post system was less under military control than its contemporary and proto-type in China is a moot question. In the beginning at least the matter of general jurisdiction was most certainly a faithful imitation.

Regulation as to the distribution of posts was again true to the Chinese pattern. Posts were to be 30 *ri*[28] apart unless surface configuration made this distance impracticable. This same qualification was carried in T'ang regulations. Japanese regulations also excepted the absence of water. The remains of post sites of this period are too few to allow much to be learned through field work. Some indication of the distribution of posts is found in

---

[26] In the above compilation the writer has resorted freely to Sakamoto, Tarō, *op. cit.*, pp. 92-97.

[27] *Ryō-no-gige, Kyūboku-ryō, loc. cit.*

[28] This *ri* was about ⅓ mile. The present *ri* is 2.44 miles, obviously too great. The shimo-michi still used occasionally in some Sea of Japan localities is 6 chō or 2,148 feet, an ancient unit.

the *Izumo Fudoki*[29] where distances between particular posts are given as 20 *ri* 180 *bu*, 21 *ri*, 34 *ri* 130 *bu*, 26 *ri* 229 *bu*, 19 *ri* and 14 *ri*.

It would seem at least in Izumo, that the distances between posts departed freely from the exact figure of the regulation. This is only reasonable. Thirty *ri* in mountain country is quite different from that on level land. Equally important is the fact that where there is a post there must be settlement with agricultural land to support it. Generally, settlement preceded the post station so that most sites were fixed at irregular distances, as were the *kuni* and *kōri* offices which also became post sites. Natural terminals on land and water routes were also predetermined sites for post stations and upset the possibilities of regular spacing.

The buildings belonging to the post station must have included a storehouse for post rice, a stable, lodging quarters and office accommodations. The post buildings of Tachihi-no-kōri in Kawachi were described as having eight storage and two residential buildings[30]—quite a sizable assembly. The buildings were said to have had plaster walls and tile roofs in a period when the use of tile roofs was generally reserved for temples. The post buildings must have been unusually impressive. The occasional mention of post gates probably means that the post buildings were on a compound. The word *ekirō* (post tower) sometimes appears but just what is meant is not clear. There seems not to have been any regulations determining the form or materials of the post buildings, but that they must be kept in good condition is quite clearly stated.

Regulations called for 20 horses at each post on the Dazaifudō, 10 on the Tōkaidō and Tōsandō and 5 on all other roads.[31] The *kuni* governors, however, had wide discretionary powers in this matter. In the Daidō era (806–809) the Sanyōdō stations in Yamashiro are said to have had 30 horses each, as did the posts of Settsu. There seems to have been constant change. As the system passed its zenith greater and greater irregularity occurred. The original regulation is notable because it departed in three important ways from that of the T'ang. First, there were fewer horses required per post. Second, there were only horses and no donkeys. And, third, the *kuni* governors exercised considerable control over post horses. On a fast post horse a man was expected to cover 10 posts in a day and on

[29] Kurita, Kan and Gotō, Kurashirō, *Hyōchū kofudoki (Izumo)*, Tōkyō, 1931, p. 377.

[30] *Shoku Nihon-kōki* (A.D. 841), in *Shintei-zōho Kokushi taikei*, III (1934), p. 123.

[31] *Ryō-no-gige, Kyūboku-ryō, op. cit.*, XXII, p. 275.

an ordinary post horse six or eight posts.[32] There were also military horses and transport horses connected with the posts and later, peasants were required to bring and feed their own horses. It is not clear how the system worked out in detail in this regard. The *kuni* governors were required to inspect all posts and post horses in their jurisdictions once each year. Old and sick horses were then to be discarded and new ones purchased. If a horse died of unavoidable causes a new one was purchased with post rice. If its death was due to carelessness the post master was responsible.

A distinctly different physical milieu in Japan brought about a different development of water posts than was found in China. Japan's highways run for the most part along the bases of great mountain masses and cross countless rapid streams at right angles. In China, on the other hand, mighty rivers provide the best natural highways over wide areas. The problem in Japan, then, was to expedite the crossing of rivers in order to continue travel by land rather than to facilitate travel upon the rivers. Two distinct developments seem to have taken place. The crossing of Japan's many rivers required ferry accommodations unless the stream was shallow enough for wading or if bridges had been constructed. Post stations might or might not be located at the point of crossing. Certainly stations were not required on both sides. Somewhat similar ferry accommodations were also needed to cross from headland to headland along the far flung coasts of Japan. There are almost countless mentions of river ferries but little is said of the means of operation and administration.

The second development was that of sea-posts. From Echigo to Sado, from Izumo to Oki, from Hizen to Iki, from Kii to Awaji, from Awaji to Awa, from Nagato to Chikuzen, etc., there was need for regular communication and special facilities were required. Boats were necessary which were safe at sea. Stations were needed at both ends of the water route so that horses could be acquired or left behind. Sea travel depended upon storm and tide and was otherwise likely to be irregular so that accommodations for travellers were essential. Post stations in such service were located where boats could land their passengers and cargoes safely and where there was shelter from storm. In addition, the *Engishiki* records four posts in *Dewa* which combined the functions of land and water stations.

---

[32] *Ryō-no-gige, Kōshiki-ryō,* in *Shintei-zōho Kokushi taikei,* XXII (1939), p. 253. This would mean that by changing to fast horses at each post a messenger could travel up to 100 miles a day or up to 80 miles on ordinary horses.

For the support of the post stations rice land was regulated in amounts of four *chō* to each post on the Dazaifudō, three on the Tōkaidō and Naka-sendō and two on all other roads. The exact area, however, seems to have varied widely. This land was cultivated by the people of the station and was under central and not *kuni* control. Its production was used to feed messengers and to defray the cost of buying and feeding of horses. The other expenses of the post were met by the central government. At first the stations were exempt from tax and frequently were subsidized. As time went on heavier and heavier burdens were placed on the people of the stations, contributing greatly to the breakdown of the entire system.

Every post station had a body of post men to do the manual labor of the post. The feeding and care of the post horses, the working of the post paddy land, the bringing back of horses left by messengers at adjacent posts, and sometimes the carrying of messengers' baggage seemed to con-stitute the chief demands of the healthy period of the post system. As time went on, more and more demands were made upon these men. "The 432 loads of annual tax from Shima are ordered to be transported by the posts of Ōmi, Iga and Ise,"[33] indicates a new and heavy burden upon the post men. The transporting of tax seems at first to have been done by post horse with a post man leading. Later, the man himself became a packer. Just how many men there were to a post is not clear. Eleven posts in Aki are recorded as having 120 men each and three posts of Suruga-gun in Suruga had a total of 400 men. Thus 120 to 130 men to a post is indicated. If this be true and we allow three post men to a house, 40 or more houses are required which approximates the traditional 50 houses of the *sato* or township.[34]

The post system and the roads themselves, in as far as the government maintained them, were solely for the promotion of government communi-cation and transportation, especially between the capital and the prov-inces. Travellers on the road, in this period, can be grouped into two classes—those with authority to command the facilities of the post sta-tions and those who had to provide for themselves. The former group in-cluded messengers of several kinds. In fact, all government officers travel-

---

[33] *Nihon-sandai-jitsuroku* in Sakamoto, *op. cit.*, p. 42.

[34] The name *sato* was used for the township at an early date and preceded the use of the name *gō*. It, supposedly, consisted of 50 families, arranged in 10 groups of five families each.

ling on government business were so classed. Some were employed, either for the relaying or through carrying of government messages between the capital and the provinces. Others were on tours of inspection, in the tax service, or going to or from their posts of duty. These people could command horses and shelter, according to their respective ranks.

The latter group included all others. Troops were moved over the roads, but except in dire emergency, no demands were made upon the post stations. Great numbers of men and horses moved over the roads employed in the transporting of taxes. Taxes were paid in kind and were mainly of three classes: (1) *so*, or land tax paid in rice; (2) *yō*, or labor tax payable in labor or in produce at a fixed rate; and (3) *chō*, or produce tax paid in silk, iron, or produce other than rice. There were also miscellaneous taxes.

The provinces were rightly regarded as the sole source of life of the growing urban populations. The splendor of Kyōto was maintained by the taxes on the provinces. Each year every province, regardless of how distant or how poor the roads, had to transport its taxes to Kyōto. Hundreds of packers and horses were required. Twenty to thirty days were necessary in case of the more distant provinces. As no facilities were provided at the post stations or otherwise along the roads, it was also necessary to transport food or goods to trade for food. Hunger and even starvation was the not uncommon lot of men so employed. For shelter they were either fortunate enough to be taken in to some peasant house or they slept under the skies. Frequent attempts were made by the central government to better conditions, but little seems to have been accomplished.

Boats were used to some extent for the transport of tax goods but government policy favored transport by land. As it became increasingly difficult to handle this transport by land, boats came to carry a greater and greater part of the tax rice, as was true centuries later under the Tokugawa shogunate. Vehicles for the transport of taxes seemed to have been used widely on the plains of China in T'ang time, but in Japan their use came late and was exceedingly limited, chiefly because of the mountainous terrain. Only locally at Ōtsu, Yamazaki, and about Kyōto is there record of their employment. As time went on increasingly heavy taxes led to the impoverishment of the people. The official classes became more and more corrupt. The people, tax goods, and the road system were exploited by them, all of which led to a decline in tribute and finally to the decline of Imperial power and the decay of all national institutions, including the road.

Another great body of men who travelled the roads were the corvee levies drawn from the provinces to work in Kyōto. These men too had to provide for their own food and shelter and their lot was as difficult as was that of the tax bearers.

It seems reasonable to believe that traders, pilgrims, priests, and common folk in general bent upon various tasks moved over the roads in even greater numbers than did official travellers. None of these people, of course, could demand the facilities of the post stations. Strangers were feared and despised by the local villagers so that the traveller had to carry his own food and provide his own shelter. Hunger and sickness were often his companions. Even in the most prosperous eras between Taika and Engi conditions were hardly better. Frequent are references to the hardship of travel. None perhaps are more vivid than the following:

> Now that I journey, grass for pillow,
> They serve rice on the *shii* leaves,
> Rice they would put in a bowl,
> Were I at home![35]

Barriers, although a thing apart from the post system, seem always to have been an integral part of the road system of Old Japan. They have changed in location, in number, and in function with political and demographic changes through the centuries, but remained to impede the free flow of communication over the roads. Built at strategic points upon the great highways, they were first designed for the defense of the capital. Later they were employed as toll-gates as well. In this early period, there were three great barriers—the Sankan. The original Sankan, from their distribution, must have been built during that brief and uncertain period when the capital was at Ōtsu. As located they would have been of little value in the defense of any other site. The three original Sankan included:

1. Fuwa-no-seki, east of Lake Biwa, near the border of Ōmi and Mino provinces. It commanded the Tōsandō and seems to have been first established in 673 A.D.

---

[35] *The Manyōshū*, No. 142. This poem is credited to Prince Arima and is believed to have been written on his fateful journey to the hot-springs of Muro in the province of Kii. The *shii* is described as the *castanopsis cuspidata*, an evergreen tree with thick oblong leaves. *The Manyōshū: One Thousand Poems, selected and translated from the Japanese*, Tōkyō, 1940, p. 9 and note.

2. Arachi-no-seki, north of Lake Biwa, near the border of Ōmi and Echizen provinces, commanded the Hokurokudō. Later the Arachi Barrier was abolished and the Ōsaka-no-seki became one of the Sankan.

3. Suzuka-no-seki in the Suzuka horst east and south of Lake Biwa on the Ōmi and Ise provincial borders, commanded the Tōkaidō.

In 789 A.D. the Sankan were abolished, probably because they had been located so as to guard Ōmi province and were of little value to the capitals which had their sites in Yamato and Yamashiro provinces.

The Imperial edict of Enryaku 8 (789) contains, in addition to the order of abolition, two illuminating statements. One reads that "the purpose of the barriers is for defense against traitors (enemies)." The barriers of the early period were essentially military institutions. The second statement recognizes the bad features of the barrier system in that "for government and private traffic the barriers cause delay, hinder business and inconvenience people." By this edict the barriers were abolished but with the death of the Emperor Kammu, the barriers were again fortified (Daidō 1–806 A.D.).

As late as 940 A.D., we read of guards from the east and west being established heavily at the Sankan during the rebellion of Taira Masakado. The original purpose of the three great barriers was the defense of the capital. The barriers were immediately closed and the guard strengthened when rebellion threatened or broke out and when an Emperor died.

Secondary barriers included:

(1) Ashigara-no-seki on the Tōkaidō at Ashigara Pass in the mountains of Sagami Province.

(2) Koromogawa-no-seki on the branch road connecting Akita castle with the Tōsandō in Rikuchū Province in Eastern Ōu.

(3) Ōishi-no-seki on the Seta River, south of Seta Bridge in southern Ōmi Province. It was established in 857 A.D.

(4) Ōsaka-no-seki on the Tōkaidō between Kyōto and Seta Bridge. This barrier was abolished in 795 A.D. but was reopened in 857.

(5) Ryūge-no-seki, also established in 857 A.D., at the border of Ōmi and Yamashiro Provinces.

(6) Tatsuta-no-seki, first established in 679 A.D., commanded the pass of the Yamato River as it flowed out of Yamato Province toward the sea.

As time went on the barriers became more and more restrictive. They added still another and often serious burden to free circulation, as the following poem so eloquently portrays:

> If it were not for the barrier
> I would perhaps return
> And making a pillow of my wife's arms
> I'd be able to sleep.[36]

As has been previously noted, at the time of the *Engishiki* the peak of the post road system had been passed. The power of the central government was on the decline and with it the national road system and its facilities. Several disintegrating forces were at work. The great powers given the *kuni* and *kōri* governors over the institutions of the road within their territories, unlike the T'ang prototype, led to ever increasing abuses. Greedy governors exploited and openly robbed the people of the post villages. Many individuals ran away and even whole villages migrated. The coffers of the central government could no longer subsidize the post people and they were compelled to turn to other occupations. With the decline of central authority, robbers increased in numbers and courage. They robbed rich and poor, governors and post stations, and kidnapped messengers and merchants. The robbers of Tōsan and Tōkai were particularly feared as were the pirates of Nankai and Seinan. It is suggestive that one whole book of the *Konjaku-monogatari* is devoted to robbers and robbery. People more and more hated to travel and messengers became less frequent on the roads. The increase of robbers stimulated the rise of a new military class. "One who wishes to be a man, must carry swords," the saying went. This, in turn, further weakened the entire national structure.

Superstition was on the increase. The horoscope, rather than the Imperial edict, came to control the pattern of travel. Taboos on defilement came to have an ever stronger hold on the people. Travellers who became sick on the road were left to die. Death defiled the area of its occurrence. Even the preparing of food by travellers called for complex rituals of purification.

As the old structure fell into decay, new institutions developed. However, in spite of danger and difficulty, circulation by road remained necessary. The post houses which for three centuries had been so large a part of the machinery of government and such prominent landscape features in

---

[36] *Manyōshū*, No. 1036.

the provinces did not all disappear. The post head became a hereditary position and the post house a private, commercial venture. The post head often became a powerful local personage. In some places, the post station became a kind of barrier and existed for the exploitation of travellers. In most cases it became a *shukueki*, post inn, where accommodations and entertainment were offered for profit. Prostitution, which had become established by the end of early Heian time, flourished at important traffic centers, but was just one way in which the post heads sought to profit from the traveller.

The post messenger function largely gravitated to the provincial governors who used their own horses and messengers to do the essential business of government.

With the establishment of the bakufu government at Kamakura by Minamoto-no-Yoritomo in 1185 came a new orientation of the national road pattern. Kamakura developed rapidly into a great city and became the national center of government and administration. Kyōto, of course, remained the Imperial home and chief culture center and so the great road of the nation became the Tōkaidō. This shift in importance from the Dazaifudō to the Tōkaidō expressed both new political and demographic loci. To the present day, the great highway of Japan connects Kinai and the south with Kwantō and the north.

The early Kamakura government adopted a progressive road policy. Passes were opened in several directions around the city and roads were extended to all regions. New regulations were promulgated for a station-road system.

It was the Tōkaidō, of course, to which the greatest attention was paid. Between Kyōto and Kamakura 62 station-inns were to be established. The names of these stations and the distances between them are known.[37]

The Tōkaidō, as of Kamakura time, ran through Mino rather than northern Ise as did the earlier Heian and later Tokugawa roads. It was something over 120 *ri* in total length and had 62 station-inns between Kyōto and Kamakura, in contrast to the 126 *ri* and 53 stations between Kyōto and Edo in Tokugawa time. Many of the stations of the Kamakura road later became post towns on the Tokugawa Tōkaidō and some have continued to become thriving towns of modern Japan. Such are Odawara,

---

[37] *Jitsugyōki* in *Dainihon Shiryō*, Book 6, Sec. 2.

Yui, Kambara, and Hiratsuka. Others were ancient, as well as modern, shrine or temple towns such as Atsuta (Miya) and Mishima. The actual development of stations and post inns fell far short of the original plan.

Yoritomo made frequent trips to Kyōto accompanied by many retainers. On such occasions temporary shelters were built at convenient places along the Tōkaidō, and food was sent ahead of the party to these points. There were also permanent buildings in a few places. High officials could have temporary shelters erected for them and could command transport for food and other conveniences. Other officials, such as provincial governors and village heads, usually planned to stay at private homes along the route. Priests could generally find shelter in temples. But the great mass of travellers were little better provided for than in preceding periods. The sky was often their only roof and they carried their own food or ran the danger of starvation. If this was true of the Tōkaidō, it is not difficult to imagine conditions on the less important roads. "At each nightly stop, whenever I quit travelling, I made a pillow of rugs and rested my traveller's eyes," wrote one traveller.[38]

Religion, in the middle ages of Japan, became a force of great significance. Many were the pilgrims to the great shrines and temples. Particularly popular became the great Kumano shrines—Kumano-gongen or san-zan. Here came not only emperors and lords, warriors and priests, but also the common people flocked here in great numbers. The great families came to have their own inns (*shukubō*) at these shrines but how the common people fared is not so clear. In the far north, the sacred mountains of Dewa also attracted their pilgrims. It would seem then that a characteristic feature of the Kamakura period was the travel of great numbers of pious people to the most distant provinces of the empire.

Robbers, the blight of the later Heian period, did not completely disappear, even in the strongest days of the Kamakura government. As this government, too, began to decline, highwaymen became so common that to travel even by day became a high adventure. Even government messengers and official parties were not immune. As a result, the use of the roads declined.

The Muromachi period, insofar as the road was concerned, was in many respects a continuation of the preceding period. It was a time of weak cen-

---

[38] *Kaidōki* in Ōnishi, *op. cit.*, p. 24.

tral government and of strong and turbulent local lords. During the later Kamakura period barriers had increased at an alarming rate. Their primary purpose was the collecting of tolls and otherwise exploiting travellers and transport. The Emperor Godaigo attempted to abolish them, calling attention to their paralyzing effects. Their number and abuses continued to increase, however, and they reached their maximum as the complete disruption of central government took place. Each feudal lord maintained barriers along the frontiers of his territories. This was partly for the collection of tolls and the control of trade, but primarily it became a means of apprehending the spies sent by other feudal lords and the stoppage of invasion. The condition of the roads varied greatly from place to place.

The stronger feudal lords who did not fear invasion improved the roads within their territories and some even attempted to facilitate communication beyond their frontiers. Others destroyed bridges and placed other obstacles in the way of free circulation as a means of defense. The road system of each province was oriented upon the castle of its lord, so that many independent road systems existed. The major consideration of all road development was to make easy the assembly and movement of troops. It is impossible to generalize upon the facilities of the road as conditions varied so widely from province to province. In some areas, inns developed and an efficient post system was maintained. In others, there was nearly complete retrogression. The temples seem to have expanded their accommodations for guest travellers. Inns for merchants came into being at several places.

The period between the final collapse of the Ashikaga Shogunate in 1573 and the establishment of the Tokugawa government in 1603 was far more important to the development of the great road system of the seventeenth, eighteenth, and nineteenth centuries than is generally believed. The end of the sixteenth century saw the unification of the nation and the pattern of a new road system established. The long fears of civil war and general anarchy preceding had led to the complete disintegration of anything like a national road system. The road beds, over wide areas, had long gone unrepaired. Many had become mere trails. One-time mountain roads had disappeared. Bridges had long since collapsed and been washed away. Travel was so dangerous and so many obstacles to free circulation had grown up that communication, except within the provinces, had reached the lowest point in many centuries.

In addition, the country was ready for change. Several forces had contributed toward this end. The decline of Kyōto had caused many of the court and church to migrate to the provinces. Social stratification had largely broken down. The influence of Europe was deeply felt. There was general dissatisfaction with the abuses of the existing system.

When Oda Nobunaga established his castle at Azuchi on the shore of Lake Biwa, he set about to create a unified road system in the territories he controlled, focusing upon this new political center. Quickly he saw that the innumerable barriers not only increased the cost of and generally retarded travel and transport, but also contributed to the sectionalism which he was attempting to destroy. He therefore ordered them to be abolished.[39] He ordered the repair and standardization of roads in the various provinces and supplemented the demand by the use of corvee labor from the agricultural classes. The great roads were to be $3\frac{1}{2}$ *ken* wide (20 ft. 9 in.) and the small ones 3 *ken* (17 ft. 9 in.). Excessively winding roads were to be straightened. Pontoon and other bridges were to be constructed and ferriage was to be made convenient. On both sides of the roads pines and willows were to be planted.[40] The old *ri* of 6 *chō* was abolished and the present *ri* of 36 *chō* was adopted. At each *ri* along the road mounds were to be built, as distance markers, and their tops planted with *enoki* (Chinese nettle tree). The beginnings of a messenger system was established. More was planned and much was actually accomplished.

Nobunaga did not succeed in conquering and unifying the entire country. The greater feudal lords still remained autonomous within their respective territories and maintained their own road systems.

What had been accomplished by Oda Nobunaga accrued to his successor, the remarkable Toyotomi Hideyoshi, who built his castle at Ōsaka and began the development of a national road system with Muromachi castle as its center. Hideyoshi always planned and executed in the grand manner. He ordered a complete land survey of the nation. He completely renovated the system of stations and at once placed them upon the long Hokurokudō. Between Ise and Sendai he established post horses and gradually extended the system northward to connect the Matsumae castle in Hokkaidō. In the course of carrying out the campaign against Korea, he

[39] *Nobunagaki*, Sec. 2. (Seki Yakusho Teishi no Koto.)
[40] *Nobunaga kōki*, book 8 in *Shiseki shūran* (1900), vol. XIX, p. 103.

ordered two swift messengers to be maintained at every *ri* all the way between Nagoya and Ōsaka.[41]

When Hideyoshi died, much was still to be done toward establishing an effective national system of communications, but much had been accomplished in that short period of three decades. Many of the features which characterized the brilliant road system of the Tokugawa period were inaugurated in the Azuchi-Momoyama period. Such was the planting of pines on either side of the road; the *ichirizuka* or mounds planted with Chinese nettles at every *ri* along the roads; the renovation of the station system, including the placing of horses and messengers; and, more important, the breaking down of the many district road systems each centered upon the local castle. As the completion of national unification was left to Tokugawa Ieyasu, so too was the completion and perfection of a national post road system.

With the Tokugawa shogunate came the flowering of Japan's post road system. Ieyasu saw clearly that if his regime were to successfully control the territories of the great feudal lords; if peace and security were to be maintained; and if the nation was to prosper, good communications must be maintained between the center and the most distant and isolated regions. Shortly after the Tokugawa supremacy was insured by the battle of Sekigahara, orders were issued that post horses be established at every station upon the great road—the Tōkaidō. When Edo was determined as the capital, plans were laid for a national road pattern centering upon that city. In the *Buke-Hattō* [Samurai Regulations] of 1635 two significant articles are recorded. Article 15 states that "Roads, post horses, boats and bridges shall be freely used by the people without interruption." Article 169 forbade private barriers on the road or the detention of vessels at ports.

The core of the Tokugawa road system was based upon the Go-Kaidō, or "Five Great Roads." These roads, like the great Roman roads which began at the Forum, all converged upon Nihonbashi, "The Bridge of Japan," in the center of Edo. The Go-Kaidō were as follows:[42]

---

[41] *Taikōki*, book 13 in *Shiseki shūran* (1900), vol. VI, p. 302.

[42] At times during the Tokugawa period, the Tōkaidō was regarded as extending beyond Kyōto to Ōsaka. As such four more stations must be added. Some contend that the Ōshū-kaidō began at Utsunomiya and extended only to Fumise. Thus it would have but 10 stations and its length would be but 57 miles.

I. *Tōkaidō*—Edo to Kyōto—53 stations—310 miles in length
II. *Nakasendō*—Edo to Kyōto—67 stations—324 miles in length
III. *Nikkō-kaidō* [dōchū]—Edo to Nikkō—17 stations—89 miles in length
IV. *Ōshū-kaidō* [dōchū]—Edo to Aomori—87 stations—465 miles in length
V. *Kōshu-kaidō* [dōchū]—Edo to Shimosuwa—44 stations—132 miles in length

In addition to the five great roads there were a number of secondary roads which were sometimes called *Waki-kaidō* or Branch Roads. Among the more important ones were the Minoji, Sayaji, Iseji, Mitoji, Nagasakiji, Hokkokuji, Sadoji, Sanindō, Sanyōdō and the roads of Shikoku. Each of these Waki-kaidō joined one or more of the main highways and served an otherwise isolated district. They were, in fact, an integral part of the central road system. There were also unofficial roads which the Japanese like to refer to as "secret" roads. They were of course known to the government and apparently tolerated. Perhaps the most famous of these avoided the ferry trip, on the Tōkaidō, between Miya [Atsuta] and Kuwana—the Shichiri-no-watashi. Many feared this seven *ri* or twenty hours of rough water as well as the uncertainty of connections. Such people went around by land or one of the two Sayaji. The Imagire-no-watashi, between Maisaka and Arai, across the neck of Lake Hamana, was another ferry trip on the Tōkaidō. This voyage of one *ri* was particularly distasteful to women travellers as the water was usually choppy. There grew up an unofficial road, known as the Hime-kaidō or Princess Highway, around the north shore of the lake.

There developed, as well, unlawful routes which attempted to avoid the barriers on the main highways. Travel, on these routes, was strictly illegal and punishable. The Hime-kaidō was, in part, of this type in order to avoid the barrier at Arai, but the government soon established a secondary barrier at Kiga.

There were also two special roads leading to the Tōshōgū Mausoleum. One, the Nikkō-onari-kaidō, served the Shōgun when he visited the mausoleum of his illustrious ancestor. The other, the Reiheishi-kaidō served the Imperial envoys, bearing presents at the time of the great April festival at Tōshōgū. The former ran parallel to and in part utilized the Nikkō-kaidō, while the latter cut across from Takasaki, on the Nakasendō, to Nikkō.

All distances in the Empire were computed from Nihonbashi. At every *ri*, ichirizuka or mounds of earth which acted as milestones, were built.

Distances everywhere on the road became official. By these markers, wages and hire for men and horses were determined. As early as 1604, officials were sent out upon the great roads to supervise their building. By regulation they were to be five *ken* square.[43] Upon this square, earth was piled and Chinese nettle trees were planted. This was obviously an idea borrowed from China where the custom dates back to at least T'ang time. A few of these markers are still preserved in Japan, but most of them disappeared in the Meiji period.

On either side of the road, evergreen trees were planted. These not only added to the beauty of the road and provided shade for the traveller, but also established the width of the road. Red or black pine or cryptomeria were used according to the soil condition of the locality. An earthen ridge, about four feet high and three feet at the top[44] was piled upon their roots, reminiscent of China's "low golden walls planted with green pine trees."[45] The use of evergreens in the Tokugawa period stands in marked contrast to the use of fruit trees in Tempyō time. The providing thus of food for travellers was no longer necessary.

The width of first class roads was regulated at six *ken* [35.8 ft.] and second class roads at 3 *ken* [17.9 ft.]. On either side of the first class roads strips of land 20 *ken* [119.3 ft.] were held by the government for the support of the road. On second class roads these strips were to be 10 *ken* [59.6 ft.]. Whether roads of these widths were ever actually established is subject to question. In 1792, it was recorded that most of the roads had lost width through the pressing in of paddy and dry fields.[46] It is probable too, that where fire destroyed houses bordering the road they were rebuilt a little farther forward. The bordering strips long ago were absorbed by the peasant if they ever actually existed. The centuries old cryptomeria and pine furnish undeniable proof that the roads, at least for a very long time, have been much narrower than the regulations provided. Between the bordering trees, distances today range between 15 and 21 feet on the lower land and in many places in the mountain country are but 9 and 10

---

[43] *Tōdaiki* in Ōnishi, *op. cit.*, p. 40.
[44] Average field measurements by writer.
[45] *Shih Chi, op. cit.*
[46] Hayashi, Shihei, *Kaikoku Heidan*, book 2.

feet. Near the castle towns, one-time centers of authority, the roads aver-age wider than at places more distant.[47]

The post station was by this time an ancient institution in Japan, hav-ing persisted in one form or another at least in some points of the country since Tempyō time. It was conceived in this period, however, in a much more complex form: a small beginning had been made, as has been noted, by Hideyoshi. In 1601, Tokugawa Ieyasu ordered 36 post horses at each station on the Tōkaidō. For the support of each horse 30 *tsubo* of land were allocated. Later, the post stations were exempted from the land tax, rice allowances were given and other privileges extended.

As the system developed, the following regulations became established: at each station on the Tōkaidō, there were to be 100 horses and 100 men; on the Nakasendō, 50 horses and 50 men, and on the Ōshū-, Kōshū- and Nikkō-kaidō 25 horses and 25 men. Again it is not clear as to whether these numbers were exactly retained at any one time. Throughout much of the Tokugawa period Seki, on the Tōkaidō, had 150 horses and 150 porters as the problem of crossing the Suzuka mountains was a difficult one. The Hakone station had 100 horses and no porters, as pasture was available but there was little arable land. There were neither horses nor porters at Arai or Misaka. To cross the river Ōi 700 porters were required at both of the stations on its banks.[48]

As demands upon the post stations increased, a system known as *su-kegō* came into being. By this means the men and horses of nearby villages were organized and compelled to assist the post stations on demand. As time went on, this system spread throughout the country and became cor-rupt. More and more came to be demanded of the peasants and their horses. The burden became so great that it led to general impoverishment of the peasants over wide areas.

At first, express messenger service was confined to government needs, but gradually private organizations developed and finally a network of private messenger routes extended over the entire country.

The post stations were planned at the traditional intervals of about 10 miles. Again the same forces were at work to establish a less regular distri-

---

[47] More than 200 measurements were made by the writer on the Tōkaidō, Nakasendō, Nikkō-kaidō and Hokurokudō.

[48] Hall, R. B., "Tōkaidō; Road and Region," op. cit., p. 366.

bution. Grouping at close intervals occurred where great rivers or rugged mountain passes had to be traversed. Exact locations were, in most places, predetermined by existing settlements, new post towns became necessary as the older ones, nearby, failed to accommodate the increasing traffic. The over-all average distance between posts on the Go-kaidō came to be about 4.83 miles.

One of the most colorful and distinguishing features of this period was the development of inns at the post towns. These were of various sorts and provided shelter for all who could pay for it. The best were known as *honjin* and were reserved for the daimyō or Great Lords. These were large and extremely fine. They stand today as landmarks and objects of admiration in many ex-post towns.

There were also *waki-honjin* or inns exclusively for samurai. There were special inns at some stations for merchants; at others, for heads of the church. There were also in each station-town, many inns—large and small —for commoners.

In the Tokugawa period, then, three important improvements over any preceding period were made. Travellers could now find food and shelter at every station; could hire horses and porters if needed; and private messages could be sent over the post roads to all parts of the Empire.

There was also far more travel upon the roads in this period than there had ever been before. Kaempfer, who travelled upon the Tōkaidō in 1691, said of it, "upon some days [it is] more crowded than the publick streets in any the most populous town of Europe."[49]

Perhaps nothing more clearly indicated the public rôle of the Tokugawa road system than the flood of maps and other illustrative materials which appeared. The maps were excellent for their time and were of several sorts. They carried a vast amount of information for the common traveller. The rates for porterage and horses, the laws of the barriers and stations, approved inns and tea houses, distances, historical sites, temples and shrines, special produce and foods of the locale, scenic views, troublesome grades and streams, the origins of place-names, names and incomes of feudal lords, dates of local festivals, and unusual natural phenomena were among the many things shown. The color prints and picture books of par-

---

[49] Kaempfer, Engelbert, *The History of Japan, 1690–1692*, translated by J. G. Scheuchzer, Glasgow, 1906, vol. 2, p. 330.

ticular roads and their stations are among the commonest prizes of the contemporary art collector. There was also a great literature of the road, of which perhaps Ikku Jippensha's *Hizakurige* was, and still is, the most popular.

In addition to the countless people who travelled upon private business, there was that unique and important feature of the Tokugawa era known as Sankin-kōdai. It was required that each feudal lord visit Edo every other year. These trips from the provincial castle to Edo and return consumed a major part of each feudal lord's income and greatly decreased his ability to cause trouble. When on these trips each lord attempted to make the best possible show of his power and rank. He was limited by law as to the number of retainers that could accompany him, but this law seems generally to have been circumvented. The greater lords were accompanied by thousands of retainers and their processions often took hours to pass a single point. These parties placed a heavy demand upon the post stations. By regulation, each *daimyō* with an income of 100,000 koku of rice or more could use 50 horses and 50 men at each station on the Tōkaidō for a two day period and 25 horses and 25 men on the Nakasendō for a three day period—all at no cost. This meant that one-half of all the porters and horses were employed for a two or three day period each time a great lord passed by. The different roads suffered different demands depending upon the areas they served and the regulations passed by the government in determining the routes of travel. In 1822, the following allocation of Sankin-kōdai processions was made:[50]

Tōkaidō	146
Nakasendō	29
Ōshū-dōchū	37
Nikkō-dōchū	4
Kōshū-dōchū	3
Mitoji	23

The Tōkaidō in this regard, as in all others, was by far the most important and heavily travelled road. It is for this reason that its accommodations were the best developed.

So much has been written of the merits of the Tokugawa road system, that the brief description preceding will suffice. More perhaps should be

[50] *Dōchū tome-gaki* in Eitarō Tamura, *Kinsei Nihon kōtsūshi* (Tokyo, 1935), pp. 284–7.

said as to the difficulties of travel in this period. This was still a military age and strategic considerations often outweighed all others. Every road had its bridgeless rivers. It is probably true that the engineering knowledge of the time would have made it most difficult to build and particularly to maintain bridges over some of the larger and more turbulent rivers. It is also true, however, that the government regarded these unbridged rivers as natural defense barriers as well. It was not uncommon for all travel to be tied up on the bank of a river in flood for days at a time. Also, in spite of the highly centralized and efficient government robbers continued to prey upon the traveller. This condition differed as to place and time. Robbery was more common in the mountain country and where the road passed through woodland. It became more common too toward the end of the era, as the government showed signs of disintegration. There were also difficulties to be faced in the post towns. The *samurai* despised the common man and often abused him. The inns exploited the traveller, as well. This practice became so wide-spread that private travellers' associations grew up which hung their signs in front of inns which could meet certain specifications.

The greatest of all deterrents to travel was the barrier. As has been noted the early barriers were established as forts to protect the capital from attack. In the Kamakura and Muromachi periods the barriers increased greatly in numbers and their main object was to levy toll. In the Tokugawa period the barriers became glorified police stations. "Iri-deppō ni de ōnna" [rifles coming in and women going out] pretty well described their chief functions. The feudal lords, in addition to their compulsory pilgrimage to Edo, had also to leave their women at the capital as hostages. To see that these hostages did not escape home and that no weapons were brought into Edo, which might serve to arm a rebellion, were the primary duties of the barriers. All who passed through were compelled to carry official passes. All persons and baggage were inspected. The gates of the barrier were open only during the daylight hours.

The important barriers guarded the approaches of Edo. On the Tōkaidō, the mountain barrier of Hakone and the water barrier at Arai were the most famous and annoying. On the Nakesendō, there were Usui and Fukushima; on the Ōshū-dōchū, Kurihashi; on the Kōshū-dōchū, Kobotoke; and on the Mitoji, Kanamachi.

It was this extensive and well organized road system which served as the

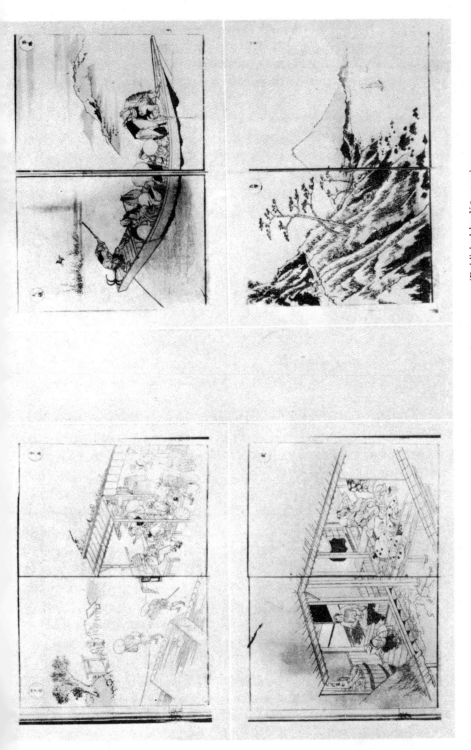

Four scenes from the "Picture Book," *Gojūsan Tsugi Dōchū Gafu*, by Hokusai, Nagoya, 1835. (Published by Kōgetsu.)

A.) The junction of the Tōkaidō and the Iseji at Yokkaichi. A stone road marker is seen to the left by the torii, while to the right is a wayside teahouse.

B.) A river ferry between Hiratsuka and Ōiso.

C.) A wayside inn after a day's travel.

D.) The Tōkaidō climbs over Satta Pass, between Okitsu and Yui. Mount Fuji rises in the background.

Four color-prints selected from different sets of the *Gojūsan Tsugi* by Hiroshige.

A.) An *ichirizuka* or earthen mound marking one *ri* of distance. On the road is a daimyō procession. The site is the Tōkaidō post station of Seki.

B.) The bridge at Okazaki. The castle is seen at the right rear.

C.) Crossing the River Ōi, the most hazardous undertaking on the Tōkaidō.

D.) The Tōkaidō winds over the hills near Shirasuka.

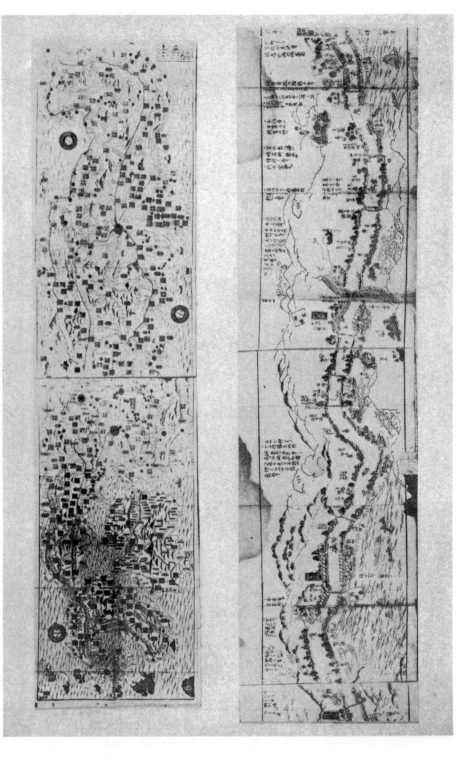

Two types of traveller's maps which were in common use.

A.) *Dai Nihon Saiken Dōchū Zukan* (dates about 1840). A cheap and popular map which ran into many editions. It carries a great variety of information useful to the traveller. It was often referred to as the "Pilgrim's Map." (7 × reduction.)

B.) The Tōkaidō between Shinagawa and Hodogaya. This is a section of a Japanese style, folding, traverse map issued by Busuke Tsuchiya about 1850. Many points of general interest are indicated, as well as a variety of information concerning rates, distances, laws, products, etc.

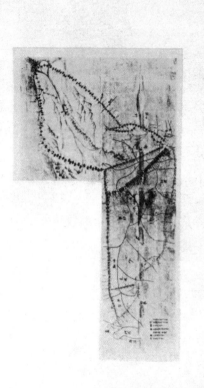
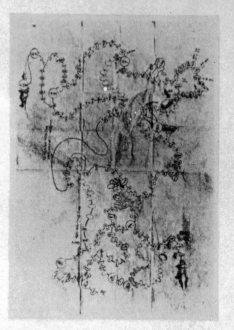
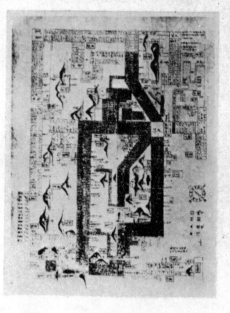

Three examples of map-like charts sold, in later Tokugawa time, for the guidance of travellers.

A.) A graphic plan of the *Go-kaidō*, showing post stations and generalized land features.

B.) A so-called "Box Map" of the *Go-kaidō*, with post station names arranged in order and sketches of famous mountains.

pattern for the transportation network of the modern era. The Meiji Restoration marked the end of a cultural development which was largely indigenous and confined to Eastern Asia. Particularly, the material culture forms of the Occident came to displace the things of past ages. Travel by foot and by horse could no longer suffice a nation bent upon becoming a world power. Railroads were an obvious necessity. The trajectories of the old roads, except in detail, proved to be the best for the new. Beginning with the Tōkaidō, there developed an efficient and far-flung system of railways, laid upon and even retaining the names of the old post roads. The old post towns responded to the new economic opportunity and account for most of Japan's modern cities. In a most interesting way, they retain the flavor of their past days. The household industries, which grew up to serve the travellers of the feudal road, have, in many places, developed into great factory industries.

Following the railways came the construction of motor roads. These have now been laid, over wide areas, immediately upon the courses of the ancient post roads and contribute to the growth and well-being of the modern towns and cities, which were the post stations of old.

Japan has become a major world power. Its transportation facilities, today, rank among the best of the world. Its towns and cities have grown at an amazing rate and include some of the world's greatest metropoli. Its population has increased from 30 to 75 million since the Restoration. The development of manufacturing industries make Japan unique in the Far East and place it among the leading industrial and commercial nations of the earth. Yet, with all this remarkable change, the fundamental distributional patterns of things Japanese—population, cities, circulation, industries, etc.—show a surprising continuity with the past. Their major lineaments, everywhere, are geared to the pattern of the ancient post roads.

ON MILTON'S CONCEPTION OF POETRY

WILLIAM ALLAN NEILSON
President Emeritus of Smith College

WRITERS on poetics have now ceased to quote the phrase "simple, sensuous, and passionate" as Milton's definition of poetry. A glance at its original context has shown them, what indeed was evident on the face of it, that here was no attempt at a definition at all, but merely a casual remark that, in contrast with logic and rhetoric, poetry is "less subtle and fine, but more simple, sensuous, and passionate." Taken as it was meant, the saying is significant enough, and affords a substantial contribution to the reconstruction of Milton's theory of his art. It assures us that, in spite of the amount of argument and theological disquisition in his epics, he was aware that the method of poetry was not logical demonstration, but that of stating truth simply and directly, of making it vivid through the medium of the senses, and of carrying it "alive into the heart by passion."

Important and sound observations these; but we must look elsewhere for the passages where Milton comes nearest to the heart of the problem of the nature of poetry, and where he betrays what is peculiar in his individual conception of it. One of these is the much quoted sentence from the *Apology for Smectymnuus:* "He who would not be frustrate of his hope to write well hereafter in laudable things ought himself to be a true poem; that is, a composition and pattern of the best and honourablest things; not presuming to sing high praises of heroic men or famous cities, unless he have in himself the experience and practice of all that which is praiseworthy." Two points are to be noted here. First, the highest poetry is apparently conceived as didactic: the true poem is a composition and pattern of the best and honourablest things. Little emphasis need be added here, for critics of Milton, and especially of the epics, have borne hard on this element in his work. The poems themselves are explicit enough. In both *Paradise Lost* and *Paradise Regained,* the Muse invoked is the Holy Spirit; the purpose of the one is to "justify the ways of God to man," of the other, "to tell of deeds above heroic, though in secret done." The didacticism of the shorter poems is hardly less marked. *Lycidas* holds up an ideal to the degraded clergy of the day; *Comus* scourges the corrupt court of Charles I, and exalts Virtue; even *L'Allegro* and *Il Penseroso* may fairly be regarded as singling out the "best and honourablest things" in two contrasted temperaments. The early *Odes*, the *Sonnets*, and *Samson Agonistes* are further evidence to the same effect. Throughout, then, the intention to teach seems not to be denied.

The second point is no less significant: the true poems must be the outcome of a true life. Here is a precept which one shall search for in vain in treatises on poetics, yet its importance to Milton is as well proved as the persistence of his didacticism. No biography of a man of letters reveals more patently than his the conviction of a mission; none tells of a more sustained effort to live up to it. The temper of Milton may be uncongenial, the tone of his controversy may be offensive, but no one can fail to see that his career was dominated by his conscience. The characteristic thing, however, is Milton's insistence that these two points are inseparable. He was convinced that what a man is and what a man does go together. We shall see in a moment that the same trend of thought appears in his attitude towards form and substance in poetry, and it is perhaps not fanciful to see it again in the so-called Materialistic Pantheism of his *De Doctrina Christiana*, with its corollary, the denial of the distinction between soul and body.

The passage, however, which is most illuminating—and the discussion of which supplies whatever justification the present note may possess—deals with another aspect of the matter, the problem of the relation of poetic content to metrical form. It occurs in what seems at first reading a curiously isolated way in the famous apostrophe to light in the beginning of the third book of *Paradise Lost*. In spite of his blindness, Milton is saying, he continues writing poetry and seeks his inspiration in scriptural story, remembering for his encouragement others who shared his lot of darkness, Thamyris and Homer, Tiresias and Phineus. He proceeds:

> Then feed on thoughts that voluntary move
> Harmonious numbers; as the wakeful bird
> Sings darkling, and in shadiest covert hid
> Tunes her nocturnal note.

Then he resumes, without transition, the lament for his loss of sight:

> Thus with the year
> Seasons return, but not to me returns
> Day, or the sweet approach of ev'n or morn,—

and so on, in the familiar moving lines.

Here we have another side of the shield turned towards us. The content, the thoughts, of poetry are no longer described by allusions to Sion or the best and honourablest things, but by their fitness for rhythmical utterance. But to speak of "fitness" is to understate his case. The important word is "voluntary"—as if the thoughts were not only fit for harmonious numbers, but were such as by their nature compelled him who would make them articulate to give them metrical form, implying that in any other form they are not the same thoughts. In an undergraduate poem he had spoken of ideas seeking expression, under another and inferior figure.

> I have some naked thoughts that rove about,
> And loudly knock to have their passage out;
> And weary of their plan do only stay
> Till thou hast deckt them in thy best array,

he said, addressing his native language. This is merely the conventional conception of words as the garment of thought, more or less fitting, but essentially separable. In the lines in the third book he has gone beyond this view, and now conceives of a relation between context and form parallel to those already referred to between the poet and the poem, and the soul and the body. The substance of poetry in this view is no longer subject to analysis into content and form: a content capable of being set forth by several among a variety of forms; a form capable of being used for a variety of contents. Content and form are merely two sides of the same fabric. And he, the poet, singing in darkness, utters his thoughts in a melody as inevitable as that of the nightingale whose nocturnal note is also her soul and her suffering.

If this interpretation of the lines in question be correct, we have here a remarkable anticipation of modern criticism. The eighteenth century, from Addison to Johnson, continued to separate in the most mechanical fashion, content and form in the discussion of poetry, and clearly never thought of the element of rhythm as other than a mere added decoration. The romantic writers, such as Hazlitt, were less mechanical, and in their enthusiastic renderings of their impressions were much more apt to deal with the total imaginative effect of a poem. But in theoretical discussions down to our own day, and especially in such as deal with the watchword of "Art for Art's sake," the fallacy which Milton, at least for the moment, saw through has continued to vitiate much thinking and writing on aesthetic problems. For "Art's sake" has most often been taken to mean "form's sake," and has implied an antithesis to "content's sake" which Milton saw did not exist, and so has led to endless battles over a false issue. So little is Milton's implication yet to be assumed as a commonplace that it is not many years since an Oxford Professor of Poetry inaugurated his tenure of office by a luminous exposition of the very question here involved.

Two questions remain: how far are the two views implied by Milton, that in the *Apology for Smectymnuus* and that in the lines just discussed, capable of being brought into harmony? and how far did either influence his practice? The second of these has been in part answered in our recapitulation of the undeniably didactic tendency of his work as a whole. But a moment's reflection shows us that it is not the didactic intent, even when that was not sectarian, that has saved Milton as a poet. It is often said that Milton's poetry survives by sheer power of music, and such criticism of it as that of Professor Saintsbury seems to proceed on that assumption. This is nearer the truth than to say that it survives through its teaching, but it is not the truth. Milton's ideas on virtue or Providence or Melancholy were, like any other ideas, transmutable into poetry only when they underwent that as yet unanalyzed imaginative process which made them "voluntary move harmonious numbers." The great and vital qualities of his poetry are not to be found in his moral or theological ideas, nor in the music of his cadences taken apart from the sense of the words or of the situation. They lie in the inseparable union of these two, and appear only when these ideas occurred in his consciousness in a mode which refused any but their unique musical expression.

Most readers feel that the imaginative process just spoken was at times imperfectly completed, that in the epics there are passages of mere theological argument thrown into blank verse. Whatever theory one may hold of the importance of subject in art, most will agree that, even if all subjects are possible, some are more difficult of treatment than others. When we consider the nature of some of the themes which Milton's didactic tendencies thrust upon him, the wonder grows, not that the process was sometimes left incomplete, but that it was so often carried to a victorious close. A careful examination will, I believe, lead to the conclusion that Milton was vividly conscious of the necessity of raising his thoughts into the region of the imagination and letting them control the rhythmical expression; and if this is so, the vast importance of the view implied in our text becomes apparent.

As Milton leaves us without an answer to the question as to *why* things conceived in a certain way demand rhythmical expression, so he leaves us uncertain as to where he found the final justification of poetry. Here, as elsewhere, Puritanism pressed hard upon the artist. At times he seems to seek to defend his art on purely extraneous grounds; but the glory of God for which he wrought meant more to him than a theological justification of the ways of Providence. The sense of beauty worked mightily in him, and he served it with infinite pains, but the moral utilitarianism of the Puritan ideal deprived us of any explicit acknowledgment from his lips that poetry is an end in itself. That this view was implicit in part of his theory, as it certainly is in his practice, seems to me to be indicated in the lines we have discussed.

HISTORICAL PESSIMISM MONTESQUIEU'S

GILBERT CHINARD
Princeton University

IN an article published in the "Revue de Métaphysique et de Morale" (1916), and entitled *Le Déterminisme historique et l'Idéalisme social dans l'Esprit des Lois*," the late Professor Gustave Lanson has made a very brilliant effort to bring Montesquieu's philosophy of history in line with the prevailing tendencies of his time. Whether or not "la vraie pensée de Montesquieu unit la tradition au progrès," such was not the judgment of his friends and contemporaries. In fact, the publication of the *Esprit des Lois* brought great distress to the camp of the "philosophes." If not openly one of them, the "président" was at least an influential ally. There was in the new and monumental work much material they could use, a store of illustrations and quotations from which they could borrow; yet the essential principles and tendencies of the book were repugnant to the main tenets of the school. Thus they were placed in a most perplexing quandary. It was to their advantage to keep the public from suspecting that there was any rift in their doctrine; to raise a quarrel at a time when the unity of front was most important, would have been exceedingly dangerous and would have brought help and comfort to the enemy. It would have been particularly infelicitous when Montesquieu was vehemently attacked and denounced as a "Spinosist and a Deist" by the "ennemis des lumières." In the words of abbé de la Roche explaining the attitude of Helvétius and his friends: "When the work appeared, and they witnessed its prodigious success, without changing their opinions, they remained silent from a respect for the judgment of the public, and for the honor of their friend." In spite of this prudent reserve, they did not remain entirely silent; but the fact that their criticisms were scattered over a long period, some of them being published almost seventy years after the first printing of the *Esprit des Lois*, may explain why they have been generally overlooked by historians and political scientists. No attempt to retrace the "fortune" of Montesquieu's masterpiece can be undertaken here, but even a very brief survey of the misgivings entertained by Montesquieu's contemporaries will help considerably in defining his attitude towards the historical development of mankind.

In his edition of the works of Helvétius, published in 1796, abbé de la Roche has related how, before publishing his manuscript, Montesquieu submitted it to his friend with whom he had already discussed it at la Brède: "When he read this work, Helvétius, who loved the author as much as he loved truth, was alarmed at the danger to which the reputation of Montesquieu was about to be exposed. Both in person and by letter he repeatedly opposed those opinions which he considered most dangerous as they were about to be laid down as political maxims by one of the finest writers in France, in a work illuminated by genius, and inculcating many important truths."

Not trusting his own judgment Helvétius consulted Saurin, "the famous author of *Spartacus*." Both agreed that the publication of the book was most unadvisable, and they presented their objections to Montesquieu who, without heeding them, went on with the publication of the *Esprit des Lois*. After mature deliberation both Saurin and Helvétius decided not to give their observations to the public; they appeared long after the death of Montesquieu and Helvétius in the edition already mentioned and published by abbé de la Roche. No less significant was the reserve of d'Holbach. His *Politique naturelle, ou Discours sur les vrais Principes du Gouvernement* (2 vols., Londres (?), 1773) is nothing but a revision and an adaptation of the main chapters of the *Esprit des Lois*, with a strong "philosophical" and systematical coloring. Yet, Montesquieu is not openly criticized and is only mentioned once under the discreet appellation of "un illustre auteur." Voltaire himself waited until 1778 to give his fragmentary *Commentaire sur l'Esprit des Lois*. Condorcet's observations on the xxixth book of the *Esprit des Lois*, dated 1780, appeared for the first time in the English translation of Destutt de Tracy's *Commentary and Review of Montesquieu's Spirit of Laws*, published by Jefferson in Richmond, in 1811, while the French text was not made available until 1816.

Of the many objections raised by the "Philosophes," I shall consider only two and discuss in some detail only one which bears more particularly on the main trend of Montesquieu's political philosophy.

Condorcet was particularly shocked by "one of the most curious chapters of the work. It is one which obtained for Montesquieu the indulgence of all the prejudiced people, of all those who detest light, of all the protectors and participators in abuse." It is also one of the shortest chapters of the *Esprit des Lois*, and will be found in Book XXIX, Chap. XVIII. It is entitled: "On Ideas of Uniformity," and ends with this striking sentence: "When citizens follow the laws, of what consequence is it whether they follow the same laws?"

The criticism of Condorcet, written in the vein which later was to become characteristic of the Jacobins, is most illuminating:

As truth, reason, justice, the rights of man, the interests of property, of liberty, of security, are in all places the same, we cannot discover why all the provinces of a State, or even all the States, should not have the same civil and criminal laws and the same laws relative to commerce. A good law should be good for all men. A true proposition is true everywhere. Those laws which appear as if it were necessary that they should be different in different countries, or exacted on objects which should not be regulated by general laws, consist for the most part of commercial regulations, or are founded on prejudices and habits which should be extinguished; and one of the best means of doing so, is to cease from giving them the countenance of laws.

The second objection, even stronger, is contained in a letter of Helvétius to which I referred previously:

You may recollect that in our discussions at Brède, I admitted that they [the principles of your work] might apply to the actual state of mankind, but I concluded that a writer, anxious to serve mankind, ought rather to lay down just maxims for an improved order of things yet to arise, than to give force or consequence to those which are dangerous. . . . To employ philosophy in giving them consequence is to give human genius a retrograde motion, and to perpetuate those abuses which interest and bad faith are but too apt to uphold. The idea of perfectibility amuses our contemporaries, offends hypocrites and men in power; but it instructs our rising generations and is a light to posterity. If our offsprings shall possess common sense, I doubt whether they will accommodate themselves to our principles of government, or adopt in their constitutions, which without doubt will be better than ours, your complicated balances and intermediary powers.

This was undoubtedly the crux of the matter. The whole of the *Esprit des Lois* was out of tune with the doctrine of perfectibility and with the optimistic belief that the world had finally emerged from barbaric conditions and that, thanks to the enlightenment coming from the philosophers, its progress was assured and a return to the previous state of ignorance, obscurantism, disorder and oppression was impossible. It would have taken an obdurate optimist or, as the French sometimes say, a bleating optimist, to derive such a conclusion from a careful reading of any of the works of Montesquieu. No ascending curve in the march of mankind could be discerned there; it was rather like the swing of a pendulum always retracing the same curve and travelling in the same path, with periods of darkness following periods of prosperity, with a monotonous and almost fatal regularity.

Such a pessimistic view of history was not new in the philosophy of Montesquieu. He had expressed it very forcibly in his first famous work; it was essentially the burden of *Grandeur et Décadence des Romains*, and it reappeared in the most striking and almost dramatic manner in the *Esprit des Lois*. It is an ever recurrent *memento mori*, like a solemn dirge which gives a sort of melancholy grandeur to his style; it expresses a fundamental pessimism, the very negation of the spirit of progress, enlightenment and "idealistic will," by which most of his contemporaries were carried away.

In his *Lettres Persanes*, it appears in a digression generally passed over by his editors and critics, but which, in my opinion, offers an early and striking illustration of one of the most important and significant tenets of Montesquieu's political philosophy.

When Usbeck, after his first days in Paris, remembering the discussions he had with his friend Mirza, undertook to settle once for all the question whether "men were born to be virtuous," instead of entering into a long and abstract disquisition, he sent to his friend a "morceau d'histoire." This is the story, or rather the history of the Troglodytes.

The Troglodytes, as Montesquieu recalls at the very beginning, were described by ancient historians as being more like beasts than men. The people whose history he is going to relate have very little in common with the tribes found in Herodotus or Pomponius Mela. "They had not fur like bears; they did not hiss like serpents; they had two eyes; but they were so malicious, so brutish that they lacked all notion of justice and equity."

Thus we do not start with the state of nature—a state in which Montesquieu was never interested, and in the existence of which he did not believe. The Troglodytes were ruled over by a king of foreign origin, who treated them severely in order to correct the wickedness of their nature. They conspired against him, slew him and exterminated his line. Then some sort of a republic was established and the people elected magistrates. But this system was of short duration and the magistrates were killed as the tyrant had been. Complete anarchy followed resulting in the almost entire destruction of the people. Only two families survived, and from them sprang a pastoral society in which the father of the family ruled, or rather in which Virtue ruled: all the citizens being perfect, society itself was perfect. But this perfection could not last. Virtue was too heavy a yoke, individual responsibility became unbearable and the Troglodytes refused to continue to assume this burden. They decided again to elect a ruler who realized that an end had come to the reign of Virtue, and that although the Troglodytes might not become criminal at once, they were bound to degenerate and decay.

This, as one can see, even from this very brief analysis, is almost a complete circle. It is at any rate a semi-historical demonstration of the pessimistic contention that it is impossible for a people ever to enjoy for any considerable length of time any form of government. The essential character of the society of the Troglodytes is mutability and instability. That they should rid themselves of tyranny is only natural; that they should be unable at first to accept magistrates and a republican state for which they were not prepared is also explainable; but when, through adversity, they have finally reached a condition which procures to the individual the maximum of happiness they are not satisfied; they want to exchange the burden of liberty for the rule of a king who will think for them and will protect their interests.

Even with the election of a good king, however, the Troglodytes did not reach real stability in their institutions. Montesquieu had planned to add a last episode to their history and to make them go through another experiment. The manuscript found in the papers of La Brède has been published by Mr. Henri Barckhausen in his edition of *Lettres Persanes* (Paris, 1913). In this last part, we learn that after the death of their first king, the Troglodytes elected, very wisely again, another king, but soon after his election they went to him and pointed out that it was desirable to establish among them "commerce and the arts." In his wisdom, the king foretold the direst calamities. As long as the use of money remains unknown, there can be no artificial distinction or superiority among the citizens; the only superiority which can be recognized comes solely from superior justice or superior virtue. As soon as riches are introduced, on the contrary, the king in order to maintain his superiority and prestige must become richer than the other inhabitants of the country, and these riches can only be obtained through taxation. In an ideal condition, with citizens eminently virtuous, the harm could be reduced to a minimum; but all chances are that if the Troglodytes are not virtuous, they will become "one of the most miserable peoples on earth."

Now the circle is completed. We can easily foresee that the Troglodytes will soon be oppressed by their ruler, and will find themselves again in a condition analogous to that of their ancestors at the beginning of their history, as recorded by Usbeck. Neither essentially good nor bad, they are unable to attain stability either in their customs or in their institutions. Already Montesquieu has reached the conclusion that all forms of government are bound to change and degenerate, for change is rarely for the better. It is not seen anywhere that a nation has ever been able to maintain itself after reaching the height of its development; it necessarily goes down the other side of the hill and there is no escape.

This appears even more clearly in the 136th letter of the *Lettres Persanes*. Rica, visiting the library of a European scholar, passes in review works on the history of Western peoples. What a sad and desolating picture! First the decay of the formidable Roman Empire, which itself had been constituted from the debris of so many monarchies and formed new monarchies when it crumpled; these in their turn, were destroyed by barbarians, or rather by men who were still free but were soon to become real barbarians, "when they lost their sweet liberty so consonant with reason, humanity and nature."

Then came the German Empire, a mere shadow of the Roman Empire. With the historians of France, we see the power of kings taking shape, the country twice almost annihilated, then reappearing only to languish through many ages, and slowly gathering strength to achieve the final stage of its development. Spain: a nation issuing from the mountains; the Mahometan princes overcome as rapidly as they had conquered; many kingdoms joined in one vast monarchy until, overborne by its own greatness and its fictitious wealth, it lost its strength and its reputation, preserving only its original pride. Italy: a nation once mistress of the world, now a common slave; her princes weak and disunited, with no other attribute of sovereignty than an ineffectual policy. Poland, which makes such a bad use of its liberty and of its right to elect its kings, that it would seem to be its intention to console its neighbors which have neither the one nor the other. England itself, although prosperous, is far from being secure, for we see "the prince always tottering upon an immovable throne, a nation impatient but prudent in its rage and which, mistress of the sea, combines commerce with power."

Montesquieu would not have said that everything is always in a state of flux, for such an expression is too easy an explanation and an excuse for ignorance; but he would have certainly admitted that nothing in human institutions can remain stable and unmovable, that it is in the very nature of things that they are constantly modified, for such is the condition of life itself.

Whether these changes and modifications are dictated by some divine intervention, whether they happen by chance, or whether they follow certain rules, and particularly whether some definite causes can be found for them, is the problem which confronts the political historian. Such will be the subject of the next two studies of Montesquieu, *Grandeur et Décadence des Romains* and the *Esprit des Lois*.

It is hardly necessary to point out that a similar conclusion can be derived from Montesquieu's dissertation on the destiny of Rome. Starting with the picture of "a settlement no bigger than those seen in Crimea" in the eighteenth century, and just sufficient to hold the booty, the cattle and the crops of primitive tribes, Montesquieu follows first the growth of the city, then of the Empire until it became corrupted because of its very size, and gradually shrunk to the point that it finally consisted of the suburbs of Constantinople, "as the Rhine, which is only a rivulet when it goes into the Ocean."

Certainly some moral and political causes can be ascribed to the ascension and fall of Rome, and these reasons, not neglected by Montesquieu, are too well known to need restatement here. But even supposing that the Romans could have corrected all their abuses and retained their old patriotism and love of liberty, it is very doubtful whether they would have succeeded in preserving their country. The fall of Rome was the very consequence of its development, for "Free States do not last as long as the others, because reverses and successes almost always cause them to lose their liberty, while the reverses and successes of a State in which the people are subjected only strengthen their servitude."

Thus, again, it seems that there is no escape, and Montesquieu offers no remedy except a pious wish that a wise republic should enter into any venture susceptible of bringing either good or bad fortune, the only good fortune which might befall it being the perpetuation of its present condition. But this is more easily said than accomplished, for "it has always happened that good laws, which cause a small republic to become great, become burdensome when the republic has grown, because they are such that their natural effect is to make a great people, and not to govern it." (Chap. ix.)

Having done its work, having reached its complete development, Rome was bound to degenerate: "In a word, here is the history of Rome: "they conquered all the people because of their maxims; but when they had succeeded, their republic could no longer be maintained; they had to change their government, and maxims contrary to the previous ones used in their new government caused the collapse of their grandeur." This process seemed to Montesquieu so certain that he did not hesitate to assume the rôle of a political prophet and to predict that other nations would follow exactly the same course: "There is now in Europe a small republic of which nobody has heard, but which secretly and silently increases its strength every day. It is certain that if it ever reaches the development which its wisdom deserves, it will change its laws; and this will not be the work of a legislator but of corruption itself."

That the course of nations is determined by inherent conditions, some of them physical and others moral, but all ascertainable and susceptible of exact study, is the contention that Montesquieu undertook to support in the *Esprit des Lois*. Many treatises on government had been written before, but most, if not all of them, were descriptions of existing governments, or formulations of the conditions which should be embodied in an ideal form of government. For Montesquieu, however, the methods to be followed in the study of government do not differ greatly from the methods of natural history. Governments, in fact, are comparable to living organisms, which are determined by their antecedents, the climate in which they live, and the very laws of their nature or species. Pure specimens of a given species are very seldom found; the species itself may degenerate; certainly the individual has no permanency and must die after reaching a certain development and a certain age.

The most striking part of the *Esprit des Lois* in this respect will be found in Book VIII, "Of the Corruption of the Principles of the Three Governments." There, it clearly appears that even if a perfect form of a republic, monarchy or despotism could be established, any of these forms would be essentially unstable and its principles soon endangered by an almost unavoidable corruption.

This is not an a priori axiom, but a conclusion derived from the consideration of history. All governments become corrupt as soon as they do not observe the essential principles upon which they are established. They are in constant danger either from the outside or from the inside: "If a republic is small, it is destroyed by a foreign force; if it be large, it is ruined by an internal imperfection. By this two-fold disorder both democracies and aristocracies are equally contaminated, whether they be good or bad. The evil is in the very thing itself, and no remedy can be found for it." (*Esprit des Lois*, Book ix, Chap. i.)

Even the most exquisitely balanced form of government ever devised by man, the government of England, cannot escape that danger, for "as all human things have an end, the State we are speaking of will lose its liberty; it will perish. Have not Rome, Sparta and Carthage perished?" (*Esprit des Lois*, Book xi, Chap. vi.) Thus the famous and enthusiastic description of the "Constitution of England" ends with the dire prophecy of its doom.

Despite Montesquieu's famous boast that he had not followed any model, "prolem sine matre creatam," the sources of many of his ideas have often been pointed out. That he was indebted both to Plato and Aristotle, among others, for his picture of the corruption of the principles of government is very likely. It does not seem however that this process of degeneration had been described by any of his predecessors with the same rigor. I hesitate to use here a term which Montesquieu did not actually employ, but remembering that he had studied natural history when a young man, and that the chapters dealing with the influence of climate are full of medical considerations, I would venture to say that this growth and decay of human institutions appeared to him almost as a biological necessity. Speaking of the Institutions of St. Louis he wrote significantly: "Ce fut le destin des *Etablissemens* qu'ils naquirent, vieillirent et moururent en très peu de tems." (Book xxviii, Chap. xxvii.) More or less rapidly, but of necessity, all living organisms are born, grow old and die, and there is little doubt that Montesquieu considered human societies as living organisms and not as arbitrary or artificial creations of man. This assumption is greatly strengthened if we refer again to the book in which d'Holbach endeavored, in 1770, to correct and to amplify, *pro bono philosophico*, some of Montesquieu's most essential principles. Significantly, he entitled the last and ninth discourse of his *Politique naturelle* "De la Dissolution des Etats." The preamble may well be considered as an explicit elaboration of the physiological views which guided Montesquieu in his descriptions of human societies:

Through its constant course, Nature drives everything that exists to its destruction; all physical or moral beings comply more or less rapidly with this unavoidable law. Human societies, their governments, their opinions, even their capital cities deteriorate and sometimes disappear. Men, these changing beings, experience continuous actions and reactions: the Citizen reacts against the Citizen; the different political bodies in a State fight almost unceasingly against one another; rulers and subjects contend continuously; nations strive constantly against other nations; passions, which affect societies as well as individuals, are the impelling forces which stir in various ways the moral world: from these constant collisions finally results the dissolution of the Body Politick.

States as well as human bodies carry in themselves the germs of their destruction: quite in the same manner, they enjoy a more or less precarious health; they are liable to suffer from crises which rapidly bring them to their end, or from chronical diseases which slowly undermine them by imperceptibly cutting at the very principle of life. As much as sick people, Societies experience fits, delirium, revolutions; a deceptive fullness of figure conceals secret ills; death itself swiftly strikes down the strongest. Ever active Nature sometimes sets up unexpectedly men who can cure the ills of a State, and make it, so to speak, rise again from its ashes; more often she brings forth, from the mass of the Nation, destructive beings that hurl the people headlong into the abyss.

This biological philosophy would easily lead to a passive acceptance of an unescapable necessity resulting from the "nature of things." With characteristic optimism, d'Holbach refused to follow this counsel of despair. He expressed the hope that future generations, wiser and better advised, would discover a cure for the inherent ailment of human institutions. Meanwhile, as doctors fight disease, even if death is the final and unavoidable end of all animated beings, all efforts must be made to study the diseases from which society suffers, and to discover some remedies.

Montesquieu was evidently less sanguine about the results to be expected from education and the "progrès des lumières." Since growth, which is the most evident process of life, results necessarily in senescence, decay and death, every possible means should be resorted to in order to maintain the status quo. The same natural law applies to nations as well as to individuals: "all governments have the same general end, which is that of preservation." (Book xi, Chap. v.) Against internal dangers that threaten the principles of government some remedies may be proposed although they are palliatives rather than real cures. In any case, the maintenance of a high standard of morality or "virtue" could not suffice to protect a small country against the aggression of a more powerful neighbor. In their efforts to preserve their very existence all nations are confronted with the same dilemma. It is in the nature of a republic to have only a small territory; but this limitation leaves it open to the danger of foreign invasion and conquest. In order to survive, it must grow stronger, it must expand, and yet it will cease to be a real republic and will lose its essential liberties as soon as it begins to grow. In a similar way, a monarchical State should be of moderate extent; as soon as it conquers additional territories it alters its institutions and becomes a despotism, for despotic authority alone can rule over a large empire. On the other hand, the principle of despotism being corrupt, it cannot endure; soon a despotic empire splits up into its component parts, each of them starting over again on a new destiny and developing new institutions after more or less extended periods of anarchy. (Book ix, *Of Laws in relation to a defensive force*.) Once again Montesquieu reaches the same pessimistic conclusions already expressed in the *Lettres Persanes* and *Grandeur et Décadence*.

If he had stopped at this point, his pessimism would be unqualified and absolute. A faint ray of hope may bring some comfort to the ailing world: some nations seem to have found a means to stay or to slow down in some degree the fateful revolution of the wheel of necessity. There exists a kind of government presenting all the internal advantages of a republican State together with the external force of a monarchy. This form of government is "a convention by which several States agree to become members of a larger State which they intend to form. It is an assemblage of societies which constitutes a new one, capable of increasing by co-opting new members, until they arrive at such a degree of power as to be able to provide for the security of the united body." A republic or federation of this kind, while able to maintain itself without internal corruption, could successfully withstand foreign aggression.

This scheme was not simply the idealistic construction of a "closet philosopher"; according to Montesquieu, whose historical interpretation was not entirely correct, it had been put into operation in the past and it was still functioning in Europe. Such associations, he maintained, had contributed to the prosperity of Greece. They had enabled the Romans to attack the universe and the universe to resist the Roman conquest. In modern Europe, they could be observed in Switzerland, in Holland and in Germany. Not that they were perfect; but the evils inherent in human undertakings had been reduced to a minimum in these alliances which could be called in a way "perpetual republics," "des républiques éternelles."

Satisfactory as this "collective security" might be in some cases, Montesquieu refused to consider it as a general means to bring about a new millennium. Condorcet had rightly discerned the fundamental relativism of the "président" when he accused him of refusing to admit that a true proposition was true everywhere, and that good laws should be accepted by all men. Although the associations advocated by Montesquieu may seem an outline of the defunct League of Nations, the organizations he had in view were far less ambitious and extensive than the League. He clearly indicated limitations which the promoters of the League might well have kept in mind. For one thing, such a federation should be composed of States of the same nature; small republics or small monarchies might unite, but a combination of republics and monarchies, be they large or small, would be unnatural and precarious. The federative system was not presented as a panacea; it was, at most, a palliative, enabling some small republics to continue to exist and to resist their powerful neighbors. It was never advocated by Montesquieu as a general organization capable of retarding considerably the inexorable march of the rise and decay of nations and empires. Even in his optimistic moods, he retained a large amount of his fundamental pessimism in his philosophy of history. The qualified exceptions he made to his general statements were too few to modify the main trend of his work and to provide great comfort for his optimistic friends.

PHILOSOPHICAL ASPECTS OF LANGUAGE

LEONARD BLOOMFIELD

Yale University

THE persons in a speech community coördinate their actions by means of language. Language bridges the gap between the individual nervous systems: a stimulus acting upon any one person may call out a response action by any other person in the community. Language unites individuals into a *social organism*.

In a way, language is to the social organism what the nervous system is to the individual. A stimulus acting upon any part of an animal may call forth a movement in any other part: the nervous system serves as a connection. Pinch a dog's tail and his mouth will snap at you. In the social organism a stimulus acting upon one person may produce a response in any other person: the connection is produced by language.

As a simple instance, suppose that Jack and Jill are walking down a lane: Jill is hungry and thirsty and she sees some apples in a tree, but she cannot climb fences or trees. So far as her own non-linguistic bodily equipment is concerned, she would have to stay hungry. However, she utters some conventional speech sounds, and at once Jack climbs over the fence and up the tree and brings her an apple. Jack has responded to the stimulus of Jill's hunger. As a speaking person, Jill commands the varied powers of many individuals—ultimately, of all the persons in her speech community and even beyond.

This instance is so simple that it may be paralleled among speechless animals. Language, however, produces very exact coöperation. Speechless animal communities are either very loosely knit, or else, as among ants or bees, they are restricted to a few rigid schemes of operation. In a human community, every child is trained in a twofold system of habits. He is taught to respond to situations not only with non-linguistic bodily movements, but also with conventional speech sounds. At the same time, he is taught to respond to these conventional speech sounds when he hears them from other persons: the other person's speech acts as a stimulus of a special sort ("stimulus-on-other-person," in our example, "Jill's-hunger").

The person who receives the stimulus and the person who acts upon it need not be near each other. If some farmers want a bridge across a river, their speech need not reach the ears of the bridge builders: many relays of speech, through a town meeting, a legislature, various officials, an engineer's office, and a contractor's staff, will finally lead to the point where workmen actually perform the movements of building a bridge.

In such ways language gives man a great biological advantage. This appears in exact coöperation in small-scale activities, such as hunting, fishing, or warding off wild animals. It leads later to the division of labor in large societies like our own. In a community of the latter kind, even the least favored individual has at his service a great variety of human performance, far beyond the strength and skill of his own body.

We do not know what connection, beyond mere coincidence, there may have been between language and the use of fire and tools; whatever the connection, it cannot detract from the import of this basic function of language.

When we say that a speech community is a *social organism*, we are not using a figure of speech. A person's membership in a speech community is not merely something superadded to his existence as a biological unit. Human behavior is entirely permeated by social factors. With the possible exception of some physiological processes, the activities of a human individual cannot be classified or predicted on the sole basis of biological equipment, but depend very largely upon the society in which he lives and upon his place in this society.

Each community is formed by the activity of language; speech utterances give us the most direct insight into its working and play a part in everything that is done. In order to observe a human group, we must understand its speech. If we want to probe deeper into the ways of the community and their historical origin, we must possess, to begin with, a systematic description of its language. In order to know anything about mankind, we must study in this way a varied set of communities. What little we know about man has come from study of this kind. Without such knowledge, we are slaves, in this matter, to rationalization, prejudice, and superstition.

The existence of an individual depends upon his membership in a speech community, to such an extent that every phase of his behavior contains linguistic elements. His *I* and *you*, his *good* and *bad*, his *will* and *must*, and so on, are largely conditioned by language and can be most plainly observed in the utterance of speech. In this sphere we may single out, on account of its cosmic importance, the power of *calculation*.

An untrained individual's response to any complex set of objects is extremely uncertain and often disadvantageous. This can be seen in the behavior of young children or of persons confronted with complexities (for example, in the way of mechanical devices) which are beyond their training. In language, however, the individual has a set of responses which have been practised by many persons and are less whimsical than untrained individual reactions. The human adult, accordingly, responds to a complex situation by a series of speech utterances (audible or internal, or, in modern times, written) which we call a *calculation*. At the end of the calculation he proceeds to make a final response, verbal or manual, whose form is dictated by the intermediate speeches. In many instances, to be sure, the conventional speeches are faulty and lead to a poor response: every community is beset with tribal superstitions, tabus, and dyspraxies. On the other hand, we find remarkably clever actions customary among savage tribes; these culminate in modern scientific procedures. In the case of these latter, the verbal calculation takes largely the form of *mathematics*.

Here again, of course, we see the division of labor: physicists, chemists, engineers, and other scientists and technical workers act for us in complex situations, and they, in turn, call upon mathematicians for the verbal reckoning. In the favorable case, then, we have the highly civilized society which meets the situations of life rationally and advantageously, for the most part by securing the operation of specialized individuals.

The social organism is the highest type of organization within our cosmos. It is wellnigh immortal, and can deal with almost any situation and secure almost any advantage. Even upon this level of biological success, the ethical consequences are self-evident. The social organism will function successfully to the extent that a stimulus upon any member will produce a response in the suitable member; for instance, if the hunger or pain of any person is speedily and smoothly dealt with by the appropriate members of the community. The social organism will function successfully to the extent that it contains enough persons who are trained to respond to its situations; for instance, if for a large population of food growers there are also enough teachers to secure rational behavior and enough physicians and sanitarians to secure the health of the community.

However, in order to draw ethical consequences, we must know what "good" is to be sought. In the light of the linguistic and coöperative character of society, this goal seems to be *variability*, both of the individual and of the social organism. The social organism, to function smoothly, must contain persons of the most various and specialized training and must set them into action appropriately and speedily. Within such an organism, the individual must perform extremely varied responses, delicately attuned to every situation—responses which, of course, in nearly every instance involve the coöperation of other individuals. It is probably the approximation to this state which we mean when in everyday speech we use the term *well-being* or *happiness*, and it is, more certainly, the inability to respond to a situation which we mean by the reverse of these terms.

Beyond all this, there is a cosmic significance to the linguistic actions of society. Modern means of recording speech utterance enable us to store up valuable responses. Here we have notably the devices of writing and printing. A great library, today, contains, recorded and available, the best responses that have been made to almost everything in the accessible world. Even now, at the dawn of civilization and with our primitive equipment, we approach the limit where everything in the accessible universe is paralleled by a recorded human response in the form of a speech utterance, and where all these records are available, at need, to any person. To the extent that irrationality and superstition are discarded, and to the extent that the social organism fosters variability in its members—and these are largely linguistic developments—to that extent will the social organism approach a state which, in contrast with the powers of less developed people, and in the eyes of such people, could be characterized as omniscience and omnipotence.

The development here is not constantly forward. Irrational and self-destructive activities are often preserved by means of language. A frequent error of societies is to make inadequate response to things, and to hope that verbal calculating will make up for imperfect observation: this is the nature of so-called *a priori* reasoning, scholasticism, and other forms of pseudo-philosophizing. Given, however, an adequate observation of things language acts to eliminate irrational patterns of behavior. For this reason, to the extent that a community carries on disadvantageous conventions, the persons or groups at the focus of disease try to prevent not only rational observation but also the free use of language. As the social organism develops, it tends more and more to abandon self-destructive actions and to conventionalize those which embody a successful response. This process depends largely upon speech—argument, debate, exposition, scientific treatises, and so on. As examples we may cite, on the one hand, the abolition of private warfare or of slavery, and, on the other hand, the rise and the conventional application of present-day physics, engineering, medicine, and sanitation.

The outline here given is based upon the treatise of Albert Paul Weiss, *A theoretical basis of human behavior* (second edition, Columbus, Ohio, 1929) and upon the same author's essay, *Linguistics and psychology*, in the journal *Language*, volume 1, 1925.

LANGUAGE AND CULTURE

FRANZ BOAS
Columbia University

THE question of interrelation between language and culture has been much discussed and the opinion is still widely held that language is an important determinant of culture. I little doubt that this opinion is strongly supported by our emotional attitude towards our mother tongue and the ease with which our most intimate thoughts find expression in our native speech. There are certainly few poets who have been able to express themselves with equal ease and force in their mother tongue and in an acquired language.

Other attempts at an evaluation of language as a means of expressing thought are based on the ground that it is difficult to formulate an abstract and logical thought in the languages of people of lower, perhaps even of an alien culture.

The problem has to be looked at from two angles, the one, in how far does language fulfill the needs of communication and of thought in a given culture; the other, in how far does language influence the line of thought, in how far does it help or hinder the development of culture.

The former question is not difficult to answer. An examination of the vocabularies of people of various types of culture shows that words exist for everything that is essential in the culture and that elaborate distinctions are found that reflect the importance of objects and activities in the lives of the people. We may observe this most readily in our own languages. The development of electrical power, of the automobile, of modern science, of new political devices, of new economic organizations, have enriched our vocabulary with terms for new experiences and objects without number. Language has supplied our needs of new symbols, even though our linguistic technique is so feeble that we had to resort to combinations of letters of the alphabet, like FDR, CIO, BMT, to convey complex groups of ideas or attitudes. The reverse of this phenomenon is our lack of knowledge of the specific vocabulary of aspects of our culture with which we are not familiar. Occupational vocabularies are on the whole confined to occupational groups and only a few words of such a vocabulary become common property. Conversely we lose the vocabulary of occupations that go out of use, and of vanishing conditions like that of falconry, of the feudal system, of weapons no longer in use. These may survive in the minds of those familiar with history, but they are no longer parts of the living vocabulary of the people.

In every culture the vocabulary reflects the relation of man to his natural environment and gives testimony of the kind of life he leads. The Eskimo uses many terms for snow: snow falling, snow on the ground, snow-drift, drifting snow, soft snow; for all these aspects are of importance in his life. These terms must be ancient, for they are not derived from a common root, but distinct in origin. The seafaring Oceanian and the inhabitants of the northwest coast of America have many terms for the sea in its various aspects as well as for canoe and canoe-building. On the other hand the modern Aztec has lost every trace of the terms related to his ancient religion. To give another example: the potlatch system of the northwest coast of America has given rise to a large vocabulary relating to borrowing, loaning, interest at various rates, indebtedness incurred in contracting marriages or in the destruction of property for the purpose of rising in social rank. A large vocabulary exists also to designate rank. In all these cases of development of a special vocabulary we may judge of its antiquity by the number of independent, specific stems. More modern terms will be found often to be derived from stems in wider use. Thus the Kwakiutl terms for rank may be of moderate antiquity, since all are derivatives of existing stems, although the grammatical form of many of them is not easily understood. The chief is "standing at the head alone," or "being at the head," the chieftainess "lifting her blanket," namely when giving a great feast when she tries to have her blanket not soiled by grease, the chief's son "the one standing in front" (of his father); the chief's daughter "the one sitting still in the house." A chief's wife of lower rank is designated by a term that cannot easily be equated with other terms but seems to be related to the term for "wealth."

This view of a correlation between the use of terms that can be derived from older stems and the relative newness of the cultural feature so designated can be supported by the frequent reluctance of speakers of native languages to adopt terms of foreign languages the general connotation of which they do not understand, and to substitute new derivatives which describe those characteristics that strike them as significant. Thus a telegraph may be called "talks along a line," an automobile "stubnose vehicle," a horse "wonderful dog," if the dog was the only domesticated animal known.

Of course, it ought not to be assumed that the etymology of such new terms remains conscious for any length of time. Proof of this is that words of this type wear down rapidly and that knowledge of their etymology is lost to the speakers. This is proved by numerous cases in which by metathesis or other phonetic processes the etymology is obscured. The words become symbols like all others which are tokens of concepts regardless of their historic origin.

I think on the basis of such data we may infer that languages are able to supply terms for new ideas as they arise and that culture determines the course of development of the vocabulary.

While this will be conceded for concrete objects, the question arises whether abstract ideas can be readily expressed in primitive languages and whether the lack of devices adapted to their formation may not hinder the development of abstract concepts.

In regard to this question we ought to consider that a great many of our abstract concepts are not an outgrowth of the language of the common people, but have arisen among the educated and have gradually found their way into the common language, not without losing in many cases their function as tokens of abstract thought. Such words as *existence, essence, character, religion, quality, quantity,* originated among literary persons and came to be adopted with the increasing complexity of culture. There are others of different character: *love, hatred, friendship, freedom, envy, thought.* Have primitive languages their equivalent? The conditions of primitive culture are such that the absolute abstract term itself can hardly ever be the subject of conversation or the object of activities. The situations talked about are always concrete. I may talk of my love, hatred, or friendship in regard to a person, but I do not talk about these attitudes in an absolute sense. Therefore, if corresponding words exist they can occur only in possessive relations. If the structure of a language permits I can say "my sympathy for his pitiable condition is great," but I cannot say sympathy is the attitude of having pity. Still, when conditions arise which require the expression of the absolute noun, grammatical devices taken from more concrete situations are generally available which make it possible to create a word, at the time of its creation unidiomatic, that will adequately express the absolute idea. The Eskimo can form an abstract noun from any verb: goodness, pity, love; but it does not occur in everyday conversation except in reference to some tangible object. In languages of different structure the abstract noun may even exist as subject acting upon a person, as "hunger acts upon me," where it is open to question whether hunger is felt an animate actor or not; or "I have pains" where it is equally uncertain whether pains are felt as an object possessed, although the grammatical forms require such formal interpretation. The endeavors of missionaries to render the many abstract terms they require, show how unidiomatic terms may be created and come to be accepted—although for one acquainted with the language they may not render in the least the thought to be expressed—and become accepted tokens when the ideas are grasped more fully.

As a matter of fact etymological investigation shows in many cases that the fundamental ideas expressed in stems are so general that they appear to us as highly abstract. Thus we have languages that have a stem meaning "movement," and all specific forms of movement, like to walk, to fly, to swim, etc., are derived from it. "To say, to wish, to think" may all be derived from the same stem, meaning "the formulation of a thought process by spoken or unspoken language." This does not mean that the generalized notions which we derive by analysis are present in the minds of the speakers for whom the words, as they exist now, are merely tokens of specific actions. It seems not unlikely that in very early times such sound complexes of very vague connotation existed and that languages as we know them now were built up on the foundation of such elements.

I think our general experience in the field of linguistic data proves that language is a reflex of culture and that there are everywhere linguistic devices that enable the language to follow the demands of culture.

There is, however, another aspect from which our problem has to be considered. We have so far spoken only of words and their relation to culture. It is another question in how far the categories of grammar and the general classification of experience may control thought. To give an example: In our speech the category of time is all-important. Whether an action was done in the past, in the present, or in the future must be expressed. We must express whether we speak about a definite or indefinite object. We must state whether we mean singular or plural. These are obligatory categories, and although a child expresses itself in the early stages of speech development without them, the adult speaker cannot omit them, except by a forced experiment, or when he has to speak a foreign language the structure of which he does not know. This condition is found in many trade jargons.

The obligatory categories of languages differ fundamentally. As just stated, number, definiteness or indefiniteness of noun, time, are obligatory in most European languages. Some Indian languages either lack the obligatory category of number, or substitute for it distributive, collective, or other similar ideas; they may lack the obligatory category of time, which is expressed when needed by devices which fulfill the functions of our adverbs; they also lack (like Latin) the obligatory category of definiteness. On the other hand, they may require a much more rigid localization than is required in our language. Location near me, you, or him may be obligatory; the source of knowledge, whether something is known by one's own sense-experience, by evidence, or by hearsay; numerous time aspects, not tenses, such as "to be in a condition, to get into a position, to be discontinually in a condition, to be repeatedly in a condition, to terminate a condition," or the corresponding terms for action, all these may be obligatory in one language or another. It is obvious that the mental picture aroused by a spoken sentence will be fundamentally different according to these categories. We could read our newspapers with much greater satisfaction if our language would compel them to say whether their reports are based on self-experience, inference, or hearsay! The strict localization of some languages creates a much more vivid picture than our indifference to localization. If I say "the children are playing," an Indian of a certain tribe could not get a clear picture of what I have in mind, because he would have to say, for instance, "children (or child) whom I see here, are (or is, were or was) playing in the woods which I see here." The speaker must be definite as to locality, but he is indefinite as to how many children there are and when they were playing. When hearing the statement the picture conveyed to him may be entirely different from the one the speaker wishes to convey. It is an exaggeration of the conditions prevailing in our own language when we are conversing. The form of our grammar compels us to select a few traits of the thought we wish to express and suppresses many other aspects which the speaker has in mind and which the hearer supplies according to his fancy, so that the more generalized the obligatory categories, the more we are apt to find differences between the complete idea the speaker wishes to convey and the situation which the hearer recreates from the speaker's utterance. In different languages some emphasize one group of categories, others others.

There is little doubt that thought is thus directed in various channels. If I say "the father built a new house for his son" and the Indian says "the son was the reason for his father's housebuilding," we stress purpose, the Indian causality. Such a tendency pervading the language may well lead to a different reaction to the incidents of every-day life and it is conceivable that in this sense the mental activities of a people may be in part directed by language. I should not be inclined to overestimate this influence, because devices for expressing finality as over against causality are ever-present, and may rise into idiomatic use.

The morphological structure of words may have a similar influence. Although the complete words are merely tokens of concepts, their structure may direct thought in certain directions. Some Indian languages emphasize in all activities the means by which the action is performed— with the hand, the mouth, by means of an instrument such as a knife, or by pulling, pushing, etc. Further, they may indicate the form of the object acted upon as long, round, flat, rope-like, etc. Although the categories may not be intensely felt, they direct the thought in certain channels when handling experiences and may in this way exert a partial control over actions.

In this sense, we may say that language exerts a limited influence upon culture. It may, however, be safely said, that when changes of culture demand new ways of expression, languages are sufficiently pliable to follow new needs. Furthermore, under new conditions, the categories that are discovered by etymological analysis become more and more mere symbols and their etymological value does no longer elicit the consciousness of the category that the analysis reveals.

Under modern conditions culture controls the growth of language; the opposite influence is slight.

All this does not touch upon the obscure problem of the processes that may have existed in the earliest formation of languages. If we may trust morphological analysis, the fundamental categories of languages were very varied and we may assume on the basis of what we observe now, that cultural activities determined largely the development of these categories. It is intelligible that forms of objects, their physical qualities, their availability for human use, should have become the basis of generalization, or that activities should have been grouped according to the parts of the body or other instrumentalities used, or that a roving people may have differentiated movements according to the character of the country traversed—but it seems impossible to determine the conditions that led to the particular variety of categories found in a given language.

THE CORRELATION OF
GREEK ARCHAEOLOGY WITH HISTORY

WILLIAM BELL DINSMOOR
Columbia University

THE archaeologist, engaged primarily in the study and interpretation of the material products rather than the verbal records of man's past, that is, the illustrations of the written text rather than the text itself, the monuments rather than the documents, often finds that he is in the enviable position of dealing with the unbiased evidence of contemporary witnesses—provided that he can interpret it—as contrasted with the textual tradition which is so often retrospective and sometimes mistaken or wilfully prejudiced. Yet illustrations and text form an inseparable whole; the one must fit the other; and the arbitration of differences is often delicate. The archaeologist, depending frequently upon ratiocination and on the underlying patterns of human behavior, may appear, if he attempts to view his chosen field in relation to the main stream of human development, to lay himself open to the criticism that "History cannot be pressed into the Procrustean bed of a System." Yet, if archaeology is to have any ultimate value, such attempts must be made.

The classical archaeologist, in particular, has a task differing from that of many of his profession in the degree to which he is surrounded, and thus both helped and hampered, by a vast wealth of written evidence. The extent to which he is thus affected must vary, naturally, in accordance with the period under investigation. For instance, a period which affords a comparatively even balance between the monumental and documentary evidence is that of rapid evolution to which the "Father of History" devoted his genius, the first thirty years of the Athenian democracy. While Herodotus supplies the main thread, Thucydides, Aristotle, Diodorus, Plutarch, and numerous others fill some of the gaps. Strictly contemporary records in the form of more or less fragmentary inscriptions,[1] while considerable in bulk, are rarely dated with the exactitude characterizing those of later times, and thus usually require archaeological inter-

---

[1] Abbreviated as *IG*² I [*Inscriptiones Graecae*, editio minor] and Agora I [inv. no.].

pretation. Contemporary monuments, likewise considerable in bulk, are usually even more disputable with respect to date; and particularly is this the case, it so happens, with the monuments of sufficient importance to have a political bearing. The present essay, in which there is room to consider only a few of the surviving monuments of this period, is a tentative effort to correlate them with the impulses that led to their creation.[2]

The stage was set by the debate between the seven conspirators who slew the Persian Magi in 521 B.C., with Otanes arguing for democracy, Megabyzus for oligarchy, and Darius for absolute monarchy (Herodotus, III, 80–83); and Darius, convincing the majority, became the Great King, ruling over a totalitarian state and all neighboring Asia and Africa, and aspiring to further conquest in Europe. At the same period the Greek cities, after brief experience of local tyrants, were beginning to drive them out. As Histiaeus of Miletus was reported as saying (*id.*, IV, 137), "It is through Darius that we enjoy our thrones in our several states. . . . For there is not one of them which will not prefer democracy to kingly rule." On the Greek mainland, Athens underwent the violent change in 510 B.C.; and the circumstantial account, by Herodotus (v, 62–63, 90) and Aristotle (*Ath. Pol.* 19), of the propaganda bureau set up by the Alcmeonids at Delphi, by means of which Spartan help was enlisted and the tyranny overthrown, is thoroughly substantiated despite Plutarch's defense of the Pythian priesthood against such accusations of venality (*Mal. Herod.* 23). We have the monumental evidence of the Apollo temple itself, with the Parian marble front contrasting with the poros limestone rear—a contrast stressed by Herodotus but invisible to Plutarch on account of the destruction of the archaic temple in the interim (373 B.C.)—and with its intrinsically Athenian pedimental sculpture which seems to betray the actual handiwork of the anti-Peisistratid sculptor Antenor.

The first three years of the Athenian democracy were not conducive to artistic progress, because of the factional strife between Cleisthenes and

---

[2] In the effort to avoid, in this brief essay, the mass of apparatus which would be required for full acknowledgement of the sources of the innumerable theories surveyed and classified, it has seemed desirable to curtail drastically the references to modern literature. With this aim, the published discoveries and views of others, whether accepted or rejected, have been presented impersonally, and with them my own observations have been interwoven without undue emphasis. I trust that my colleagues are not unwilling to share with me this anonymity in the interest of simplicity.

Isagoras. The latter became archon in 508–507 B.C., whereupon Cleisthenes made his bid for popular support by proposing the redistribution of the four tribes into ten, and enlargement of the Council. Isagoras countered by summoning Spartan aid and driving out seven hundred families of the Alcmeonid party: "Cleomenes, the Lacedaemonian king, again banished them from Athens in a time of civil strife by the help of the opposite faction, expelling the living and disinterring and casting forth the bones of the dead" (Thucydides, I, 126). A monumental relic of this vandalism is the huge grave stele of Megacles in the Metropolitan Museum (New York), which had been intentionally broken up at just this time and used for making a grave with double-T clamps and black-figured pottery. To the same movement may be due the erasure of the name of another Megacles, the nephew of Cleisthenes, and the substitution of Gla[uc]y[t]es on a votive painted terracotta panel on the Acropolis.[3]

When the Athenians, overthrowing the rule of Isagoras after a two-day siege of the Acropolis in 507 B.C., recalled Cleisthenes and his followers from exile, quiet was restored and the democracy was established on a firm basis. At this moment, it would seem, the state repaid its debt to Delphi.[4] Our only historical record of the Treasury of the Athenians, to be sure, treats it as a memorial of Marathon (Pausanias, x, 11, 5); and such a date, in fact, receives the approval of its modern discoverers. And it is true that the phrase "first-fruits of battle from the Medes at Marathon" actually occurs in the dedicatory inscription on the long trophy base erected beside the south flank of the Treasury; but this inscription (undoubtedly the source of Pausanias's phrase "from those who disembarked at Marathon") is not on the Treasury itself, nor was there ever such an inscription on the Treasury, nor is there any intimate physical connection between the trophy base and its foundation on the one hand, and the corresponding portions of the Treasury on the other. Indeed, the physical evidence would require the Treasury to be already in place, or

---

[3] The usual supposition that, since this Megacles was ostracized in 486 B.C. (Aristotle, *Ath. Pol.* 22), the substitution of the name would have occurred at this time, seems less reasonable in that ostracism was merely a political maneuver and not a case of *damnatio memoriae*.

[4] That is, the previous completion of the temple of Apollo had been a private venture of Cleisthenes.

at least begun, before the trophy base; but whether the time interval was two weeks or twenty years remains problematical.

The internal architectural evidence, because of the scarcity of comparative material of this period, is fairly noncommittal. Much stress has been laid on the profile of its Doric capitals as representative of the spirit prevailing at Aegina, which is true enough but of little assistance, because we do not know whether these capitals are earlier or later than those at Aegina, or whether Aegina was more or less provincial than Athens, or even the exact date of the temple at Aegina (which vacillates in modern theory between 510 and 480 B.C.). It has been argued that the profiles of the mouldings at Delphi seem later and favor a post-Marathon date; but again the scarcity of comparative material suggests that judgment be withheld. One architectural trait, the concavity of the under surface of the sloping pedimental cornice (earlier examples being simple planes, as in the Peisistratid temple of *ca.* 530–520 B.C. on the Athenian Acropolis), might be regarded as evidence of lateness, were it not that the same concavity appears in the Peisistratid Hall of the Mysteries at Eleusis (*ca.* 520–514 B.C.) and apparently also at Aegina. In short, the architectural evidence would be as suitable for a date before Marathon as for one after the battle. And, with regard to technique, we seem to have a significant indication in the use of Cycladic island marble and island dovetail clamps, both of which would have been anachronistic in an official Athenian structure dated later than 490 B.C., and such clamps would not have been employed at Athens itself after 530 B.C. In other words, we seem to be concerned with an instance of itinerant stonecutters being imported along with their material from the island quarries at a period before the state quarries outside Athens on Mt. Pentelicon were exploited on a large scale, that is, before 490 B.C. The sculptural criteria are more elusive and therefore more subjective in interpretation, with the result that we have two distinct schools of thought, one favoring the decade 510–500 and the other 490–480 B.C.; but here again, comparing certainly dated sculpture of 490–480 B.C. from the Athenian Acropolis, such as the pouting maiden dedicated by Euthydicus, it becomes fairly obvious that state sculpture of this decade could hardly have been as archaic as the heads in the metope frieze of the Treasury.

Now it happens that some years earlier, within a year of 525 B.C., had been born a certain Leagros, an exact contemporary of Themistocles, an important citizen of Athens and killed when general in 465 B.C.; Leagros in turn had a son Glaucon who was a general in 441–440 B.C. Both are mentioned many times as "beautiful boys" on painted vases dated stylistically about a generation apart, 510–500 and 480–470 B.C., so that there can be no doubt as to their identity; and through this prosopographical evidence may be exactly dated, within the period 515–500 B.C., a group of more than a hundred black-figured and red-figured vases painted when both techniques were still employed concurrently, and characterized by ornamental borders consisting of circumscribed plumply-petaled palmettes set diagonally, and often with an alternating wig-wag movement. Nothing like this ornament had been employed earlier; and nothing like it recurs later except, in the following generation, a few sporadic imitations distinguished either by anaemic hairline palmettes or by elongated palmettes with lancet-shaped central petals. Consequently, when we meet this very un-architectural ornament as part of the decoration of a building we may be certain that it was derived from vase-painting; and when we observe that there is only one instance of such architectural employment, and that with the ornament in its pristine form, on the interior cornice of the Athenian Treasury for which the preponderance of evidence has already suggested the very period of this stage of vase-painting, we seem to have definite confirmation of a date considerably before rather than shortly after Marathon. In other words, the appropriate date of 507 B.C., when the young democracy could officially reward the Pythia for her intervention, may be regarded as a firmly established landmark in the development of sculpture and architecture.

Slightly later, when a coalition between Sparta, Boeotia, and Chalcis threatened new dangers for the infant democracy, the Spartan occupation of Eleusis collapsed through the defection of their Corinthian allies and one of the Spartan kings, while the Boeotians and Chalcidians were successively defeated on both shores of the Euripus on the same day in 506 B.C. "The chains wherewith they [the Boeotian and Chalcidian captives] were fettered the Athenians suspended in their citadel, where they are still to be seen in my day, hanging on walls scorched by Median flames,[5]

---

[5] The inference that these were walls or terrace walls associated with the Peisistratid temple of Athena, which would be the "megaron facing toward the west," seems to be confirmed not only by the peculiar plan of that temple and by the coincidence that its remains are actually scorched by the Median flames, but also by the analogy of the "fetters still in my day preserved at Tegea where they hung round the walls of the temple of Athena Alea" (Herodotus, I, 66).

opposite the megaron which faces toward the west. And they dedicated
a tenth part of the ransom-money, setting up a bronze quadriga which
stands at the left hand immediately on entering the Propylaea on the
Acropolis" (Herodotus, v, 77).[6] The inscription on the quadriga as quoted
by Herodotus is preserved on two pieces of white Pentelic marble (IG^2 I
394 I); but these are letters of the middle of the fifth century, dating from
a Periclean renewal of the destroyed monuments, probably in 446 B.C.,
commemorating the conquest of Euboea (Thucydides, I, 114, 3). But a
fragment of the original inscription in earlier letters (IG^2 I 394 II), which
Herodotus never saw, is on black Eleusinian limestone and shows that the
first and third lines of the original epigram were later interchanged. Of
special importance from the archaeological standpoint are the exactly
dated official lettering of 506 B.C. and the authenticated use of black
limestone in Athens at this early date.[7]

---

[6] Cf. Diodorus, x, 24; Pausanias, I, 28, 2; *Anth. Pal.* VI, 343. I believe that too much has
been made of the use of the present participle "on entering" by Herodotus in an effort to
show that he saw the quadriga on the left *before* entering the Propylaea, whereas Pausanias
saw it on the left *after* entering (but mentioned it on the way out), where it had undoubtedly been originally erected. This assumed triple location, inside, outside, and then inside
again, has caused an unnecessary amount of argument, and also leads to an impossible
situation in that, if Herodotus saw it on the left outside, in a Periclean renewal, it must
have been either at the very top of the west slope on the rock directly in front of the present entrance—where Pericles would hardly have planted it as late as 446 in view of the
coördinated plans for the entire Acropolis—or at the left on the terrace of the Agrippa
monument—a terrace which did not exist until about 432 B.C., fourteen years after the
renewal. These alternatives may be dismissed even without raising the very improbable
theory that Herodotus ever came back to Athens after 443 B.C. and saw the present Propylaea. The use of the latter term (which first became official in 434 B.C.) could easily have
been due to revision at Thurioi, and is quite in line with other revisions such as the mention of the flight of Zopyrus from Persia to Athens (III, 160), which according to Ctesias
occurred just before the death of Artaxerxes and so in 426 or 425 B.C. Nor is there any like-
lihood that a hypothetical Propylon northwest of the Parthenon, necessarily small if indeed one ever existed, would have been designated by Herodotus at any time by this more
complicated and plural term, Propylaea. The only plausible solution is that Herodotus
passed through the Old Propylon and, following the usual direction toward the northwest
corner of the Parthenon, saw at the left, inside the Acropolis, the renewed Periclean pedestal almost if not quite where the original monument of 506 B.C. had stood, and exactly
where Pausanias saw it six hundred years later.

[7] The significance of the latter point may be better appreciated in the light of recent
arguments that black Eleusinian limestone was not employed outside Eleusis before 437

"Thus did the Athenians increase in strength. And it is plain enough, not from this instance only, but from many everywhere, that freedom is an excellent thing. . . . As soon as they got their freedom, each man was eager to do the best he could for himself. So fared it now with the Athenians" (Herodotus, v, 78).

The earliest buildings erected by the democracy at Athens itself were naturally those for civic purposes; and of two of these, the old Bouleuterion erected on the west side of the Agora and the Pnyx of Cleisthenes high on the Museum hill, the plans have recently been recovered by excavation. By a coincidence, another assembly place, the theatre, is known to have been reconstructed at this very time on account of a collapse of the wooden bleachers (Suidas, *s.v.* Pratinas); but we are ignorant of its plan and location, whether it stood in the Agora or on the site of the theatre of Dionysus. Much less impressive was the erection of religious buildings; a simple temple of the Mother in the Agora has recently been uncovered, but even this was closely related to civic use since she was the protectress of the state archives. By contrast, the huge Doric temple[8] of Zeus Olympius laid out by the Peisistratids was abandoned (Aristotle, *Pol.* v, p. 1313b; Vitruvius, VII, pr. 15) and remained a deserted ruin for centuries, a memorial of the thwarted ambitions of the tyrants. And on the Acropolis the two temples of Athena, the Peisistratid temple or *Archaios neos* at the north and the more primitive Hecatompedon at the south, were given no further attention or embellishment at this time.[9]

The democracy was eight years old when it was subjected to the first

---

B.C., and that, in consequence, all structures containing this material must be dated after 437 B.C. (the beginning of work on the Propylaea). Just why the use of this material in the Propylaea should be regarded as the earliest instance we are not told. In any case, among the list of examples of earlier date, we may cite not only the Chalcidian quadriga (506), but also the Athenian Stoa at Delphi (497), the pedestal of a younger Hipparchus at Ptoon (480?), the Athena Promachos statue pedestal at Athens (463–454), and the Zeus statue pedestal and impluvium at Olympia (454–448).

[8] I purposely say Doric; in spite of the current opinion that it was to be Ionic, the forms and proportions of the column drums tell a different story.

[9] This fact needs to be emphasized because of the prevailing opinion that the so-called Hecatompedon *had been* the northern temple and had disappeared before this time, being replaced by the Peisistratid temple, and also because most investigators consider that the southern temple was begun in a new form, as the Older Parthenon, under Cleisthenes (but see below).

important test. Revolt of the Ionian cities from Persian rule had been instigated by Aristagoras of Miletus in the autumn of 499 B.C., and during that winter he sought assistance from Sparta (Herodotus, v, 38, 49–51), the chief military power of the Greek mainland, as had many before him, including Croesus (I, 69, 81), Smyrna (I, 152), the Scythians (VI, 84), and the Samian exiles on two occasions (III, 45, 148). But Sparta refused to send her boys across the sea to die on foreign shores. Argos, next to receive the appeal, likewise declined on the advice of the Delphic oracle (VI, 19, 77). Not so, however, was the appeal received at Athens: convinced that the first line of defense of the democracies was on the Asiatic shore, she sent an expeditionary force of twenty ships, supplemented by five from Eretria (v, 55, 65, 97). "These ships were the beginning of mischief both to the Greeks and to the barbarians," pessimistically remarks Herodotus (v, 97), who is thereupon taken to task by Plutarch (*Mal. Herod.* 24) for thus audaciously discrediting the Athenians "because they endeavored to deliver so many and so great Greek cities from the barbarians." A large part of the year 498 B.C. must have elapsed before the conclusion of these debates and preparations, and it so happens that such a date coincides with the evidence for a structure which seems to have been erected to propitiate Poseidon on the occasion of this earliest foreign naval venture. For concentrically under the Periclean marble temple of Poseidon at Sunium lies an earlier and barely smaller poros limestone temple, which apparently had been carried up to its complete height but remained unfinished and was finally demolished. Work presumably ceased because of some political convulsion or warlike occurrence, and the two Persian invasions of 490 and 480–479 B.C. at once come to mind as the most logical causes, though a date in the eighties is less suitable than one in the nineties for the erection of such an important temple in poros limestone rather than marble. Assuming that it was damaged by a Persian landing party in 490 B.C. as the fleet rounded the cape from Marathon in its fruitless attempt to capture Athens, one may attempt to deduce the foundation date, some years earlier, by means of the principle of orientation, assuming that its axis was laid out in the direction of sunrise on the morning of the annual temple festival. Collation of the angle of deviation from true east and of the observed level of the horizon in that direction, with the sun's course on the various days of the Julian calendar projected back to about 500 B.C., shows that the phenomenon would then have occurred on

February 26/27 or October 30/31 (Julian); and these in turn could have coincided with the eighth day of a lunar month (the sacred day of Poseidon), as projected back from the known solar eclipse date of October 2 = Boedromion 29, 480 B.C., only in the case of the autumn event in 495— probably too late for the foundation of a temple which may well have been nearly complete even before the abortive Persian invasion of 492 B.C.— or in 498 B.C. The latter, with October 31 = Pyanopsion (rather than Boedromion) 8, would have been the most suitable occasion; Pyanopsion 8 was also the day of the Theseia and of the safe return of Theseus from Crete (Plutarch, *Theseus*, 36), preserved by his reputed father Poseidon (called Soter in a later Sunian inscription, *IG*² II 1300), just as the latter was now entreated to bring back the Athenian fleet safely.

The events of the six years of the Ionian Revolt (499–494 B.C.) are described by Herodotus (v, 35–vI, 30), not in the annalistic fashion with which he treats subsequent events, but with reference to three geographical areas; and we are not told how many campaigns occurred in each area nor whether they coincided with those elsewhere. It is generally admitted that the actions thus recounted are insufficient to fill the period of the war; but since the first engagement recorded by Herodotus is the march on Sardis and the burning of the city, followed by the battle of Ephesus and the withdrawal of the Athenian fleet (v, 100–103), these events by common consent have been assigned to the first real campaign of 498 B.C. If, however, we take into account some events omitted by Herodotus such precipitate change of policy by the Athenians seems most improbable. Particularly abbreviated are the earlier stages of his story; there is no mention of the first siege of Miletus by the Persians from the land side, and of the interception of the Phoenician fleet, coming to assist from the sea, by the confederated Ionian fleet off the Pamphylian coast, a victory in which the Athenian and Eretrian contingents participated (Plutarch, *Mal. Herod.* 24).[10] "Then turning back and leaving their ships at Ephesus, they invaded Sardis and besieged Artaphrenes, who had fled into the castle, that so they might raise the siege of Miletus." The Pamphylian victory and the burning of Sardis might have occurred in 498 B.C., but

---

[10] Lysanias of Mallus, whom Plutarch quotes as his authority, was referring primarily to the five Eretrian ships; but it is obvious, both from Herodotus (v, 99) and from the sequel, the burning of Sardis and the Persian plans for revenge, that the Athenian and Eretrian contingents were united.

the following year seems more probable; and there is no evidence that the battle of Ephesus was immediately followed by the Athenian withdrawal, which might have been delayed even until 496 B.C., after the collapse of Cyprus. In any case, we have sufficient evidence for an Athenian victory over an Asiatic fleet at this time, the earliest encounter of the sort and one which must have created a strong impression.

In this connection we are preferably to consider the Athenian Colonnade at Delphi, which our sole literary evidence associates with an impossibly late event, Phormion's naval victory of 429 B.C. Pausanias (x, 11, 6), as in the case of the Treasury, plainly drew an erroneous inference from two subordinate dedications, in this case the trophies of Phormion dedicated inside the Colonnade, which he himself describes, and presumably also a trophy of Leuctra (371 B.C.), the shield of Asopichus (Athenaeus, XIII, 605), whom he mistook for Phormion's father.[11] Modern scholarship has rejected this date, because of the early character of the lettering of the true dedicatory inscription on the upper step of the Colonnade, and has substituted one of six alternatives: (A) a hypothetical naval victory over the Spartans on the occasion of the double victory over the Boeotians and Chalcidians in 506 B.C.; (B) the hypothetical conclusion of a naval war with Aegina in 487 B.C.; (C) the battle of Salamis in 480 B.C.; (D) events of about 475 B.C.; (E) the battle of the Eurymedon in 469 B.C.; or (F) a victory over the Aeginetan fleet in 458 B.C. Of these, however, the last four are far too recent for such archaic letter forms as the cross theta in the inscription, particularly in view of the fact that this is an official monumental inscription. On the other hand, the two first cited occasions are hypothetical and yielded no reasonable excuse for naval trophies;[12] and, in addition, that of 506 B.C. seems too early for such letter

---

[11] Pausanias was prone to such confusion of different persons with identical names; other notable instances were his assumption (1, 22, 4) that the two horsemen at the entrance to the Athenian Acropolis represented the sons of Xenophon because the name of (a much earlier and unrelated) Xenophon appears in the inscriptions, and his confusion (1, 23, 3–4) of a statue of Dieitrephes with the career of his grandson.

[12] The chronology of the early wars with Aegina (Herodotus, v, 82–88 for the first; v, 81, 89, for the second; vi, 87–94, for the third; cf. Thucydides, 1, 14, 41) is not only uncertain but also seems to contain nothing that can be regarded as an Athenian victory. In any case, it can be said that the date 487 B.C. is meaningless, since the mention of a thirty-year pause by the oracle need not mean that the Athenians actually waited so long and affords no

forms as the alpha. The true occasion is apparently to be recognized in one of the events omitted by Herodotus, and consequently overlooked by many recent investigators, namely, the above-mentioned victory of 498 or 497 B.C. in the Pamphylian Sea, when an Athenian fleet for the first time met a foreign foe, and won. It is not inappropriate to assume that this earliest Athenian building in the Ionic style, with black limestone steps and white Parian marble columns supporting a wooden entablature,[13] was intended as an allusion to the Ionian shores which had been the scene of the fleet's activities.

The disheartening effect of the defeat at Ephesus, or possibly a renewal of threats from Aegina, caused at Athens a resurgence of the isolationist party, remnants of the old followers of Isagoras, who reasserted their sympathies toward the Peisistratid house—which might have appeased Persia—by electing Hipparchus the son of Charmus to the archonship for 496–495 B.C. Hipparchus, not being an immediate descendant of the first Peisistratus but one of the collateral members of the family, had been allowed to remain in Athens, though it was primarily with him in mind that Cleisthenes had framed the still unenforced law of ostracism (Aristotle, *Ath. Pol.* 22). An immediate result was the recall of the twenty Athenian ships. To the same year of Peisistratid ascendancy may belong a well-known inscription (*IG²* I 761), that on the altar of Apollo Pýthius at Athens.

According to Thucydides (vi, 54) this altar, of which part of the cornice was discovered near the Ilissus River, was erected at the same time as the altar of the Twelve Gods in the Agora by the younger Peisistratus, grandson of the tyrant, during his year of archonship. "The Athenian people afterwards added to one side of the altar in the Agora and so concealed the inscription upon it; but the other inscription on the altar of the Pythian Apollo may still be read, though in indistinct letters, as follows:

---

justification for reckoning back from the attack in 457 B.C. And, even if 487 B.C. were accepted, the fact that the event in question was merely a refusal on the part of the Athenians to declare war could hardly have been sufficient cause for erecting a colonnade to commemorate a naval victory.

[13] While the column bases are of Parian marble, the present column shafts are of Pentelic, possibly necessitated by repairs (of which there are signs) after the earthquake of 373 B.C. The use of Parian marble rather than Pentelic might be taken as another reason for dating the Colonnade earlier than 490 B.C.

'Peisistratus the son of Hippias dedicated this memorial of his archonship in the sacred precinct of the Pythian Apollo'," the very words which still survive on the pieces of the marble cornice. Thucydides remarks that "the family of Peisistratus took care that one of their own number should always be in office; among others who thus held the annual archonship at Athens was Peisistratus, a son of the tyrant Hippias, . . . and he dedicated the altar during his term of office." It seems clear that this archonship was some year before the expulsion of the tyrants in 510 B.C.; and, in view of the fact that Peisistratus was one of the five sons of Hippias and yet presumably at least thirty years old when archon, there has been a tendency to assign him to the latest year possible, if not 511–510 (occupied by Harpactides) at least the otherwise unoccupied year 512–511 B.C. But even such a date seems far too early for the embarrassingly late lettering which also, despite Thucydides, is still reasonably clear to the modern archaeologist's eye. The latter difficulty is hardly explained by the theory that the adjective may mean "obsolete" or "old-fashioned"; it is more plausible to assume that Thucydides was accustomed to the sight of more deeply cut letters, and that the red paint once filling them had faded. And the former difficulty is hardly to be met by the recent suggestion that Peisistratus should be dated in one of three later years (499/8–497/6) for which we know only one or two claimants, and presumably in the latest of these (497–496) after a change of policy resulting from the defeat at Ephesus. For Thucydides plainly cites the archonship as an instance of the practice *during* the tyranny, and so *before* 510 B.C. Moreover, the name of the younger Peisistratus, as a direct descendant of the tyrant, must have been among those of the five sons of Hippias read by Thucydides (VI, 55) on the stele commemorating the banishment set up in 510 B.C. on the Acropolis;[14] and it is most improbable that he

---

[14] There seems to be no valid reason for the recent suggestion that the "stele of dishonor" on which were engraved the names of the banished Peisistratids in 510 B.C. (Thucydides, VI, 55) was identical with the bronze stele set up beside the *archaios neos* in 507 B.C. to contain the names of the three hundred banished followers of Isocrates (Schol. Aristophanes, *Lysistrata*, 273; cf. Herodotus, V, 72; Aristotle, *Ath. Pol.* 20, 28), or with the bronze stele made from the melted statue of Hipparchus the son of Charmus in 487 or 479 B.C., on which "they voted to inscribe the names of criminals and traitors [and] the name of Hipparchus himself" Lycurgus, *Against Leocrates*, 117–119). There seem to have been several such stelae of dishonor located between the statue of Athena Promachos and the *archaios*

would ever have revisited Athens after 510 B.C.,[15] since even as late as the end of the Peloponnesian War the descendants of Peisistratus were specially prohibited from returning to Athens (Didymus, in Marcellinus, *Thucydides*, 32). It seems certain that the younger Peisistratus was archon during his father's tyranny, 527–510 B.C., in one of the otherwise unoccupied years 522/1–512/1 B.C.;[16] and since, according to a recently discovered inscription from the Agora (I4120), the archon for 522–521 B.C. was . . . . . stratus, the coincidence suggests that we should restore [Peisi]stratus—unless a vague and not yet verified trace of the fifth letter should prove to be another sigma, in which case Peisistratus should descend to one of the following ten years. Such a date would be in accord with the carved heart-and-dart ornament, which belongs in the cycle of the Siphnian Treasury (*ca.* 530–524 B.C.) and hardly seems much later; and the double-T clamps would be contemporary with the earliest use of this form in the upper parts of the Peisistratid temple of Athena on the Acropolis of Athens. I believe that we should not hesitate to date this altar at or shortly after 522–521 B.C. The extant lettering, however, must date from a period considerably later than the expulsion of the tyrants,

---

neos, including such later examples as the stelae of Arthmius (*ca.* 461) and of Phrynichus, Androtion, and Archeptolemus (411).

[15] It has been suggested that Peisistratus may have been allowed to remain in Athens and thus have obtained the archonship in 497–496 B.C., and that he may have been the Peisistratus against whom was cast a vote of ostracism (represented by one extant sherd), necessarily in or after the beginning of 487 B.C., the date of the earliest ostracism. Both suggestions seem contrary to the implications of the "banishment stele"; and the Peisistratus of the ostrakon may have been another of the same name, if indeed the sherd is really an ostrakon and not a mere graffito. I can see no grounds whatever for the suggestion that one of the brothers of Hippias, namely, Thessalus, was allowed to return to Athens and take up citizenship; this seems to be based on an effort to explain an ancient confusion between Thessalus and Hegesistratus—sometimes assumed to be one and the same (Aristotle, *Ath. Pol.* 17)—and has little probability in its favor.

[16] It seems not impossible to assume that Peisistratus was born as early as 552–542 B.C., since his father Hippias, without surpassing Marshal Pétain, might have been born as early as 575–572 B.C., having been very old at the battle of Marathon (Herodotus, VI, 107; Thucydides, VI, 59) and dead before he could return home (Suidas, *s.v.* Hippias). Under these circumstances, it is preferable to follow Thucydides (who claimed to have unimpeachable information that Hippias was the eldest of the sons of Peisistratus, I, 20 and VI, 55) and Aristotle (*Ath. Pol.* 18), rather than the contrary tradition that Hipparchus was the eldest.

and so can only be interpreted as an addition or renewal, the original inscription having been either omitted or placed on a different part or, if on the cornice, merely in painted letters which had faded. Whatever the cause, the fact that the present inscription is an addition seems evident from an almost imperceptible detail, the letters being set in a narrow and slightly smoother band of their exact height.[17] Whether some merely scratched or painted letters were erased by abrasion—either because of inappropriate political sentiments[18] or because the slightest allusion to the benefactions of the tyrants was offensive immediately after 510 B.C.[19] —or whether the stonecutter adjudged the existing surface unsuitable for his purpose,[20] it now seems evident that the inscription is not contemporary with the altar. We may suppose that, in accordance with usual custom, the letters would be in the style of the time of renewal, and this style agrees exactly with that of the Athenian Colonnade at Delphi, differing from the latter only in the use of an angular rho—not necessarily a sign of greater age since it recurs in the Marathon cenotaph and in the Hecatompedon inscription of 485–484 B.C. The only appropriate time for such a renewal of a reminder of the benefits of tyranny would have been during the momentary ascendancy of the same party—and family—in 496–495 B.C. As such, the Peisistratid altar becomes a memorial of the isolationist victory in 496 B.C.

In the second year following, the autumn of 494 B.C., the confederated Ionian fleet was defeated at Lade (Herodotus, VI, 7–17) and Miletus, besieged by the Persians for the second time, finally succumbed and was laid waste, its inhabitants being enslaved and transported to Mesopotamia, "six years from the time when the revolt first broke out under

---

[17] Only photographs taken under certain lighting conditions show this band, which is invisible on other photographs and on squeezes—and the original is now inaccessible.

[18] Compare the less successful erasure in the upper line of the Charioteer base at Delphi. It is obvious that even the change of a single word in a metrical inscription might require the erasure and rearrangement of the whole.

[19] Compare the concealment of the Peisistratid inscription on the altar of the Twelve Gods as recorded by Thucydides, and also the excision of all references to Macedonia and her kings in Athenian inscriptions set up before 200 B.C.

[20] Compare the smoothed band sunk barely below the stippled surface for the second (Aeschylean) epigram on the cenotaph of Marathon.

Aristagoras" (VI, 18–20). The isolationist policy of Athens seemed for the moment to have been justified; and when the murmurings of conscience found vent, the following spring, in the presentation of the *Capture of Miletus*, "the whole theatre burst into tears" and the author Phrynichus, prosecuted by the aristocratic government of that year (archon Pythocritus, 494–493), was fined one thousand drachmas for a breach of the peace (Herodotus, VI, 21).[21] Meanwhile, after passing the winter of 494–493 B.C. at Miletus, the Persian fleet set forth for the purpose of mopping up the islands and shores of Ionia and the Hellespont (Herodotus, VI, 31–33), so that Miltiades was forced to abandon his local principality in the Chersonese and to flee to Athens (VI, 34, 41, 104). But here, as an enemy of the Persians, he was forced by the aristocrats to stand trial on the curious charge—curious in view of their own inclinations and of the non-Athenian environment of his "crime"—of tyranny in the Chersonese (VI, 104). It was the last effort of the isolationists. Themistocles of the anti-Persian party was elected archon (for 493–492 B.C.); Miltiades was acquitted "and was thereupon made general of the Athenians by the free choice of the people."[22] The preparations for the inevitable war, evidenced in monumental form by the creation of the Peiraeus harbor and fortifications (Thucydides, I, 93), now proceeded apace.

Marathon, apparently fought on Boedromion 16 = October 11, 490 B.C., left few scars in Attica, and these were speedily forgotten in a general spirit of elation. "We, first and alone, dared to engage with the barbarian at Marathon" (Thucydides, I, 73). Even the Spartans, who arrived too late, "gave the Athenians all praise for their achievement" (Herodotus, VI, 120). Only at Sunium, apparently, was there any serious destruction,

---

[21] Herodotus actually says, "for recalling to them their own misfortunes." But the trial probably had a deeper and more political meaning, and is to be associated with the trial of Miltiades later in the same spring.

[22] It has recently been argued that the Persians did not reach the Hellespont until 492, that Miltiades fled to Athens in that year and stood trial in 492–491, being thereupon acquitted and elected general for the year 491 when, according to this theory, the battle of Marathon is supposed to have been fought. But the postponement of the Persian arrival at the Hellespont and the antedating of Marathon both seem incredible and contrary to all evidence; the illusory advantage of continuity in the career of Miltiades is based on the supposition that he was elected general only for the year of Marathon, whereas he was probably elected two years before Marathon and then, like Pericles, reelected annually.

that of the poros limestone temple considered above;[23] and here, after the retirement of the Persians, was adopted an expedient which became characteristic of the more serious invasion a decade later. Beside the damaged temple was erected a makeshift structure in order to house the cult statue and offerings pending the construction of a new temple, a process deferred until 444 B.C. And in this temporary structure, of simple rectangular plan fronted on the east by an apsidal porch, the secondhand column drums of the temple's interior were utilized as the skeleton of the walls, forming a sort of "half-timber" work with rubble filling. Such an explanation best fits this mysterious structure, which must be later than the partial destruction of the poros temple and yet earlier than the erection of its marble successor.[24]

To Delphi, apparently immediately after the battle, were sent the "first-fruits of battle from the Medes at Marathon," and these were set up along the south flank of the Athenian Treasury, on a long pedestal of which the later alterations do not concern us here. It is sufficient to note that its construction is not only quite independent of that of the Treasury but also very different, in hard gray limestone rather than marble, while the clamps in the foundation course, instead of being dovetail, are double-Γ in the front row and double-T in the rear row of blocks, both rows being contemporary.[25]

---

[23] Compare the devastation of the sanctuaries of Naxos (Herodotus, VI, 96), Eretria (VI, 101) and Delium (VI, 118), the last being deprived of a goldplated statue of Apollo which Datis afterwards ordered to be returned.

[24] The excavators have suggested that it was a later building; but the terrace of the marble temple intersects it, and an assumption that it was so built as to lean against or mask the lower half of an open temple colonnade seems incredible, and even impossible if we consider the different floor levels.

[25] This use of contemporary double-Γ and double-T clamps should serve as a warning against the current tendency to regard these two varieties of clamps as characteristic of distinct periods. The double-Γ form was merely the simpler type and therefore was invented first (with the ends of the iron bar bent horizontally rather than vertically as in the Ionic type of reinforcement in dovetail clamps), but it survived as a more economical type side by side with the more efficient but costly double-T (with the ends of a dumbbell shaped bar reheated and shaped or "upset" as separate processes), and so was used even in later work with cheaper construction or poorer stone. Thus the double-Γ and the double-T forms show purposeless intermingling in the platform at Aegina, while higher in the same temple the double-T clamps appear in the heavy bottom blocks and the double-Γ clamps in the smaller upper blocks of the walls; so also the frieze blocks have double-Γ clamps while the

At Athens, the earliest notable landmark of the decade following the battle is the cenotaph of Marathon, its base characteristically dressed on the face with a stippled panel surrounded by smoothed borders in the same plane, the upper border containing the two lines of the epigram by Simonides (Agora I 303 + IG^2 I 763). In this we have the work of an official stonecutter, so that the forms of the letters, and the individualistic punctuation with a row of three tiny circles with central dots, assume special importance. The fact that the two additional lines, forming the epigram by Aeschylus, are engraved within a band subsequently smoothed across the stippled surface clearly demonstrates their later origin, and the lettering also is more careless; but the date can hardly be later than about 485 B.C. since the monument was one of the victims of the Persian occupation of 480–479 B.C. Very different is the lettering of a private dedication by the polemarch Callimachus, killed at Marathon, and so probably completed by his son, with two vertical lines of writing in adjoining flutes of an Ionic column (IG^2 I 609). Though the date may be regarded as assured, the character of the lettering (with the old cross theta) would seem to be twenty years earlier than that on the Marathon cenotaph or even considerably earlier than that on the altar of Peisistratus of the preceding decade. The discrepancy is undoubtedly due to the essential difference between public and private monuments; in the monument of Callimachus the work was apparently done by a very conservative stonecutter. Not only, then, have we another epigraphical landmark of value; but the recent identification of the Ionic capital which fits the shaft, and of the marble statue of Nike which fits the cutting on the capital, furnish equally important evidence for the development of architecture and sculpture. Another private dedication which probably belongs to the same period is the statue base erected against the outer curb of the altar of the Twelve Gods in the Agora by the very Leagros (Agora I 1597) whose youthful popularity has enabled us to date the Athenian Treasury. The circumstances of discovery suggest that the statue was removed during the

---

architrave below and the cornice and pediments above contain the double-T form. The double-Γ form appears also in the lower Tarentine base (*ca.* 490–485) and the Argive niche of the Epigonoi (*ca.* 482) at Delphi, the sill course of the old shrine of Athena Nike on the Acropolis (*ca.* 478, with double-T clamps above), the Argive base of the Seven against Thebes at Delphi (*ca.* 456), the upper parts (*ca.* 447–425) of the temple at Bassae (with double-T clamps *below*), and even in the Thessalian niche at Delphi (after 373 B.C.).

Persian occupation, the top thereafter forming part of the trodden surface of the Agora; and a date in the decade 490–480 B.C. would agree not only with the surface tooling with the stippled panel and smooth borders, and with the lettering (as advanced as in the official inscriptions of the decade, though the theta has the special peculiarity of a tiny concentric circle), but also with the career of Leagros, then about forty years of age.

As for monumental building, it has been argued that none could have been attempted during the years of "alarm and preparation" between the two Persian invasions of 490 and 480 B.C. Similar arguments have been employed against the assumption of building operations during the Archidamian War with its annual Spartan invasions (431–421 B.C.); but in that case we possess the contrary words of Plutarch (*Aristeides*, 24) and the evidence of the monuments; and it would hardly seem that such an objection can ever again be raised by those who recall the attitude of the democracies in the face of totalitarian threat between 1935 and 1940. We may, therefore, in considering the warmly debated question of the reconstruction of the Acropolis, give proper weight to the evidence that this, too, was intended as an outward symbol of the new importance of the state resulting from Marathon, executed in a new material which now for the first time was made available on a large scale, Pentelic marble. We are concerned primarily with two buildings, the marble Older Parthenon and the marble Old Propylon, the predecessors, respectively, of the present Parthenon and Propylaea which formed the corresponding portions of the building program of Pericles.

What stood on the site of the Parthenon, even earlier than the construction of the marble Older Parthenon, has likewise been a debatable question. Three concrete theories have so far been presented as to the form of the earliest temple, the grandfather of the present Parthenon, so to speak. (A) It was a primitive apsidal structure, rectangular only on the east front, though the rear end is supposed to have been subsequently squared and thus to have accommodated an additional sculptured pediment. (B) It was a rectangular temple of poros limestone, with open porticoes at both ends but with solid walls on both flanks, with sculptured pediments at both ends. (C) It was a peripteral temple of poros limestone, with columns on all sides, but remained an abortive scheme so that everything above the foundations existed only on paper. The dates assigned to these alternative ancestors vary in accordance with the investigator's attribution of extant fragments. Scheme A, for instance, has been assigned to about 600 B.C. on the assumption that this would be a suitable date for the sculpture to be attributed to its original east pediment. Scheme B likewise depends upon the style of the architectural sculpture assigned to it and hitherto dated, on grounds quite independent of attribution to any definite building, as between 600 and 560 B.C. Scheme C, lacking sculpture as a guide, and lacking even architectural remains except the foundations, has been dated more subjectively, as (a) about 540 B.C. during the third tyranny of Peisistratus, (b) between 527 and 510 B.C. during the tyranny of Hippias, (c) about 510 or 506 B.C. upon the foundation of the democracy by Cleisthenes, (d) about 489 B.C. after the battle of Marathon, or (e) about 479 B.C. after the battle of Plataea. It is to be observed that the evidence for schemes A and C is so different that the two schemes might be united, a primitive apsidal temple (A) being succeeded by the plan for a peripteral limestone temple (C), both anterior to the Older Parthenon.

All these possibilities are seriously upheld at the present time. But when we consider them in detail, it becomes evident that scheme C, including all its subvarieties, must be eliminated, because the foundations, the sole evidence for its existence, are inseparable from the Older Parthenon itself and were clearly planned for the latter rather than for any hypothetical predecessor. The courses wrongly regarded as the lower steps of scheme C were in reality intended to be, from the very beginning, the receding coping of a high podium, with a broad terrace surface extending from the coping to the bottom step of the Older Parthenon, as is shown by the construction with exceptionally long blocks; no covering steps were ever planned at this point. And the earth packed around the foundations, down to the very bottom, contained potsherds dating as late as 500–490 B.C., and similar potsherds of this date were even trodden into the top of the black earth covering the surface of the Acropolis before the foundations were begun. Hence the foundations (the evidence for the assumed scheme C) were not begun until just after 490 B.C., and since the marble Older Parthenon was in process of execution several years before 480 B.C.,[26] it is obvious that the lack of any time interval corroborates the structural evidence showing that foundations and Older Parthenon are inseparable. The case of scheme A is even more difficult. The chief evi-

---

[26] See below.

dence for its existence is a rock cutting which proves on examination to date from the time of the present Parthenon, a century and a half later. The few architectural and sculptural fragments assigned to scheme A may be shown to belong to the great mass of architecture and sculpture which once formed the temple known as the Hecatompedon, whether the latter be placed toward the northern or toward the southern edge of the Acropolis. Thus schemes A and C are both deprived of all support, and we are left with the possibility of scheme B.

Now, on the other hand, our evidence becomes more favorable. For the pieces of architecture and sculpture constituting what is generally regarded as the Hecatompedon, including, as we have seen, the few pieces erroneously isolated for scheme A, have generally been assigned to an assumed earlier stage of the structure toward the north, which for the sake of distinction may be designated as the Peisistratid temple or the *Archaios neos*. There have been two theories regarding the restoration of the Hecatompedon on the existing northern foundations, (a) occupying only the narrow inner rectangle, or (b) utilizing the outer wider concentric rectangle. But the total number of fragments now recovered requires a temple wider than the inner rectangle; and the spacing of the architectural units is such that it cannot have been as wide as the outer rectangle. Furthermore, both concentric rectangles of foundation, though differing in material, are identical in the technique of dressing masonry, and this technique, particularly the use of the toothed chisel, is far too late for the early archaic sculptural and architectural style of the Hecatompedon fragments, in which no traces of the toothed chisel appear. Nor are there any suitable foundations at a lower level under the Peisistratid temple. Still another difficulty with the northern site is the date at which the Hecatompedon, if it had stood there—whether on the inner or the outer foundations or below them—must have been taken down to make room for the Peisistratid temple, namely, at about 530–525 B.C., whereas all the pieces of the Hecatompedon were recovered in contexts of 490–469 B.C. The only other possible location on the Acropolis is the southern site now entirely concealed by the foundations of the Older Parthenon, so that complete verification can never be obtained except by boring or tunneling. Such processes, however, could do little more than reveal some actual remains, and consequently the exact location, of the imbedded older foundations, of which the existence may be deduced from the distribution of the existing architectural and sculptural fragments. For most of these were recovered from the terrace fill south of the Older Parthenon foundations, dated by the potsherds found in it as shortly after 490 B.C.; many of the marble metope slabs were employed for lining the forecourt of the Old Propylon, also dated shortly after 490 B.C.;[27] two other metope slabs, containing the "Hecatompedon inscription," actually bear the date 485–484 B.C.;[28] and several architraves and wall-blocks are built into the lower part of the Cimonian south Acropolis wall of 469 B.C. The piece which had wandered farthest, one of the sculptured heads from the pediments, was recently found on a well on the north slope of the Acropolis filled with debris from a general clearing of the surface of the Acropolis itself, either during the reorganization after 490 B.C. or after the Persian destruction of 480–479 B.C.; but the absence of any burnt or scorched potsherds in this well implies that it was the earlier of these occasions. For all these reasons we may assume that the Hecatompedon—which was in any case the traditional name of the cella of the Parthenon—occupied the site later covered by the Older Parthenon and thus was the grandfather of the present Parthenon; in other words, we may adopt scheme B.

The date of the marble Older Parthenon has been, and still is, even more variously interpreted than that of its predecessor. Apart from the general attributions to a pre-Persian date by its discoverers a century ago, specific periods are being advocated at the present time, as follows: (A) about 530 B.C. during the tyranny, (B) about 510 B.C. immediately after the tyranny, (C) about 489 B.C. after the battle of Marathon, (D) about 485 B.C. in order to leave room for a predecessor after the battle of Marathon, (E) about 479 B.C. after the battle of Plataea, and (F) about 469 B.C. at the time of the Cimonian south wall of the Acropolis *or* in order to leave room for a predecessor after the battle of Plataea. Of these various theories, however, we are undoubtedly to eliminate schemes A and B, since the temple could not be earlier than the foundations on which it rested; and these, as we have seen, date from just after 490 B.C. For similar reasons we may eliminate schemes E and F, because, as we have seen, the Older Parthenon and its foundations were designed as an integral whole; and it is most unlikely that, if the foundations were

---

[27] See below.
[28] See below.

erected as late as 479 or 469 B.C., there would have been no potsherds in the earth fill later than 490 B.C. An additional difficulty with schemes E and F is that the incomplete Older Parthenon was destroyed by fire, which at this period and in view of all the other evidence can only be interpreted as the Persian conflagration of 480 B.C.[29] As for scheme D, which was created merely to leave time for a presumed earlier use of the foundations, the mere fact that foundations and temple are now seen to be contemporary equates it with scheme C, to which we are henceforth limited. And with scheme C, dating just after the battle of Marathon, all our evidence agrees: the potsherds in the earth fill against the foundations, descending to 500–490 B.C. but no further; the traces of fire on the temple and on its scattered remains, as well as the stratum of burned debris above the earth fill against the foundations, giving 480 B.C. as the lower limit for the date; the identity in marble technique, stippled panels and smooth borders in the same plane, with numerous monuments of the decade 490–480 B.C., including the Marathon cenotaph and the Leagros base; the coincidence that most of the Hecatompedon fragments were buried in the earth fill at the very moment that others were inscribed with the "Hecatompedon inscription" of 485–484 B.C.; and many other details which harmonize with this general picture. With the knowledge that the temple and its foundations were begun shortly after 490 B.C. but considerably before 480 B.C. (since above the thirty-five feet of foundations the steps and columns. had been erected to an appreciable height before the destruction), it is reasonable to suppose that the great scheme was designed in the archonship of Aristeides ("supervisor of public revenues," Plutarch, *Aristeides*, 4) in 489–488 B.C., and begun with proper ceremony at the Panathenaic festival of 488 B.C. And that date has the additional confirmation of the principle of orientation; for, of all the years between 490 and 480 B.C., it was only in 488 B.C. that the sunrise could have occurred exactly along the line of the temple's axis on the third day from the end of Hecatombaion (August 31, Julian, 488 B.C.), as ascertained both by calculation and by actual observation on the proper morning in the temple itself. Thus the Older Parthenon is to be regarded as a memorial of victory over the Persians, which the Persians themselves demolished upon their return.

The first marble entrance to the Acropolis, the Old Propylon, so obviously belongs to the same building program as the Older Parthenon

---

[29] For the traces of fire, see below.

that, ever since its remains have been recognized, it has in general followed the fluctuations of the main temple. Thus, after a general attribution to the pre-Persian epoch by its discoverer on account of the traces of a great conflagration, it was more definitely assigned to the following successive periods: (A) about 540 B.C. during the tyranny of Peisistratus, (B) about 489 B.C. after the battle of Marathon, and (C) about 469 B.C. during the ascendancy of Cimon. The principle of identity of date with the Older Parthenon still holds, so that we are now limited to (B) about 489 B.C., or more probably 488 B.C. like the temple. But in view of the fact that the Propylon was erected largely on bedrock so that the level of the marble work was quickly reached, we may infer that the structure was erected to its complete height before the fire of 480 B.C., though the surfaces were never dressed down and finished. Thus it was actually the first building to be erected in Pentelic marble.[30] This priority seems to be confirmed by the undeveloped character of some of the precautions taken to protect the surfaces, more akin, in the Old Propylon, to those in soft poros limestone; but in the Older Parthenon, with longer practice, a more effective technique was evolved. Outside the Propylon was laid out a forecourt of the same date,[31] lined with steps and a marble bench with a dado consisting of secondhand marble metope slabs from the dismantled Hecatompedon, turned upside down with the ornament chiseled and rubbed off.

In connection with the Old Propylon, for more reasons than one, must be noted the so-called "Hecatompedon inscription" (IG I² 3/4), discovered in the Persian debris on the Acropolis and, in spite of its fragmentary condition, exactly datable because of the survival of the archon's initial (Ph- and Phi-) at two points, one of them definitely requiring ten letters and so fitting only Philocrates of 485–484 B.C. We are, therefore, concerned with one of the years of the erection of the Older Parthenon and Propylon, and in view of the fact that the inscription is carved on two of the marble metope slabs of the Hecatompedon, dismantled in 489 B.C. to make room for the Older Parthenon, and also because the inscription

---

[30] For the use of other materials, see the discussion of the fire, below.

[31] Too much emphasis has been laid on the existence of two double-Γ clamps in the otherwise unclamped poros enclosure of the forecourt of the Propylon, as evidence that it should date from the tyranny of Peisistratus. As we noted in connection with the Marathon base at Delphi, this was merely an economical form used in later times together with double-T clamps, and is not to be regarded as an infallible sign of early date.

regulates conduct within the Acropolis, it would be tempting to assume that these stood in line with the numerous other secondhand metope slabs of the same series lining the entrance forecourt of the Propylon. Such, however, could hardly have been the case: the vertical joints between the slabs lining the forecourt are carefully smoothed for close contact and are decoratively beveled, while those of the "Hecatompedon inscription" are rough with irregular protrusions preventing close contact. While we must conclude that these regulations did not form part of the architectural scheme, a location near the entrance is most plausible; and in any case they constitute a most important landmark in early Athenian epigraphy. The use of the dot theta is now firmly established in official inscriptions; and in this example, with its beautifully designed and spaced letters and with its characteristic punctuation in rows of three or nine tiny circles, we see the work of the same hand that executed the epigram of Simonides on the Marathon cenotaph four years earlier.

Meanwhile, as the threat to civilization became more evident, and as the Persians prepared their land army for the great march from the Hellespont, the Athenians and Spartans sent out envoys with the aim of preparing a united defense. "For if all Greece join together in one, there will be a mighty host collected, and we shall be a match for our assailants; but if some turn traitors, and others refuse their aid, and only a small part of the whole body remains sound, then there is reason to fear that all Greece may perish" (Herodotus, VII, 157). Nevertheless, placing their trust in the expanses of sea lying between them and Hellas, the islands of Crete, Corcyra, and Sicily adopted a policy of isolation; Crete bluntly refused aid on the advice of the Delphic oracle (VII, 169); Corcyra spoke brave words, that "the ruin of Greece was a thing which they could not tamely stand by and see," but retained their fleet in the west (VII, 168); Sicily merely sent out ships "to watch the war and see what turn it would take" (VII, 163). Even on the mainland, as in the Peloponnesus, a large proportion desperately maintained their neutrality and "stood aloof from the war, and by so doing, if I may speak freely, they in fact took part with the Medes" (VIII, 73). And others, as Thessaly and Thebes, less fortunately situated, frankly submitted and even assisted the enemy with all their forces. The dream of a united stand quickly faded; but at least Athens had Sparta by her side, and many lesser states.

The chronology of the invasion must be worked out with reference to the single fixed point in this half of the century, the solar eclipse of October 2 (Julian), 480 B.C., just after the battle of Salamis. Slightly more vague are the dates of Salamis itself, "in the twenties of Boedromion" (Plutarch, *Camillus*, 19) just after the Eleusinia (Herodotus, VIII, 65)— and so, considering the state of the moon, probably on September 27[32]— and of Thermopylae, coinciding with the Carneia in Sparta (ordinarily in the Attic month Metageitnion) and with the Olympic games in Elis (Herodotus, VII, 206; VII, 26) which in this year seem to have culminated on August 26. During the intervening thirty days Athens was taken.

The story of the capture of the Acropolis by the Persians, a few days before the battle of Salamis, may be illustrated by numerous archaeological remains. Thus the well-known oracular response from Delphi, "safe shall the wooden wall continue for thee," interpreted by Themistocles to refer to the wooden hulls of the fleet, was regarded by "certain of the old men" as proof that "the citadel would escape, for this was anciently defended by a palisade" (Herodotus, VII, 140–144). The exact form and location of this so-called "palisade" are problematical, for it hardly conforms to our knowledge of the Pelasgian wall which at this time formed the Acropolis defenses; but it seems clear that Herodotus was referring to the west end of the Acropolis, where the credulous few, "having fortified the citadel with planks and boards, . . . imagined themselves to have discovered the true meaning of the oracle uttered by the Pythia, which promised that 'the wooden wall' should never be taken—the wooden wall, they thought, did not mean the ships, but the place where they had taken refuge" (VIII, 51). For "the Persians encamped upon the hill opposite [i.e., to the west of] the citadel, that called the Areopagus by the Athenians, and began the siege of the place, attacking the Greeks with arrows whereto pieces of lighted tow were attached,[33] which they shot at the barricade. And now those who were within the citadel found themselves in a most woeful case, for their wooden rampart betrayed them; still . . . they stoutly refused all parley, and among their other modes of defense rolled down huge masses of stone upon the barbarians as they were

---

[32] On the very same day, according to tradition (Herodotus, VII, 166), the Carthaginian end of the Axis, having seized the opportunity of invading the great island which formed the western outpost of democracy, was decisively thrown back at the battle of Himera.

[33] At Thermopylae in 1939 were found actual examples of these incendiary arrow heads used by the Persians.

mounting up to the gates" (VIII, 52). Thus the scene can be localized at the great west bastions of the Pelasgian wall and the intervening Old Propylon at the head of the west slope. And in this very building chance has preserved the scanty traces of the wooden wall.

It has been frequently observed that the inner face of the marble dado of the flank wall of the Old Propylon—being imbedded in the Pelasgian wall, there is no outer face—is cracked and flaked and reddened by fire, and that such traces recur on the marble anta which faced toward the now missing columns. These traces must date from the destruction of 480 B.C., since they are partially concealed by repairs (stucco and inserted poros blocks) of the style characteristic of the work of 479–478 B.C., described below. It has been less frequently noted that above the dado is still one small piece of a marble belt course $3\frac{3}{8}$ inches (0.086 m.) high, a treatment typical of walls only if the upper portions were to be painted.[34] Whenever it was feasible, moreover, the upper parts of such walls concealed by paint were economically constructed of inferior material; and such was obviously the case in the Old Propylon, where the rough top of the marble belt course would hardly have supported another course of stone. On such a bed only mud bricks could have rested satisfactorily. But there is more than this: on the top of the belt course is cut a socket $1\frac{1}{8}$ inches (0.028 m.) deep. The front face of the belt course is now a separate fragment which rarely remains in place, being thrust forward by each annual growth of weeds; but when one retrieves it from the ground below and adjusts the fracture to the rear piece, it becomes evident that the socket was $8\frac{1}{8}$ inches (0.205 m.) square and set $3\frac{1}{4}$ inches (0.082 m.) behind the face of the wall. In other words, we have the footing for a vertical timber 8 inches square, apparently one of several set at regular intervals and forming half-timbered work with mud bricks filling the intervals; and since this half-timbered wall recedes from the face of the marble below, we must assume that most of the difference was taken up by planks about $2\frac{1}{2}$ inches thick nailed horizontally across the upright studding. Such, in any case, must have been the mode of construction;[35] and, being unique on the Acropolis, we

---

[34] As in the northwest wing (Pinakotheke) of the Propylaea, the Hellenistic reconstructions of the Tholos and Odeum of Pericles, and several late stoae both at Athens (those of Eumenes II, Attalus II) and Pergamon (that of Eumenes II around the temple of Athena Polias).

[35] Other evidence, though secondary, is the collection of "old masters" subsequently

may infer that the wooden walls of the Old Propylon were those which misguided the few defenders.

"At last, however, in the midst of these many difficulties, the barbarians made discovery of an access . . . Behind the gates . . . where no watch was kept . . . a few soldiers mounted from the sanctuary of Aglaurus." The location of this obscure entrance, and the traces of the wooden stairway wedged into the cleft between the main rock of the Acropolis and an enormous flake which had slipped off during the dim geological past, have long been known but were only recently excavated and studied in graphical detail. We are now enabled to picture every movement of the few assailants to the point where they reached the summit; and on seeing them "some of the Athenians threw themselves headlong from the wall, and so perished, while others fled for refuge to the inner part of the temple. The Persians rushed to the gates and opened them, after which they massacred the suppliants. When all were slain, they plundered the temple and fired every part of the citadel" (Herodotus, VIII, 53).

The traces of the conflagration are still visible, not only on the remains of the Old Propylon, but also on its companion the Older Parthenon, and also on the scattered blocks of the temple *par excellence* (the Peisistratid temple or *Archaios neos*) to which Herodotus refers—as, for instance, the great poros Doric capitals dug up from the terrace fill west of the Parthenon. Traces of fire on painted roof terracottas from the lesser buildings, and on archaic marble votive sculptures and on fragments of painted vases

---

exhibited in the northwest wing (Pinakotheke) of the later Propylaea. For some of these, as catalogued in the lost book by Polemon and also by Pausanias (I, 22, 6–7), particularly the *Achilles with the maidens of Scyros* and the *Odysseus with the maidens of Scheria* by Polygnotus, were older than the actual date of the Propylaea (437–432 B.C.) and must be presumed to have been sawn out of the wooden revetment of some earlier walls. A plausible conjecture would be that they had been piously rescued from the walls demolished in 437 B.C., having been painted by Polygnotus on the wooden walls of the Old Propylon, which had been restored after 479 B.C., as the remains indicate, practically in its original form. It is impossible, in any case, to admit the curious modern theory to the effect that the Pinakotheke was erected sufficiently earlier than the rest of the Propylaea to have permitted Polygnotus to execute these as mural designs on the marble walls. For, even though the Pinakotheke was planned to have mural paintings, the construction shows not only that such were never executed (so that the collection must have consisted solely of panel pictures) but also that the erection was simultaneous with the rest of the building, that is, after 437 B.C.

which had been dedicated in the sanctuaries, bear witness to the violence of the destruction, as do the layers of ashes and charcoal met by the excavators in 1835–1836 and 1886–1889. Much of this evidence has been deprecated by the advocates of post-Persian dates for such buildings as the Older Parthenon, who argue that the fire stains and fissures on the poros limestone are due rather to dead algae contained within the natural stone, and that the similar stains on the marble are natural discolorations existing when the marble was quarried and that the fissures are the results of wind and frost. It is stated that poros if subjected to fire should be white rather than pink, and that marble if subjected to fire should be gray rather than pink. To be sure, when poros is subjected in the laboratory to the intense flame of a Bunsen burner it becomes white; but experiments have shown that when burning wood is the agent the stone can be transformed to any desired shade of pink, and it would be difficult to explain otherwise the coincidence that the fire-swept ruins of ancient buildings of this material, such as the temple of Heracles at Acragas[36] and the capitals of the Peisistratid temple on the Acropolis, are characterized by pink and even purple tones as well as flaking, while those not so devastated are buff or brown. As for marble, it must be admitted that the back of the west pediment of the Parthenon, again subjected to fire, yields a general impression of gray; but one should also take into consideration the effect of the east wind on a surface exposed for centuries at this lofty height,[37] as contrasted with more protected surfaces on low levels uncovered comparatively recently by excavation; and in any case we may adduce actual examples of marble colored pink by fire, such as the walls of the Old Propylon described above.

The lower city of Athens appears to have suffered only incidental rather than systematic destruction in the course of the brief Persian occupation in 480 B.C. Xerxes withdrew his army a few days after Salamis (Herodotus, VIII, 113), and it was not until ten months after the first capture, and so about July, 479 B.C., that Mardonius reoccupied it (IX, 3). This summer, like the preceding winter, passed in vain efforts by the

---

[36] It has been argued independently, to be sure, that likewise in these ruins at Acragas the pink color is a natural mineralogical effect. Since, however, it occurs there in conjunction with surfaces which have obviously been flaked and destroyed by fire, I can see no excuse for separating the causes of discoloration and destruction.

[37] Compare the white, gray (verging on black), and golden brown tones characterizing the different sides of the Parthenon columns.

Persians to isolate Athens with offers of a separate peace, territorial compensations and restoration of the burnt temples (VIII, 136–144). Sparta countered by promising Athens—though with the reminder that "'twas by you that this war was kindled at the first among us, our wishes being in no way consulted"—to serve as the arsenal of democracy (VIII, 141–142). Athens decided, "So long as the sun keeps its present course, we shall never join alliance with Xerxes" (VIII, 143). Until that decision "Mardonius had neither ravaged their territory nor done it any the least harm; for till now he had cherished the hope that the Athenians would come to terms with him. As, however, he found that his persuasions were of no avail . . . he determined to withdraw from Attica . . . and first to burn Athens, and to cast down and level with the ground whatever remained standing of the walls, temples, and other buildings" (IX, 13). The traces of this destruction, though wreaked upon less monumental buildings constructed with ephemeral materials, have not entirely vanished. The excavator meets layers of burned debris, containing fragments of artifacts of dates appropriate for the destruction of 479 B.C., in such areas as have not been disturbed by his ancient or modern predecessors, as, for instance, under the buildings along the west side of the Agora—the Stoa of Zeus Eleutherius (where the old sanctuary of Zeus Soter was destroyed), the temple of the Mother and the archaic temple of Apollo Patrous, the early municipal buildings under and near the Tholos and the road to the southeast—and also on the hill above—the scorched earth under the Hephaesteum and the deposits of burned debris further west. Masses of such deposit (some of course thrown down from the Acropolis above) are likewise encountered on the north slope of the Acropolis. Gravestones and bases of monuments, injured at this time and subsequently broken up for second-hand building material, are everywhere encountered. "Of the old line of walls but a small part was left standing; most of the houses were in ruins, a few only remaining in which the chief men of the Persians had lodged" (Thucydides, I, 89). All Attica suffered as well, either then or on the preceding occasion (Herodotus, VIII, 50). The burning of Eleusis (IX, 65) has left its mark in layers of carbonized debris and scorched roof-tiles. The half-burnt ruins of the temples of Hera on the road to Phaleron and of Demeter at Phaleron were described by Pausanias (X, 35, 2) more than six centuries later.

As the Athenians who marched from Attica to meet Mardonius at

Plataea were afterward able to say, "We went forth from a city which was no more, and fought for one of which there was small hope; and yet we saved ourselves, and bore our part in saving you" (Thucydides, I, 74). The Spartans, better than their word, were now staunch allies, and to them the Athenians willingly confided the unified command. The battle roll is still legible on the coils of the serpent column removed from Delphi to Constantinople. And before engaging combat on the fateful day of September 26, 479 B.C., the allies swore the Oath of Plataea which was ever afterward solemnly repeated by the Athenian youths: "I shall fight as long as I live, and I shall not prefer life to liberty; nor shall I abandon my company commander nor my platoon commander whether living or dead; . . . and those of my companions who may have died I shall bury on the very spot, and not one shall I leave unburied. And after fighting the barbarians victoriously I shall exact a tithe from the city of the Thebans . . . And of the sanctuaries which have been burnt and thrown down by the barbarians I shall not rebuild anywhere a single one, but shall leave them as monuments of the impiety of the barbarians. And if I abide steadfastly by what is written in the oath, our city will be healthy, not sickly; our land will bear crops, not be fruitless; . . . our flocks will yield increase like to their progenitors, not monsters."[38]

Since the day when the fate of Europe, and of the world, hung in the balance just as it did at Tours in 732, thirty years passed in intermittent conflict with Persia, while Athens still considered herself bound by the terms of the Oath of Plataea, though this weighed more heavily on Attica than on any other territory. Not only were religious observances impeded by lack of accommodation, most of the sanctuaries lying deserted, encumbered by ruins serving as quarries for secondhand building material (as the Peisistratid temple on the Acropolis and the Older Parthenon) or

---

[38] This oath, like the Peace of Callias, has been branded as apocryphal by the anti-Athenian historian Theopompus and hence by nearly all modern commentators, merely because it is not mentioned by Herodotus or Thucydides. But we have numerous references to it, and even versions of it, from the fourth century B.C. and later; only by considering it genuine can we understand the proposals of Pericles for its abrogation thirty years later—so far as the burnt sanctuaries were concerned—on the occasion of the abortive Panhellenic Congress; and only its strict observance explains the consistent failure to rebuild the sacked temples for periods ranging from thirty years to more than a century, or, in some cases, their perpetual preservation as unrestored ruins.

containing mere temporary shelters (as under the Erechtheum and, presumably, near the Hephaesteum, as well as at Sunium). In addition, despite the impulse given to the less spacious arts by the increased prestige and prosperity of Athens, there was a danger that the new spirit of monumental architectural design inaugurated by Aristeides would stagnate and be suffocated. It is true that a few special temples, apparently in all cases modest, were erected as direct consequences of the war, as those of Artemis Aristoboule founded by Themistocles in the deme of Melite (Plutarch, *Themistocles*, 22; *Mal. Herod.* 37) and of Athena Nike on the Acropolis (existing under the present temple), or to fulfill urgent needs, as the Telesteria at Phlya (Plutarch, *Themistocles*, 1) and Eleusis (as shown by extant foundations). There were also some repairs, which may be regarded as semi-religious, in the cella of the Peisistratid temple (apparently now transformed into a treasury known as the Opisthodomus) and in the Old Propylon. For the rest, architecture consisted only in the erection of secular and civic buildings (such as the Tholos) and of fortification walls. It was to remedy this situation that, immediately after the signing of the Peace of Callias with Persia in the spring of 449 B.C., marking the final victory of democracy after fifty years of hostilities, Pericles took the step of calling the Panhellenic Congress at Athens for the purpose of debating the reconstruction of the sanctuaries burnt by the Persians, the completion of the vows made to the gods during the course of the Persian Wars, and the freedom of the seas (Plutarch, *Pericles*, 17). The second step, the Congress having failed, was the abrogation of the self-imposed Oath of Plataea, so far as it pertained to the burnt sanctuaries. Next came the decree of Pericles, proposing that moneys accumulated by the Delian League, now no longer required solely for warlike purposes, should provide the means of rebuilding the temples. The first of these, appropriately enough, was to have been the outward symbol of the victorious peace, the reconstruction of the little temple of Athena Nike on the Acropolis in more costly material and richer design, as evidenced by a decree (*IG*² 1 24) which seems to have been passed by the Council before June 22 of 449 B.C. But new and larger plans for the reconstruction of the entire Acropolis as a memorial of the successful conclusion of the Wars, and the resulting necessity of coordination, suspended operations on the little temple before a single stone had been laid; and the model and specifications thus left in abeyance were evidently employed for the fulfillment of another vow of the period of the Persian Wars, the erection of a temple to Artemis Agrotera on the bank of the Ilissus River, the sanctuary at which was celebrated the annual festival commemorating Marathon. In furtherance of the main project, the Acropolis itself, Pheidias was recalled from Olympia and Ictinus from Bassae; both were associated with Callicrates, and to all three was equally due the crowning glory of Athens, the Parthenon laid out on the morning of the Panathenaic festival of July 28, 447 B.C., to be speedily followed by the Propylaea and the other marble buildings of the Periclean age. Thus, in a sense, the building program of Aristeides was that actually carried out by Pericles, though in much more grandiose form, and Demosthenes (XXII, 13) was not wholly unjustified when he stated that the present Parthenon and Propylaea were built from the spoils of Marathon: they exemplified in monumental and matchless form the ultimate victory of democracy.

SOME NOTES ON THE ECONOMIC INTERPRETATION OF HISTORY

FRANK H. KNIGHT

University of Chicago

IT has already long been recognized that one of the intellectual vices of that far-off age, the nineteenth century, was the excessive "rationalization" of human behavior and human nature. The economic interpretation of history was a phase or product of this error. The modern rationalistic world-view may be said to have come in with the European Enlightenment; but it was given a special twist by the empirical-practical English mind in utilitarianism, of which the classical economics, the science of the economic man, was essentially an application, after considerable logical purification. Marry this to the German-romantic rationalism, or rationalistic romanticism, of Hegel, and the Marxian interpretation of history is the natural, reasonably predictable, offspring.[1] The doctrine of our title is already well on its way to the discard and might before now have become a topic of historical interest only, if it had not got into politics. In that field, almost as in religion, a theory retains its truth, and even a degree of untouchable sanctity as long as a large number of people will abide by an agreement once made to believe in it.

A convenient approach to the issues raised by our topic is afforded by a well-known small volume of lectures by Professor G. N. Clark of Oxford University, entitled *Science and Social Welfare in the Age of Newton*. The third chapter, on "Social and Economic Aspects of Science," is explicitly a reply to an essay on "The Social and Economic Roots of Newton's Principia" by the Russian Professor B. Hessen, which is a polemical interpretation of the English seventeenth century movement in terms of orthodox Marxism.[2]

---

[1] It is notorious among critical students of economics that Marx and Engels got the main points in their position, and especially their most palpable economic fallacies, by copying from the Ricardian economics but paraphrasing in a somewhat more rigorous, and "consequent" or thorough-going presentation.

[2] Clark, *op. cit.*, Oxford University Press, 1937. Hessen's paper is published in the volume

Professor Clark's work is also suited to bring out other relations between history and economics, and to illustrate the type of reasoning one may expect to encounter in this field of discussion. Writing as a historian, the author on one hand rather adequately demolishes the Marxist error but on the other hand himself falls into economic fallacies of equal magnitude, in addition to missing the main point (according to this writer) of the subject he is discussing. His economic reasoning is of a kind which is characteristic of historians and of educated people generally, a fact which is at once the main practical reason for teaching economics, and the despair of those whose profession it is to do it. It would hardly be possible to imagine a "better bad example" than is afforded by a couple of sentences taken from near the end of Professor Clark's second chapter: "Again, technological improvement was most active . . . in those industries in which there was international competition . . . the export industries, which each state now tried to foster in order that its dependence on imports might be lessened, and its exporting power increased." Obviously, the fostering of export industries would *increase* a country's dependence on imports—unless the exports were given away to foreigners, which is not customary. And importation is the only intelligible motive for fostering exports, as well as its natural consequence. There are other hardly less "flagrant" sins against facts and logic, such as the observation that a labor-saving invention is a "synonym for unemployment," but we must turn to the main subject of the present essay.

* * * *

In arguing against Professor Hessen's economic interpretation of the scientific movement in which Newton was the most dramatic figure, Professor Clark admits that the economic interest plays an important rôle in the activities of men, and hence in social change. But he argues that five

---

Science at the Crossroads, (Kniga [England] Ltd., London, 1932—see pp. 151–212) with other items presented by members of the Russian delegation at an international scientific congress held at London in 1931. (The fullest and best discussion in English of our subject as a whole is probably the volume of M. M. Bober, *Karl Marx's Interpretation of History*. Cambridge, Harvard University Press, 1927. See also Seligman, E. R. A., *The Economic Interpretation of History*, 2nd Ed. Rev., 1924; and Sée, Henri, same title (Trans. M. M. Knight) New York, 1929. This last, as well as Bober's work, has extensive bibliographic notes.

other types of interest, distinct from the economic, have also to be recognized as playing rôles, which are of comparable importance. The first of these is the *health* interest, underlying medical science. He admits that this is "utilitarian," but distinguishes it from the category of economics. Clark's second non-economic interest, he says, is not even utilitarian, unless "everything is utilitarian"; this is the interest in the *fine arts*, particularly painting and music. The third is *war*. The fourth is the *religious* interest, to which the discussion centering around the life work of Max Weber has drawn so much attention. The fifth is the pure *intellectual* interest in science, the desire for knowledge for its own sake. The validity of the distinction between the scientific and utilitarian interests is explicitly argued in connection with mathematics and the motives and personalities of the leaders in that field; but a reasonable person must surely admit its reality in connection with any branch of inquiry.[3]

* * * *

In attempting to build upon this analysis, and to get beyond it, we may start from the question which will undoubtedly be raised by anyone disposed to advocate the economic interpretation—the question whether these various interests or motives are really distinct from the economic. The thesis of this paper is that this question itself rests on a fallacy, so that no answer to it can be correct. Properly speaking, there is no distinctively economic motive, or end or value. We may speak of an economic *interest*, but only if we are careful to understand that what we mean by it is not an interest in doing any particular thing or kind of thing, or in achieving any particular kind of end; it is merely the interest in doing "economically" anything that one does at all, i.e., in acting efficiently or effectively. These terms, "economic" and "efficient," which are closely synonymous, refer to the use of means or resources or "power" in any form, in the pursuit of any given end, regardless of its nature. Any activity or problem is, then,

---

[3] The story is often told that the great mathematician K. F. Gauss once closed a paper before a public meeting by giving vocal thanks to God that no one could possibly make any use of the theorem he had demonstrated.

Professor Clark recognizes a kinship between the scientific and esthetic interests, but still holds that they are different. He quotes Arbuthnot, a writer contemporary with Newton: "Truth is the same thing to the understanding, as music to the ear, and beauty to the eye."

"economic," or is affected by the economic interest, in so far, first, as it involves the use of resources or power, and secondly, in so far as the problem is actually and realistically one of "economizing" the available means or power.

No yes-or-no answer can be given to the question whether any problem is economic or not; at most it is a matter of degree, and at bottom even this form of the question embodies a misconception. Every human activity involves the use of means or power, and the degree of satisfactoriness of any activity is always in some sense a matter of success in achieving what is attempted, and hence a matter of the efficiency or effectiveness with which means are used. All human capacities, and time itself, a dimension of all activity, are, formally speaking, means or "resources." And all activity involves economizing human capacity or time, as well as more tangible means and resources which are practically always involved to a greater or less extent in any project or problem of action. This is clearly true of all the activities which are contrasted with the economic by Professor Clark. All of them involve the use of what we call material means, in the loose general sense of the word "material." This is apparent if one goes through the list; doctors, artists, soldiers, ministers of religion, and scientists have their economic problems, and so do institutions concerned with these fields of activity. Professor Clark must be aware that universities have them, and by all report it is as true of armies, hospitals, art schools and museums, and "even" of churches.

To begin with, "one must live," as a familiar aphorism says, as a condition of pursuing any of these "higher" activities; and "living" is universally recognized as an economic problem. But this undisputed fact glosses over the deeper issues. Some of these are uncovered by asking what is included in a living, and attempting to relate that category in turn to the activities to which it is alleged to be prerequisite, such as health, art, war, religion, and the pursuit of truth—and others which, as will be noted presently, might be added to this list. The complexity of these issues may also be suggested by an aphoristic question regarding the means-and-end relations of eating: Do men eat to live or live to eat? It is obvious that they universally do both, and in a multiplicity of senses. And the same is true in every conceivable degree of curing disease, searching for truth, and of all the higher activities; they are both ends and means.

The question whether any activity is economic or not is, to repeat, the question whether, or how far, it makes sense to regard the *problem* involved as one of economizing means in realizing some end, given in advance. Living, in the large, does not seem to fit the means-end relation to any specific activity, but rather to *consist* of an indefinite aggregate of activities and interests, which are mutually means and ends to each other. In particular, it needs to be emphasized that that "living" which is prerequisite to any of the so-called higher activities cannot possibly be defined in biological terms. Human living is always a complex mixture of the higher activities themselves. Living, at the human level, means living in some way, according to some standard. This is clear if we reflect that in our own culture a relatively small fraction of what is nominally spent for "food" even by people classed as poor, really represents the cost of physiological nourishment, while a still smaller part of the cost of clothing, shelter and other budget items ministers to animal needs, to physical life and health, or to "comfort." The human value even of "subsistence" is esthetic and social.

* * * *

It is possible however, to make some headway in the analysis of the general problem of what is meant by the economic as a category, as a more or less distinct form of motivation. To begin with, there are two aspects of economic activity, or of economizing, in ordinary common-sense usage. The first aspect is "technical" or technological; there are various concrete, manipulative ways of using any means to any end, which are "effective" in various degrees. But economics, as a recognized special science or subdivision of knowledge, is not concerned with technological problems. These belong to the various branches of technology as such, including the fine arts and the crafts. Every art or craft has its technique—not merely the fine arts and the professions, engineering, etc., but also agriculture, business management, cookery and the most menial occupations, in the home and outside of it. Economics is not concerned with these techniques. It deals with another aspect of economic activity, which—putting the matter in crude, common-sense terms to begin with—is that of employing means or resources for more important rather than less important uses or immediate ends.

Refining the conception somewhat, economics deals with the *apportionment* of resources among various modes of use. The science takes its rise from the empirical fact that (in consequence of the principle of "diminishing utility") the effective use of resources commonly involves such apportionment. Hence there is a problem of "correct" apportionment, in order to secure the "best" results, or what is called in economic jargon, "maximum satisfaction of wants." Much of the difficulty of economic theory as a science inheres in this conception of a generalized end of activity, called "want satisfaction." It means simply the common denominator of the more specific and concrete ends of action, the perfectly abstract general end to which all concrete ends are means.[4] We do compare these prospective results as quantities, insofar as we choose "rationally," in deciding how much of our total expenditure, in money or productive capacity, is to be allocated to each. "Want satisfaction" commits one to no theory of motive or the good; it is merely the term which has become conventionalized to refer to *that which* any individual is trying to "maximize," to get *more* of in preference to less, in choices between different ways of using means.

It will now be clear that it is at best a vague question of degree, how far any problem of action, or the effective motivation in any human activity, is "economic." It is a matter of judgment, of one's feeling as to how far it is good sense, or is realistic, to view any type of action problem as one of economizing means. Of the five interests discussed by Professor Clark, religion and the fine arts are perhaps least realistically described as economic, in the problem they present; war and medicine would surely be "more" economic, with scientific activity somewhere between. Writing poetry surely is not primarily a matter of economizing paper, ink, and "labor," and neither is religious worship. The need is first to understand what statements about economy mean, and then to realize the vagueness and subtlety, amounting to sheer paradox, in the means-end relation. When we say, for example, that the ministry of religion, or musical composition, is not primarily an economic activity, we mean only that we do not ordinarily think of the problems involved as problems of the allocation or effective use of means. Under critical scrutiny, it is evident that we "could" do so; and sometimes and within limits we do. Thus the validity of usage or of our thought habits as a test of the nature of things becomes

---

[4] Want satisfaction is not really the *summum bonum* of the moral philosophers, since ethical or other critical evaluation is excluded from economic comparison, which is quantitative only. But logical definition runs in much the same terms, and utilitarianism and pragmatism virtually reduce all ethics to economics.

questionable. Worship and the creative arts certainly involve the use of means, and specifically of what are unquestionably classed as economic resources; and these can be used more or less "effectively." Moreover, economic resources certainly are apportioned between these activities and other (competing) uses, and a "margin of indifference" is determined upon. The apportionment of resources between "higher" and "lower" uses is presumably made, or people try to make it, in such a way that at the indifference margin all the different uses are "equally important." This makes the meaning of importance itself something of a paradox. But there is no escaping the logic which makes this equalization of the importance of all alternative uses of any means, "at the margin," the *meaning* of economy (in the aspect of apportionment; technical efficiency is another meaning).

Before leaving Professor Clark and his list of five interests, it must be emphasized that while undoubtedly useful for the author's purpose in making it clear—as against Hessen and naïve or dogmatic economic interpreters generally—that other interests than the economic must be recognized, this list itself will not stand scrutiny as an analysis or classification of the ends, motives, or interests which must be taken into account by the historian or other student of social life. It seems doubtful whether anyone can make a clear analysis of human motives, or one which will stand much critical scrutiny. It must suffice here to point out that this list has nothing to say about such fundamental interests as play, self-expression, and self-development; of activity and achievement for their own sake; or of social interests, including emulation and personal and group likes and dislikes, as well as sociability as such—all in highly various forms.

The play interest seems to be especially important, and seriously neglected in discussion. It seems to stand at the opposite pole from the economic interest, however defined, and is indeed largely anti-economic in principle; and yet it also contains its economic element. In play as well as in "work," one is always trying to do something, to achieve some objective, and to do it effectively. And yet, as someone has remarked, the first step in organizing a football game according to the ideal of economic efficiency would be to put all the men on the same side; it is wasteful and absurd to have half of them struggling with all their might in opposition to the other half. Moreover, an element of the play interest is probably universal in all voluntary activity. Reflection upon the meaning of these facts is sufficient in itself to reduce any economic interpretation of conduct as a universal principle literally to "foolishness."[5] In addition, all interests are suffused with a desire for *power*, dominion over men and over things. But power as an end, apart from any desirable result to be obtained by its use, is outside the concept of economy or economic rationality.

In sum: Economic thinking deals with the problem of using given means to realize given ends. Its scope is limited in one direction by critical reflection about ends, in contrast with the problem of getting things wanted, and in the other by the unconscious or mechanical cause-and-effect aspect of behavior. The means available to any individual (or to any group, considered as an economic subject) are at any time "really" given; but the end is not given or is given only in a partial and provisional sense. There is no final end in conduct, in any concrete and intelligible meaning. Such terms as want-satisfaction, or "happiness," or self-realization, as general ends, are little more than names for the fact that, for our thinking, activity is at any moment directed to *some* purpose beyond the concrete end immediately in view. All concrete ends are really means, as one realizes the moment any end is questioned; and the ultimate end is simply "the good life!" And "the good" must include many species, which resist analytical differentiation. Moreover, the means-and-end relationship is complicated by the indisputable fact that means—or more properly the procedures by which means are used, i.e., activities as such—may evidently be good or bad *per se;* they are subject to value judgments, about as much as are ends themselves.

Again, even the immediate, concrete end or objective, in a particular limited problem or project, never is fully given at the beginning. It is always subject to re-definition during the process of its realization. This is true in all degrees. In the limiting case at the opposite extreme from the concept of economic behavior, the end is not given at all; the essential motive of the action is "curiosity," it is to find out what the result will be. Such activity is *explorative*. And all activity seems to involve this motive as a factor. For example, we would never read a book or listen to a lecture if we knew in advance exactly what book we are going to read—its content—or what we should hear the speaker say, though to be moved to ac-

---

[5] Sociability, of course, combines with more concretely directed activities, in which the play and work interests on one hand, and coöperation and conflict interests on the other, stand out as two sets of polarities.

tion we must have some idea of what is to be expected. And all creative activity above absolute drudgery is more or less explorative and creative. Worse still, reflection about play makes it clear that in a very large measure the end is really instrumental to the activity, rather than the converse. We deliberately set up an end for the purpose of making the activity interesting. This is also true in all degrees, of "economic" life in the empirical sense, both in production, or "business," and in consumption. Activity in either of these fields may have as much the character of a competitive sport as that of satisfying wants, as a specific and final consequence of the use of means. Or, the motivation may be that of play in games of solitaire. There is no clear distinction between work and play, and the concept of economic activity has no clear relation to either. All economic activity is affected by the creative and explorative interests, which have much in common with play, and by numerous social and individual motives which do not enter into the make-up of the hypothetical "economic man." In short, the economic interest is an aspect of conduct in general, varying widely in importance relative to other aspects. It does not pertain to any distinct field of action or class of activities.

It is a particularly serious fallacy, associated with the economic interpretation, to think of economic activity as the only field in which conflicts of interest occur, between individuals or between groups, or as the only field in which conflicts reach the proportions of a major problem. Candid reflection will rather make it seem doubtful whether the abolition of all economic problems—say by a fairy gift to every adult of the power to work physical miracles—would ameliorate social conflict, or would even change its form in any important respect. All the "higher" activities are both competitive and coöperative, including religion and pure sociability, as well as science and philosophy, and it is doubtful whether the competition and power relations in other fields, and particularly in politics, are morally better or tend less to conflict than those of the business world, or whether they are essentially different.

* * * *

The application of this brief and sketchy theoretical analysis must be briefer still. The quest of the historian, as a philosopher, or as methodology-conscious, is for causes, forces, laws, uniformities of sequence, or elementary concepts in some form, which will serve to make historical writing intelligible, to "explain" the past, and in some degree, as he fondly hopes, give an inkling as to what may be expected in the future. A classification of the possibilities in this direction should undoubtedly begin with a dichotomy. The first question is to decide as to the relative importance in historical process of motivated and unmotivated behavior, or deliberate action as against unconscious "social forces." Surely, this is a matter of degree; neither sort of causality can be excluded, or have fundamental importance denied to it. And the same will be true of numerous sub-heads under each of these general categories; especially on the side of motivated action, one must recognize many kinds of ends, good and bad, rational and irrational.

In teaching economics, and writing for economists, who are notoriously afflicted with a naïvely utilitarian, rationalistic, and individualistic bias, it is the unconscious and social element which needs emphasis. The writer's favorite procedure has been to insist upon some reflection on the part of students about language and the scientific study of language. Linguistics is recognized as perhaps the most "scientific" and intellectually satisfactory of the *"Geisteswissenschaften."* The outstanding fact in the study of linguistics is that no one proposes to explain or interpret the evolution of language in terms of conscious or rational individual motivation. Indeed, it is something of a paradox that, although language is evidently one of the most important instrumentalities or tools of social life— and hence of all human life—and is consciously and purposively used as a tool, effort to increase the functional efficiency of language is found to play a relatively small part in linguistic change. Even the struggle for existence and selective survival among variations hardly seems to work toward the "improvement" of language.

In the respect indicated, language is only a somewhat extreme example of features in which all social-cultural phenomena share in greater or less degree. Next to language in this respect would doubtless come the law. In fact the same statements made about language would apply literally to the law through most of its history. It is only in fairly advanced civilizations that laws are "made," or changed, by "taking thought," or that they even become subject to conscious observation and criticism on the part of the mass of the people who live under them; and even here the historical school of jurisprudence denies or minimizes the effective reality of legislation.

We might go through any working list of departments or forms of social behavior, and show that tradition, subject to slow, unconscious modification, is the basic element in all of them, though this is decreasingly so, in most fields, as we approach the conditions of today. Language still obstinately remains exceptional; we do indeed see efforts made to improve language or make it more "scientific," but they do not get far. In primitive society, conscious motivation seems to function almost exclusively in a conservative sense, in all fields; it acts to resist change, to enforce conformity to tradition.

It would seem that this unconscious and highly conservative form of change, called "drift" by the linguists, and custom or tradition by sociologists, is the proper meaning of the "historical," as a distinct type of causality or process, and as a category of interpretation. Thus it is largely antithetical to the category of the "economic," as understood by economic theorists, for the latter refers to behavior of a conscious, highly deliberative and "rational" type.[6] In this usage, a "historical" interpretation of history is the antithesis of the "great man" interpretation, to which the "economic" interpretation would be closely related.

But this is not the way in which the terms are commonly used; and surely the supreme need is for the removal of ambiguity in usage, and establishment of some consistent terminology. Most history, as actually written, is primarily biographical; its main problems and its method of explanation run in terms of individual motivation, though not, for the most part, of "economic" motivation, as defined by the economist. The chief motive recognized by historians is the desire for political power.[7] On the

---

[6] But as we have seen, the economic is by no means the extreme antithesis to tradition or historical causality. The economic view of behavior assumes that the end of action is given, as well as the means and knowledge of procedure; i.e., it abstracts from deliberation about ends, and consequently does not apply to behavior as affected by problems of evaluation—"truth, beauty, or goodness." Thus scientific, esthetic, and moral activities, in which ends are not given but problematic, are rational in a higher sense than the economic. The latter, as already noted, is bounded in an upper direction on a scale by critical evaluative action, on the lower side by unconscious or non-deliberative behavior.

[7] It is true that in the "new" or "social" history this is less true than in the older and more exclusively political history. But it is perhaps still predominantly true, even in these newer writings, at least that the motives of action are conscious interests, though a broader range of such interests is taken into account.

The relation between political and economic power is an important topic, but must be

other hand, what *historians* (and Marxists, in the dialectical aspect of Marxism) mean by the *economic* interpretation is a species of what we have called the "historical" category *per se*. The economic interpretation, commonly so-called, consists in selecting a particular field of activity, and thread of change, called the economic, but defined vaguely or not at all, and making that, conceived as a drift, the "independent variable" in historical process, and treating other types of behavior and threads of change as causally dependent upon it.[8]

In the field of economics, it is important to note, we find a situation which may be regarded as either parallel, in a sense, with that found in history, or inverse, according to taste. That is, we find a succession of "historical schools" of economics, beginning especially in Germany about the middle of the nineteenth century, and with the *"Neo-Historismus"* of Weber, Sombart, *et al.*, in Germany, and "institutional economics" in America, as current or recent phases. Thus, while historians have been running to an economic interpretation of history, many economists have been advocating an historical interpretation of economics. It would be interesting, if space limits allowed, to subject this situation to philosophical scrutiny. A combination of these two opposite views or approaches would make a good starting point for a real discussion of the general subject of social and historical interpretation.

*   *   *

Finally, there is space for only the briefest indication of the lines along which it would be interesting to develop a critical analysis of the economic interpretation of history as itself a phenomenon of intellectual and

---

passed over; it is obvious that each is in varying degrees a means to the other, with economic power growing in importance in modern times.

[8] The best meaning for the expression "economic interpretation of history"—if one were given the task of finding a definite, particular meaning for it—is surely to take it (as the American Marxist Calhoun has argued) as the application to human history of the Darwinian principle of selective survival on the basis of biological efficiency. This gives in effect a technological interpretation, which is the evident meaning of Marx and Engels in many passages, and undoubtedly has much truth in it. It also has limitations, among them its incapacity to explain decadence, which is a historical fact as real and as important as progress. The important but puzzling pretentions of Veblen to be the apostle of the Darwinian method in economics come to mind in this connection, but can only be mentioned.

cultural history. We mean, of course, the theory— not really originated by Marx and Engels (who ever originated anything?!)—but which at least was forced upon the attention of scholars and of the public chiefly by their writings and the work of their followers. Marx and Engels, and the "scientific" socialists, shifted somewhat recklessly between the expressions, "materialistic" and "economic" interpretation or conception (*Auffassung*). The background is of course Marx's "flirtation" with the Hegelian dialectic, in which he more or less playfully, as he said, stood the dialectic on its head, or, in his own view, on its feet. "Dialectical materialism," is another stock designation of the position. It would be easy to show—in fact it hardly seems to need demonstration—that the three concepts, materialistic, dialectical, and economic, if clearly defined, are mutually exclusive, that they belong in different universes of discourse, with no intellectual bridge between any two of them.[9] All three undoubtedly have reality, and all three are valuable, even necessary, in the discussion of historical process, stability and change. But in so far as a phenomenon belongs in any one of these categories, it does not belong in either of the other two. This means that a highly pluralistic conception of history is unescapable, at least until philosophy and metaphysics have made enormous progress, beyond anything either yet achieved or in sight for the future, in the way of unifying the ultimate concepts used in our thinking.

But this is by no means the end of the confusion in Marxism. For the Marxian Scientific Socialists, all three of the categories mentioned are intellectual preliminaries to their real interests—one might even say a kind of smokescreen. What they have been trying to promote is, in the first place, a "class struggle" theory of history. But it is evident, first, that in "struggle" and "class" struggle we have two more categories, irreconcilable as principles, either between themselves or with any of the prior three. And second, even these theories of history are still preliminary, a part of the propaganda for the real objective, which is the practical political one of fomenting a conscious class struggle, which did not exist or pre-

---

[9] A dialectical interpretation of history is "practically" equivalent to a mechanistic view, the difference being purely a matter of metaphysical theory. The "rationality" referred to at the outset has become in Hegel "absolute" reason, which is so far from human reason that they are antithetical. The same paradox is found in connection with economic process; "absolutely" economic behavior is conceptually identical with mechanical sequence; without liability to error, purposiveness is unthinkable.

dominate before, or it would not need to be promoted. Incidentally, critical examination would show the notion of an economic class to be so vague and shifting that it can hardly be used in any scientific discussion of *political* struggles.

The vital fact is that any single scientific or positive theory of motivation is self-stultifying, especially in connection with any sort of propaganda. For any general theoretical explanation of behavior or motive must apply to the activities of the (explainer and) propagandist himself, and any intellectually satisfactory explanation reduces his propaganda to nonsense, to selling talk, if not to mere noise. The suggestion of an economic interpretation of the economic interpretation is all that should be needed as an answer to it, if taken in a thorough-going and inclusive sense. The "victims" of the propaganda must be kept from thinking of that possibility—which in fact has an embarrassing amount of validity! For the real motive back of any political propaganda is largely the quest of power on the part of those who are carrying it on. The propagandist can usually see this clearly in connection with every propaganda except his own. To the Marxists, as to most reformers, it has been only their opponents who have been actuated by selfish or "class" interests. *They* are asking nothing for themselves—except supreme power and the perquisites thereof! From an impartial or objective historical and political point of view, perhaps the most interesting fact in connection with the Marxist theory of history is the paradox that, human nature—and specifically human political intelligence—being what it is, one of the most effective ways of securing active support for a cause is to "prove" that it will "inevitably" triumph, that in fact there is nothing that anyone can do about it. Predestinationism in religion (Islamic fatalism) is an earlier conspicuous illustration of the same psychological principle.

What seems most philosophically significant about Marxism is its bearing upon the problem of ethics. For what it primarily means in practice is the complete futility and even the unreality of any intellectual-moral discussion, especially of group policy. It teaches that economic self-interest is the exclusive principle of human action (except that of the teacher?) that all human conduct is to be understood in terms of such interests, backed up by force. It is essentially the repudiation of real discussion and of reason (except in so far as dialectical process means the will of the Absolute, really expressed in "my" will) and direct appeal to violence in behalf of group self-interests. Since the same phenomena of class division and struggle would undoubtedly reappear within any "class," however composed, as soon as it became dominant (by "liquidating" its opponents) the doctrine finally spells the *bellum omnium contra omnes*, or complete social chaos.

In conclusion: Any unique or monistic interpretation of history is a delusion and a snare. But the "economic interpretation" particularly needs to be combatted, above others, because, while it contains a large portion of truth, this is so obvious, and so much in line with the dominant trend of oversimplification in modern thought, that it naturally tends to receive too much recognition and emphasis. The "economic factor" is both assumed to have a much more definite meaning than can properly be given to it, and is also assigned a far greater rôle in comparison with other principles than is possible, if it is separated from other principles in any defensible way. It is the limitations in favor of other principles, and the danger of oversimplification in historical analysis in general, which call for emphasis.

INVENTIONS, POPULATION
AND HISTORY

WILLIAM FIELDING OGBURN
University of Chicago

THE thesis of this paper is that inventions affect the size of populations and in this manner influence history. That inventions have helped shape the events of past history is obvious but not always appreciated. However, in the assessment of factors affecting the events of the past it is believed that invention has not received the emphasis it should have received if the various factors were given their proper weighting. For instance, America would hardly have been discovered and settled by white peoples if there had not been a boat of adequate size. Sails and a compass also were essentials in making the settlement of the New World, but the usual account gives no credit to these inventions although the names of the ships are recorded. This is natural. Historians, of course, attribute this discovery to Columbus. Indeed, more credit is given to Queen Isabella of Spain than to the invention of the boat.

Inventions, of course, are not wholly neglected by historians. It is the custom, for instance, to mention in history how armies fighting with gun powder overcame those equipped with bows and arrows. But in the main, inventions are not greatly emphasized by historians in their concern with particular events.

In establishing the control of England over the seas in the 19th century the deeds of her great naval heroes such as Lord Nelson are recounted and properly so; but it remains a fact that the success England derived from her great empire rested in large part on attaching the steam engine to her ships; and the greatness of the premiers of England in foreign policy during the long reign of Queen Victoria rests in large part upon England's early attainment of the armored war ship propelled by steam.[1] There is even a tendency to associate this Golden Age of England with the leadership of Queen Victoria herself. No doubt Queen Victoria was a good queen, but it is also probable that the greatness attributed to her is

---

[1] Brodie, Bernard, "Sea Power in the Machine Age," 1941.

due to the remarkable success of England as a world power during her reign. The queen was the symbol of a great era; the achievements of the time really were determined by a series of successful inventions adopted by England before the other states of Europe acquired them.

I

That the success of leaders is sometimes due to possession on the part of their followers of superior mechanical techniques is one of the main points in the controversy over the rôle of the great man and of social forces in history. The tendency to explain history in terms of great men has been frequently discussed. Indeed, it is quite natural to describe achievements in terms of leaders. Medals are given to men for conspicuous deeds but no one has ever heard of a medal being pinned upon an invention.

Such mechanical and hidden forces as inventions tend to elude the pen of writers. The working of some machine is not inherently as interesting as the human drama of war, debate, exploration, intrigues or ambitions. These social forces are usually seen as economic, and there is a great body of literature concerned with the economic interpretation of history,[2] and there has grown up a great school of economic historians who are concerned with these impersonal and hidden forces that have determined the events of the past. But back of economic forces are inventional changes as Karl Marx rightly emphasized. The inventional interpretation of history is, indeed, like the economic interpretation of history, only one step removed.

There are, though, two kinds of economic interpretations of history that have not in general been adequately distinguished in critiques of this type of history. One is the history which posits the movements of man as being essentially concerned with selfishness. This rôle of selfish interest is especially noted in class situations in society. An illustration of this type of economic interpretation is the work of Charles Beard on the origins of the constitution of the United States.[3] Ordinarily the framers of the constitution of the United States have been thought to be seeking in a somewhat noble and disinterested manner a document which

---

[2] Seligman, E. R. A., "Economic Interpretation of History," 2nd ed. rev., 1924.

[3] Beard, Charles A., "An Economic Interpretation of the Constitution of the United States," 1935.

would be the basis of the welfare of the common people of a democracy, whereas the work of Beard indicates that the framers were seeking selfishly their own class interest which would prosper best without too much control being given over to the people.

The other kind of economic interpretation of history is one which does not emphasize the selfish motive so much as the force of economic factors. On this plane of analysis the great force in modern history was capitalism,[4] a monetary economy resting upon a great variety of economic organizations such as corporations, banks, trust companies, exchanges and labor unions. These economic structures were made possible by such social inventions as the division of labor, wage system and rates of interest. Thus, much of the activity of the nineteenth and twentieth centuries in Europe and America which is the subject matter of modern historians is to be accounted for in terms of these economic forces centering around capitalism.[5] This second type of economic interpretation of history concerns the materials of economic history. Usually, however, economic historians describe the economic trends without relating the super-structures of political and social organizations with this economic organization. Such a task of correlating cause and effect in economic forces and political consequences is very difficult if scientific standards be maintained.

If this analysis were carried one step further back of the economic organizations, there would come a technological interpretation of history. The argument here presented is that the explanation of history would be somewhat better achieved if there be added a further explanation of the inventional influence back of the rise and variations of economic forces.

A very good illustration of the inventional interpretation of history is the history of the Great Plains[6] area in the United States which in its early development was essentially on open range country for cattlemen. There were no woods and the rainfall was too slight for agriculture. The westward movement of population passed it by because the woodland culture which they possessed was not adapted to the plains. Conquering of the plains came later largely through three inventions—the six shooter pistol, barbed wire and the wind mill.

---

[4] Sombart, Werner, "Der Moderne Kapitalismus," 1928.

[5] Hacker, Louis M., "The Triumph of American Capitalism," 1940.

[6] Webb, Walter Prescott, "The Great Plains," 1931.

II

Since the technology back of the economic organizations rests upon invention it is desirable to discuss the characteristics of invention. The word *invention* as used here carries a broad meaning and covers not only the concept of mechanical invention but also discoveries in applied science. Thus the discoveries regarding anti-toxins and the germ theory of disease would be classed under this broad concept as inventions. So also the domestication of cattle is of the general nature of inventions. In general, discoveries in pure science would not be thought of as inventions affecting history until these discoveries became practicable. Thus the discovery of the Herzian waves did not become an influence in society until it acquired some practicable form as in the radio. It is, therefore, the radio that influenced history rather than the discovery of the Herzian waves.

The idea of invention is sometimes extended to include social invention. New types of social organization, of new art or of religious forms as, for instance, the League of Nations or the literary essay or the religious revival meeting would then be called social inventions. It is quite desirable under some conditions to so extend the concept as to cover social organizations and new patterns in the non-material culture. Such is particularly the case in studying social change, but it is necessary in this paper to eliminate from the idea of invention these extensions into the field of non-material culture.

Another characteristic of invention is its evolutionary nature. To most users of the term an invention appears to be born fully developed like Venus out of the sea. In fact, however, the birth of an invention requires a period of gestation and a long period of development. For inventions to have widespread influence they must be relatively durable, simple to operate and easy to repair. Hence, their appearance in the past is not quite as quick and dramatic as is customarily described. It took a long time for gun powder to be used effectively in cannons. It seems to have been thus used as early as the fourteenth century, but gun powder did not become a significant force in history until a century or more later when it was influential in changing the feudal system. This slow development of inventions may be part of the explanation as to why their appreciation as forces in history tends to escape historians. The sudden, quick and dramatic events of history, especially those centering around personal achievement and deeds, are more readily observable than these slow movements.

Particularly likely to be missed by writers is the influence of small inventions. The steam boat, for instance, was a large and spectacular one, and hence, difficult to overlook. The terms large and small in being applied to inventions do not refer to their physical dimensions but to their influence. Large inventions are those that are significant in their social effects. The small inventions are measured in the millions while the larger inventions are measured in the thousands. While the illustrations and discussions that follow will be chosen mostly from the large inventions it should not be forgotten that the cumulative force of small inventions is significant for history, too.

Inventions are seen in the theory here being set forth as a force. How can so material an object as an invention be a force? If the course of history is determined by social forces, how could technology be a social force? History is, by common agreement, the record of the behavior of human beings and the forces of history are the activities of mankind. In other words, if there were no human beings and hence no human behavior, there would be no history. Social forces, therefore, flow from human beings and groups of individuals. When the phrase "the force of invention" is used or when "technological forces" are implied what is meant is that invention or technology serves as a new stimulus for groups of individuals to behave in different ways. The force is always resident in the physiological structure of the human organism, but inventions set up new customs, and new social institutions because human beings react to inventions in new ways. Thus, railroads were a force in building cities. In fact, railroads ushered in the era of cities. Before then the proportion of population in cities in any country was quite small. Now the railroad is the result of a mobile steam engine on a roadway made of two rails. Human beings react to these iron rails and mobile engines as stimuli by building cities. It is in this sense, therefore, that inventions become a force in history. They stimulate human activity.

III

The foregoing remarks sketch out quite generally a theory of inventions and history. The purpose of this paper, however, is not to explore this whole general field of the relation of invention to history but rather to discuss a limited part of it. This part concerns the effect of invention on population, that is, numbers of people. Since population aggregates of various sizes affect history then inventions influence history indirectly by varying the size of human populations.

In exploring this thesis, populations are thought of as units of various sizes. At certain times in history the significant unit of population is the local community. At other times the significant unit may be the population of a large area such as a state. Another population unit is an army. There are, then, a great variety of population units differing in kind and size.

The influence of population changes on history lies in the shaping of general processes rather than being the direct and immediate cause of unique events. The term *history* will be used not so much as a record of events as an account of social movements and of civilizational developments. A particular event such as the decision of President Wilson to attend the Peace Conference in Paris is not illuminated very much by any statistics of population. On the other hand, the rise of the United States as a power among nations distinctly rests upon population. That history, so conceived, is affected by population will be readily admitted. The population of France in the seventeenth century was probably four or five times the population of England at that time while in the twentieth century they were about equal in numbers. The historical relationships of these two countries were undoubtedly affected by the ratio of their populations. For the exposition of this thesis it then becomes desirable to describe the ways in which inventions affect the sizes of populations and ensuing historical movements.

As a first point it may be observed that some inventions affect population directly. A very good illustration is contraceptives. This invention in its modern form was adopted in France in the early part of the nineteenth century and not in the other countries of the world until the latter part of the nineteenth century, thus producing differentials in population growth that were significant for history. Thus at the time of the beginning of the first World War the birth rate of Germany was very much greater than that of France, and may have been a factor in causing it. The population of northwestern Europe and, indeed, of the United States will become a diminishing population within a few decades largely because of this invention. It does not seem probable that this will be the case so soon with the Slavic countries or possibly with southern and southeastern European nations. Nor is the birth rate of Japan and the Orient likely to fall soon to so great a degree.[7] Consequently, it will produce new differentials between the size of the populations of the various states which will undoubtedly influence the history of the coming years especially in the competitive rivalry of states.

Another illustration is the epochal discoveries of the past century in medicine which have reduced the number of deaths. The result of these discoveries plus the development of sanitation has been a reduction of the death rate from thirty or forty per thousand to almost a third these rates. The effect of the reduction of deaths had, of course, been compensated for in population growth by the reduction of births which occurred at the same time and at nearly the same rate for a time; but in the future the death rate will rise while the birth rate will probably fall in the countries of the western world. This control of disease makes possible, of course, the settlement of regions otherwise difficult, such as had been the area of the Panama Canal.

Another way in which inventions affect population is through food. At the time that Malthus wrote and earlier, variations in the food supply caused significant changes in populations. Today the actual changes in the amount of food probably do not cause such great changes in numbers, though always food is necessary to maintain populations. Hence, inventions affecting food affect population. There have been in the past thousand years many inventions relating to the supply of food such as fertilizers, the rotation of crops and the storage of food. These agricultural inventions applied somewhat more successfully to the population of France than to the population of Italy and led to the power of France during the late Middle Ages. Again, England's population has recently become the equal in numbers to that of France because of inventions affecting food. The British are able to obtain a much larger food supply by importation than they could if they were dependent upon their own agricultural land.

The idea of importation leads to a consideration of another way in which invention affects population, namely, transportation. Transportation affects the size of an area in two ways, by bringing food and by

---

[7] Thompson, Warren S., "Danger Spots in the World's Population," 1929.

moving human beings. Transportation, for instance, has abolished famines; and urban populations would be impossible if it were not for transportation, since the city is a local unit where the inhabitants are not able to raise the food they eat but must import. There are, of course, other inventions affecting the city but food supply by railroads, boats and trucks is quite essential. Cities are also a phenomenon resting upon the migration of human beings, that is to say, their transportation. Cities do not maintain their populations since either the death rate is higher than the birth rate or the birth rate is lower than the death rate. Mathematically these statements are the same but not sociologically. In medieval London, for instance, it was impossible for the birth rate to equal the death rate for the death rate was very high. In modern London the birth rate is so low that the death rate cannot be made to equal it. Hence, cities maintain themselves by migrations from farms and smaller places. Therefore, inventions affecting transportation affect populations. Other illustrations of more historical significance might be cited. The settlement of the New World could only have taken place under conditions of good transportation. In Asia and Europe the horse has led successive migrations from the Arabian desert and from the steppes of Russia which have profoundly affected the course of European history. The coming of the Norsemen depended upon the excellent boats possessed by the Vikings. Thus, the rôle of the Norsemen in medieval Europe was the result of inventions related to transportation by sea.

Still another influence of invention on population occurs through the manufacturing of tools. This is very well illustrated by that great collection of inventions which gave rise to the industrial revolution of the nineteenth century. The population of Europe doubled during this century. At the same time it distributed her sons and daughters all over the world. This phenomenal multiplication of population during the past century and a half is attributed by students to the inventions centering around steam power and to the accompanying achievement in medical progress.[8] The development of manufacturing and the various organizations of the capitalistic system meant employment for larger and larger numbers of workers. This increase in workers could only have been possible with the increase in the food supply either by imports or by agricultural improve-

---

[8] Thompson, Warren S., "Population Problems," 2nd ed., 1935.

ment. That the coming of the machine age to the Orient will lead to a similar expansion of population is not certain, because of the spreading of another invention, contraceptives, which was subsequent to the Industrial Revolution in England. Birth control might even precede factories in China. It is possible to have an industrial revolution in the Orient without an increase in population if numbers be kept down by contraceptives.

Still another way in which inventions affect population is through war. This is seen in the conquest of America by the whites. When the Spaniards came in contact with the American Indians, they possessed the horse, armor, sword and gun, none of which the Indians had. It was, therefore, relatively easy for Cortez to conquer vast numbers of Indians with a handful of Spaniards so well equipped. The invention of the stirrup was especially significant in the development of cavalry, thus enabling the horse to play a very great rôle in history. Indeed, the domesticated horse even without the invention of the stirrup was one of the greatest war instruments known in early times since it made quick attacks and quick get-aways possible.

The bombing airplane and tank give advantage to those larger countries possessing them in numbers which is comparable in some ways to the superiority of the Spaniards over the Indians or the horsemen of the Arabian desert over the sedentary populations.

From the preceding paragraphs it can be seen that inventions affect population in a variety of ways, directly and indirectly, through birth rates and death rates, and by migration and distribution. It is only by the recognition of the variety of ways in which these different inventions influence population that we can appreciate their significance for history.

IV

The subject has been discussed from the point of view of inventions that affect population. It is now desired to approach the subject from the other end, that is, to note certain significant changes in history and observe how they have been produced by changes in population and in inventions. The first illustration concerns the rise and fall of states. At any one time in history one state is predominant over another. Sometimes one people is thought of as carrying the "torch of civilization" which is later passed to another people. Thus Greece was at one time in the lead, at another Rome, and so on. Perhaps the torch of civilization is not the right symbol; perhaps it would be better to speak of one state being an economic vanguard. In any case, the economic prominence of the eastern Mediterranean area rested upon a fortunate concurrence of a number of inventions occurring within a few thousand years. These were copper, bronze, iron, the alphabet, the horse, cattle, the wheel and the boat. The peoples in other parts of the globe had no such happy concurrence of inventions. Hence, the Mediterranean peoples were given a tremendous lead over the other peoples of the world by the possession of such a remarkable set of great inventions. The definite proof and establishment of why one country takes dominance over another cannot be demonstrated, of course, without a great deal of research and investigation on the part of many workers but the general theory can be illustrated quite briefly. It can hardly be questioned that England's priority in the nineteenth century was due to the power inventions producing the Industrial Revolution, to inventions in shipping plus the fortunate location, of course, of the island and the possession of coal and iron. This in no way minimizes the character of the English people. Explanations of the prominence in history of one people or country can be approached from this point of view rather than from the point of view of racial abilities. But Greece and Rome could not possibly assume the lead over England after the inventions using steam because they had no coal and iron. Other inventions will produce other shifts among peoples in the future.

The history of the medieval and modern world was, as a further illustration, greatly affected by the inventions producing a series of agricultural revolutions. One of these is taking place at the present time. It is the application of mechanical power to the farms. During the Industrial Revolution mechanical power was supplied to the handicrafts. Farms were only indirectly affected, for mechanical power was not applied to the plow and hoe as it was to the handicrafts. Now, a hundred years later, farms are experiencing this same application of mechanical power, through the gasoline engine though instead of through the steam engine.

In earlier times there was the agricultural revolution that attended the discovery of the three field system. Indeed, it is argued that the practices that were developed with the transfer from the two field to the three field system in northern Europe increased agricultural efficiency enormously. Some interpreters of history, indeed, are disposed to explain the shifting of economic power from the Mediterranean to northwestern Europe as a result of agricultural revolutions, that is to say, of inventions improving agricultural production. The three field system was not especially suited to low rain fall and general climatic conditions of the Mediterranean. The heavy plow also favored northern Europe as compared with the Mediterranean area. Parenthetically, the reader should remember that such great changes can only be made by clusters of inventions but writers have acquired the shorthand method of signalizing these by the central invention. Thus the Industrial Revolution is thought of as due to the invention of the steam boiler and steel making. So the agricultural revolution rests upon various subsidiary inventions among which are the iron plow, which really might be considered a major invention as would also be the knowledge of fertilizers and the restoration of nitrogen to the soil by certain legumes.

Another phenomenon of history resting on population and invention is the shift of power from farms to great cities. The urban population of any large area before the railroads was probably never more than ten or fifteen per cent, if so much. It was the railroads and the factory system that brought in the cities. Today, of course, we have a great urban nation and a great urban civilization which has really furnished for man a quite new type of environment. Wealth is in industrial centers rather than on the farms. The cities are further being changed in the twentieth century by the automobile into what are called metropolitan areas. The cities of the nineteenth century, produced by the railroad, are being changed into metropolitan areas of the twentieth century by the automobile.

V

Great historical phenomena have then been brought about by clusters of great inventions. It is now desirable to go further back than the historical period and to see how certain developments before written records have been the result of inventions.

The earliest culture of mankind that we know is hunting and food gathering without benefit of seed planting and domestication of animals. Man in very early times hunted not only wild animals and game of various sizes but he probably spent more time gathering roots and herbs than he did trapping, killing and fishing, except in special localities. This stage of culture is usually known as the period of lower hunters. It rested upon relatively simple tools such as those possessed by the Australian natives or the Tierra del Fuegans. They had some traps, spears and throwing sticks. There was no pottery but some basketry. Their clothing was generally of the simplest. The effect of this simple technology on population was to maintain only very small groups, often five or six families of twenty or thirty individuals. With such small groups it can be seen that the elaboration of social life into other groupings, classes and associations could not be very great. Furthermore, these small bands did not live generally in one place very long, or if they did, wandered out as hunters from a central location as a base. Hence, the wandering life meant a restriction of social institutions. This culture rested upon a simple technology with very few mechanical inventions. History was quite different with peoples on so slender a technological base from what it is with us possessing such an elaborate structure.

Among other hunting people the technology became more elaborate. There were bows and arrows, sleds and other means of transportation, the domesticated dog, quite elaborate traps and fishing devices. In the case of the higher hunters the population unit was a good deal larger. It was sometimes a hundred or more individuals. Hence, there was more division of labor in their social system. A priest class began to arise. There were age societies and further elaboration of sex and age divisions in the group. As to more exact population statistics, Murdock has computed the average population of a community or band of hunters (lower and advanced), but with no agriculture and herding. The average population of a band for ten such peoples was forty-five persons. The population of a unit of hunting peoples was, furthermore, not very large because they had no way of storing food. Their economic life was essentially one of feast and famine.

Presently, however, a very important discovery was made, the domestication of large animals which in a few localities led to a life of herding. These animals were not at that time located on farms. Herding of domesticated animals meant a more reliable supply of meat than could be obtained by hunting wild animals. The population unit increased in size. Murdock finds an average of 160 persons.[9]

As the domestication of animals led to a more continuous supply of

---

[9] From a paper not yet published, made available to the author.

meat the domestication of plants led to a more abundant supply of plant food. The discovery of the planting of seeds and the invention of the digging stick led to agriculture in a simple form. The digging stick was used for resetting roots or for planting grass seeds. With such arts the food supply became more stable. Thus again the numbers of the population were increased. Villages were then the rule and with a stable village life came possibilities of further specialization and division of labor among social groups. This type of agriculture is known as the hoe culture and Professor Murdock's figures show an average community of three hundred and thirty persons. Among primitive peoples who have both agriculture and hunting, the size of the population unit is still larger. It becomes, according to Murdock's figures, a village of about four hundred and fifty persons.

Eventually there appeared another significant invention—the plow, which was quite superior to the hoe. It was more productive, led to a greater yield per unit of cultivated land and made possible the applications of animal power to agriculture. The plow culture produced villages that are not greatly different from those we know today and to a social life that was not so markedly different from that found in hamlets and villages in Colonial America, for Colonial America was a plow culture in the advanced stages. With the plow and domestication of animals farming could support villages of several hundred or even thousands of population. Consequently, a new order of social life was ushered in.

The boat became a very effective invention when coupled with the plow culture. Primitive peoples who live on water have some kind of water transportation. The simplest form is log or a dugout but when agriculture is fairly highly developed and when the wheel has appeared, the boat has by this time become a fairly elaborate instrument for travel. The combination of all these makes cities. The plow culture distributed civilization along the fertile river valleys. The hunting peoples lived in main on the edges of woodlands. The boat, wheel and plow shift the population to the water edges either of big rivers, big lakes or small seas. Thus the locale of historical events was again shifted in the direction of water transportation. Eventually came the steam boiler and steel which produced another great shift already described. Mechanical power tends to move the center of civilization again to the regions which have access to coal and iron. The predominance of the river valley nations is lessened with the coming of steam. The age of steam is not focused on any narrow area but rather shows its greatest manifestations in some big area that is relatively close or has access to coal and iron. The area is large because of the accompanying development of transportation.

VI

This theory has concerned history, history as a record of the past. Hence, it is not very appropriate to speculate concerning the rôle of invention and population for the future. But if the principle is once established and found to be widespread, namely, that inventions affect the size of populations and the size of populations affects historical developments, then it is to be expected that these same forces will shape the future as they have shaped the past.

It is beyond the province of this paper to say what the future may be like because of inventions but it is certainly to be expected that the inventions of electricity which distributes power so easily will be a factor. It is also thought that the chemical inventions which are coming so rapidly to transform one substance into another will be very influential. Steam power was able to transform the shape of one object into another. Chemistry transforms one material into another. Chemistry has greatly influenced the nationalism of Germany, for instance. Then again the inventions which are the most brilliant of our present era are the communication inventions—radio, television, facsimile transmission, motion picture, sound recording—all of which will be influential in the distribution of population. The twentieth century is also characterized by great developments in transportation. We are only seeing the beginning of the airplane. Its effect upon war is particularly spectacular and it is apparently having an effect upon the amalgamation and enlargement of governmental units. When steep flight air craft are developed a wider distribution of population around cities is to be expected. Indeed, significant inventions seem to be coming with greater rapidity than in the past and it is hoped that the historians of the future will put emphasis on the social forces that arise from inventions.

ICONOGRAPHY OF OLD DETROIT

RANDOLPH G. ADAMS
University of Michigan

WHAT did Detroit look like when it was young? In the nearly two centuries and a half that have elapsed since it was founded, almost every vestige of old Detroit has disappeared. The few logs from an old stockade which are preserved in the Detroit Trust Company Building and at the Detroit Public Library probably do not date from Cadillac's time, but from nearly a hundred years later. We therefore must fall back upon maps and pictures drawn, painted, or printed during the early period of Detroit's history. Efforts to portray old Detroit, made many years after the period they are supposed to represent, do not greatly excite the iconographer. He wants maps and pictures done by a contemporary cartographer or artist at the time they are supposed to illustrate. Anything else is apt to be akin to what lawyers call hearsay evidence.

We shall confine ourselves to the period between the acts of two Frenchmen: the founding of Detroit by Antoine Laumet de la Mothe Cadillac in 1701, and the invention of photography by Louis Jacques Mandé Daguerre in 1839. Pictorial representation in Cadillac's day was the work of the artist who made an image (icon) representing as accurately as possible what he thought he saw. Daguerre's discoveries and inventions fundamentally affected the graphic arts because they eliminated the chance of human error. Accuracy, to the iconographer, is much more important than mere artistic self-expression.

Since we propose to deal chronologically with our subject, it is exceedingly difficult to avoid discussing "firsts." What is the first map of Detroit? What is the first picture? Bibliographers well know that as soon as an item is designated a "first" and that allegation published, someone is apt to produce another which is indisputably earlier. No wonder that during the Harvard Tercentennial Samuel E. Morison somewhat ruefully remarked that he had to spend a great deal of his time "killing priorities." So, in what follows, the reader will please supply the words "alleged," "reputed," "believed to be," "earliest now recorded," etc., etc., wherever need be. This is a tentative essay, a trial balloon. It is to be hoped that it will bring forth additions, corrections and emendations. Thus the record may be made more accurate and more adequate.

The city of Detroit was put on the map by the French geographer, Guillaume Delisle. It is obvious that the words "le detroit" mean "the strait," or narrows which connect Lake Saint Clair with Lake Erie. "Detroit," meaning Cadillac's village, could not have been put on a map before Cadillac founded it in 1701. In the very next year, 1702, Delisle drew his manuscript "Carte du Canada et du Mississipi," upon which in the proper place is the conventional mark for a town, and immediately above it the words "le Detroit."[1] These words are entirely within the area of the present state of Michigan and probably refer to the settlement and not the strait.

But a manuscript is seen only by a few. Such data as it contains do not become "news" until it is manifolded and published. Delisle lost but little time in doing just this. In 1703 he had engraved, printed, and published two maps apparently based on the manuscript mentioned in the preceding paragraph. Both locate Detroit. One was his "Carte du Canada ou de la Nouvelle France et des Decouvertes qui y ont été faites."[2] The other was

---

[1] This manuscript map was last reported to be in the *Archives du Ministère des Affaires Etrangères*, in Paris. There is a photograph in the Karpinski Collection, Clements Library, University of Michigan, No. 356 (New York Public Library 111). The "Karpinski Collection," which will be frequently mentioned in this paper, refers to a collection of 773 photographs of manuscript maps relating to America in European archives.

While traveling in Europe in 1924, Professor Louis C. Karpinski of the Department of Mathematics of the University of Michigan, conceived the idea of photographing every manuscript map of America in French, Spanish and Portuguese archives. This ambitious project received the enthusiastic support of Regent William L. Clements, who appreciated the foresight and energy of Professor Karpinski, and who helped to finance the work. Many priceless cartographic sources on American history, long neglected by librarians and historians, were thus brought to light and made available to American scholars.

The following libraries subscribed to the entire series of the Karpinski reproductions: The William L. Clements Library, the Library of Congress, Harvard College Library, the New York Public Library, the Ayer Collection at the Newberry Library and the Henry E. Huntington Library. Other libraries have since subscribed to parts of the collection. In this study we have given the numbers assigned by the New York Public Library to the maps in the Karpinski Collection, as well as the Clements Library numbers.

[2] Of this 1703 Delisle "Carte du Canada," there are several variant editions, because

his "Carte du Mexique et de la Floride."[2a] Which of the two, the "Carte du Canada" or the "Carte du Mexique" was issued first, we do not as yet know. The former seems based on the northern part of Delisle's manuscript map of 1702, mentioned in the preceding paragraph, and the latter on the southern part. Either may be the first printed map upon which Detroit appears.

The problem of what Detroit, the stockaded fort and trading post, looked like is still a moot point. In the library of the *Service Hydrographique* in Paris there is a manuscript map of the whole region from Lake

---

the original copper plate was revised from time to time. Tentatively we may list the editions of the 1703 edition as follow:

A. With the cartouche reading in part, "Par Guillaume Del'Isle Geographe de l'Academie Royale des Sciences A PARIS Chez l'Auteur Rue des Canettes prez de S[t]. Sulpice . . . 1703." A lower section of the cartouche contains the scales of distances in which the word "Echelle" stands alone. Copy in the Yale University Library.

B. With the cartouche reading in part, "Par Guillaume Del'Isle Geographe de l'Academie Royale des Sciences A PARIS chez l'Auteur sur le Quai de l'Horloge a la Cour[ne]. de Diamãs . . . 1703." In the lower section of the cartouche the word "Echelle" has been lowered and above it appears: "et se trouve a Amsterdam chez L. Renard Libraire prez de la Bourse." Credit for identification of this variant belongs to Dr. O. O. Fisher of Detroit, Professor Karpinski and Colonel Lawrence Martin. The map, formerly in the possession of Dr. Fisher, now belongs to the Clements Library.

C. Wording of the entire cartouche agrees with "B" except that Delisle's address has been changed to "Quai de l'Horloge a lAigle dOr." Copy in the Clements Library.

D. Wording of cartouche agrees with "C," but words "et se trouve a Amsterdam chez L. Renard Libraire prez de la Bourse" have been erased. Copy in Library of Congress.

E. Wording of the entire cartouche agrees with "D" except that the word "Geographe" following Delisle's name has been deleted and "et Premier Geographe du Roy" has been inserted above "A PARIS." This indicates issue after 1718. Copies in the Clements Library and the Library of Congress. (See page 260, below.)

[2a] The "Carte du Mexique" also exists in variant editions. So far we have been able to identify:

A. With Delisle's address in the cartouche "A Paris Chez l'Auteur Rue des Canettes pres de St Sulpice . . ." Copy in the Library of Congress.

B. With Delisle's address in the cartouche "A Paris Chéz l'Auteur sur le Quai de lHorloge." The word "Horloge" is so crowded that we may conclude the words "Rue des Canettes" were erased and the plate corrected. Copy in the Clements Library.

Huron to Lake Erie,[3] upon which a small square fort with bastions at the corners, represents the settlement at Detroit. But the map lacks title, date and any evidence as to the cartographer. For the sake of convenience, we will call it the "Buffalo Map" because upon it an Indian is driving a herd of buffalo into Lake Erie near the site of modern Monroe, Michigan. This map is reminiscent in style of the crude maps which appear in the printed narratives of Hennepin and Lahontan, and because of its crudity and general inaccuracy, we give it an early position in the iconography. A great deal more study ought to be devoted to this "Buffalo Map" which, incidentally, may be the first map of Lake Saint Clair.

Sometime, probably between 1728 and 1734, the little stockade appears on a manuscript map of the region between Lakes Huron and Erie which is signed by Henri Louis des Champ de Boishébert, commandant at Detroit between those years. The stockade is now definitely "fort des françois," and is oblong.[4] Another manuscript, exhibiting the same inaccuracies and distortions as the Boishébert map, but undated and unsigned, also exists.[5] It locates for the first time the "Grand Marais" which is so well known to modern Detroit realtors who have developed the Grosse Pointe district. On this map "Fort des françois" is square with bastions at the corners.

The earliest detailed map of Detroit, showing streets and houses, is a matter of controversy. I will mention first a manuscript map in the *Archives du Ministère des Colonies* in Paris, which shows a square structure, with large Vauban-like bastions at the corners, and locates with some care and detail the various buildings inside the stockade—"Leglise," "Maison

---

[3] BSH 71-B4044 (Karpinski Collection, Clements Library, No. 356, New York Public Library 442).

[4] When last reported, this manuscript map "Carte du détroit Erié remontent jusqúau Lac huron" was in the library of the *Service Hydrographique*, Paris, No. 4044-B. There is a photograph in the Karpinski Collection, Clements Library, No. 698 (New York Public Library 441). For a sketch of Boishébert, see J. C. Webster, *Charles des Champs de Boishébert*, 1931.

[5] "Carte du Detroit et Partie du Lac Erie, et du Lac S^te. Claire . . . " last reported in *Archives du Ministère des Colonies*, Paris, No. 545. There is a photograph in the Karpinski Collection, Clements Library, No. 759 (New York Public Library 502).

du Commandant," "Maison de M.ʳ de Tonty," etc.[6] There is in the Bibliothèque Nationale a manuscript memorandum, which may be by Tonti, which describes Cadillac's original fort as "d'un arpent en quarré."[7] Mr. Quaife argues that the memorandum tends to fix the date of the map as early as 1701 or 1702. On the other hand, Father Jean Delanglez of Loyola University, Chicago, who has also devoted much time to the collation of the map and manuscript, argues that the map may have been done by someone in Paris who never saw Detroit, and any date up to and as late as 1749 may be assigned to the map. The map itself bears neither title, nor name of cartographer, but clearly, on its face, bears the date "1749" in another handwriting. If this date is correct, this map which has been frequently used as the earliest representation of Detroit, does not deserve that credence.

It is with a great deal more security that we approach the very interesting group of maps of the Detroit region done between the years 1749 and 1755 by the engineer, Joseph Gaspard Chaussegros de Léry, 1721–1797, son of the engineer Gaspard Chaussegros de Léry. Three of these are detailed manuscript plans of an oblong stockaded town with small corner bastions. The best of the three, "Plan du fort du detroit . . ." is clearly dated "20 aoust 1749."[8] In the *Archives du Ministère des Colonies* in Paris is an equally satisfactory plan of Detroit dated "1749" and bearing the notation "Ce Plan a eté levé Sur les lieux en 1749 par ordre de M.ʳ le M.ⁱˢ de la Galissoniere Commandant General en Canada par le S.ʳ de lery fils offi-

---

[6] This manuscript map was last reported as being in the *Archives du Ministère des Colonies*, Paris, No. 550. There is a photograph in the Karpinski Collection, Clements Library, No. 762 (New York Public Library 505).

[7] The alleged Tonti memorandum was last reported in the Bibliothèque Nationale, MSS. fr. 9097. R. G. Thwaites (*Wisconsin Historical Society Collections*, xvi, 127–130) and Clarence M. Burton (*Michigan Pioneer and Historical Collections*, xxxiii, 131–132) both published abridged translations. But M. M. Quaife points out that Messrs. Thwaites and Burton both used an incomplete transcript and hence missed the date "20.ᵉ 7ᵇʳᵉ. 1701," which is on the original. Photostats of the complete original are in the Library of Congress and the Clements Library.

[8] Father Honorius Provost of Laval University prepared for the Clements Library photostats of all these Chaussegros de Léry maps at Quebec. They have been dealt with adequately and reproduced in *Rapport de l'Archiviste de la Province de Québec pour 1927–1928*. Miss Louise P. Kellogg's sketch of Chaussegros de Léry is in the *Dictionary of American Biography*.

cier d'infanterie faisant les fonctions d'Ingenieur au dit Payis et remis au Depot par le meme officier en 1752."[9]

We are also indebted to Chaussegros de Léry for two manuscript maps of the entire Detroit River, from Lake Saint Clair to Lake Erie showing the "ribbon farms" above and below Detroit, all of which are now inside the city limits of modern Detroit. One of these maps, "Carte de la Riviere du Detroit," shows the vegetation and no less than forty geographical locations named, and clearly indicated. It is dated and signed "le 22 octobre 1749. Lery fils."[10] The other, "Carte de La Riviere du detroit depuis le Lac Erie jusques au Lac Ste Claire," is clearly marked "Donné par mr de Lery fils 1752."[11] This is a precious document because it indicates the names of fifty-two property owners, the proprietors of the "ribbon farms" of old Detroit. The original manuscript of this map is in the *Service Hydrographique* in Paris. It was examined with care by Professor Karpinski and photographed. After subsequent study it was rephotographed and studied by Messrs. Karpinski, M. M. Quaife, Abel Doysié and the present writer. They have been able to decipher fifty of the fifty-two names.[12]

Chaussegros de Léry's manuscript maps were the basis for the first printed map of Detroit. In 1764 the cartographer Jacques Nicolas Bellin published in Paris his *Le petit atlas maritime* in five volumes. Plate twelve in volume one is based upon Chaussegros de Léry's "Carte de La Riviere du detroit," 1752, with his "Plan du fort du detroit . . . , " of 1749, as an inset.[13]

But by 1764 when the first printed map of Detroit was published,

---

[9] Last reported in the *Archives du Ministère des Colonies*, Paris, No. 549. There is a photograph in the Karpinski Collection, Clements Library, No. 761 (New York Public Library 504). Father Jean Delanglez believes this map was made in 1749, and the notation added in 1752 when Léry went to Paris and turned it over to the French government.

[10] Original manuscript map last reported in *Archives du Ministère des Colonies*, Paris, No. 547. There is a photograph in the Karpinski Collection, Clements Library, No. 760 (New York Public Library 503).

[11] Original manuscript last reported in the library of the *Service Hydrographique*, Paris, No. 4044ᵇ68. There is a photograph in the Karpinski Collection, Clements Library, No. 696 (New York Public Library 439).

[12] A redrawing of the map clearly showing the names of the property holders is at the Clements Library.

[13] There are two variants of this Bellin map: one having "Tome I. No 12." at upper right, and the other lacking that notation. Both variants are in the Clements Library.

France had lost Canada, including Michigan and Detroit. As is well known to every reader of Francis Parkman's classic *The history of the conspiracy of Pontiac*, Britain had a good deal of trouble making good its title to Detroit. During Pontiac's siege in 1763 and 1764, Detroit was fortunate in having as one of its defenders one of the most distinguished engineers in the British army, John Montresor. Apparently during the siege he made an exquisite water-color manuscript map of the Detroit River from Belle Isle to the site of the modern Ambassador Bridge, showing clearly the oblong "Town" and "Pondiacs Encampments."[14]

There is among the Additional Manuscripts in the British Museum a curious map showing the environs of Detroit at the time of the British occupation and locating the Battle of Bloody Run—"Capt Dalyelle le 3me Juillet." It has been dated 1768. This is not a very important map. We mention it only because it has been used in historical studies.[15]

The period of the American Revolution in Detroit left for the iconographer a little "Survey of the Comons," dated and signed "Detroit 22nd Oct 1776 James Sterling Surveyor." It shows the "ribbon farms" of Legras, Alexis Campau, Widow Dumai, Robt. Navarre Junr, Jacques Godfroy, Alexis Delisle and Widow Chesne—names all well known in Detroit history. The area is that of the Potawatomi village, near the site of the present army post of Fort Wayne, Detroit.[16]

Turning from maps to pictures, the rightful claimant to the title of the "first picture of Detroit" appears to be a wash drawing showing a few buildings and a stockade. It was found among the John Askin Papers by Clarence M. Burton, the historian of Detroit. Mr. Burton ascribed the drawing to Captain David Meredith, Askin's son-in-law, who was in Detroit about 1790. Mr. Burton further believed that the picture represented "Fort Lernoult" which the British built just back of the old French stockade during the American Revolution. This picture deserves a great deal more study.[17]

---

[14] A redrawing of the Montresor map was used as end-papers in Calvin Goodrich's *The first Michigan frontier*, Ann Arbor, 1940. The original is in the Clements Library.

[15] B. M. Add. MSS. 21686. See also H. R. Holmden, *Catalogue des cartes.* . . . Ottawa, 1912, No. 1639. We suggest that this be called the "Sandusky map" because of the prominence given Sandusky Bay in an inset.

[16] A copy of the original manuscript is in the Burton Historical Collection, Detroit Public Library.

[17] Mr. Burton tentatively dated the document "1780." But Miss Louise Rau of the

The original French stockaded town was variously called "Fort du De-troit" and "Fort Pontchartrain." It was simply a wooden walled town on the banks of the Detroit River. In 1778, Lieutenant Governor Henry Hamilton, British commander at Detroit, set out to regain the Illinois posts captured by the American, George Rogers Clark. Instead, Hamilton himself was taken prisoner at Vincennes (Indiana) early in 1779 by Clark, who then planned to attack Detroit. The British garrison, learning of these plans, began a new and stronger fort on an elevation back of the town and called it "Fort Lernoult," after the British officer then in com-mand.

What is possibly the first map to show this extension of the stockaded town is to be found in the George Washington Papers. Sometime late in 1780, "Henry Bawbee" (possibly one of the Detroit "Babys"), an Indian half-breed, sketched both the "old fort," and the "new fort," showing in detail the location of buildings and points of military significance of both. Bawbee seems to have been one of those spies who would serve either side. In any case, he delivered the map to Daniel Brodhead, at Fort Pitt, who promptly relayed it to General Washington. The locations of buildings in the old town agree with other maps, but those in the new fort do not—from which one may infer that the barracks and other houses were at first hastily constructed, and later re-arranged.[18]

Returning to pictures, the first undoubted picture of old Detroit is a water-color painting showing the west end of the town, the waterfront stockade, and the west gate. This painting is entitled "A View of Detroit, July 25th 1794." It was discovered in England, about 1923, by Lady Nancy Astor and by her presented to the City of Detroit.[19]

Some time about 1796 when the French were trying to make up their minds whether or not to try to interest themselves in their lost American

---

Burton Historical Collection, thinks it is later, as Meredith came to Detroit after that date.

[18] The map and Brodhead's letter transmitting it to Washington is in vol. 159 of the Washington Papers at the Library of Congress. I am grateful to Col. Lawrence Martin for calling my attention to this map. I must also thank Dr. St. George L. Sioussat and Mr. Donald Mugridge, who procured for me photostats of Bawbee's map and Brodhead's letter.

[19] The painting bears the initials "E. H." and is in the Burton Historical Collection, Detroit Public Library. It is reproduced in color as the frontispiece of M. M. Quaife's *John Askin Papers*, vol. 1.

possessions, there were a good many French "observers" in the United States. Among them was General Georges Henri Victor Collot. Some of the data given him for use in his travels were submitted to Létombe, French consul general at Philadelphia, who drew from them a very large "Plan Topographique Du Détroit Et des eaux qui forment la jonction du Lac Erie avec le Lac Saint Clair." Accompanying this is a good-sized view (18 × 24 cm.) of the Detroit waterfront as it appeared in 1796.[20]

Although by the terms of the Treaty of 1783, the British agreed to surrender Detroit to the United States that post was not actually secured until the army of General Anthony Wayne took possession in 1796. With Wayne there came Major John Jacob Ulrich Rivardi, an engineer in the United States Army. He made what is probably the most beautiful and accurate map of old Detroit showing its streets and gardens, the church and government buildings, as well as Fort Lernoult with its barracks, buildings, walls, bastions, and the like. Rivardi probably did not finish this map until after he had been transferred from Detroit to Niagara for in the lower border of the map is the legend, "drawn by J. J. U. Rivardi.— Niagara March-29-99."[21]

The last picture of old Detroit is probably the one painted by the English surgeon, Dr. Edward Walsh, who was stationed with the 49th Regiment in Upper Canada, 1803–1805. From the Canadian shore he painted a water-color, "A View of Detroit and the Straits, taken from the Huron Church June 22nd 1804."[22]

We call the above-mentioned picture the last of old Detroit because in the next year, 1805, almost the whole of the old French town was de-

---

[20] A full-sized re-drawing of this map (the original is 135.5 × 181 cm.) was prepared for Clarence M. Burton through Whitelaw Reid, when American ambassador at London. This re-drawing now hangs in the main reading room of the Burton Historical Collection, Detroit Public Library. The original manuscript was last reported in the *Archives du Ministère de la Guerre*, Paris (État-Major, L.I.D.no 7-B-61). Photograph, in several sections, in the Karpinski Collection, Clements Library, No. 445 (New York Public Library 202). The view of the Detroit waterfront was redrawn in black and white and reproduced in 1889 in Silas Farmer's *The History of Detroit and Michigan*, Detroit, 1889, I, 367; and again in C. M. Burton's *The City of Detroit, Michigan*, Detroit, 1922, II, 959.

[21] For Rivardi, see *American State Papers, Military affairs*, I, 87–93. The original watercolor manuscript map is in the Clements Library.

[22] A color collotype facsimile by Jaffé has been published by the Clements Library, which owns the original painting.

stroyed by fire. It was then that the new plan for a new Detroit was adopted. It followed the system of the circle and radiating boulevards similar to that which Pierre L'Enfant had designed and which he was using at that time in the building of the capital city on the banks of the Potomac.

So the iconography of modern Detroit begins with what is sometimes known as "Woodward's Plan," sometimes as the "Governor and Judges Plan." It looks like a symmetrical spider's web, surrounded by a perfect hexagon, each side of which is planned as another hexagon containing another spider's web. Mathematically it is beautiful. The center of the original hexagon can still be seen in Grand Circus Park with its radiating boulevards as depicted upon "A Plan of the City of Detroit Drawn By Abijah Hull Surveyor of Michigan January 1807."[23]

But the military fortification of Detroit could not wait upon the realization of the spider-web plan. In that same year of 1807, someone, apparently a United States Army engineer drew "A Plan of the fortification, now erecting at Detroit, which encloses all the buildings in the Town, with the plan of the Town which falls within the pickets Augt. 19, 1807." This shows the relation of the old town on the river with Fort Lernoult. This map is less satisfactory than Rivardi's map of 1799, but does show a detailed drawing of the kind of block-house used for the defense of the town.[23a]

Someone whose initials are either "L A R" or "I A R" made a pen-and-ink sketch of the western end of the town and waterfront, with legend "No 8 Detroit. April 23d 1809 I[L?]AR." Harry MacNeill Bland, the historical print expert, conjectures that the artist may be one Robertson, because of some similar drawings of other towns in the Finley collection at Knox College. But what the series was of which this picture of Detroit is "No. 8" we do not yet know. The drawing deserves much more study.[24]

In this same year, 1809, Aaron Greeley executed a manuscript survey

---

[23] A photostat of the worn and torn manuscript of Abijah Hull's map is in the Burton Historical Collection, sent to C. M. Burton by J. Franklin Jameson in 1909. The present whereabouts of the original, despite diligent investigation, eludes the iconographer. There is a reduced facsimile in G. N. Fuller, *Economic and social beginnings of Michigan*, Lansing, 1916, opp. p. 124.

[23a] This map was found among the records of the Corps of Engineers in the War Department and was transferred to the Map Division of the Library of Congress.

[24] The original sketch is in the Clements Library.

which is important because it shows the city after the fire, yet locates many old landmarks which existed before that catastrophe.[25] Greeley's surveys then became the basis for his all-important "Plan of private claims in Michigan Territory," which again shows the "ribbon farms" and the names of the owners. This map has been extremely important in fixing the ownership of real estate and making possible the abstracts of title which are essential to modern realtors.[26]

The War of 1812 should have produced a number of maps of Detroit. But if it did, they elude the iconographer. There exists a rather ragged manuscript map, showing the "Main Street" and the fort, and also three batteries of three twenty-four pounders close to the waterside. It has no title, and is dated 1812 in an unknown hand. C. M. Burton seems to have been of the opinion that this map was drawn by one William Evans during the War of 1812, but upon what authority does not appear.[27] So far, no proof has been advanced tending to support the idea that it is a contemporary document.

In John Melish's *Military and topographical atlas of the United States*, 1813, there is a map of the whole Detroit River from Lake Saint Clair to Lake Erie, reminiscent of the Collot map of 1796, and useful for tracing the military actions around Detroit during the War of 1812. This map was engraved by Henry S. Tanner.[28]

About 1820 an American army engineer, George Washington Whistler, was in Michigan and executed a famous water-color painting of Detroit from the Canadian shore, showing the "Walk-in-the-Water" passing the town. "Walk-in-the-Water" was the first steamboat to travel on the waters of the Great Lakes west of Niagara. Whistler's painting is best known

---

[25] "A Map of the Military Ground at Detroit, in the Territory of Michigan; shewing the situation of the old public Ground, and as it is surveyed by the request of Colonel Burbeck. 13ᵗʰ April 1809. Aaron Greeley Dpᵗʸ. Surveyor." This original manuscript is in the General Land Office, Department of the Interior, Washington, D. C.

[26] "Plan of private claims in Michigan territory as surveyed by Aaron Greeley D. surveyor in 1810." This is a large map with an inset listing names and holdings of Detroit land owners.

[27] The manuscript map referred to is in the Burton Historical Collection. To it is pinned a newspaper clipping of 1826. The map is reproduced in C. M. Burton, *The City of Detroit, Michigan*, Detroit, 1922, II, 1025.

[28] "Map of Detroit River and adjacent country, from an original drawing, by a British engineer." The identity of the British engineer awaits further investigation.

through two lithographs, one entitled "Detroit in 1820, from an original sketch made in 1820 by George H. [sic!] Whistler C. E. with view of 'Walk-in-the-Water.' Arrived at Detroit May 20th 1819. Job Fish commander." This was published by The Calvert Lithographing Company of Detroit in 1871. The other is entitled "Detroit in 1820, with view of 'Walk-in-the-Water,'" and was produced by Corrie's Detroit Lithographic Office at about the same time as the Calvert picture. The Calvert picture is a colored lithograph, while the Corrie is black and white. Some copies of the Corrie print have been hand-colored.[29]

I trust the reader will pardon a moment's reflection on why the iconographer is more interested in a painting as a document than in a painting as what I have called "mere artistic self-expression." George Washington Whistler had a famous son—James Abbott MacNeill Whistler. Yet, from the point of view of the iconographer of Detroit, the little painting by Whistler *père* is more interesting, more significant, more important, than all the great artistic works of Whistler *fils*.

The Detroit skyline, as seen from the Canadian shore across the River, commended itself to successive artists for obvious reasons. Next after Dr. Walsh's effort in 1804 came that ascribed to Alexander Macomb. Detroit was the headquarters of a United States military district when Macomb was in command for several years up to and including 1821. In that year he may have painted a rather exquisite little water-color, on the back of which appears "City of Detroit in 1821, painted by Gen! Alex. Macomb."[30]

The quarter century of Detroit after the fire of 1805 yields surprisingly few maps. The fancy spider-web drawn by Abijah Hull in 1807, certainly does not appear to have made much headway when Greeley's survey was

---

[29] The original Whistler painting is owned by Mr. William Van Dyke of Detroit. Copies of the two lithographs are not uncommon—both are in the Clements Library. The story of the publication of the two prints seems to be somewhat as follows. The Calvert company published its lithograph, based rather faithfully on the Whistler painting. Then a rival firm, the Corrie Company, desiring to share in the profits of a popular print, issued its lithograph. But lest it be charged with infringing the copyright of the Calvert Company, the Corrie artist changed many details—the rig of the ships in the Detroit River, the figures in the foreground, etc.

[30] This painting is owned by Mrs. R. L. Stanton of Grosse Ile. It was reproduced in the Detroit *News-Tribune*, February 25, 1906. A drawing of it in black and white appears in [C. M. Burton] *Centennial celebration of the evacuation of Detroit by the British*. Detroit, 1896, opp. p. 97; and also in G. B. Catlin, *The Story of Detroit*, Detroit, 1923.

made in 1809. In fact it does not appear to have been so generally carried out as to be recorded on a map of something actually in existence until the publication of the "Plan of Detroit by John Mullett 1830." This is a really satisfactory chart showing the area from Randolph to Cass streets, and from Grand Circus Park to the River. There were two editions of this map, and it had to be supplemented in 1835 by the "Map of the western addition to the city of Detroit, as surveyed into lots by John Mullett...." This map covers the area from Cass to Seventh streets and from "Chicago Road" [Michigan Avenue] to the River.[31]

In both the historiography and cartography of Detroit, the name of Farmer will always be noteworthy. John of that name drew maps in the first half of the nineteenth century, while Silas wrote history in the last half. In 1825 the elder Farmer produced a manuscript map of that part of Detroit which is bounded by Bates and Brush streets, Jefferson avenue and the River. It shows actual pictures of many of the buildings. (This is in the nature of a "stop-press." The map was bought by the Burton Collection while I was reading proof on this article. I am exceedingly grateful to Miss Elleine Stones, librarian of the Burton Collection.) John Farmer's "Map of the surveyed part of the territory of Michigan . . ." first appeared in 1826, and was followed by many editions. What rather concerns us is his "Map of the city of Detroit . . ." which appeared in 1835. It includes the central area shown on Mullett's map of 1830, includes the western supplement to Seventh street published by Mullett in 1835, and adds a corresponding area to the east as far as Russel street, including the whole area from Gratiot avenue to the River.[32]

Heretofore we have been dealing with maps, both manuscript and printed, but with pictures done only by hand. What is the first print of Detroit, i.e., the earliest picture manifolded by one of the processes of

---

[31] Of the two editions of Mullett's "Plan of Detroit . . . 1830," one bears the imprint "Engraved & published by J. C. Lewis" (copies: Kenneth L. Moore, of Detroit, and the Burton Historical Collection), while the other bears the imprint, "Bowen & Cos. Lith! Philad!" (copy: Clements Library). The "Map of the western addition" is in the Burton Collection. This map shows that "J. Mullett" owned a good piece of property on the River between Seventh and Eighth streets. John Mullett designed the seal of the University of Michigan in 1825, and that of the city of Detroit in 1827.

[32] John Farmer, "Map of the city of Detroit . . ." " . . . according to act of Congress . . . 1835." Copy in the University of Michigan Library.

printing? So far the answer seems to be a "View of the city of Detroit, M. T." painted by one C. F. Davis, engraved on stone by one A. Fleetwood, and published by the lithographer M. Bancroft in New York. Unfortunately it is not dated. But it does not show the Baptist Church and City Hall which were built about 1835. Michigan was not called "M[ichigan] T[erritory]" after that date. So until another claimant appears, this may be the "first print of Detroit," in the sense that no picture reproduced by either printing, lithography or engraving seems to precede it. Tentatively, we ascribe to it the vague date "circa 1835?"[33]

The next artist who depicted Detroit's skyline from across the River was the landscapist William James Bennett. His oil painting of Detroit can be dated, from internal evidence, about 1836.[34] But it is a question as to whether Bennett painted Detroit "from life" or from a sketch by someone else. For in 1837, there appeared an engraving of the Bennett painting, which is "painted by W. J. Bennett from a sketch by Fred^k Grain." F. B. Richardson, of the Detroit Institute of Arts informs us that Grain was a fairly well known draftsman of the period; that Bennett was a busy and successful artist; that it is quite conceivable that Bennett did not want to take the trip from New York to Detroit; that he sent out Grain to make a preliminary sketch; and executed the painting from Grain's sketch. Anyway by 1837 the Bennett painting was published in an engraved print, of which the iconographer has to recognize two variants, one bearing the imprint of Henry I. Megarey of New York, and the other of John Levison of the same city.[35]

There is another water-color painting of Detroit done about this same time. All we know about it is that Robert Fridenberg, the well known New

---

[33] The only copy with which I have met is in the Phelps Stokes Collection at the New York Public Library. See Stokes and Haskell, *American historical prints*, N. Y. 1932. Harry Mac Neill Bland had this print before it went to Mr. Stokes, but tells me he has no record of its provenance.

[34] The original Bennett painting is owned by the Detroit Institute of Arts. It was purchased and presented to the Institute in 1935 by the Fred Sanders Company—well known to every Detroit epicure.

[35] See Stokes and Haskell, *American historical prints*, N. Y., 1932, p. 137. Both variants of the engraving are available in the New York Public Library, the Detroit Institute of Arts and the Burton Historical Collection. Although Dr. W. R. Valentiner testifies that the original Bennett painting cost only $320 in 1934, certain print dealers are trying to sell the prints for as high as $1500.

York dealer, billed it to the Clements Library as "Detroit, August, 1838," that the presence or absence of certain buildings tends to support Mr. Fridenberg's opinion as to its date, and that it deserves a great deal more study.[36]

The invention of photography supervenes at this point. We will leave to a future monographist the problem of when the first photograph in or of Detroit was taken. Of course, engravings, paintings and the like continued to be made. One of the most charming of about this period is a picture of Detroit on a blue and white china platter with a flower and scroll border, in the Detroit Institute of Arts.[37] The invention of photography by Daguerre revolutionized not only the whole business of making pictures and maps—it revolutionized the business of manifolding them. We began this essay with the work of a Frenchman. Thus do we end it. After all, Dr. Leland has spent a good deal of time revealing to American scholars the French influences on American history.

---

[36] The picture now hangs in the Michigan Historical Collections, at the Rackham Building, University of Michigan.

[37] See S. Laidacker's notes on the "American City Series," in *The American Antiques Collector*, II, 34 (1940).

(Note 2, pp. 247–248 continued)

F. Wording of cartouche agrees with "E," but the map has an additional line in lower left corner reading "Ph.Buache P.G.d.R.d. l'A. R.d S. Gendre de l'Auteur. Avec Privilege du 30 Au. 1745." Copy in Clements Library.

G. Cartouche re-engraved so as to read ". . . par Guillaume Del'Isle Premier Géographe du Roi et de l'Académie Royale des Sciences. Revue et Augmentée en 1783. A Paris chez Dezauche Successeur des Srs. Del'Isle et Buache Rue des Noyers prés alle des Anglois." The Buache imprint at lower left is changed to read "Avec Privilege du Roi."

Editions A to G above are all printed from the same plate, many times corrected and re-engraved in the details mentioned.

Another edition, printed from an entirely different plate, appeared "A Amsterdam chez Iean Covens et Corneille Mortier Geographes Avec Privilege," about the year 1733.

MOODY'S *SCHOOL OF GOOD MANNERS:* A STUDY IN AMERICAN COLONIAL ETIQUETTE

R. W. G. VAIL
The University of the State of New York

ANYONE with a sense of humor and a taste for early American manners and customs can spend an enjoyable half hour and learn considerable about the daily life of his colonial ancestors by examining a copy of Eleazar Moody's *The School of Good Manners. Composed for the Help of Parents in teaching their Children how to behave during their Minority*. If we turn to the section which treats "Of their Behaviour at the Meeting-House," we find a vivid picture of the discomforts of the unfortunate boys and girls who were compelled to sit through a two-hour sermon in a cold church with such admonitions as these adding to their misery:

Decently walk to thy seat or pew; run not or go wantonly.

Shift not seats, but continue in the place where your superiors order you.

Fix thine eye on the minister; let it not wildly wander to gaze on any person or thing.

Be not hasty to run out of the meeting-house when the worship is ended, as if thou wert weary of being there.

Walk decently and soberly home, without haste or wantonness, thinking upon what you have been hearing.

Having finally reached home after the frigid service, the small boy of Colonial New England was still compelled to mind his manners for he had often been told:

Make a bow always when you come home, and be instantly uncovered..

Never speak to thy parents without some title of respect, as, *sir, madam*, &c.

Quarrel not nor contend with thy brethren or sisters, but live in love, peace and unity.

Bear with meekness and patience, and without murmuring or sullenness, thy parents' reproofs or corrections.

Being a normal, healthy youngster, our Colonial small boy could hardly wait for the bountiful Sunday dinner but he had to remember these further admonitions of his stern though loving parents:

Come not to the table without having your hands and face washed, and your head combed.

Be sure thou never sittest down till a blessing be desired, and then in thy due place.

Ask not for any thing, but tarry till it be offered thee.

Speak not at the table; if thy superiors be discoursing meddle not with the matter; but be silent, except thou art spoken unto.

Dip not thy meat in the sauce.

Take not salt with a greasy knife.

Spit not, cough not, nor blow thy nose at the table, if it may be avoided: but if there be necessity, do it aside, and without much noise.

Blow not thy meat, but with patience wait until it be cool.

Smell not of thy meat, nor put it to thy nose.

Throw not any thing under the table.

Foul not thy napkin all over, but at one corner.

Pick not thy teeth at the table, unless holding up thy napkin before thy mouth with thine other hand.

As soon as thou shalt be moderately satisfied, rise up from the table, though others thy superiors sit still.

When thou risest from the table, having made a bow at the side of the table where thou didst sit, withdraw.

Dinner being over, and the company having reassembled in the withdrawing room, the children of the family were still somewhat ill-at-ease, for they knew that they must:

Stand not wriggling with thy body hither and thither, but steady and upright.

When thou blowest thy nose, let thy handkerchief be used.

Spit not in the room, but in the fireplace, or rather go out and do it abroad.

Let thy countenance be moderately cheerful, neither laughing nor frowning.

Be not among equals froward and fretful, but gentle and affable.

Though they might be ever so eager to join in the conversation, they knew that courtesy required that they should:

Among superiors speak not till thou art spoken to, and bid to speak.

If thy superior speaks to thee while thou sittest, stand up before thou givest any answer.

Speak not without *sir*, or some other title of respect.

If thy superior be relating a story, say not, "I have heard it before," but attend to it as though it were altogether new to thee. Seem not to question the truth of it. If he tell it not right, snigger not, nor endeavour to help him out, or add to his relation.

Interrupt not any one that speaks, though thou be his familiar.

Let thy words be modest about those things which only concern thee.

At last the long New England Sabbath came to an end and the small boy was glad to escape to school the following day. But here, again, he had to remember that he must always:

Bow at coming in, pulling off thy hat; especially if thy master or usher be in the school.

If any stranger come into the school, rise up and bow, and sit down in thy place again, keeping a profound silence.

At no time quarrel or talk in the school, but be quiet, peaceable and silent. Much less mayest thou deceive thyself, in trifling away thy precious time in play.

If thy master speak to thee, rise up and bow; make thine answer standing.

Bawl not aloud in making complaints. A boy's tongue should never be heard in the school but in answering a question, or saying his lesson.

Go not rudely home through the streets, stand not talking with boys to delay thee, but go quietly home, and with all convenient haste.

Divulge not to any person whatever, elsewhere, any thing that hath passed in the school, either spoken or done.

It must have been hard for the small boy to observe this last rule when he wanted so much to tell his friends about the birching given to one of his chums by the master or to explain to his mother how sorry he was for one of the girls who had to stand in the corner in a dunce cap. Even when school was out, the youngster had certain rules to follow on his way home, some of them reminiscent of the Elizabethan courtesy books, as for example:

Always give the right hand to your superiors, when you either meet or walk with them; and mind also to give them the wall, for that is the upper hand, though in walking, your superior should then be at your left hand. But when three persons walk together, the middle place is the most honourable; and a son may walk at his father's right hand, when his younger brother walks at his left.

Pull off thine hat to persons of desert, quality or office; shew thy reverence to them by bowing thy body when thou seest them.

Go not singing, whistling or hallooing along the street.

Run not hastily in the street, nor go too slowly; wag not to and fro, nor use any antick or wanton postures, either of thy head, feet or body.

Offend not the master or scholars of another school.

Adventure not to talk with thy companion about thy superiors . . . Children must meddle only with the affairs of children.

As to the supposed author of these wise but severe regulations for the deportment of the Colonial youth of America, we learn from Samuel Sewall's diary that he sent his son Samuel to Moody's school in Boston in 1688. This was a writing school which the worthy pedagogue conducted near Prison Lane (now Court Street), on the west side of "the Highway" (now Tremont Street). Young Sewall also attended the grammar school, so he was obliged to go to the writing school either at noon or after five o'clock in the afternoon. Moody, who was also well known as a scrivener, was in Boston as late as 1706 and died in Dedham in 1720.

Though *The School of Good Manners* is attributed to Eleazar Moody, and it is probable that he adapted it for use in New England, this interesting work has a much earlier origin. Of course there have been courtesy or etiquette books for the use of schoolboys, and a very few for schoolgirls, ever since the middle ages. In fact, such guidebooks also appear in the classical literatures of Greece, Rome, Egypt, India and China, as well as in Latin, Italian, French and German during the thirteenth century and continuously thereafter.

It is probable, however, that only the French manuals had any considerable influence on the courtesy books of England, which began, in various forms, only a little later than those of the Continent. There are many famous treatises for the guidance of the young to be found scattered through English literature, from Caxton's *Book of Courtesy* and Sir Thomas Elyot's *The Governour* on down to Lord Chesterfield's *Letters to his Son* but we are only concerned with the literary ancestors of our American Colonial manual.

In this brief paper, we cannot trace the origin of the well known French courtesy book, the *Civilité Puérile* which we find forming the essential part of the first direct ancestor of *The School of Good Manners*. But it is probable that the edition which descended, with many changes, to Eleazar Moody was the following:

L' A, B, C, ou instruction pour les petis enfans. Après laquelle s'ensuit La Civilité Puérile. A laquelle auons adiousté la Discipline & Institution des enfans. A Anvers. Ex L'imprimerie de Christophle Plantin, Mil. D. Lxiiii. [1564].

The only known copy of this early French juvenile was described in catalogue 62 of William H. Robinson of London, 1937, item no. 98 as a 12mo bound in limp vellum. It appears to have been translated by William Fiston (or Phiston), an Englishman who flourished between 1570 and

1609, whose translation appears in the Stationer's Register as licensed to William Jones, March 14, 1595. From this entry and from the title and preface of the following edition we may reconstruct the title of the lost first edition of this work as follows:

A.B.C. or, the first schoole of good manners. London: W. W.[hite] *for William Jones, 1595.*

The earliest edition which has survived (and that in a single copy) has this title:

The schoole of good manners: or, a new schoole of vertue. Teaching children and youth how they ought to behaue themselves in all companies. Also the manner of seruing and taking vp a table: With divers godly prayers for mornings and euenings; and certaine new graces: very necessarie to be vsed both of old and young. Newly corrected and augmented, By W. F. Imprinted at London by W. W.[hite] *for William Iones and are to be sold at his house at the signe of the Gunne neare Holborne Conduict.* 1609. Unpaged, A–E in eights, small 8vo. (5½ by 3½ inches).

The only known copy was presented by J. O. Halliwell-Phillipps to Henry Huth on February 7, 1876. It was sold at the Huth sale at Sotheby's, June, 1913, no. 2916, to Bernard Quaritch for 25 pounds. Quaritch sold it to Mr. W. A. White who gave it with a portion of his library to Harvard College Library.

Our reason for believing that this is a translation of the foregoing French work is found in the author's preface to this edition, where he says: "Now having of late happened upon a little booke in French, concerning children's manners, I hauing more leysure then I well liked, thought good to expell my languishing idleness, by translating, and (in places needfull) correcting, this treatise which I haue intituled an A.B.C. or, the first Schoole of good Manners."

In Hazlitt's *Handbook* and in the *Dictionary of National Biography*, this translation by Fiston is credited to Francis Seager (or Segar), who flourished between 1549 and 1563, as the probable author. Seager was, indeed, the author of a similar but versified manual of prayers and precepts and this work may have been used by Fiston in his adaptation of the French work for English readers, but the two works are quite distinct and probably not by the same hand.

Seager's manual, which went through at least a dozen editions, has the following title, taken from the British Museum catalogue:

The schoole of vertue, and booke of good nourture for chyldren and youth to learne

*theyr dutie by. Newly perused, corrected, and augmented by the fyrst auctour F. S. . . .
London: Wyllyam Seares,* 1557. 28 leaves, 8vo. Reprinted in Early English Text
Society Original Series 32, 1868.

Fiston's *The schoole of good manners* was published in at least four
editions, the last in 1629, and appears to have been revived by J. Garretson in 1685 under this title:

The school of good manners. By the author of English Exercises. [J. Garretson]
London, 1685.

According to Dr. A. S. W. Rosenbach's *Early American children's
books,* no. 41, this "frequently reprinted" work was the immediate source
of the book attributed to Moody. We have been unable to find any other
reference to Garretson or to any other edition of his book.

We now come to the work by the New England schoolmaster Eleazar
Moody and, again, the first edition has not survived. The title is given,
however, in an advertisement in Joseph Moss: *An election sermon. New
London: Timothy Green,* 1715, where it is described as "lately printed . . .
sold by T. Green," with the title given as follows:

*The school of good manners. Containing, (1) Sundry mixt precepts. (2) Rules
for childrens behaviour at the meeting house, at home, at the table, in company, in
discourse, at school, abroad: With an admonition to children. . . . Some prayers
for children; with graces before and after meat.* [New London ?, 1715?].

No copy of the first or second edition has survived but Evans no. 2699
mentions a third edition printed in New London by Timothy Green in
1725 and Sabin no. 77825 lists a fourth edition with the imprint: Boston:
Sold by B. Eliot, 1732. Rosenbach no. 41 describes his copy of the fifth
edition as follows:

*The school of good manners, containing I. Twenty mixt precepts. II. One hundred
and sixty three rules for childrens behaviour. III. Good advice for the ordering of
their lives; with a baptismal covenant. IV. Eight wholesome cautions. V. A short,
plain & scriptural catechism. VI. Principles of the Christian religion. VII. Eleven
short exhortations. VIII. Good thoughts for children, a compendious body of divinity; An alphabet of useful copies; and Cyprian's twelve absurdities, &c. The fifth
edition. New-London: T. & J. Green,* 1754. 42 leaves, A–G in sixes. 24mo.

In this edition, and presumably in the first four as well, there appears a
preface signed by T. Green, the printer, in which he states that the work
was: "compiled (chiefly) by Mr. Eleazar Moody, late a famous School-
Master in Boston." The popularity of this work is evident from the fact
that there were at least 34 editions published between 1715 and 1846.

An edition published in New London about 1801 states on the title that it is by "the Preceptor of the Ladies' Academy in New London." Since the teacher of the Ladies' Academy at that time was William Green, a native of the town and a graduate of Dartmouth in 1791, it is probable that this version of the old classic may be attributed to him. An abbreviated and versified version by the author of "Good girl's soliloquy," etc., was published in New York in 1822 and later reprinted without date.

It is a long journey from Plantin's A B C book of 1564 and Moody's *School of Good Manners* of 1715 to the Emily Posts of our day but it is interesting to watch, in the changing pages of the old courtesy books, the development in the manners and social customs of our people. When George Washington, in his boyhood *Rules of Civility and decent behavior in company and conversation*, wrote in 1745 that one should "Kill no vermin as Fleas, lice, ticks &c. in the Sight of Others," he did not realize that what he wrote would sound strange or unusual nearly 200 years later. His set of rules, which may well be an amplification of Moody, not only seem curious to us, but paint a vivid picture of the daily life of the boyhood of our first president and of the time in which he lived. In the same way, a study of the other old manuals of civility bring us a rich reward of knowledge of former days.

BIBLIOGRAPHY

The Plantin A B C Book

L' A, B, C, ou instruction pour les petits enfans. Après laquelle s'ensuit La Civilité Puérile. A laquelle auons adiousté la Discipline & Institution des enfans. A Anvers. Ex L'imprimerie de Christophle Plantin, Mil. D. Lxiiii. [1564]. 12 mo.

Title from catalogue 62, William H. Robinson of London, 1937, item no. 98. 45 pounds.

Francis Seager

The schoole of vertue, and booke of good nourture for chyldren and youth to learne theyr dutie by. Newly perused, corrected . . . London: Wyllyam Seares, 1557. 28 leaves, 8vo.   BM.

A versified manual of prayers and precepts, perhaps one of the sources used by Fiston.

Same, London: H. Denham, 1582.   Sir R. L. Harmsworth.

Same, London: R. Jones, 1588. Licensed to R. Jones, 1586.   Herbert.

Same, London: R. Jones, 1593.   HEH.

Same, London: Edw. All-de for Edward White, 1620. Described by Hazlitt.

Same, London, 1621. HCL.

Same, London: M. Flesher for Robert Bird, [1626]. Licensed to Brewster & Bird, 1626. Bodleian, HEH.

Same, London: M. Flesher for Iohn Wright, [circa 1630]. Corser sale, March, 1869, no. 804.

Same, London, [circa 1640]. Eng. Bk. Auct. Rec., Vol. 15, p. 490; V. 21, p. 483.

Same, London, [circa 1660]. Eng. Bk. Auct. Rec., Vol. 15, p. 490.

Same, London, 1677. Mentioned by Hazlitt.

Same, London, 1687. Bodleian.

Same, The second part. [By Richard West] London: Edw. Griffin for Nathaniel Butter, 1619. Mentioned by Hazlitt.

William Fiston (or Phiston) (Fl. 1570–1609)

A. B. C. or, the first schoole of good manners. London: W. W.[hite] for William Iones, 1595. Supposititious title of lost first English edition from French original, based on the entry in the Stationer's Register where it was licensed to William Jones, March 14, 1595.

The schoole of good manners: or, a new schoole of vertue. Teaching children and youth how they ought to behaue themselves in all companies. Also the manner of seruing and taking vp a table: With divers godly prayers for mornings and euenings; and certaine new graces: very necessarie to be vsed both of old and young. Newly corrected and augmented, By W. F. Imprinted at London by W. W.[hite] for William Iones and are to be sold at his house at the signe of the Gunne neare Holborne Conduict. 1609. Unpaged, A–E in eights, small 8vo. (5½ by 3½ inches). HCL.

The schoole of good manners. London: Printed for J. Wright, 1618. Supposititious title of lost edition, based on the entry in the Stationer's Register where it was licensed to J. Wright on September 17, 1618.

The schoole of good manners, or a new schoole of vertue, teaching children and youth how to behaue themselves in all companies: Also the manner of caruing and taking up a table with diuers godly prayers for mornings and euenings and certaine new graces very necessary to be vsed both of young and old. Newly corrected and augmented by W. F. London, Printed for Iohn Wright, and are to be solde at his Shop at the signe of the Bible without Newgate. 1629. 8vo. Title from Hazlitt's Handbook. Bodleian.

J. Garretson

The school of good manners. By the author of English Exercises. London, 1685. Title from note in Dr. A. S. W. Rosenbach's Early American Children's Books, Portland, 1933, p. 22, no. 41.

Eleazar Moody

The school of good manners. Containing, (1) Sundry mixt precepts. (2) Rules for childrens behaviour at the meeting house, at home, at the table, in company, in discourse, at school, abroad: With an admonition to children. . . . Some prayers for children; with graces before and after meat. [New London ?, 1715?]. Advertised as "lately printed . . . sold by T. Green," on the last leaf of Joseph Moss: *An election sermon.* New London: Timothy Green. 1715, a copy of the latter being at HCL. Trumbull 1334. Presumably the lost first American edition of William Fiston's *School of good manners.*

The school of good manners. Third edition. New London: Printed by Timothy Green, 1725. Title from Evans 2699 who probably copied an advertisement.

The school of good manners. . . . Fourth edition. Boston: Sold by B. Eliot, 1732. 18mo. Title from Sabin 77825.

The school of good manners, containing I. Twenty mixt precepts. II. One hundred and sixty three rules for childrens behaviour. III. Good advice for the ordering of their lives; with a baptismal covenant. IV. Eight wholesome cautions. V. A short, plain & scriptural catechism. VI. Principles of the Christian religion. VII. Eleven short exhortations. VIII. Good thoughts for children, a compendious body of divinity; an alphabet of useful copies; and Cyprian's twelve absurdities, &c. The fifth edition. New-London: T. & J. Green, 1754. 42 leaves, A–G in sixes. 24mo. Title from Rosenbach No. 41. Rosenbach.

The school of good manners. Composed for the help of parents in teaching their children how to carry it in their places during their minority. Boston: Re-printed and sold by T. & J. Fleet, at the Heart & Crown in Cornhill, 1772. 79, [1] p., 24 mo. A–E in eights. Rosenbach, No. 75. BPL, Rosenbach.

The school of good manners. Composed for the help of parents in teaching their children how to carry it in their places during their minority. Boston: Printed and sold by John Boyle in Marlborough-Street. 1775. 78, [1] p., 32 mo. AAS, BPL.

The school of good manners. Composed for the help of parents—teaching children how to behave during their minority. Portland: Printed, and sold, by Thomas B. Wait. 1786. 58 p., 32 mo. Rosenbach 112. AAS, Rosenbach.

The school of good manners. Composed for the help of parents—teaching children how to behave during their minority. Hartford: Printed, and sold, by Nathaniel Patten. M, DCC, LXXXVII. 36, 12 p., 12 mo. AAS, A. C. Bates. Second title: Mr. [Samuel] Moody's discourse to little children. The fourth edition. Hartford: Printed and sold, by Nathaniel Patten, M, DCC, LXXXVII.

The school of good manners. Composed for the help of parents, in teaching their children how to behave during their minority. Boston: S. Hall, 1790. 27 leaves. Small square 8 vo. Title from Rosenbach, No. 149. Rosenbach.

The school of good manners. Composed for the help of parents, in teaching their children how to behave during their minority. The seventeenth edition. Windsor: Re-Printed by Alden Spooner. M, DCC, XCIII. 40 p., 24 mo. AAS.

The school of good manners. Composed for the help of parents in teaching their children how to carry it in their places during their minority. [wdct. of a woman teaching a boy and girl] Printed by B. Edes & Son, in Kilby-Street,

Boston, 1794. 92 p., 24 mo. Rosenbach, No. 183; Sabin 77825.   AAS, BPL, NYPL, Rosenbach, Mrs. Arthur Greenwood.

The school of good manners, composed for the help of parents, in teaching their children how to behave in their places, during their minority. The first Troy edition. Troy, Printed by Gardner and Billings. MDCCXCV. [2], 94 p., front. and wdcts., 32 mo.   JCB.

The school of good manners. . . . Boston: Printed by Manning & Loring. [1796]. Title from Evans 30808. There is no such edition. Evans incorrectly described the 1805 edition from a copy at AAS with the date torn off.

The school of good manners. Composed for the help of parents, in teaching their children how to behave in their places, during their minority. Dover: Printed by Samuel Bragg, jun., 1799. Evans 35832.   NNHS.

The school of good manners. Composed for the help of parents in teaching their children how to carry it in their places during their minority. [three line quotation from Proverbs] [n.p.] Printed in the year 1801. 48 p., 24 mo.   AAS.

The school of good manners. By their Preceptor of the Ladies' Academy in New London. New London: Samuel Green, [n.d., but circa 1801] 12 mo. Title from Anderson auction catalogue 1602, November 14, 1921, No. 289. Sold for $20. "On the inside cover is an inscription by a former owner, dated 1804." There was a "Ladies Academy" at New London from 1799 to 1834. The first teacher of this school was William Green, a native of the town and a graduate of Dartmouth, 1791. He ran the school until his death on December 26, 1801 and so was probably the author of this variant of *The school of good manners*.

The school of good manners. Composed for the help of parents in teaching their children how to carry it in their places during their minority. [three lines quoted] Haverhill: Printed by Galen H. Fay. 1802. 40 p., 12 mo.   AAS, BPL, EI, HCL, HPL.

The school of good manners. Composed for the help of parents in teaching their children how to behave during their minority. Printed and sold by Manning & Loring, No. 2, Cornhill, Boston, 1804. 94 p., 24 mo. Manning & Loring's first edition.   AAS.

The school of good manners, composed for the help of parents in teaching their children how to carry it in their places during their minority. [wdct.] [quotation from Proverbs] [Boston?:] Printed in 1805. 48 p., 32 mo. Sabin 77826.   BPL.

The school of good manners. Composed for the help of parents in teaching their children how to behave during their minority. Printed and sold by Manning & Loring, No. 2, Cornhill, Boston. 1805. 95 p., 24 mo. Manning & Loring's second edition.   AAS, BPL.

The school of good manners. Composed for the help of parents in teaching their children how to behave during their minority. Newburyport, Published by W. & J. Gilman, Printers & Booksellers, No. 2, Middle-street. [1805?]. [48] p., wdcts., 24 mo. Advertised as "for sale at this office, wholesale and retail" in W. & J. Gilman's *Merrimac Magazine*, January 4, 1806.   AAS.

The school of good manners. Composed for the help of parents in teaching their children how to behave during their minority. Printed and sold by Manning & Loring, No. 2, Cornhill, Boston. 1808. 95 p., 24 mo. Manning & Loring's third edition. AAS, HCL, LC.

The school of good manners, composed for the help of parents in teaching their children how to carry it in their places during their minority. [wdct.] [quotation from Proverbs] Exeter: Printed by Morris & Sawyer, and sold at their Book Store. 1808. 48 p. 24 mo. W. M. Stone.

Same title, imprint and collation, 1813. U. Ill.

The school of good manners. Composed for the help of parents in teaching their children how to behave in their minority. Printed and sold by Manning & Loring, No. 2, Cornhill, Boston. Sold also by Samuel T. Armstrong, and by Lincoln & Edmands, 1813. 95 p., 24 mo. Manning & Loring's fourth edition. AAS, BPL, LC, Mrs. Arthur Greenwood.

The school of good manners. Composed for the help of parents in teaching their children how to behave during their minority. Windsor, Vt.: Jesse Cochran, Printer. 1815. 47 p., including front., 24 mo. Sabin 77826. AAS, H. G. Rugg, LC.

The school of good manners. . . . John Babcock and Son. New Haven. S. & W. R. Babcock. Charleston. [circa 1818–1825]. Mrs. Arthur Greenwood.

The school of good manners. By the author of "Good girl's soliloquy, Poetic tales, Little ditties for little children, Present to little children," &c. &c. New York: Published by Samuel Wood & Sons, No. 261, Pearl-Street; and Samuel S. Wood & Co. No. 212, Market-St. Baltimore. 1822. 46 p., wdcts., square 32 mo. A versified and much abbreviated paraphrase of the original text. AAS.

Same title, imprint and collation. [n.d.]. NYPL, Yale, Mrs. Arthur Greenwood.

The school of good manners. Composed for the help of parents, in teaching their children how to behave during their minority. Windsor, Vt. Published by Simeon Ide. 1829. 64 p., illus., 24 mo. Title from detached cover at AAS, collation from W. M. Stone copy. W. M. Stone.

The school of good manners. Composed for the help of parents in teaching their children how to behave in their youth. Revised and amended . . . Written for the Massachusetts Sabbath School Society, and revised by the committee of publication. Boston: Massachusetts Sabbath School Society, 1837, 62 p., 18 mo. Title from LC printed card. HCL, LC, NHHS.

Same title and imprint, 1846. 72 p., 18 mo. Title from Sabin 77827. HCL.

INTERNATIONAL LAW IN A
TROUBLED WORLD

JESSE S. REEVES
University of Michigan

TO put within the limits of a short article any adequate treatment of conflicting theories of international law is a problem of compression analogous to that of the supposititious composer who undertook to express an entire symphony by means of a single chord. As soon as the concept of the law of nations began to appear, debate began as to its nature, its obligations, whether or not it was law, what, if any, were its sanctions—and there has never been any substantial agreement as to its jurisprudence. Grotius attacked this problem in the "Prolegomena" to his work on *The Law of War and Peace*, and not yet has the problem been solved by universal acceptance as to any one theory. Nor is it likely that there will be any agreement upon the theory of international law until there is a generally accepted theory of the state. Whatever the theory of international law may be, it rests upon the fundamental hypothesis of the state. What the state is believed to be, or what the state ought to be— Aristotelian or Platonic, Kantian or Hegelian, totalitarian or democratic —largely determines the conviction as to what international law is or ought to be.

At the core of every theory of the state is the problem of sovereignty. International law does not furnish its own major premises or its own categories. They are derived, we say, from state practices, from the decisions of competent tribunals, from the writings of learned jurists. But these practices, decisions, and opinions are themselves derived from the theories of the state, which are either rationalizations after the facts, or the more or less conscious putting into practice of dogmas and ideas which have been deduced from earlier rationalizations. It would be to no purpose to labor the matter as to who is the founder of modern international law, whether Vitoria, or Gentilis, or Grotius. We are probably safe if we say that the thinking which we characterize as modern international law begins with the appearance of the modern state. The century which heard Vitoria, Gentilis, and Grotius was the century in which was first expounded the doctrine of sovereignty by Bodin. All four of these great thinkers were the product of an era which gave the training, direction, and color to the age in which we live, the age of the modern territorial, national state. Bodin rationalized the as yet imperfect realization of the unified nationalistic state, France. Vitoria, son of a unified Spain, saw its expansion over seas. Gentilis, exiled from Italy—then and for long after, a geographical expression—was an expatriate in a strongly nationalistic England, while Grotius, in origin intrinsically provincial rather than nationalist, found refuge in the France which Bodin rationalized. Neither Vitoria, Gentilis, nor even Grotius seriously attacked the problem of sovereignty.

With the Europe which began with the Peace of Westphalia in 1648, the acceptance of the doctrine *cujus regio, ejus religio* rested upon the fundamental definition of Bodin: "Majestie or Sovereigntie is the most high, absolute, and perpetuall power over the citizens and subjects in a Commonweale . . . that is to say, the greatest power to commaund."[1]

What Bodin undertook to demonstrate was that which later came to be designated as internal sovereignty: "The first and principal function of sovereignty is to give laws to the citizens, generally and individually," and, incidentally, it is true he admitted the duties of sovereigns to each other under the Law of Nations, but insisted that a prince is not "more bound by the Law of Nations than by his own laws, except in so far as the former are in agreement with the laws of nature and of God." In the Bodinian system the range of sovereign will is limited to the area of the sovereign's competency—namely, within the state. The will of one sovereign might, and did, co-operate with the will of another sovereign in compact, or treaty, for such was directed by the law of nature: *pacta sunt servanda.*

The important thing is that the Bodinian concept of sovereignty was adopted in 1648 as the foundation of what came to be called the public law of Europe—a treaty-law, wherein the will of each was supreme within and limited by compact without. That part of international law derived from the law of nature or from international custom was ancillary to the main structure. The so-called European family of nations was based upon compact, or rather by various series of bilateral compacts, the work of those great diplomatic gatherings which came to be known as congresses. The multilateral compact was long in coming into being. It was the invention

---

[1] From the only English edition, 1606, p. 84.

of the nineteenth century, and had its climax in the World War peace treaties and the Covenant of the League of Nations.

The theory of international law, then, is closely bound up with a theory of the international community. The problem strongly resembles the problem of political obligation within the state, and this has ever been to find a tolerable way of passage or bridge from the individual to the sovereign state. The individual completely free, his will untrammeled, is a negation of the state, it is anarchy. The will of the sovereign, supreme and omnicompetent, reduces the individual to the status of a cell in an organism, existing only for the good of the sovereign. Such was once called despotism. Now it is totalitarianism. Some *via media* is to be discovered between anarchy and absolutism. The most familiar one is based upon the action of the individual wills—the social compact—of Hobbes, of Locke, or of Rousseau, resulting in the great *persona ficta*—the State. Opposite to this is that which may be called the de-facto-group origin of the state, examined and elaborated by Gierke, and made into a modern theory by the guild socialists, Figgis and G. D. H. Cole. One is the product of acts of will and is in a sense artificial. The other is more or less "found to be," and is, in a sense, "natural." Society is antecedent to the state. The state is but one aspect of society. The legal order and society are coexistent. Neither produces the other. Neither could exist without the other. "*Ubi societas ibi jus est*"; but this *jus* is not necessarily a product of will any more than *societas* is. "Man is a social animal."

The naturalness of the international community is not associated with any theory of sovereignty such as that of Bodin. It was not something thought into being by the wills of sovereigns: it was self-existent, not ordained. "The world as a whole," said Vitoria, "being in a way one single state, has the power to create laws that are just and fitting for all persons, as are the rules of international law." It is, again, the thought of the Spanish jurist Suarez, whose work was published in 1612, some thirty-odd years after Bodin first printed his book on the Commonwealth, and thirteen years before Grotius's work appeared in Paris:

The human race, however divided into various peoples and kingdoms, has always not only its unity as a species but also a certain moral and quasi-political unity, pointed out by the natural precept of mutual love and pity which extends to all, even to foreigners of any nation. Wherefore although every perfect state, whether a republic or a kingdom, is in itself a perfect community composed of its own members, still each state, viewed in relation to the human race, is in some measure a member of that universal unity. For those communities are never singly so self-sufficing but that they stand in need of some mutual aid society and communion, sometimes for the improvement of their condition and their greater commodity, but sometimes also for their moral necessity and need, as appears by experience. For that reason they are in need of some law by which they may be directed and rightly ordered in that kind of communion and society. And although this is to a great extent supplied by natural reason, yet it is not so supplied sufficiently and immediately for all purposes, and therefore it has been possible for particular laws to be introduced by the practice (*usu*) of those same nations. For just as custom (*consuetudo*) introduces law in a state or province, so it was possible for laws to be introduced in the whole human race by the habitual conduct (*moribus*) of nations. And that all the more because the points which belong to this law are few and approach very nearly to natural law, and being easily deduced from it are useful and agreeable to nature, so that although this law cannot be plainly deduced as being altogether necessary in itself to laudable conduct (*ad honestatem morum*), still it is very suitable to nature and such as all may accept for its own sake.[2]

Grotius gave many names to this "moral and quasi-legal community" of Suarez. It was "the common society of the human race," that "perpetual common society of the human race," "human society," "that great community," "that great corporateness," "that mutual society of nations," "that great society of states," "that commonwealth of the world," "the society of the world," a natural association and not a super-state. Within that great society, however, the law was at least in part the product of the wills of its constituent members. The absolute and ideal qualities of the law of nature were mixed with custom by Grotius, tempered if not compromised by the relative and realistic elements which come to be called positive.

Pufendorf, seeking to set forth an ethical system with the exactitude of mathematics, limited the operation of the will within the state and practically abolished it in the field of international relations. "All states were as to each other as in a state of nature." This doctrine, it is true, was formulated by Pufendorf, but it must be remembered in justice to him that in all the circumstances of the state of nature, all states were under the duties of the law of nature or the supreme code of ethics and morals. In such a state of nature states had the analogy of what Locke later de-

---

[2] *Tractatus de Legibus et Deo Legislatore*, 2, 19, 9; quoted by Westlake, *Collected Papers*, pp. 26–27.

veloped as the natural rights of the individual within the state—the primordial and essential rights of independence and equality.

But a state of nature involves the absence of a society. Abstract from such a state of nature the rights and duties of the law of nature and the state is a free agent, with unfettered will, subject to no limitations but those imposed by itself, and international law becomes either the positive international morality of the Austinian school or else it rests upon consent, express or implied, of the Positivists. Again, if states are as to each other only as in a state of nature, the concept of the international community being eliminated, international law becomes a static system derived from a few so-called absolute international rights and duties.

It may be objected that to deny the fundamental rights of states is to deny the right of the state to be, and to forbid the realization of nationalistic demands. No one, however, would nowadays seriously assert that the displacement of the doctrine of natural rights for one of social control entails the juristic destruction of individual personality. Every theory of social progress, whether collectivist or individualistic, rests ultimately upon the idea of human, that is, individual, perfectibility, associated with that of individual moral obligation. The state is but one, although traditionally the highest one, of the means by which these foundations are laid. Since the time of Plato it has been recognized that only in the state can the individual achieve the realization of himself. The state can act only through government, its concrete political organization. Government, however collectively it may be organized, can work only by the co-operation of individuals.

Within our own memory we have seen the state undertake to subject groups within it to the standards of individual morality as expressed in terms of law. The corporation is no abstraction, but a real entity operating only by the co-operative exercise of individual wills. Group morality is becoming identified with individual morality, not because the state as power commands it, but because society, organized in the state, demands that equal standards are necessary for the protection of the individual and hence of itself. So with states. The state as power is the negation of moral, as well as of legal, obligations. None within can have rights against it; therefore, it lies under no duties. But as states are the concrete realizations of organized society, they owe duties to all within and to each other. These duties of external action are moral only until there is a recognition of a status quo, and then they become legal. The growth of law is predicated upon the progress from the dynamic and moral to the static and legal, whence new moral duties emerge, which in turn become legal. New relationships create new responsibilities. These beget new moral duties and moral rights. As these, again, become legal, new relationships result with greater and greater complexity and sweep.

One may go even further and assert that to posit the doctrine that states are "naturally" in a state of nature with one another and also to eliminate the law of nature results in the acceptance of the doctrines that the state will is unlimited not only internally but externally, that the state is a "law unto itself," that the state is power, unfettered by law, that treaty limitations are matters of policy and convenience merely, and the world takes on the features of Hobbes's state of nature in which "life is nasty, brutish, and short."

As with the theorists of the state, there is the way out by the effort of will, in contracting out of the state of nature. Wolff was the first to set forth the international social compact, an implied compact by which was created the *Civitas Maxima*. The multilateral treaties of the post-Napoleonic period undertook to do the same by express compact and there were created the Holy Alliance and the Confederation of Europe. But as the nineteenth century progressed, the doctrine of nationalism developed as never before. Along with it came theories of the state, mostly German, which apotheosized the state, struck from the operation of its will all the limitations of law and morality. Fichte and Hegel were the philosophical pioneers, and Treitschke the popular expositor, of the doctrines which have led to the destruction of the international community *in esse* and of the breakdown of international law as "that body of rules which states habitually observe in their mutual relations."

While the English positivists deny that international law is law—because of the narrow Austinian concept of law—they have not failed to stress the necessity that states are under the moral law. Woodrow Wilson, who was to some extent Austinian, insisted that the moral obligation of a state was even stronger than any mere legal obligation; the latter rested upon the former. The German positivists, however, would exclude the attribution of all moral values to the sovereign state—or rather would contend that the sovereign state creates its own moral values. So Laski:

Here, its effect is to justify the positivist theory by arguing that the state has an absolute moral value beyond which we cannot go; that, therefore, the validity of international law must necessarily consist in its furtherance of that value. And, since the only judge of this furtherance must be the State (for, otherwise, it would cease to be itself the embodiment of absolute moral value), it follows that the State, in judging whether it should or should not accept as binding a proposed rule of international law, need have regard to its own interests only. In doing so, by reason of its assumed nature, it realizes the highest purposes at which it can aim. For in securing its own self-interest it is securing, also, the interest of that absolute value which it embodies.[3]

To accept, however, any positivist position completely is to forsake those who take the side of intellectualism against anti-intellectualism in that eternal struggle; it is to take that compromising position which Benda has indicated in his "Trahison des Clercs," it is pragmatic, realist, and relative. The international jurist, freeing himself from the claims of the here and now must declare for the eternal verities of truth and justice. "Here I stand, God helping me, I can do no other!" "Common sense" suggests the expedient. Truth and Justice do not involve the calculus of utilitarian expediency, nor are they to be measured by it.

Positivism, or relativism, or realism looks askance at the ideal—whether it be the ideal of the essential one-ness of humanity or of the essential one-ness of a world legal order. The fact of the unity of humanity, and of the world legal order is now nonexistent. The idea remains. To that idea we as jurists, not apologizing, nor benumbed by defeatism, must be loyal. The greater the descent into the abyss of crime and indecency, the greater the need for that highest loyalty, namely faith in the everlasting truths of the moral code. The more international law is flouted, the greater the need is to be loyal to the ideas of international justice; the more the international community ceases to exist, the greater the need is for that faith by which alone it is to be realized. The legal order in its ideal is at one with the moral order. Both rest upon the faith that truth and righteousness will prevail. Without that faith, man returns to the brute, and the rule of the jungle is the rule of existence, not life, over man the animal. The true, the beautiful, and the good, that glorious trinity, through loyalty to which man, noble by being reasonable and reasoning, demonstrates his manhood, alone make man free. It is this loyalty upon which international justice rests, and upon this international justice provides the unassailable and ever secure foundation of international law.

---

[3] H. J. Laski, *The State in Theory and Practice* (New York, 1935), p. 195.

JOHN HERSCHEL'S PHILOSOPHY
OF SCIENCE

C. J. DUCASSE
Brown University

IN Sir John Frederick William Herschel's *Preliminary Discourse on the Study of Natural Philosophy*, published in 1830, we have, the late Professor Minto points out, "the first attempt by an eminent man of science to make the methods of science explicit."[1] The *Discourse*, however, attempts something more than this. It formulates Herschel's philosophy of science. Although its discussion of scientific method is doubtless its most significant part, it considers also the nature of the objects of the natural sciences, the relation of such objects to the cognitive powers of the human mind, the tasks of these sciences, and the values for human society of the study of science. The work is divided into three parts. The third, which deals with "the subdivision of physics into distinct branches, and their mutual relations," adds little or nothing to the theory of science contained in the first and second parts and may therefore be left out of consideration here. The first part is entitled "Of the general nature and advantages of the study of the physical sciences." What it has to say concerning the objects studied by these sciences and the questions they ask about those objects will be considered in connection with the contents of Part II. The point of chief interest otherwise in Part I is found in what Herschel has to say about the effects of advances in science on the improvement of the condition of mankind. The "more abundant supply of our physical wants, and the increase of our comforts" are not the only or even the greatest benefits resulting from these advances: "the incalculable advantages which experience, systematically consulted and dispassionately reasoned on, has conferred in matters purely physical, tend of necessity to impress something of the well weighed and progressive character of science on the more complicated conduct of our social and moral relations. It is thus that legislation and politics become gradually regarded as experimental sciences; and history . . . as the archive of experiments,

---

[1] W. Minto, *Logic, Inductive and Deductive*, 1904. P. 257.

successful and unsuccessful, gradually accumulating towards the solution of the grand problem—how the advantages of government are to be secured with the least possible inconvenience to the governed." The power which we now know a scientific approach to any problem confers may ultimately enable us "to bear down those obstacles which individual shortsightedness, selfishness, and passion, oppose to all improvements, and by which the highest hopes are continually blighted, and the fairest prospects marred."[2]

Part II of the *Discourse*, in seven chapters, sets forth and illustrates "the principles on which physical science relies for its successful prosecution, and the rules by which a systematic examination of nature should be conducted." It is chiefly to this that we must turn for Herschel's philosophy of science, which we propose to outline and examine in what follows.

Herschel's direct predecessor in the attempt to formulate a philosophy of natural science is Francis Bacon, whose best known work, the *Novum Organum Scientiarum* appeared some two hundred years earlier (1620). It should be mentioned at the outset that Herschel was thoroughly familiar with this celebrated work and thought highly of the doctrine contained therein. Indeed, facing the title page of the *Discourse*, we find transcribed the famous first aphorism of the *Novum Organum*, "Homo, naturae minister et interpres, tantum facit et intelliget quantum de naturae ordine re vel mente observaverit: nec amplius scit aut potest"; and on the next page there is reproduced an engraving of a bust of Bacon.[3] Laudatory references to Bacon, and sympathetic interpretations of the teachings of the *Novum Organum* are found in many parts of the *Discourse*, which in the history of the philosophy of science may well be regarded as the direct descendent of the *Novum Organum*. Almost every one of the general precepts of method which Bacon formulated but could not adequately illustrate, reappears in the *Discourse*, and, interpreted in the light of the concrete scientific achievements of the intervening two centuries, is given its true perspective and clearly related to actual and fruitful scientific practice. It may not be amiss here to call attention to one or two passages in the third chapter of the second part of the *Discourse*, which are of importance in throwing light on the place of Francis Bacon in the history

---

[2] Sec. 65.   [3] Cabinet Cyclopaedia Edition, London, 1840.

of the philosophy of science. Since Herschel is himself one of the most notable writers on scientific method, his mere opinions as to Bacon's importance in the history of the subject constitute so many facts in evidence concerning the influence Bacon has actually had on one at least of his successors in this field. Referring to the process he like other writers calls *Induction*, which he describes in Section 95, Herschel says: "It is to our immortal countryman Bacon that we owe the broad announcement of this grand and fertile principle; and the development of the idea that the whole of natural philosophy consists entirely of a series of inductive generalizations, commencing with the most circumstantially stated particulars, and carried up to universal laws, or axioms, which comprehend in their statements every subordinate degree of generality, and of a corresponding series of inverted reasoning from generals to particulars, by which these axioms are traced back into their remotest consequences, and all particular propositions deduced from them. . . ."[4] Further on in the same chapter Herschel writes: "By the discoveries of Copernicus, Kepler and Galileo, the errors of the Aristotelian philosophy were effectually overturned on a plain appeal to the facts of nature; but it remained to show on broad and general principles, how and why Aristotle was in the wrong; to set in evidence the peculiar weakness of his method of philosophizing, and to substitute in its place a stronger and better. This important task was executed by Francis Bacon, Lord Verulam, who will, therefore, justly be looked upon in all future ages as the great reformer of philosophy, though his own actual contributions to the stock of physical truths were small, and his ideas of particular points strongly tinctured with mistakes and errors, which were the fault rather of the general want of physical information of the age than of any narrowness of view on his own part; and of this he was fully aware . . . it is not the introduction of inductive reasoning, as a new and hitherto untried process, which characterizes the Baconian philosophy, but his keen perception, and his broad and spirit stirring, almost enthusiastic, announcement of its paramount importance, as the alpha and omega of science. . . ."[5]

Estimates of the importance of Bacon's writings on scientific method have been widely divergent—some judging them negligible and others pronouncing them epoch-making. For lack of space in these pages to ad-

---

[4] Sec. 96.   [5] Sec. 105.

duce the relevant evidence, the present writer can only record his opinion that Herschel's estimate just quoted, of both the merits and the defects of Bacon's contribution is much more just than either of those extremes.

Another influence which can be traced in the *Discourse* is that of the doctrine of method briefly formulated by Newton in a few passages of the *Principia* and of the *Optics* and so brilliantly applied in his own scientific work.[6] This influence is apparent, for example, in the stress Herschel lays on the method of hypothesis-deduction-verification. It is true that, notwithstanding the common opinion to the contrary, Bacon, before Newton, had described and advocated this method; but of course Bacon did not have the clear understanding possessed by Newton of the manner in which this method is to be employed in practice. It is the example of Newton's *use* of it, much rather than the brief description of it in the *Optics*, or the statements of Bacon, which brought about the adequate recognition of the great importance of that method.[7] Newton's influence is also apparent in the many references in the *Discourse* to the requirement that the causes to which one appeals be *verae causae*. Herschel's interpretation of the meaning of this term, however, is somewhat broader than that which Newton appears to have intended to place upon it.

The examination of Herschel's views we shall now undertake will consist of an exposition of and commentary on the contents of Part II of the *Discourse*. A more systematic treatment than would otherwise be possible will result if we allow ourselves to deviate at times from the order followed by Herschel. We shall therefore arrange our exposition under the following five headings: I. Observation, Experiment, and Classification, II. The Uniformity of Nature, III. The Analysis of Phenomena, IV. The First Stage of Induction, V. The Second Stage of Induction. We pass now to the first of these.

I

Part II of the *Discourse* opens with some remarks repeating in effect those made by David Hume in Section IV of his *Enquiry Concerning Human Understanding*, where he points out that the objects of inquiry

---

[6] The relevant passages in the *Optics* are in Qu. 31, and in the *Principia* in the section entitled *Regulae Philosophandi* and, at the end of the book, in the *General Scholium* where occurs his famous "*hypotheses non fingo.*"

[7] Cf. Bain, *Logic*, Vol. II, p. 408. Jevons, *Principles of Science*, pp. 581 ff.

are in all cases either "relations of ideas" or "matters of fact." Inquiry into
the first, Hume says, gives us the mathematical sciences, whose conclusions have demonstrated certainty. Inquiry into the second begets
the sciences of nature. Their inferences are not demonstrative for they are
all based on the relation of Cause and Effect, and we obtain knowledge
of this relation not through reason but only through experience. Herschel
similarly contrasts the abstract with the natural sciences. The truths of
the abstract sciences, e.g., of mathematics, can be arrived at independently
of perceptual observation because such truths are necessary in the sense
that denial of them involves one in self-contradiction. But in natural
science, where we are concerned with causes and effects, and with laws
which "for aught we can perceive might have been other than they are,"[8]
the great and ultimate source of our knowledge must be human experience.[9] This can be acquired in two ways: either by the mere passive
observation of facts as they occur—but when for any reason science is
limited to this, progress is usually very slow—or actively by *experimentation*, that is, "by putting in action causes and agents over which we have
control, and purposely varying their combinations, and noticing what
effects take place."[10] Whenever this has been possible the progress of
science has been rapid.

"Experience once recognized as the fountain of all knowledge of nature," we must clear our minds of all prejudices concerning what might
or what ought to be the order of nature in any proposed case, and determine to stand and fall by the result of direct appeal to facts and of strict
logical deduction from them. Such prejudices are of two sorts: prejudices
of opinion and prejudices of sense. The first are false opinions which we
have come to receive without adequate evidence, and which, from being
constantly admitted without dispute, have obtained the strong hold of
habit on our minds. The second are not so much errors of sense as judgments in which we mean to report no more than we actually sense, but in
which we in fact assert much more—and this more, false—without realizing that we are doing so until appropriate checks are used. These remarks
of Herschel's are obviously reminiscent of Bacon's discussion of the
Idols.

The fourth chapter of the second part of the *Discourse* is concerned

---

[8] Sec. 66.   [9] Sec. 67.   [10] Sec. 67.

with "The observation of facts and the collection of instances." Herschel there declares after Bacon that "whenever . . . we would either analyze a phenomenon into simpler ones, or ascertain what is the course or law of nature under any proposed general contingency, the first step is to accumulate a sufficient quantity of well ascertained facts, or recorded instances, bearing on the point in question . . . the more different these collected facts are in all other circumstances but that which forms the subject of enquiry, the better; because they are then in some sort brought into contrast with one another in their points of disagreement, and thus tend to render those in which they agree more prominent and striking."[11] In the remainder of the chapter, Herschel describes and illustrates the characters such recorded instances must have, to be of scientific value. The facts, and also the circumstances that were present when the facts occurred, must be accurately observed; and the record then made of them must be literal and faithful in the sense of not allowing what are really inferences, however natural or plausible, to creep into the record. Again, precise numerical statements should be given in every case where they are possible, and should be obtained from actual counting or measurement, since the quantitative reports of the unaided senses are untrustworthy. It is true that even with fixed standards (e.g., of length, weight, etc.) some error unavoidably enters into our measurements, but we can always assign a limit which such error cannot possibly exceed. Moreover we can increase the accuracy of our measurements almost without limit by repeating them many times and taking their mean.[12] Lastly, when our laws have been formulated on the basis of them, we can find out whether our formulations are vitiated by errors of observation, or on the contrary are trustworthy, by deducing predictions from these laws and observing whether or not the facts verify them.

The fifth chapter is concerned with Classification and Nomenclature. The number and variety of objects and relations that observation reveals in nature is so great as to confuse and bewilder us unless we limit our observation at any one time to a few facts, or to a number of facts so bound together by resemblance as virtually to constitute one fact. Any such fact, that appears important, should receive a name. This will insure to it a correspondingly important place in our thought and will

---

[11] Sec. 109.   [12] Secs. 227 ff.

serve there as a nucleus around which further information that we obtain may be systematically organized. As soon, however, as a considerable number of objects in a given field, and their relations, have been observed, arbitrary proper names will no longer serve. We must have names essentially relational, which will not only serve to identify the objects but will at the same time indicate their relations to others of the given field; so that "the direct relation between the name and the object shall materially assist the solution of the problem 'given the one, to determine the others'."[13] Now, "any one may give an arbitrary name to a thing, merely to be able to talk of it; but, to give a name which shall at once refer it to a place in a system, we must know its properties; and we must *have* a system, large enough, and regular enough, to receive it in a place which belongs to it and to no other."[14] Nomenclature cannot therefore usefully at any time be given much more system and precision than our knowledge itself possesses; else we run the risk of mistaking the means for the end by sacrificing convenience and distinctness to a rage for arrangement.

II

Attention must now be called to a character which Herschel, in the fourth chapter, states facts must have if they are to possess any scientific value, and which is of a very different order from the others already mentioned. Herschel's words on the point are as follows: "The only facts which can ever become useful as grounds of physical enquiry are those which happen uniformly and invariably under the same circumstances . . . for if they have not this character they cannot be included in laws."[15] Whether a given fact be anomalous only in appearance, owing to our having failed to detect some difference in the circumstances; or whether it be really anomalous, owing to caprice, i.e., owing to "the arbitrary intervention of mental agency"—in either case all we can do with anomalous facts is to record them as curiosities or as problems awaiting explanation, but "we can make no use of them in scientific enquiry."[16]

This character of being regular is obviously not one that is a possible matter of observation in any individual instance, and cannot therefore be used as a guide in the selection of instances. The practical consequence

---

[13] Sec. 130.   [14] Sec. 132.   [15] Sec. 110.   [16] Sec. 110.

Herschel draws from the above remarks is only the one already mentioned, namely that not merely facts themselves, but also the circumstances under which they occurred must be carefully observed and recorded. But the broader import of his remarks as above quoted concerns the status of the so-called Principle of the Uniformity of Nature. They present uniformity, in effect, as a postulate definitive of the scope of science. Herschel does not say that we know nature to be wholly or partially ruled by law; neither does he directly say that we have to assume it to be so for practical purposes. The import of his words is merely that so far and so far only into nature as there may happen to be regularity, does the realm of science extend. This follows directly from his view that science essentially consists of a body of general propositions. Science is the study of such phenomena as are governed by laws.

III

We now come to what Herschel, in the second chapter of Part II of the *Discourse*, calls "the analysis of phenomena." A large portion of the chapter is given by him to the discussion of some of the terms in which his methodological doctrine is stated, and of some of the assumptions that underlie it. An examination of these terms and assumptions, as considered by Herschel at this and other places in the *Discourse*, is indispensable to an understanding of his doctrine, and in particular has to be more or less closely combined with any critical exposition of the part of it that concerns the analysis of phenomena.

The term *phenomenon* is explicitly defined by Herschel as follows: "Phenomena . . . are the sensible results of processes and operations carried on among external objects, or their constituent principles, of which they are only signals."[17] What he means by this is explained by him in the following words: "As the mind exists not in the place of sensible objects, and is not brought into immediate relation with them, we can only regard sensible impressions as signals conveyed from them by an . . . inexplicable mechanism to our minds, which receives and reviews them, and by habit and association, connects them with corresponding qualities or affections in the objects."[18] This situation is compared by Herschel to that of a person who, having constantly observed that a certain tele-

---

[17] Sec. 76.   [18] Sec. 74.

graphic signal was sure to be followed by the announcement of the arrival of a ship, would connect the two facts by a link of the same nature as the link which connects the notion of a large floating building filled with sailors with the impression of the outline of a ship on the retina of a spectator on the beach.[19]

Herschel here obviously deals in summary fashion with the classic philosophical problem of our knowledge of the "external world." Since he was writing as a methodologist of science, it was of course not incumbent on him to undertake a full discussion of that problem; but since he nevertheless touches upon it and attempts to state his methodological doctrines in terms of the answer to it which he sketches, it is necessary at least to make as explicit as possible the import of his words on the subject.

Herschel intends to use the terms "sensible impression" and "phenomenon" synonymously; also, the words "objects" and "sensible objects," as synonymous. "Sensible object" seems to mean in Herschel's usage an object *qua* causing or susceptible of causing an impression, i.e., a sensation: "We know nothing of the objects themselves which compose the universe, except through the medium of the impressions they excite in us, which impressions are the results of certain actions and processes in which sensible objects and the material parts of ourselves are directly concerned."[20] The sensation or impression, then, constitutes the "signal" of the existence and of the nature of the object, in the sense in which any effect observed may be described as for us a signal of its cause. The objects themselves are declared by Herschel not to be known by us otherwise than through the sensations they cause in us. The nature of the objects, as distinguished from that of the sensations that signify them, is known to us, he seems to hold, because the qualities and affections of the objects "correspond" to the sensations in us. But these "corresponding" qualities in the object are, so far as can be gathered from Herschel's words, merely such qualities as in our minds have become habitually *associated* with given sensations. The question then arises, whence our ideas of these *objective* qualities, if our sensations are all we ever directly experience. The status of associate of some sensation of ours could be acquired by an objective quality only *after* we had had experience of the quality itself, and

---

[19] Sec. 74.   [20] Sec. 109.

this he believes we never have, since he holds that all we ever are directly acquainted with are our own sensations. It would seem then that if this is the situation, the nature of the objects must forever remain a mere X to us; i.e., all we can then know of them is that they are the sorts of entities, if any, of which our sensations are signs.

Herschel's illustration of the telegraph and the ship does not clarify the situation, for the analogy between it and the relation of "phenomena" to "objects," as the latter is abstractly described by him, does not hold. In the case of the telegraph signal, *both* the sight of the motion of the telegraph and the sight of the arrival of the ship have been "sensible impressions." We have thus here two terms first *given*, and *then* a relation of association established between them. In Herschel's abstract description, however, we are supposed to *construct* the second term purely out of a relation (habitual association) of it to the first, notwithstanding that this relation can come to exist only *after* the experience of the second independently of the relation.

With regard to the other illustration—the connection between the "notion" of a large floating building filled with sailors and the impression of the outline of a ship on the retina of the spectator on the beach—the following may be said. If Herschel means by "the outline on the retina" just what he says, viz., the same sort of physical fact in the eye as occurs in any other physical camera and not the *sensation* this fact in the eye causes in the mind, then the "connection" between the outline on the retina and the "notion" of a large floating building is something very different from the sort of connection called association of ideas. It is, namely, connection between the stimulation of nerve endings and the occurrence of mental states. If on the other hand Herschel means by "the outline on the retina" the sensation caused in the mind by the presence of this outline on the back of the eye, then that sensation can become associated with the "notion" of a large floating building only if this notion has already been acquired; and the question then remains *how* it was acquired. Obviously, association between the sensation and the notion is not a possible answer to it. Herschel's statements quoted above thus wholly fail to provide an intelligible account of the relation of phenomena to objects.

When, however, we pass to actual cases of the "analysis of phenomena" as offered by Herschel we find another story, which must be taken to represent his true thought much rather than does the short and precarious venture into epistemology we have just examined. The "analysis of phenomena" in these concrete cases turns out to be not as first announced a "rendering sensible" of objective processes which the mind was assumed incapable of sensing, but merely an analysis of complex objects or objective processes into simpler. These, however, are referred to by Herschel at a number of places in the chapter as themselves "phenomena" —inconsistently, let it be noted, with his initial definition of phenomena as the sensible *results in the mind* of processes and operations among external objects. For example, in Sec. 79, the propagation of motion from one body to another is termed a "phenomenon." At most places, indeed, Herschel seems to use the word "phenomenon" to mean any objective event susceptible of being somehow "observed." Moreover, the relation between a complex(?) phenomenon (e.g., the sensation of sound) and the simpler "phenomena" into which it (?) is analyzed by Herschel (e.g., the rapid vibratory motion of the parts of a bell, the communication of it to the air, by the air to our eardrum, ossicles, etc., and ultimately to the auditory nerve—this then exciting sensation), turns out to be not of the nature of an association of our ideas resulting from habit, but a causal relation among external objects, where one process causes another *to occur*, not merely to be thought of.

Discussing the "analysis" of the phenomenon of sound just given, Herschel goes on to say that "two other phenomena, of a simpler, or, it would be more correct to say, of a more general or elementary order,[21] into which the complex phenomenon of sound resolves itself" are brought to light: (a) the excitement and propagation of motion, and (b) the production of sensation. Again, the communication of motion from body to body is resolvable into several other "phenomena": the original setting in motion of a material body; the behavior of a moving particle when it comes in contact with another; the behavior of that other—the last two in turn pointing to another phenomenon which must also be considered, namely, the connection of the parts of material masses, by which the parts influence each other's motion. "Thus . . . an analysis of the phenomenon of sound leads to the enquiry, first, of two *causes*, viz., the cause of motion, and the cause of sensation, these being phenomena which (at least as human knowledge stands at present) we are unable to analyze fur-

---

[21] Cf. Bacon, *Novum Organum*, II. 4.

ther; and therefore we set them down as simple, elementary, and referable
. . . to the immediate action of their causes. Secondly, of several questions
relating to the connection between the motion of material bodies and its
cause, such as, *What will happen* when a moving body is surrounded on all
sides by others not in motion? *What will happen* when a body not in motion is advanced upon by a moving one?"[22] The answer to such questions
consists in *laws of motion*, in the sense attributed by Herschel to a law
of nature, viz., "a statement in words of what will happen in such and
such general contingencies." Lastly, we are led to the two other general
phenomena of the cohesion, and the elasticity of matter, which, until
means are found to analyze them further, must be regarded "as *ultimate
phenomena*, and referable to the direct action of causes, viz., an attractive and a repulsive *force*."[23]

By the above concrete picture of the "analysis of a phenomenon," what
Herschel means by the phrase is made clearer than by his abstract description. But it makes clear also that what is then analyzed is not a "phenomenon" in the sense he has specified for this term. To complete the
account of his views on this particular part of the task of science, we may
add his declaration, in Section 88, that no general rules can be given for
the analysis of phenomena, "any more than . . . general rules can be laid
down by the chemist for the analysis of substances of which all the ingredients are unknown." As to the utility of the analysis of phenomena
in the development of science, Herschel goes on to say that it principally
"enables us to recognize, and mark for special investigation, those (phenomena) which appear to us simple; to set methodically about determining their laws, and thus to facilitate the work of raising up general axioms,
or forms of words, which shall include the whole of them;[24] which
shall, as it were, transplant them out of the external into the intellectual
world, render them creatures of pure thought, and enable us to reason
them out *a priori*," this often leading to the discovery, by deduction, of
previously unsuspected particular facts.

Herschel's use of the terms Cause, Force, and Law, now calls for separate examination. There seem to be some four distinguishable senses in

---

[22] Sec. 80.   [23] Sec. 80.

[24] The example of Bacon in using the word "axiom" to designate the laws of nature is
followed by Herschel. Also often by Newton. See Dugald Stewart, *Philosophy of Mind*,
Vol. ii, Ch. iv.

which the term Cause is employed by Herschel in the *Discourse;* but as
he does not appear to have realized that he was in fact using the term
in more than *two* different senses, the four, in spite of their distinctness
from one another, can hardly be exhibited by means of wholly separate
quotations from his work. There will accordingly be a certain amount of
overlapping in our remarks concerning each of them.

The first of the four is that in which a cause is conceived as an *act
of will.* According to Herschel there is one case and only one where we
have an "immediate consciousness" of an "act of direct *causation,*"[25] and
this is "the production of motion by the exertion of force"[26]—"we feel
within ourselves a *direct* power to produce" motion of our limbs. But our
original impression of the nature of force is independent of any perception
of motion; it is received from "our own effort and sense of fatigue," for
when, for instance, "we press our two hands violently together, so as just
to oppose each other's effort, we still perceive, by the fatigue and exhaus-
tion, and by the impossibility of maintaining the effort long, that something is going on within us, of which the mind is the agent, and the will the
determining cause."[27] This internal consciousness, Herschel claims, gives
us "a complete idea of *force.*" That force as so understood is the cause of
motion, however, and that motion can therefore be regarded as the *signal*
of the exertion of force, is something which we come to know only by
finding that the same action of the mind, which, when our limbs are en-
cased in plaster enables us to fatigue and exhaust ourselves by the tension
of our muscles, puts it in our power, when our limbs are free, to move
ourselves and other bodies.[28] The conclusion Herschel draws from these
remarks is that since the *process* by which the exertion of force causes
motion of our limbs remains obscure to us even in the case where the force
is exerted by ourselves, there is very little prospect that "in our investigation of nature, we shall ever be able to arrive at a knowledge of ultimate
causes." This "will teach us to limit our views to that of *laws,* and to the
analysis of complex phenomena by which they are resolved into simpler
ones, which appearing to us incapable of further analysis, we must consent to regard as causes."[29]

---

[25] Sec. 78.   [26] Sec. 77.   [27] Sec. 77.   [28] Sec. 77.

[29] Sec. 78. The "cause" of sensation is declared by Herschel to be "much more obscure"
still than that of motion (Sec. 82). As thus obscure, the "cause of sensation," e.g., of

Here, then, we find Herschel speaking of "the exertion of force" as the cause of motion of our limbs through an intervening process; also, of the *will* as the "determining cause" of the fact that something (viz., muscular tension) is going on within our body. In a passage to be quoted below, moreover, Herschel clearly identifies the exertion of force with the act of volition by stating that when a nerve is cut, the exertion of force occurs without any muscular tension resulting.

We come now to a second sense of "cause," that in which a cause is conceived as an *ultimately simple phenomenon*. In the passage quoted above Herschel uses the term "ultimate causes" to mean, apparently, the elements which would be revealed by a complete analysis of the process through which the exertion of force (act of will) causes tension or motion of our muscles, if such analysis were possible. An ultimate cause, as so conceived, is thus an ultimate phenomenon—a phenomenon which does not merely seem to us unanalyzable and simple, but really is so. More-over, the exertion of force (act of will) of which he speaks above is not the cause in *this* sense of what takes place in the muscle, since what he regards as obscure is not the nature of force as exerted by us (of which we have "a complete idea"), but the *process* through which it causes the change in the muscle. We have then already two different senses of the word cause in the passages quoted: In one, cause means the exertion of force or act of will; and in the other, cause means the simple, unanalyzable phenomena of which the process intervening between the act of will and the resulting motion, ultimately consists.

That we have no knowledge of causes in the second of these two senses (ultimate causes), however, is a thesis which assumes that our act of will is not the immediate cause of what occurs in the muscle, but causes it only through an intervening mechanism. And the ground of this assumption in Herschel's mind appears to be that "when we put any limb in motion, the seat of the exertion seems to us to be *in* the limb, whereas it is demonstrably no such thing, but either in the brain or in the spinal marrow; the proof of which is that if . . . a nerve, which forms a com-

---

auditory sensation, cannot be taken to refer to the vibration of such objects as bells, or of the air, of course. Herschel, indeed, makes it clear in Sec. 82 that by the "cause of sensation" he intends something which has to sensation a relation analogous to that of an "effort of memory or imagination" to the images which that effort causes to appear in our minds!

munication between the limb and the brain, or spine, be divided in any part of its course, however we make the effort, the limb will not move."[30] The intervening mechanism of which Herschel thinks can then only be the nerve which connects the place of motion, viz., the muscle, with the place of the exertion of force, viz., supposedly the brain or spinal cord. But Herschel is here on very precarious ground, as will appear from the following considerations.

That the act of will or effort, in Herschel's sense of fact of consciousness directly known to introspection, is *located in* the brain or spinal cord is an assumption the correctness of which is in no way evidenced by the experiment of cutting the motor nerve ending, say, in the muscles of the arm. For one thing, it seems impossible without absurdity to take literally the relation "being in" or "being the seat of" in any case where the terms of it are supposed to be not both of them material, space-occupying objects, but on the contrary one a material object (the brain) and the other a state of consciousness as directly known to introspection (not the hypothetical molecular brain process which "corresponds" to it). The absurdity which would be involved in taking it literally is of the same sort as that in speaking, say, of transfixing on a pin the feeling of dizziness. Then, "being in" must be taken figuratively and loosely, to mean the relation, whatever it may be (parallelism, or interaction, etc.) that obtains between the psychical act of will and its constant bodily correlate. But this correlate may well be neither the contraction of the muscle (say the biceps) which would occur if the effort "succeeded" nor the molecular processes in the nervous connections of this muscle, but very possibly on the contrary either a contraction in some *other* muscle,[31] or the molecular process in the nerve connections of this other muscle, which of course the severing of the motor nerve leading to the biceps leaves wholly untouched.

Be all this as it may, however, it would seem to have no applicability to the case of inorganic nature, where no nervous system at all is involved in the production of motion. The "exertion of force," let it be remembered has been defined by Herschel only in terms of volition as directly introspected. Therefore, unless he means to assume that when one billiard ball

---

[30] Sec. 77.

[31] E.g., as some psychologists have suggested, in the muscles of the breathing apparatus. See Smith and Guthrie, *Chapters in General Psychology*, Ch. VI.

pushes another, it "exerts force" in the sense of having the state of consciousness which consists in willing that the other move, the occurrence
of motion in inanimate nature cannot be taken as the signal of the "exertion of force" *as defined*. But if not, force then remains undefined so far as
inanimate nature is concerned; and therefore so does the "cause" of motion in inanimate nature if that cause is meant to be something not observed but hidden and inferred. Herschel declares *both* that the cause of
motion in inanimate nature is force, *and* that the forces of nature are
never observable, but are only inferred from their effects by means of an
analogy to the human will as fact of consciousness. This analogy, however, if it is to hold, presupposes some sort of pan-psychism. Herschel
seems to have had some awareness of this, but it is not clear whether he
accepts it or not. His most explicit statement bearing on the point is this:
"Of force, as counterbalanced by opposing force, we have . . . an internal
consciousness; and though it may seem strange to us that matter should
be capable of exerting on matter the same kind of effort, which, judging
alone from this consciousness, we might be led to regard as a mental one;
yet we cannot refuse the direct evidence of our senses, which shows us
that when we keep a spring stretched with one hand, we feel our effort
opposed exactly in the same way as if we had ourselves opposed it with
the other hand."[32] If Herschel is not willing to say that the spring *wills*
what it then does as ourselves will to stretch it, then "force" as exerted
by the spring constitutes a third sense in which he uses the term Cause.
Attention to the examples Herschel gives suggests that "force," in the
case of a "force of nature," is thought of by him not much more clearly
or significantly than as a *deus ex machina*. I have already quoted the end
of Sec. 80, where he speaks of the cohesion and elasticity of matter as,
so far as we now know, "*ultimate phenomena* and referable to the direct
action of causes, viz., an attractive and a repulsive *force*." From this, the
meaning he really attaches to "ultimate cause" can easily be construed:
An ultimate phenomenon is one that cannot be further analyzed, and an
ultimate cause is the cause of an ultimate phenomenon in the sense of
"cause" in which an attractive or cohesive force is the cause of cohesion—
which sense, let us add, is also that in which the famous *vis dormitiva* of
opium is the cause of sleep! In other words, when we find anything T

---

[32] Sec. 81.

behaving in a particular manner M under given conditions C, and cannot answer the question why T so behaves by pointing to an intermediary I which is caused by C and itself in turn causes M (that is, by giving an analysis of the phenomenon), we answer by saying: T behaves in manner M because there exists an X such that X causes T to do M in the presence of C. And a *deus ex machina*—an X of this sort defined *merely* as such a cause as would produce an effect such as we suppose it to cause—seems to be all that Herschel, without realizing it, really means by a force in external nature. This is a third sense in which he uses the term "cause," since it is here not as before the ultimately simple phenomena that are spoken of as causes but the non-phenomenal forces to the "direct action" of which these phenomena are to be "referred."

We come now to the fourth and most fruitful of the several conceptions of Cause to be found in the *Discourse*, viz., that of *proximate cause*, where that which causes is some phenomenon antecedent in time to its effect. Section 83, in which Cause in this sense is introduced, opens with these words: "Dismissing, then, as beyond our reach, the enquiry into causes, we must be content at present to concentrate our attention on the laws which prevail among phenomena, and which seem to be their immediate results." Towards the end of the same section Herschel then writes as follows: "Thus, in a modified and relative sense, we may still continue to speak of causes, not intending thereby those ultimate principles of action on whose exertion the whole frame of nature depends, but of those proximate links which connect phenomena with others of a simpler, higher, and more general or elementary kind. For example: we may regard the vibration of a musical string as the proximate cause of the sound it yields, receiving it, so far, as an ultimate fact, and waving or deferring enquiry into the cause of vibrations, which is of a higher and more general nature."

When Cause is so conceived, the two terms of the causal relation are both then phenomena and are one temporally sequent to the other. For example, in Sec. 138 Herschel says: "Experience having shown us the manner in which one phenomenon depends on another in a great variety of cases, we find ourselves provided, as science extends, with a continually increasing stock of such antecedent phenomena, or causes (meaning at present merely proximate causes) competent under different modifications, to the production of a great multitude of effects, besides those which originally led to a knowledge of them." He goes on to tell us that he has in mind what Newton called *verae causae,* which he takes to mean phenomena "which experience has shown us to exist" and "to be efficacious in producing similar phenomena" (to those they are called upon to explain).[33] He then gives the following three illustrations: the elevation of the bottom of the sea till it becomes dry land, as cause of the presence of shells in rocks at a great height above the sea; the sinking of old continents and the elevation of new, as a possible cause of great changes in the general climate of large tracts of the globe; the increase of the minor axis of the ellipse that the earth describes about the sun, as cause of the diminution of the mean temperature of the surface of the earth.

We may now for purposes of contrast, recapitulate briefly the four meanings of the term Cause that we have discerned in Herschel's text: In the *first* sense examined, the relation of a "cause" to its "effect" is the sort of relation that subsists between an act of will (as known in introspection) and the tension or motion of a muscle that accompanies it. In the *second* sense "causes" are the genuinely simple phenomena into which a complex phenomenon is theoretically analyzable. In the *third* sense, the relation of "cause" to "effect" is that of a postulated noumenal "force" to its phenomenal manifestation, e.g., of "cohesive force" to cohesion as observed, or of "soporific power" to the phenomenon of sleep. Such "causes" are always "forces" postulated *ad hoc;* they are never directly observed but supposedly only "inferred" from their so-called effects. In the *fourth* sense, the relation of a "cause" to its "effect" is that of an event to another event sequent to it in time and following it "necessarily." What "necessarily" means here, Herschel explains when in Sec. 145 he enumerates "the characters of that relation which we intend by cause and effect." What these are we shall examine later in detail. Suffice it to say here that "invariable connection" is the character most nearly inclusive of its various features. This fourth sense of causation is that to which Herschel's formulation of the principles which since J. S. Mill have been called the Methods of Agreement and of Difference, and of their derivatives, is relevant.[34]

Before turning to an examination of them, we must first say a few words

---

[33] Sec. 141.

[34] Cf. Leuckfeld, "Zur logischen Lehre von der Induction," Archiv für Geschichte der Philosophie, Vol. 10, p. 351.

concerning the use of the terms *Law*, and *Induction* in Herschel's *Discourse*. A number of passages in which the term Law occurs have already been quoted. We may recall that the answer to such a question as "What will happen when a body not in motion is advanced upon by a moving one?" constitutes, Herschel says, a "law of motion." Again, in Sec. 89, he says "A law of nature, being the statement of what will happen in certain general contingencies, may be regarded as the announcement in the same words, of a whole group or class of phenomena. Whenever, therefore, we perceive that two or more phenomena agree in so many or so remarkable points, as to lead us to regard them as forming a class or group, if we lay out of consideration, or *abstract*, all the circumstances in which they disagree, and retain in our minds those only in which they agree, and then, under this kind of mental convention, frame a definition or statement of one of them, in such words that it shall apply equally to them all, such statement will appear in the form of a general proposition, having so far at least the character of a law of nature," for instance "Double refracting substances exhibit periodical colors by exposure to polarized light."

A law of nature, such as this proposition constitutes may, Herschel goes on, be regarded in one of three ways;

1. "As a general proposition, announcing, in abstract terms, a whole group of particular facts relating to the behavior of natural agents in proposed circumstances."[35] For instance, the law stated above includes "among others the particular facts that rock crystal and saltpetre exhibit periodical colours."

2. "As a proposition announcing that a whole class of individuals agreeing in one character agree also in another"; for instance, here, as declaring the constant association between double refraction and exhibition of periodical colors.

3. "As a proposition asserting the mutual connection, or in some cases the entire identity of two classes of individuals"; for instance, here, "if observation had enabled us to establish the existence of a class of bodies possessing the property of double refraction, and observations of another kind had, independently of the former, led us to recognize a class possessing that of the exhibition of periodical colours in polarized light, a mere comparison of lists would at once demonstrate the identity of the two classes, or enable us to ascertain whether one was or was not included in the other."[36]

Laws may thus in Herschel's view briefly be characterized as *general*

---

[35] Sec. 91.   [36] Sec. 93.

facts, as distinguished from particular facts. Such general facts are themselves susceptible of being grouped into classes, i.e., "included in laws which, as they dispose of groups, not individuals, have a far superior degree of generality, till at length, by continuing the process, we arrive at *axioms* of the highest degree of generality of which science is capable."[37]

As to the relation between Laws and Causes, Herschel is not very definite. We have seen that Cause, in the last of the senses distinguished above, appears to mean for him a fact antecedent to another which follows it "necessarily," and that by "necessarily" he appears to mean, broadly, *according to a law*. Note also the end of the following passage, which seems to regard the notion of causes as bound up in that of Law: "Every law is a provision for cases which *may* occur, and has relation to an infinite number of cases that never have occurred, and never will. Now, it is this provision, *a priori*, for contingencies, this contemplation of possible occurrences, and predisposal of what shall happen, that impresses us with the notion of a *law* and a *cause*."[38] As definite a statement as can be found in the *Discourse* as to the relation between Cause and Law is the following: "Whenever two phenomena are observed to be invariably connected together, we conclude them to be related to each other, either as cause and effect, or as common effects of a single cause."[39] In this statement the words "we conclude" probably are not intended by Herschel to mean that the invariability is *evidence of* something other than itself, called Causation. Rather, he probably means to adhere to Hume's view, according to which invariability *constitutes* the relation called causation.

If so, however, *all* laws could then be spoken of as causal laws. They would all be such that the pairs of events that can be subsumed under them would *eo ipso* be related either as one the cause of the other, or both as effects of some antecedent third. This would have to be so even in the case of "empirical laws" as defined by Herschel, that is, "Laws . . . derived, by the direct process of including in mathematical formulae the results of a greater or less number of measurements."[40] He describes such laws, it is true, as "unverified inductions" and says that until they have been verified "no confidence can ever be placed in them beyond the limits of the data from which they are derived." But what he has in mind for

---

[37] Sec. 94.   [38] Sec. 26.

[39] Sec. 92. Cf. however, Sec. 162.   [40] Sec. 187.

them is verification "theoretically by a deductive process," not, as one could fairly expect, verification by observation of the "invariability" which he seems to equate with causation. Like J. S. Mill after him, and like anyone else who accepts Hume's identification of causation with regularity of conjunction, Herschel can be confronted here with the objection that according to this view we should have to class as causal certain relations which he like anyone else would, as a matter of common sense, refuse so to class. These would include not only such a relation as Ohm's law describes between electrical current, potential and resistance, but also such a case as that of the close covariation over a good many years, which Morris Cohen mentions somewhere, between the death rate in the state of Hyderabad, India, and the membership in a certain mechanics' union in New York.

But whatever may be Herschel's view of the relation between Law and Cause, he declares in Sec. 95 that the process of formulating laws "is what we mean by induction." Induction may, he holds, be carried on in two different ways: either by noting the agreements and disagreements of ascertained *classes;* or by considering the *individuals* of a class and seeking what character they have in common beside that which constitutes them one class. The latter employs the division of labor and is better adapted to the infancy of science; the former, which is more suitable to the maturity of science," mainly relies on individual penetration, and requires a union of many branches of knowledge in one person."[41]

IV

In the sixth and seventh chapters, Herschel passes to a direct enunciation of the methodological precepts that are to govern induction. He distinguishes two broad stages in induction: at the first, science is concerned with the discovery of "proximate causes" and of laws of the lowest degree of generality, and with the verification of these laws. At the second stage the inductions of science have for their material no longer individual facts, but on the contrary general facts, viz., the laws themselves and the causes, which, in the first stage, were obtained from the examination of the individual facts. The results of this second stage of induction consist

[41] Cf. Bacon, *New Atlantis*, the end.

in laws of a higher generality, to which he gives the name of Theories, and which must, like the others, be verified.

In our examination of what Herschel has to say concerning the first stage, it is worth while to note first of all that the problem he has directly in mind when he approaches the formulation of his "rules of philosophizing" and throughout the exposition of them, is that of the *discovery* of causes. The problem of *proof* of causal connections, on the other hand, is for him that of verifying—by deduction of predictions and comparison of the predictions with observed facts—the *causal hypotheses* that resulted from the use of the method of discovery: " . . . when the cause of a phenomenon neither presents itself obviously on the consideration of the phenomenon itself, nor is as it were forced on our attention by a case of strong analogy . . . we have then no resource but in a deliberate assemblage of all the parallel instances we can muster; that is, to the formation of a class of facts, having the phenomenon in question for a head of classification; and to search among the individuals of this class for some other common points of agreement, among which the cause will of necessity be found."[42] If more than one such point of agreement appears, we must then devise "crucial" experiments where—some of these points of agreement being absent and the phenomenon nevertheless still present—we find evidence adequate to the rejection of such absent points from the cause.

According to this broad prefatory description of the course of scientific investigation, the rôle assigned by Herschel to experimentation appears to be that of eliminating from a number of possible hypotheses as to the cause of a phenomenon those which are incorrect; and, eventually, that of devising more and more severe verifications of the adequacy of the hypothesis which has survived this process of elimination. That Herschel is directly concerned with the discovery of causal hypotheses is further evidenced by the following words, which immediately introduce his detailed presentation of principles of method: "When we would lay down general rules for guiding and facilitating our *search*, among a great mass of assembled facts, *for their common cause*, we must have regard to the characters of that relation which we intend by cause and effect."[43]

Let us now examine these defining characters of the causal relation, and the rules of practice Herschel bases upon them. These characters are:

---

[42] Sec. 144.   [43] Sec. 145. Italics mine.

1st. Invariable connection, and, in particular, invariable antecedence of the cause and consequence of the effect, unless prevented by some counteracting cause. To this are appended some remarks concerning the difficulty of deciding which one, of two phenomena, precedes the other, when the cause and the effect either are gradual changes—so that a late stage of the cause coexists with an early stage of the effect—or else occur in almost instantaneous succession.

2nd. Invariable negation of the effect with absence of the cause, unless some other cause be capable of producing the same effect.

3rd. Increase or diminution of the effect, with the increased or diminished intensity of the cause, in cases which admit of increase and diminution.

4th. Proportionality of the effect to its cause in all cases of *direct unimpeded* action.

5th. Reversal of the effect with that of the cause.

On the basis of these characters of the causal relation, Herschel then formulates ten observations which may be considered as "rules of philosophizing."[44] Thus, he says, we conclude:

1st. That if in our group of facts there be one in which any assigned peculiarity, or attendant circumstance, is wanting or opposite such peculiarity cannot be the cause we seek.

2nd. That any circumstance in which all the facts without exception agree, *may* be the cause in question, or, if not, at least a collateral effect of the same cause: if there be but one such point of agreement, this possibility becomes a certainty; and on the other hand if there be more than one, they may be concurrent causes.

The third observation is an injunction against *a priori* rejection of a cause in favor of which we have a unanimous agreement of strong analogies, merely because we do not see how such a cause can produce the effect, or even can exist under the circumstances of the case.

4th. That contrary or opposing facts are equally instructive for the discovery of causes with favourable ones.

5th. That causes will very frequently become obvious, by a mere arrangement of our facts in the order of intensity in which some peculiar quality subsists; though not of necessity because counteracting or modifying causes may be at the same time in action.

For example, the rapidity of vibration of a medium, and the pitch of the note heard are judged to be causally connected owing to the correspondence between the series of frequencies and the series of pitches.

---

[44] Secs. 146–162.

6th. That such counteracting or modifying causes may subsist unperceived and annul the effects of the cause we seek, in instances which, but for their action, would have come into our class of favourable facts; and that, therefore, exceptions may often be made to disappear by removing or allowing for such counteracting causes.

7th. If we can either find produced by nature, or produce designedly for ourselves, two instances which agree *exactly* in all but one particular, and differ in that one, its influence in producing the phenomenon, if it have any, *must* thereby be rendered sensible. If that particular be present in one instance and wanting altogether in the other, the production or non-production of the phenomenon will decide whether it be or be not the only cause: still more evidently, if it be present *contrariwise* in the two cases, and the effect be thereby reversed. But if its total presence or absence only produces a change in the *degree* or intensity of the phenomenon, we can then only conclude that it acts as a concurrent cause or condition with some other to be sought elsewhere.

Herschel adds here that although such cases of single difference are rare in nature, they are easily devised in experimentation, which becomes the more valuable as it more closely approximates the requirement of having exact agreement in all its circumstances but one.

8th. If we cannot obtain a complete negative or opposition of the circumstance whose influence we would ascertain, we must endeavor to find cases where it varies considerably in degree.

9th. Complicated phenomena, in which several causes concurring, opposing, or quite independent of each other, operate at once, so as to produce a compound effect, may be simplified by subducting the effect of all the known causes, as well as the nature of the case permits, either by deductive reasoning or by appeal to experience, and thus leaving as it were, a *residual phenomenon* to be explained.

Herschel concludes these observations by noting that:

10th. The detection of a *possible* cause, by the comparison of assembled cases *must* lead to one of two things: either, 1st, the detection of a real cause, and of its manner of acting, so as to furnish a complete explanation of the facts; or 2ndly, the establishment of an abstract law of nature, pointing out two phenomena of a general kind as invariably connected; and asserting, that where one is, there the other will always be found.

The application of these rules is then illustrated by a number of examples—the investigations of Wells into the cause of dew, particularly, being discussed at length.

In the remainder of the sixth chapter, Herschel deals mainly with the verification of inductions of the first stage. The manner in which we seek for possible causes or laws, although important in practice, is theoretically of no moment: "provided only we verify them carefully when once detected, we must be content to seize them wherever they are to be found."[45] In practically every case, however, the statement of a law of nature that we frame goes beyond the cases actually examined; and we cannot rely on its thus "enabling us to extend our views beyond the circle of instances from which it was obtained, unless we have already had experience of its power to do so; unless it actually *has* enabled us before trial to say what will take place in cases analogous to those originally contemplated.[46] To examine whether it thus actually enables us to predict is to *verify* it. Thus "the successful process of scientific enquiry demands continually the alternate use of both the *inductive* and *deductive* method";[47] and the confidence which we may justifiedly place in the universality of a law is proportionate to the severity of the verifications made, extreme cases affording particularly convincing tests.[48] But "The surest and best characteristic of a well-founded and extensive induction . . . is when verifications of it spring up, as it were, spontaneously, into notice, from quarters where they might be least expected, or even among instances of that very kind which were at first considered hostile to them. Evidence of this kind is irresistible, and compels assent with a weight which scarcely any other possesses."[49]

Empirical laws, "derived by the direct process of including in mathematical formulae the results of a greater or less number of measurements," cannot be trusted beyond the limits of the data from which they are derived, and even within those limits must be carefully scrutinized, to ascertain whether the differences between their results and actual facts may fairly be attributed to errors of observation.[50]

Herschel then remarks that "in forming inductions, it will most commonly happen that we are led to our conclusions by the especial force of some two or three strongly impressive facts, rather than by affording the whole mass of cases a regular consideration,"[51] and he devotes the remainder of the chapter to concrete illustrations from modern science of some of the chief kinds of such "prerogative instances" described by Bacon. But he observes that although much is usually made of this part of Bacon's

---

[45] Sec. 170.   [46] Sec. 176.   [47] Sec. 184.   [48] Sec. 177.
[49] Sec. 180.   [50] Sec. 187.   [51] Sec. 191.

work, the classification of them under various headings, however just, is
not of much practical help, for the misfortune is that the choice of those
that would be most useful does not rest with us: "we must take the instances as nature presents them."[52]

V

The seventh and last chapter is devoted by Herschel to the higher degrees of inductive generalization, and to the formation and verification of
theories. "As particular inductions and laws of the first degree of generality are obtained from the consideration of individual facts," he tells us,
"so Theories result from a consideration of these laws, and of the proximate causes brought into view in the previous process, regarded all together as constituting a new set of phenomena." . . . "The ultimate objects
we pursue in the highest theories are the same as those of the lowest inductions" and the means are closely analogous in both cases.[53]

An important part of the knowledge we seek of the hidden processes of
nature depends on the discovery of the actual structure of the universe
and its parts, and the agents concerned in these processes. But "the mechanism of nature is for the most part either on too large or too small a
scale to be immediately cognizable by our senses, and her agents in like
manner elude direct observation, and become known to us only by their
effects.[54] Are we then in such cases "to be deterred from framing hypotheses and constructing theories" because we find it difficult to decide between
rival theories or because we "find ourselves frequently beyond our depth"?
"Undoubtedly not," Herschel answers. "Hypotheses, with respect to
theories, are what presumed proximate causes are with respect to particu-

---

[52] In view of De Morgan's opinion (expressed in his *Budget of Paradoxes*) that Bacon's
writings neither influenced Newton nor could have been of any possible value to him, and
even that Newton had probably not read them, it is interesting to note Herschel's statement with regard to one of Bacon's "travelling instances," that, "in reading this, and many
other instances in the Novum Organum, one would almost suppose (had it been written)
that its author had taken them from Newton's Optics"! The correspondence that Herschel
notes—though it obviously cannot be construed as evidence either that Newton "borrowed" from Bacon or even that he had read his work—at least shows that Bacon's observations were not all as intrinsically worthless as the expressions of some of his critics
would lead one to believe. Cf. McVey Napier. Trans. Royal Soc. of Edin., Vol. 8, p. 384.

[53] Sec. 201.   [54] Sec. 202.

lar inductions: they afford us motives for searching into analogies," and if well constructed frequently lead to additional steps in generalization. In certain cases, even, "such a weight of analogy and probability may become accumulated on the side of an hypothesis, that we are compelled to admit one of two things; either that it is an actual statement of what really passes in nature, or that the reality, whatever it be, must run so close a parallel with it, as to admit of some mode of expression common to both, at least in so far as the phenomena actually known are concerned."[55]

Herschel then goes on to discuss the process of constructing theories:

> In framing a theory which shall render a rational account of any natural phenomenon, we have *first* to consider the agents on which it depends, or the causes to which we regard it as ultimately referable. These agents are not to be arbitrarily assumed; they must be such as we have good inductive grounds to believe do exist in nature, and do perform a part in phenomena analogous to those we would render an account of; or such, whose presence in the actual case can be demonstrated by unequivocal signs. They must be *verae causae*, in short, which we can not only show to exist and to act, but the laws of whose action we can derive independently, by direct induction, from experiments purposely instituted; or at least make such suppositions respecting them as shall not be contrary to our experience.

As an instance of an agent that is such a *vera causa*, Herschel mentions "force, or mechanical power" in the theory of gravitation.[56] This is hardly a happy illustration since the description of a "force" always turns out, on examination, to be a statement that objects of a certain kind are such that circumstances of certain sorts cause them to behave in a certain manner. That is, a force is essentially a causal law; and a law—even a causal law— never *itself* functions as a cause. A true example of an agent which is a *vera causa* in the sense specified by Herschel would be the *atom*.

But *secondly*, we have to consider "the laws which regulate the action of these our primary agents; and these we can only arrive at in three ways: 1st, By inductive reasoning," that is, by examining all the particular cases, piecing together the results of our observations, and generalizing from them; "2dly, By forming at once a bold hypothesis, particularizing the law, and trying the truth of it by following out its consequences and comparing them with facts; or 3dly, By a process partaking of both of these

---

[55] Sec. 208.   [56] Sec. 209.

. . . viz., by assuming indeed the laws we would discover, but so generally expressed that they shall include an unlimited variety of particular laws; —following out the consequences of this assumption . . . comparing them in succession with all the particular cases within our knowledge; and lastly *on this comparison*, so modifying and restricting the general enunciation of our laws as to *make the results agree.*"[57]

Thirdly, in cases where the laws which regulate the actions of our ultimate causes do not apply at once to the materials and directly produce the result (as in the instance of gravitation), we have to consider "a system of mechanism, or a structure of parts through the intervention of which [the effects of our ultimate causes] become sensible to us."[58]

As to the estimation of the value of a theory, i.e., the "verification" of a theory, what is important to know "is whether our theory truly represent *all* the facts, and include *all* the laws to which observation and induction lead."[59] While theories are best arrived at by the consideration of general laws, they are "most securely verified by comparing them with particular facts, because this serves as a verification of the whole train of induction, from the lowest term to the highest";[60] but these particular facts must be widely diversified and include extreme cases if reasonable probability of detecting error is to be afforded. "When two theories run parallel to each other, and each explains a great many facts in common with the other, any experiment which affords a crucial instance to decide between them . . . is of great importance."[61]

Except in point of generality, the inductions of the second stage are thus not conceived by Herschel to differ markedly from those of the first stage. They are still, ultimately, *obtained from* experience, as well as verified by appeal to experience. Even when guessed at by a bold stroke of genius, the guess is still one that springs from examination of the facts, rather than from the spontaneous demand of man for intellectual tools adapted to his logical needs. That is, for Herschel, it is an act of *discovery* rather than of invention.[62] Whewell, on the other hand, urges a few years later that the

---

[57] Sec. 210.   [58] Sec. 214.   [59] Sec. 216.   [60] Sec. 219.   [61] Sec. 218.

[62] Herschel even says, in Section 86, that "the axioms of geometry themselves may be regarded as in some sort an appeal to experience, not corporeal, but mental . . . these axioms, however self-evident, are still general propositions so far of the inductive kind, that, independently of experience, they would not present themselves to the mind. The only difference between these and axioms obtained from extensive induction is this, that

task of science as it actually presents itself in many cases is to be described much rather as that of inventing a way of stating the facts observed that shall satisfy our logical demands.

VI

In the light of this examination of Herschel's *Discourse*, what can we now say of his place in the history of the philosophy of science? For one thing Herschel—unlike his contemporary Whewell whose *Novum Organon Renovatum* represents the influence of Kant in this field—clearly belongs in the line of British empiricists which may be considered to begin with Francis Bacon and to include as principal figures Locke, Berkeley, Hume, and John Stuart Mill.[63]

Herschel, of course, was not like Locke, Berkeley, and Hume concerned to formulate an epistemology, but the theory of scientific method is so intimately connected with epistemology that, as we have seen, he finds himself led at times into epistemological excursions. These are improvised on empiricistic and associationist principles, but they remain amateurish and contribute nothing to the solution of the epistemological problems concerned. Herschel's definition of "phenomena," for instance, is as we have seen at variance with his own actual use of the term; and his account of the relation of phenomena to objects is unacceptable. Again, he mistakenly believes that a force can be a cause; that in acts of will the ultimate nature of force is evident to our observation; and that the forces of nature are essentially akin to volitions. Again, as already pointed out, Herschel, like Hume before him and Mill after, never distinguishes clearly between the two notions of cause and of law. On this account, many of the statements in which he uses the terms have the sort of obscurity confusion breeds. His conception of theories as simply wider laws, having to narrower ones a relation analogous to that of the latter to the particular facts they

---

in raising the axioms of geometry, the instances offer themselves spontaneously . . . and are few and simple; in raising those of nature, they are infinitely numerous, complicated and remote."

[63] In the thirteenth century Roger Bacon exhibited a more genuine empiricism and a greater practical mastery of scientific method than did Francis Bacon in the seventeenth. But Roger's example did not influence his contemporaries or his successors as it would have done had he lived three hundred years later.

generalize is inherited from Bacon and is unsound. However, the question of the nature of theories and of their relations to laws is a difficult one. Whewell, whose *Philosophy of the Inductive Sciences* was published ten years after Herschel's *Discourse*, exhibits a sounder insight into it; but it is not until comparatively recent years that a clear answer can be said to have become available.[64]

On the credit side are to be placed Herschel's statements on the subject of Observation, Experiment, Classification, Hypothesis, and Verification; not, however, because particularly original since even in Bacon's writings rather similar remarks are to be found, but rather because of the clear light thrown on these scientific procedures by the true concrete illustrations of them Herschel furnishes. His remarks on terminology, and the relation to the scope of science which he assigns to the postulate of the "Uniformity of Nature," are also sound and valuable. His greatest contribution, however, is undoubtedly to be found in the ten "rules of philosophizing" already quoted. It is in them and in the remarks which accompany them that we find, for the first time both distinctly enunciated and amply illustrated, the famous four methods of Agreement, Difference, Concomitant Variations, and Residues. These names, by which they are now universally known, are due to John Stuart Mill; but Mill himself declares that in Herschel's *Discourse* alone, "of all the books which I have met with the four methods of induction are distinctly recognized."[65] And at least one logician, W. S. Jevons, has expressed his preference for Herschel's discussion of them over that of Mill.[66] These methods, nowadays often referred to as "Mill's Methods," would, if they are to be tied to any man's name, therefore seem better described as Herschel's Methods. The history of at least some of them, however, can be traced back as far as Aristotle. Bacon had discerned the first three (which are the most significant) and

---

[64] See for instance Norman Campbell's *Physics, the Elements*, 1920; and more recently J. H. Woodger's *The Technique of Theory Construction*, 1939. The various judgments above as to errors and confusions in Herschel's *Discourse* have had to be expressed dogmatically here since any attempt to justify them would have required far too much space. The grounds on which the writer bases most of them may, however, be found in his *Causation and the Types of Necessity*, 1924, and in a paper recently published, entitled *The Nature and Function of Theory in Ethics*. (*Ethics*, Vol. LI, No. 1, October 1940.)

[65] System of Logic, Bk. III, Ch. IX, §3.

[66] *Pure Logic and other minor works*, p. 251, note.

was fully aware of their great power, although the material to which he proposed to apply them was inappropriate and barren.[67] A very clear statement—the best prior to Herschel's—of the first three is to be found in Hume's *Treatise of Human Nature* (1739);[68] although the conception of Cause implicit in the rules Hume there gives is, without his being conscious of it, different from that of Cause as event observed to have been regularly followed by a certain other, which is the conception he explicitly adopts.

The clear and abundantly illustrated discussion of these four methods given by Herschel would be sufficient to assure him a permanent place in the history of the philosophy of science; but this place is further assured by the fact that his *Discourse* contains much the best and most comprehensive formulation up to its date of the methods of scientific investigation, and strongly stimulated or influenced the labors in this field of his contemporaries Whewell and J. S. Mill.

---

[67] *Novum Organum*, II, Aphorisms 11, 12, 13, 15, 18, 20; also among the *Prerog. Inst.* aph. 22.

[68] Bk. I. Part III. Sec. XV "Rules by which to judge causes and effects."

SCIENCE IMPLIES FREEDOM

CHAUNCEY D. LEAKE

University of California

ACADEMICALLY trained people often suffer acutely from the sickening realization that their traditional ideals may lose value for them. What profit honor, unless all are honorable, or can be made to be so? Can ideals have value beyond the lowest common denominator of their acceptance?

Growing from Greek rationalism and the good will moralities of Jesus, nourished by ancient guilt and punishment notions from racial childhood, flowering in the fears of economic and political insecurity in declining Rome, coming to rich fruit in the glow of chivalry, ripening in the fierce sun of scholastic zeal and Church authority, mellowing in the Renaissance, and beginning to shrivel in the Age of Reason, only a few of these ideals have really clung to the tree of our culture after the shaking of democracy and the steady winds of science. The rest are merely memories for nostalgic discomfort. Spenglerly ominous is the lack of blossoms for fresh rich fruit on that tree!

Currently we *feel* that Nazism *must* be wrong, but it seems difficult for us to muster confidence and ability enough to *know* and *show* that it is wrong. Perhaps science, whose business is to get at the truth of things, may help us.

Most people have no idea what science is about. In order to obtain popular recognition that science implies freedom, there may still be some excuse in a democracy for trying to acquaint the public with the spirit behind scientific endeavor. For this is the permeating essence in whatever pleasing fragrance science may have. But it is rarely noticed in the impressive displays of its practical applications so freely advertised from every university, institute, industry, Treasure Island, and World of Tomorrow. Too few of those who call themselves scientists are familiar with it. When the spirit of science is appreciated then it becomes easy for the initiated to understand the many emotional factors which inhibit acceptance of it by neophytes.

One might readily catalogue a long list of specific instances in which various agencies have interfered with the freedom of science. One may note historically the badgering of such humanistic scientists as Socrates, Archimedes, Hypatia, Vesalius, Servetus, Spinoza, Bruno, Galilei, Lavoisier, Priestley, Simpson, Darwin, Einstein, and Freud. In our own sweet land of liberty the now-forgotten LaFollette Committee might expose much fanatical imposition of social inhibitions and taboos by religious and health cults, much political control of scientific research and its findings, much ridiculous legal bigotry over what may be taught about birth control, alcohol, evolution, and over what may be done experimentally with animals. But these are merely illustrations of errors in judgment arising from factors which threaten scientific freedom everywhere and when.

For science is a way of thinking. Free expression of scientific ideas can only follow wide popular sympathy for scientific thinking. It might be presumed that such sympathy exists. Unhappily it does not. Unreflecting enjoyment of material benefits of applications of scientific knowledge brings no more interest in the fundaments of science than occasional horror that this same knowledge is also applied in racketeering and warfare. There is little tolerance for the aim, spirit, and method of science since most humans not only are ignorant of them but even cheerfully prance with conditioning against them, like bumptious drum majorettes.

WHAT SCIENCE IS ABOUT

Definitions of the spirit, method, and aim of science have been attempted by Edwin Grant Conklin, Emeritus Professor of Biology at Princeton University, once President of the potent American Association for the Advancement of Science, and Executive Secretary of the American Philosophical Society. Enjoying more the vivid account of himself in *Time* (July 3, 1939) than any adulation for greatness, he insists in *The Direction of Human Evolution* (New York, 1921) that the spirit of science is freedom to seek and to find the "truth." By this abused idea-symbol, he means an objectively demonstrable and intellectually coherent explanation of ourselves and our environment. Going on, he emphasizes that the spirit of science implies not only freedom to hold and to express any view for which there is rational evidence, but also recognition that knowledge of ourselves and our environment is incomplete and subject to revision, and that there is no legitimate compulsion to belief beyond the voluntary acceptance of demonstrably rational evidence.

About the method of science there often drifts an odor of confusion over Aristotelian "deductive" and Baconian "inductive" reasoning. The successful pragmatic scientist, however, is merely uncommonly sensible. He may proceed over either of two broad paths. On one he is mainly rationalistic and tries to build by experimental reasoning within the rigid limitations of logical consistency a coherent ideal structure with which some details of the universe about us may be found to correspond. Here he follows a mathematical way. On the other he becomes more empirical. He observes and describes as accurately as he can his environment and himself, and then offers a tentative explanation of ways by which he and his environment may operate; whereupon he devises experiments to test the validity of these explanations, and confirms or modifies his ideas in accordance with the results of these experiments. This is the way of the life sciences.

Conklin identified the aim of science with that of religion, to know the "truth" about ourselves and our environment, with confidence that even unwelcome "truth" is better than cherished error, that the welfare of humanity depends upon the extension and diffusion of knowledge among men, and that "truth" alone can make and keep us free.

Even in this very practical and busy era some attention may be merited by this declaration of faith. For we order our lives on the basis of what we believe. One may find this a sane and inspiring *credo*. Most of the enormous difficulties of people may be traced to beliefs which are the antithesis of this in being chiefly smug expressions of fond hopes, pathetic desires, and anxious wishes oozing from such primordial nervous slime responses as are referred to ordinarily as greed, jealousy, and fear.

The social advantage of an appreciation of the scientific faith becomes more pressing as thoughtful people consider the various uses to which our scientific knowledge may be put. We have acquired knowledge about ourselves faster than control over ourselves. Scientific information and conclusions may readily be applied for the welfare of society, but if used for selfish gain at the expense of others they may weaken or destroy social co-operation. Obstacles to the freedom of science seem certain to mushroom whenever the implications of unwelcome knowledge conflict with the selfish purposes of individuals. Meanwhile sound reasons are developing for believing that full freedom for science will be found to add to the broader and more lasting satisfactions of all people, that is, that science has moral value.

A BIOLOGICAL BASIS FOR ETHICS

It is remarkable that three great American biologists, representing the east, mid-continent, and west, should come to about the same conclusions at the same time regarding a biological basis for ethics. Different approaches have led to the same general position on the part of Conklin C. Judson Herrick, Emeritus Professor of Neurology at the University of Chicago, and Samuel J. Holmes, Professor of Zoology at the University of California. Conklin says (*Scientific Monthly*, 49: 295, 1939): "Biologically life is maintained by continual balance, co-operation, compromise, and the same principles apply to the life of society. The highest level of human development is attained when purpose and freedom, joined to social emotions, training and habits, shape behavior not only for personal but also for social satisfactions. Conduct bringing the broader and more lasting satisfactions is the better." According to Herrick (*Scientific Monthly*, 49: 99, 1939): "That social stability upon which the survival and comfort of the individual depend and that moral satisfaction upon which his equanimity, poise and stability of character depend arise from the maintenance of relations with his fellow men which are mutually advantageous." Holmes opines (*Science*, 90: 117, Aug. 11, 1939): "Morality becomes just one phase of the adjustment of the organism to its conditions of existence. As a good body is one which runs smoothly and efficiently in the maintenance of its vital functions, so a good man is one whose conduct not only maintains his own life on an efficient plane, but conduces to the enhancement of the life of his social group." Both Conklin and Herrick would agree with Holmes in saying, "Peoples may believe that their moral customs derive from a supernatural source, but one potent reason for their adoption is their conduciveness of survival."

These distinguished biologists discern survival value in social and ethical fitness as well as in physical. There is a better chance for continuing existence for that individual or group which adjusts itself in harmonious conduct toward others with mutual satisfaction and benefit than for that which does not. The wider this adaptation becomes, and the more groups it includes, the more it contributes to the welfare of all mankind. Here is ethical motivation for promoting the appreciation of the spirit of science and of the necessity for its freedom. Only under such freedom may knowledge become readily available for making the wiser choice of goals and of the means of reaching them. This seems to involve that matter of "human engineering" which so aroused Alfred Korzybski.

In his 1937 presidential address before the American Association for the Advancement of Science, Conklin elaborated this idea with favorable comment from the press. He said: "Of all the possible means of rapidly improving social conditions, ethical education is probably the most promising. Ethical habits especially are dependent on education, and in all normal human beings it is possible to cultivate unselfishness, sympathy rather than enmity, co-operation rather than antagonism. Human nature can be improved by human nurture."

At the Philadelphia meeting of the Association in December, 1940, agreement was reached on the formulation of an objective scientific principle, operative in an ethical manner, but independently of metaphysical implications or considerations. While this principle seems obvious enough when it is even casually expressed, failure to recognize and to remember it may be the cause of many of our troubles. This principle is a sort of scientific expression of the Golden Rule: *The probability of survival of a relationship between humans or groups of humans increases with the extent to which the relationship remains mutually satisfying.*

This statement is a special case of the more general principle: the probability of survival of individual, or groups of, living things increases with the degree with which they harmoniously adjust themselves to each other and their environment. As a biological basis for ethics, our formulation is thus a corollary of the Darwinian principle of evolution. Practically, it may become as significant as the formulation of the principle of gravity, if we will but recognize it. It operates, anyway, like gravity, independently of our opinions about it, whether we like it so, or not. And, as in the case of gravity, we can function so much better if we recognize it and take advantage of it.

SCIENCE AND DEMOCRACY

The current problem of the freedom of science has provoked some interest on the part of intelligent observers. American scientists have been urged editorially by the *New York Times* to try with their British brethren to publicize the aim and spirit of science in order to help preserve its freedom. Pointing out that the essence of democracy and science is freedom of thought and of expression, the editor warns sharply of the current peril to that freedom. He emphasizes the importance of cultivating the objective attitude of science in approaching social and international problems and calls for a world association of scientists to offer the opportunity of promoting the spirit of science to all people.

To this appeal, J. McKeen Cattell, the brilliant editor of *Science* and *The Scientific Monthly*, replied that the American Association for the Advancement of Science had already adopted at its Boston meeting of 1933 a "Declaration of Intellectual Freedom." Study of this indignant but platitudinous "Declaration" reveals that it proposes no way by which the freedom of science is to be preserved in the face of rising dangers against it. These threaten democracy generally. Science and democracy are complementary, the essence of both being freedom to hold and to express opinions for which rational evidence may be produced. This presumes Voltairean tolerance for such opinions, even if they be unwelcome; but tolerance in the sense of fair and critical appraisal, not merely apathetic acquiescence. The roadway of democratic freedom is laid broadly enough for two-way traffic. If there were no road-hogs or similar beasts there would be little need for traffic cops.

The program which science and democracy may undertake to preserve freedom would seem best to be one of education with patient and understanding direction against conduct and judgment built chiefly on emotional and sentimental factors. That sensory stimulations and responses conditioned to them drive us as well as other animals is evident from the studies begun by Russia's Nobelate physiologist, Ivan Pavlov. However, such responses and conduct generally may be guided into socially approved channels. If such training is lacking, individuals and social groups may be utterly deaf to reason when pushed by passion. Walter Cannon, Harvard's great Nobelatent physiologist, demonstrated the resulting brainless behavior to be like that which one sees in animals with active spinal reflexes and endocrine glands divorced from cerebral control.

In ironic contrast to intelligently guided conduct, this brainless behavior wild-fires through a group: a dog-fight gets every dog in the alley snapping; a steer frightened by the shadow of an aeroplane stampedes the herd; an excited monkey puts the whole cage in an uproar; an effective "tear-jerker" brings out every handkerchief in the audience; an hysterical outburst about blood on a white dress sets off a lynching bee; a Hitler gang inflames legions to mob sadism, and a "war spirit" sweeps a nation. Wittily Conklin suggests that the dictator who blares "We think with our blood!" already "sees red," and that he who "feels it in his bones" acknowledges ossification of thought. Biologists insist it was brains not brawn that enabled primitive men to survive the huge carnivora which once abounded, and it is intelligence directed toward the welfare of society as a whole that alone can guarantee civilization.

To be effective in helping us to adapt ourselves successfully to each other and to our environment so that we may survive decently, our intelligence must be free—free to seek the demonstrable limitations of ourselves and our environment. This knowledge, which is science, may be reasonably applied to the choice of ideals of conduct conducive to mutually beneficial adaptations and thus to decent survival. It may also be applied to the selection of appropriately satisfying methods of moving toward these ever receding ideals. The Greek trinity of truth, goodness, and beauty (whatever those words may mean!) may be revived in the ethical and esthetic implications of the aim and spirit of science. Science proves the unity of logics, ethics, and esthetics, in the same sense that "the exception proves (tests) the rule."

SCIENCE AND SOCIETY

Not being fanatical, the spirit of science fails to inspire heroism in the struggle for freedom. Conklin says, "The scientist realizes that his knowledge is relative and not absolute, he conceives it possible that he may be mistaken, and he is willing to wait in confidence that ultimately truth will prevail. Therefore, he has little inclination to suffer and die for his faith, but is willing to wait for the increase and diffusion of knowledge. But he knows better than others that the increase and diffusion of knowledge depend entirely upon freedom to search, experiment, criticize, proclaim."

The situation, then, seems to be that scientists, that is those who need intellectual freedom the most, are the very ones least willing to fight for it, or least able to assure it, except through the voluntary co-operation of the rest of society. This implies trust and confidence on the part of society in the aim and spirit of science. Such a trust, if given generously, might become the most powerful compulsion to scientists to remain worthy of it and to justify it.

Herbert Evans' History of Science Club in Berkeley recently discussed factors contributing to the gradual extinction of the ancient Greek scientific spirit of free inquiry. James Westfall Thompson summarized them as thinking based on ignorance and emotion, and authority based on revelation. These factors conquered critical curiosity by the 4th century A.D., and freedom from them has not yet been won. A dazzling picture of the conquest and its persistence may be visioned in Merejkowski's brilliant trilogy, *Julian the Apostate*, *The Romance of Leonardo*, and *Peter and Alexis*.

Attempts at scientific effort, which achieved such success with Plato, Aristotle, Archimedes, Euclid, and Galen, faltered under the stresses of adversity. Discarding reason in favor of emotion, substituting allegory and symbolism for criticism, those capable of thinking forsook the unpleasant rigor of philosophy for the alluring fascination of mysticism. Man, failing to appreciate fully the value of his intellectual disciplining, in effect threw up the sponge when he realized the menace of his changing environment, and indulging in self-pity and self-comfort, retorted, "You can't keep me from dreaming." Gilbert Murray's conclusion seems justified: "The search for truth was finally made hopeless when the world, mistrusting reason, wary of argument and wonder, flung itself passionately under the spell of a system of authoritative revelation, which acknowledged no truth outside itself, and stamped free inquiry as sin."

Emotional reflexes fed by ignorance, fear, and greed remain in our cultural heritage. Perhaps they still may retain biological value in regard to self or group preservation in crises, but whenever there is no effective intelligent guidance of them toward a broader social welfare they tend to bring us anguish and distress. A promising way of overcoming the handicap of this heritage is by disciplined application of the scientific spirit and method toward the goal of obtaining individual control of emotional energy. Then it may be directed toward mutually satisfying and thus socially beneficial adaptations, in the realization that the broader social welfare is the more conducive to lasting gratification both for the individual and for the group. Such a program requires an opportunity for everyone to become acquainted with the spirit, aim, and method of science. It also requires freedom of thought and expression.

At one of the recent meetings of the American Association for the Advancement of Science there was a series of spirited sessions on "science and society." Opinion agreed on a way by which the spirit and aim of science may be presented so as to attract the interest of the public. It is to offer science in a cultural and historical light, stressing its part in shaping our society and civilization, and emphasizing its opportunities for a free and rational faith based on demonstrable evidence about ourselves and our environment. Unfortunately unnewsworthy, such offerings are possible only in books or magazines which fail to reach the masses.

This idea has long been cultivated by George Sarton, the erudite Belgian humanist, who has devoted his life to promoting a scholarly concern for the history of science. This is necessary, he feels, in order to provide the teachers who may be able to inspire humanity with the significance of the aim and spirit of science and of the social and ethical potentialities of scientific effort. He established two scholarly periodicals, *ISIS* and *OSIRIS*, in support of this notion, and he has been partly supported by the Carnegie Institution and Harvard in the compilation of a comprehensive survey of the history of science, modestly called an "Introduction." Practically unknown to the public, his work lacks appreciation even from those scientific executives who think that something like it should be done. The ethical spirit of his campaign in behalf of science is apparent in all of his writings. It was well expressed a little while ago in an essay on the "Unification of Good Will" (*Isis*, 27: 211, 1937).

In this Sarton calmly considers how the good-will of people may be unified without physical or moral restraint, without unfair proselytism or indiscreet propaganda. He thinks that the crucial problem of our time is to harmonize freedom with unity of socially beneficial purpose. In commenting on the universal failure of the policy of forcible conversion in religion, he points out that humanity now realizes "that religion has no value unless it be the individual's own, discovered or continued in freedom, without bribes or fears." He urges each of us to continue a patient search for whatever part of "truth" may be of interest, and to encourage our neighbors to do the same. Culture, he says, is similar to democracy and science, in that its most significant feature is attitude of mind, which to be shared, like good-will and happiness, must be appreciated freely by each person.

SCIENCE AND HUMANITY

The problem of interference with the free spread of scientific ideas is thus seen to be a very fundamental one. It is implicit in all the difficulties of humanity in its pathetic quest for a harmonious way of adjusting itself to itself and to its environment. Perhaps an inspirational appeal to reason in behalf of the scientific proposal may be made so powerfully that it may be followed confidently and patiently by the mass of men. If such an appeal is to be heard, it would seem to have a better chance of being effective were it to be made by co-operative effort from leaders in science, government, education, and religion.

Co-operation between these leaders seems necessary if humanity is to promote social harmony among its different individual groups so that peace, good-will, and lasting satisfactions may prevail. Freedom for scientists is a prime requisite if we are to have as full and exact knowledge about ourselves and our environment as possible. We may not like this information when we get it, but we can't even plan intelligently, let alone build until we know a great deal more than we do now about the strength and character of our human materials, and their potential behavior under various kinds of stress and strain.

Before indulging ourselves fruitlessly in dreams of what we would like to be, let us first consider what is possible for us to be. To make this estimate a reasonable one, our scientists must be free to get facts on which to start. Recently Julian Huxley, in the first exchange lecture between the British and American Associations for the Advancement of Science, pointed out that "wishful thinking issuing in unpractical schemes is one of man's unique biological attributes." It is also within man's unique biological power to realize how this comes to be, and to try to correct it, if desired.

Claiming that the ideals of science form the foundation for a natural religion, Conklin suggests that they may serve as a set of principles to assist in guiding conduct. As a basis for ethics he would include faith in the universality of a system of law and order in nature; belief that nature is intelligible and that by searching our knowledge of it may be increased; recognition that this knowledge is not absolute but relative; realization that there is no way to avoid temporary error, since in this process we learn by trial and error; confidence in the necessity of freedom, open-mindedness and sincerity in seeking this knowledge; faith that relative "truth" about ourselves and our environment will ultimately be agreed upon by all reasonable people; realization that "truth" cannot be established by compulsion, nor error overcome by force, and finally belief that the long course of evolution leading to man and society, intelligence and ethics, is not finished, and that man can take an intelligent part in directing his future course.

If these articles of faith appear suitable for a shipyard in which to build a new ark for humanity, we had better hustle our plans accordingly, for our forty-day travail approaches. It is for the social leaders in each community to determine whether or not to set the example of acceptance. Theirs is always the responsibility for maintaining culture, but in this matter with greater consequences than in any other. This appeal in behalf of the spirit and freedom of science is not for votes, not for money, not even for distributing pamphlets or the use of a name on a letter-head—it is merely for intelligence, which is often the hardest to give.

COÖPERATION IN THE STUDY OF POLITICAL SCIENCE

JOSEPH P. CHAMBERLAIN
Columbia University

LIKE the practice of medicine and engineering, so the practice of government may be said to be an art based upon science, and it is not always the persons who understand best the science who can be the best practitioners of the art. The practice of the art should be the more successful if it is based upon the ground work of principle and of organized experience which form the science, and the sounder the science the more successful should be the practice of the art. The end of the art is to assure the smooth operation of governmental institutions by political means to advance an opinion or point of view and to set up institutions which will realize a control in the affairs of men deemed advisable or advantageous by those who hold a particular opinion. Training in this art is a worthy subject for academic instruction, as is the preparation for other arts not more necessary for the wellbeing of individuals and the prosperity and good order of society. Its successful practitioners attain high honor, and whether the ends to which they have devoted their skill are considered admirable or not in particular cases, the methods by which they achieve them and the organizations devised by the practitioners deserve perhaps a more sympathetic consideration than they have always received at the hands of those who, often with justice, criticize the results which have been attained in a particular country or in a particular situation.

In its way the study of the art of politics is the study of coöperation, a coöperation of men of many different skills and different points of view, but all under the inspiration and direction of the practitioner of the art of politics. His object may be the maintenance of his party in power, it may be the overthrow of an opposition party, it may be the accomplishment of a reform which he believes required for the welfare of the people or of the party, and his personal fortunes as a politician or an individual in many cases may depend on his success. The student of the art of politics is, however, less concerned in the object than in the method, and the skill shown in pursuing an end, the use of means of persuasion or of compulsion, are the matter of his study.

Political science is based on a wholly different motive than the art of politics. Its purpose is the advancement of knowledge and of understanding. It differs from the art of politics in the same way in which all science differs from the practical arts in that it is not concerned in accomplishing a particular practical object, nor in advancing a special theory, but is concerned in the study of political phenomena, in the development of theory, and the testing of that theory by observation of the facts of political and social action. The theory may involve the organization of government on a large scale, the operation of the judiciary or the legislative or executive, for instance, the government of a federal and of a unitary state, and the political conditions under which one or the other might be successful. It may involve the study of a single political institution such as the device of workmen's compensation and of the governmental organ best fitted to assure the smooth functioning of the device. It is upon this scientific work that the modern political practitioner is learning more and more to depend when he is faced by the problems of a modern industrial society in competition with other industrialized societies on an international scale.

The skill of the practitioner is not sufficient, nor will his practical knowledge enable him to make the decisions upon which important interests, social, economic, and political, depend. It is more and more necessary in small adjustments as in great that he lean upon a great body of knowledge organized and thought through by the political scientist, himself frequently, perhaps usually, incapable of successfully practicing the art of detecting opinion and of making the concessions and compromises which are essential to the functioning of any society and more especially one with a democratic form of government.

Political science so understood must go far beyond even a scientific study of the government of one state or of a particular function of government. It should be based on observation of the devices of government and the functioning of government in other countries, thrown against the social organization and the historic background of those countries. The scientist must not, as does the politician too often, assume that the form of government of his country and the governmental devices of the society with which he is familiar are to be set up as a criterion against which those existing elsewhere in the world are to be checked. But to understand the government of another country is no easy matter. The student may be familiar with the constitution and the form of that government, but this is not enough for the political scientist, who must understand why institutions that may seem to him inefficient or wrongly conceived and constructed have come into being, whether they are continued in response to a felt need of the dominant forces in the state or are merely a historic survival, no longer corresponding to the need which may have called them into being and which may be ready to disappear. This knowledge a foreigner can acquire only from discussion with experienced persons in the country which he is studying or by reading the judgments of such men on their own political scene. Thus he may come to understand as a scientist the political organization of the country he is studying and to surprise even its own people with his understanding. Such books as Bryce's *American Commonwealth* and Lowell's *Government of England* are cases in point.

An understanding of government and political organization should be based, it would seem, on coöperation of scholars of different countries. Just as scientific men and economists recognize the universality of their sciences, so it is important that the political scientist recognize that his science can be based soundly only on a worldwide study of phenomena which may be better carried out in different countries by the men of each country, in a scientific and not in a nationalistic spirit, who will then share by conversation or by exchange of books or articles the results which each has found. It is not the purpose of the political scientist to devise governmental machinery. That is the work of the practitioner, but the more firmly he can stand on scientific findings the better his work will be. It is the task of the political scientist to study the functioning of governmental and political organization on a wide and a narrow scale, so as to build a body of knowledge which will contribute to the understanding of man as a political animal and to the direction of his action as such an animal.

The science of politics must go further than a study of contemporary government. It should involve a study of the political forms which have existed in other countries. Some have sprung up quickly and have withered and disappeared with equal speed, leaving little behind. Others, like the Chinese and Byzantine Empires and the French Monarchy, have struck their roots deep in the soil of the society in which they developed and have left an enduring impression on the political structures of the world. These are merely examples of historic governmental institutions which have a double value to the political scientist. In the first place, they are an indication of a form of government which grew and developed in a particular form of society and which has had a long enough experience for the accumulation of a great mass of facts in regard to its operation but which has had its growth, its rise, modifications and decay, so that it can be dissected with less danger of prejudice affecting the scientific consideration of its functioning than would be the case of any existing or recent government. All national governments and national governmental forms have their zealous partisans. It is easier to look at them with the eye of the politician than with that of the scientist. A critical study of these ancient governments will, however, arouse less feeling than will a taking apart of the government of an existing state, and that particularly in a time like the present, when feeling is so strongly aroused for and against political ideals, with a fervor in many instances approaching that with which religious principles have been attacked and defended at different periods of the world's history. A study of governments in the past requires a thoughtful examination of the social conditions under which those governments existed and flourished and the changes in social conditions during the course of their long history which required modifications in governmental forms. The political scientist should know also of the movements of peoples, of the rise of dynasties and states, of the coming into an organized and civilized community of people with a different form of political organization and a different social organization. These, however, are proper studies for the historian, so that a political scientist trying to examine and evaluate the political organization of a past era must depend on the coöperation of the historian. It is not intended to imply that this collaboration can be limited only to the past. The historical approach and the historical method of assembling and organizing facts is just as necessary to the political scientist who is studying modern political institutions as if he were studying the bureaucracy of the Byzantine or of the Chinese Empires or of that which formed perhaps the backbone of the Bourbon Monarchy. Even in the international sphere the study of the forms of world organization which have been taking shape quite rapidly in certain economic and social situations which, it has been discovered, cannot be satisfactorily dealt with by national states separately or by common action through foreign offices and by the old diplomatic methods, the political scientist is apt to go astray if he has not the coöperation of historians.

But he needs the help of other disciplines than that of history. In the field which has just been mentioned, that of developing international control of the actions of individuals through treaties and agreements, more nearly approaching acts of a legislature than the treaties of the 18th and early 19th centuries, a knowledge of economics on an international scale is just as essential as is drawing on the experience of economists and businessmen in the preparation of statutes to regulate the people of a national state. A political scientist trying to advance the knowledge of international relations and of an understanding of the international society and of the means of control which have come into being in response to its needs must draw upon the knowledge, the experience, and the trained judgment of the economist. In this field as well as in the national field there must be the same relation between the political scientist and the practitioner of the art of politics. The scientist, the student of politics, should be alive to "the difference between the advancement of knowledge and the direction of opinion," a pregnant phrase from the pen of President Keppel of the Carnegie Corporation, which was cited by Professor Ogg on page 333 of his *Research in the Humanistic and Social Sciences*. He may have convictions which will lead him in the rôle of a practitioner to advance opinions or which will lead him to advise those who themselves are practitioners advancing opinions in which he agrees, but he must realize that it is his rôle to collect materials and to analyze and organize them in cold blood as his service to the cause of learning and through learning for the advancement of humanity. It is for the practitioner, under the pressure of public opinion and of the circumstances, to determine when an international organization is necessary and the form which it shall take.

The political scientist, the economist, and the historian complement each other in the study of the phenomena of the modern world. Each has a different approach, a different object in his study, but each needs, it would seem, the advice and criticism of the other disciplines if he is to have a just understanding of the complicated life history of national and international organisms whose atomic construction is that of individual human beings with their desires, their prejudices, and the historic setting in which they live their lives.

The psychologist has his place, and perhaps a more important one than has often been assigned to him, in this coöperation for better understanding of the phenomena arising from the life of the human being in society.

Other disciplines are too apt to disregard the atom, the individual man, and to think of the great movements of masses of men or of masses of goods or of services. The demand of the human being for order, for a degree of liberty, for security, for a chance to exercise his spirit of enterprise arises from the individual himself. Conflicts between these great motive desires arise also from the needs and feelings of individual human beings, and it is the contribution of the psychologist to the study of the political scientist, both to force on his attention the importance of the atom, man, and to explain the reasons which motivate the activity of that atom, the basis of all society. The more accurate the information which can be given him by the psychologist the better work can the political scientist accomplish in his own field.

It would draw out this short article to too great length to dwell upon the other disciplines which must be drawn on by the political scientist, both to aid his general thinking and to aid his thought in respect to particular situations and particular political organizations. As an example, the development of the political organs set up for the control of narcotics has required close coöperation not only with all the disciplines already mentioned but has also required the help of chemists and medical scientists. Only recently a substantial volume has appeared under the imprint of the National Research Council, a *Report of the Committee on Drug Addiction*, dealing with various scientific and medical questions which have been found important to a full understanding of the problem and to make possible the devising of a system of control which will be effective and not too narrowly regulatory of the practitioners of the art of medicine. No student of political science could possibly have done the research necessary to collect the material in this imposing volume, nor could he understand the technical scientific papers contained in it. He must have the coöperation of the natural scientist, however, not only to collect the material but to interpret it to him. It is necessary that he have this information if he is to comprehend the bearing on the science of politics in its international aspect, of the phenomena attending the use of narcotics, and of the devices to regulate human activity which have been used and which have been suggested, in dealing with it by governments separately or by governments through international agencies backed up by governmental action. It is not necessary here to do more than point out how essential to the practitioner of the art of politics would be the collaboration of the scientific scholars who prepared the papers contained in this volume, nor would it be necessary to point out that the practitioner as much, perhaps even more than the political scientist, must have the coöperation of scientific men not only in making the studies but in advising him as to what they really show and what use may be made of them as guides in devising methods of control.

The place of the sociologist as a coöperator with the political scientist is clear. It is said that man is a political animal, but it has already been pointed out that his action as a political animal is only part of his action as a social animal. A study of the political organization of China, for instance, without an understanding of the family, the village, and the guild, would merely result in advancing knowledge of a form of government, interesting enough as a form, but without taking into consideration the social pressures which made it effective and which limited its action. Interesting and important in itself as a form of government which has endured longer perhaps than any other on the earth, but as has been already remarked, only to be brought into a truly scientific study of political phenomena if it is interpreted in the light of the social phenomena and the social organizations which underlay it.

The geographer, the anthropologist, the geologist represent other disciplines which must be called on by the political scientist in his study both of broad principles and of particular situations, and their aid is essential to the political practitioner who is devising ways and means to regulate and control human activities. As an example of the service of the anthropologist may be mentioned the importance of knowledge of the tribal customs of the African peoples in setting up a governmental institution, or even a great agricultural or industrial enterprise, in the Dark Continent. These customs may or may not be adopted in whole or in part into the organization which the dominant modern civilization requires for successful functioning in its own interest, but difficulties will arise should they be left out of consideration by governmental officers or sympathetic reformers.

The value of coöperative work among scholarly groups and organizations is apparent in the important field of the collection and preservation of materials and of devices to make them more readily available for research. The joint committee of the American Council of Learned Societies and the Social Science Research Council on materials for research is an evidence that this need is understood by leaders of scholarship in this country and an evidence of a community of interest recognized by scholar of all the disciplines represented on the two Councils. For there is no sharp line of demarcation between material which is of value to the economist and that which can serve the purposes of the political scientist or the historian or the sociologist. A particular document may be principally of use to one of the disciplines, but the same reasons that make coöperation among scholars so important in the discovery of truth will apply to the joint use of the materials which they assemble. Coöperation in the various devices for making available material which has been jointly collected is important as an aid to productive scholarship. So also the examination of the various mechanical means for facilitating the preservation and the use of materials of research can best be done by coöperation of the scholars of the various learned associations, so that each will have his say in the development of these new means of aiding creative scholarship. In this field the importance of the large organizations comprising different scholarly associations, such as the American Council of Learned Societies and the Social Science Research Council, is especially evident, and the work which has been set on foot by them and their agencies is a worthy fruit of scholarly coöperation.

With the importance of collaboration among scholars, not only scholars of different disciplines but scholars of the same discipline, the problem of the organization of research assumes formidable proportions. First there must be achieved coöperation between scholars without hampering the freedom of the individual scholar to carry out his own work in his own way and without dictating to individual scholars what subjects they should investigate. This is particularly true at the present time in political science, a discipline in which freedom of research and freedom of expression are so sharply curtailed in countries where they formerly flourished and produced most valuable fruits.

Studies in the field of politics by competent and independent scholars were never more important. Stress has been laid on the increase in the activities of government and on the need for new organs or adaptation of existing organs to meet the need. More spectacular and of growing importance is the need of work by political scientists to study the conflicting principles and theories of political and governmental action which occupy the minds of people, and which are preached by protagonists without any consideration of their consequences to society or searching criticism of the assertions upon which they are based. We are constantly being confronted by theories and by the enunciation of principles in the form of slogans which catch the ear of agitated and frightened people who are apt to be led astray by promises and by immediate advantages offered to them without considering whether in the long run the loss will be much greater than any present gain. Not the political scientist alone but scholars in all the social sciences may do a great service to humanity in developing by their coöperative work a knowledge and an understanding of social phenomena which will bring hope for the better social and political organization of the society of the future, both national and international. Despite the great number of government research agencies and the excellent work which they are doing, it is on the independent scholar that the main burden of thinking through and analyzing the problems of political science must rest. The government agencies are equipped to collect information in a way which no private group or any combination of private groups can hope to rival. Without drawing on their experience there can be no understanding of governmental problems, but in the interpretation and organization of their material they must too often take into consideration the requirements of practitioners of the art of politics, so that it is the private scholar who must assume the great share of the burden of the advancement of knowledge in the interest of knowledge itself.

Coöperation among scholars can produce its best fruits only if the younger men can be taught not only the need for coöperation but how it can be best accomplished by the experience of working themselves in a group investigating together a problem of interest to all its members. Such association in work with men of other disciplines is one way, and not the least important, of stemming the tide toward specialization of which we hear much in these days of great accumulation of material for research and of knowledge in each of the disciplines. A student of political science or of economics or of sociology may realize as a matter of principle that he has much to learn from men of other disciplines, but he may find that his own work and his own line of study are so engrossing and take so much of his time and energy that he yields to the tendency to dig deep in his own field and to pay only cursory attention to the fields which he considers belong to his neighbors. This is understandable and even commendable, for no one scholar can expect to be a master in the many disciplines represented by the constituent organizations of our great learned societies. Nor should the political scientist think of himself as an economist or a geographer or a sociologist or a psychologist. However wide his knowledge and however great his devotion to study, he can never become a master in so many fields, nor would it be easy for him through his own efforts fully to understand the position of his discipline in the complex of so many branches of scholarship. If, however, a young man can become associated with a group working on a problem, he can learn the technique of utilizing scholars in other branches of learning in helping him to work out a problem in his own and to feel that he is helping them to understand their place as well as his own, in the great republic of letters. If there is to be scholarly coöperation there must be training in scholarly coöperation, and training of the young men in particular. Through their research and through their teaching they can spread the idea and the practice, so that there can be a better understanding of the part played in the acquisition of knowledge by each of the different disciplines and the importance of their working together if there is to be a knowledge of social phenomena, and not a knowledge of phases of these phenomena, in the minds of many scholars.

The association of scholars to promote research and the pooling of the results of research and the protection at the same time of the individual freedom and initiative which is the cornerstone of all scholarship is an important object of the association of American scholars both within their disciplines and in the broader scope of the American Council of Learned Societies and the Social Science Research Council. These organizations testify to the realization among American scholars of the need of organization with individual liberty. These great groups, however, cannot themselves either carry on research or direct research. They can assure the protection of the individual scholar, and through their organs and through discussion at the meetings of the Council of the ACLS can exercise an effective criticism of plans for research and of suggestions for the use of funds for research. In the wide field of political science, in the still wider one of social science in general, and in the almost limitless field of coöperation between disciplines in the study of man and his environment, there is clearly need for groups which will take a broad view of the needs and of the possibilities and will either plan wide projects for research or select among those suggested to them the most appropriate and most valuable. Which are the most appropriate and the most valuable projects and which are the wide projects which can best be set on foot in view of limits in financial resources are, however, often determined by a judgment as to the ability of individual scholars to carry out the work which they suggest or in finding the scholars who can take a share in realizing a broad program. These two great organizations early found it necessary to organize their committees on the planning of research and to advise as to projects on a greater or lesser scale. They have been alert to discover the more neglected branches of learning and to devise ways and means to fill certain of the gaps which they have found. But a particular piece of research, once it has been planned for and organized, must be put in charge of an *ad hoc* group, whose capacity needs to be carefully considered, both for scholarly qualifications and for the personal qualities which lead to effective group action. It is in this delicate task of organizing groups and of unobtrusively urging them toward the result hoped for that a very real service to scholarship has been accomplished, a service that is recognized by many scholars and which must be appreciated by the great foundations which wish to see their money used effectively. The qualities of the administrative officers of the great scholarly societies have been well expressed by the Director of the American Council of Learned Societies in his Memo for Guidance of the Advisory Board, February 1928. What he set forth as necessary qualities of members of that board applies even more sharply to the administrative officers of the Council. A member of the board, he wrote, should have "insight to discover what is significant, practical sense, and constructive imagination." I should like to add the qualities of persuasiveness and modesty, a willingness to sink his own personality in the interest of the Council and its constituent associations, and I think that we have a fairly good picture of the mind of the Director. Very nearly the same may be said of his administrative assistants, who like the Director have been willing to devote their talent for creative scholarship to facilitating the scholarly achievement of others. The sum of the accomplishment of the Director can only be cast by reckoning in the share in the work of the many who owe suggestion and inspiration to him and who have profited by the materials which could scarcely have been available to them except for what he has done.